THOMAS B. LARSON has been a Senior Fellow at the Russian Institute, Columbia University, from 1966–1968. He is the author of numerous articles, and co-editor of *Soviet Politics Since Khrushchev*. As a former Foreign Service officer, Larson served in both Moscow and Paris. He has also served as Chief of Research on the USSR and Eastern Europe for the Department of State.

DISARMAMENT
AND SOVIET POLICY,
1964–1968

THOMAS B. LARSON
Columbia University

PRENTICE-HALL, Inc.   *Englewood Cliffs, N. J.*

This report was prepared under contract (ACDA/E–115) with the United States Arms Control and Disarmament Agency. The judgments are those of the author and do not necessarily reflect the views of the United States Arms Control and Disarmament Agency or of any other department or agency of the United States government or of Columbia University.

PREFACE

An earlier study of Soviet attitudes toward arms control and disarmament was completed in 1964 at the Russian Institute of Columbia University under contract with the United States Arms Control and Disarmament Agency. This project brought together, in 1963, a group of leading Western experts on Soviet affairs and disarmament questions, who discussed extensively the rationale of Soviet attitudes and behavior. With the assistance of other participants, Alexander Dallin prepared the report on the project, which was published as *The Soviet Union and Disarmament: An Appraisal of Soviet Attitudes and Intentions* (New York: Frederick A. Praeger, Inc., 1965). The completion of this study coincided with the end of the Khrushchev era.

Again with the support of the United States Arms Control and Disarmament Agency, the Russian Institute agreed to organize a broad study of Soviet trends from 1964 relevant to arms control and disarmament. To provide a starting point, specialists in various spheres of Soviet activity were commissioned to write papers analyzing trends in the USSR since October, 1964. These papers are published in a separate volume, *Soviet Politics Since Khrushchev*, edited by Alexander Dallin and Thomas B. Larson (Englewood Cliffs, N. J.: Prentice-Hall, Inc., 1968). The papers also served as the basis for discussions at a conference held on Nantucket Island, Massachusetts, April 1–5, 1967. The participants, who included most of the authors of the papers, represented a broad range of American and Western European specialists on Soviet affairs in various disciplines. The present report, written after the Nantucket conference, was reviewed in draft form at a smaller meeting held in New York City on November 30–December 1, 1967.*

The report presented here does not pretend to summarize the views of the specialists involved in the project, although all the participants had an opportunity to comment on the earlier version. No attempt was made at either of the conferences to achieve a consensus or even to count noses for and against debatable propositions about Soviet atti-

* A list of the participants of the two conferences is appended.

tudes and behavior on arms control and disarmament. Nevertheless, in preparing the report, the author drew freely upon the papers prepared for the project and upon the discussions at Nantucket and New York. At appropriate places the report calls attention to the existence of divergent opinions on important issues.

Professor Dallin commented thoughtfully and in detail on the draft report, as did some of the other conference participants. In addition, Robert Lambert and Nadia Derkach of ACDA and Robert Baraz and Herbert Block of the Department of State offered valuable suggestions on the text. None of those involved in the project, however, would probably want to endorse without reservation the analysis and conclusions presented here.

In addition to those mentioned, others performed indispensable services in carrying on the project. Liaison with the United States Arms Control and Disarmament Agency was handled by Kent K. Parrot, who offered help and encouragement and facilitated the progress of both the project and the report. Thomas P. Raynor, Assistant Director of the Russian Institute, served as rapporteur at the Nantucket conference, and David Hepinstall performed a similar function for the New York meeting. Barry H. Steiner compiled the bibliography and chronology. Alan C. Lopez did useful research on priorities in Soviet policy on arms control and disarmament. Elizabeth A. Pond deserves thanks for her editorial assistance, and Mildred O'Brien for her expert typing of the report in both its draft and final versions. Constance A. Bezer, administrative assistant for the project, handled many thankless tasks with charm and efficiency. My wife, Helen R. Larson, went over a preliminary draft of the manuscript to improve the sense and the style.

Thomas B. Larson

CONTENTS

INTRODUCTION

Issues regarding the Soviet Union and disarmament have gained in importance since October, 1964, despite the disappearance from the scene of Nikita Khrushchev, the inveterate, garrulous, and ebullient champion of "general and complete disarmament." Whether or not Khrushchev thought that a radical disarmament scheme could be negotiated, he certainly believed that a campaign emphasizing general disarmament would promote Soviet interests.

Leonid Brezhnev and the other leaders who have guided Soviet policy since 1964 talk much less about disarmament than did Khrushchev. The war in Vietnam and resort to violence elsewhere have made the times less propitious for such talk. In addition, Khrushchev's successors are a cautious lot, not easily inspired to grandiose visions and grandiloquent expression. They have been singularly less inventive than Khrushchev in originating new models of broad disarmament schemes, and also in casting and recasting proposals for separate measures of arms control and disarmament.

Despite these differences, the USSR under the new leadership has engaged in serious arms control negotiations, and the achievements recorded since 1964 compare favorably enough with the earlier agreements. Avoiding the euphoric attitude regarding the United States that occasionally infected Khrushchev and made him vulnerable to the charge of misjudging the principal world rival of the USSR, the Brezhnev group has nevertheless continued to act on the principle that "you can do business with America."

In arms control, the "business" accomplished since 1963 under both Khrushchev and his successors contrasts strikingly with earlier failures. Yet in relation to the dangers presented by the augmentation of nuclear arsenals in the hands of rival and antagonistic states, the progress often seems slight. Furthermore, a new dimension to the arms competition among major powers was added when Communist China joined the nuclear weapons club, for Chinese interests clashed with those of both the Soviet Union and the United States. Nor will China necessarily be the last country to acquire nuclear weapons.

1

Technology itself proved unsettling. The explosion of the first atomic bombs in 1945 and the testing of the first intercontinental ballistic missiles (ICBMs) in 1957 were followed by periods in which these technological developments were absorbed into the military establishments of the two chief military rivals. Particularly after 1957, when the great destructive power of nuclear warheads was mated to the rapid delivery system of ICBMs, there seemed to be a prospect of a relative stabilization of technology, which could provide the basis for stability in Soviet-American power relationships.

This breathing spell (a spell of rather uneasy breathing, to be sure) now seems to be disappearing. Although no single innovation appears to be as important as those that gave rise to nuclear weapons and ballistic vehicles, a number of separate developments threaten to change the calculus of relations between the superpowers and to give a new lift to arms competition. These include the initial deployment of antiballistic missiles (ABM), development of mobile ICBMs, the perfection of multiple warheads to be launched by a single missile against separate targets (MIRV), and experimentation by the USSR with a satellite designed to release a nuclear weapon from orbit (MOBS or FOBS).[1]

A striking discrepancy thus exists between the rapidity of the major powers' advances in increasing the sophistication and power of their armaments and the slowness of progress in establishing agreed limitations on national arms policies. Yet the situation is not hopeless. For the technical advances of the past two decades concerned weapons whose military use has become less and less plausible, and arms competition involving such weapons has assumed an eerie quality.

Before the age of nuclear weapons, armed forces coming into possession of novel armaments and vehicles could usually test them in battle without having to wait very long for an opportunity to demonstrate what the new machinery could (and could not) do. Since Hiroshima and Nagasaki, there has been no demonstration in warfare of an atomic (or nuclear) weapon or of any of the advanced vehicles tailor-made for these warheads.

There is no assurance, of course, that such weapons will not be put to military use in the future. Nevertheless, powerful disincentives, notably the prospect of mutual destruction on an unparalleled scale, in-

---

[1] MIRV (multiple independently guided re-entry vehicles) is the Pentagon's term for an American development involving separately targetable warheads launched by a single missile. These are to be used either from land (as with the Minuteman) or from under water (in the case of Poseidon submarines, based on remodeling of Polaris submarines). FOBS (fractional orbital bombardment system) is the American designation for a Soviet-developed system of launching a weapons-carrying vehicle into a low orbit, from which it drops off the pay-load before completing a single orbit. MOBS (multiple orbital bombardment system) refers to a similar satellite weapons carrier designed for multiple orbits.

hibit rival leaders from pressing the button to inaugurate nuclear war. Despite the fact that these weapons systems were integrated into the rival military establishments, their only "utilization" has been in the politico-psychological realm.

The public disclosure of post-atomic innovations in weapons systems testifies to the importance of this psychological aspect. The United States developed the first atomic bombs in greatest secrecy, in order to spring them on the enemy in World War II. Subsequent weapons developments, however, have had to be made public; this has allowed them to pay their way as a means of "deterrence" prior to, and possibly without, any military application. Even the Soviet authorities, who are far more reserved in this respect than their American counterparts, have incentives to advertise their weapons achievements in order to translate these into political payoffs.

It is precisely in this sphere of psycho-politics, to which the influence of the new weapons systems has been so far confined, that the modest arms control achievements of the past few years have had their greatest impact. This political impact has been disproportionate to the importance of the actual limitations on arms. It seems likely that if further arms control agreements can be concluded they too will be more important in gradually altering the expectations of rival statesmen and peoples than in drastically limiting the armaments and arms policies of the major powers.

The prospects for further agreements depend, for an essential part, on Soviet receptivity to various measures of arms control. It is to this question that the present study is addressed. It seeks to analyze the impact on Soviet arms control and disarmament policy of significant trends of the past four years, outside and within the Soviet Union. The study is thus designed as a successor to a report on Soviet attitudes toward disarmament in the Khrushchev era (*The Soviet Union and Disarmament*, by Alexander Dallin and others).

The present report considers the changing character of decision making and of decision makers in the post-Khrushchev USSR, and examines trends in ideology, foreign policy, economic development, and military affairs bearing on disarmament prospects. It pays less attention to some of the "constants" of Soviet behavior and policy than did the earlier volume, for that analysis of those basic factors remains valid today. In contrast, the present work focuses more attention on the specifics of arms control negotiations, particularly Soviet proposals and Soviet positions on American and other proposals. Finally, in a look at the future, this report evaluates the prospects for future agreements on various measures in the disarmament field.

A word on terminology is in order. The vocabulary of the subject is both controversial and imprecise. The venerable term "disarmament" has become increasingly unsatisfactory for the central concept, because it is weighted toward the idea of liquidating military forces and weapons in a period in which many of the measures discussed, and almost all the progress made, has concerned other types of limitation. As a supplement, the term "arms control" made its way into official and unofficial discussion, particularly in the United States. Thus, reference to "arms control and disarmament" was institutionalized in the title of the government agency principally concerned with the subject. Nevertheless, Soviet spokesmen object strongly to the term "arms control." [2] When President Johnson in his 1967 State of the Union address referred to "the common interests between Russia and the United States" in "arms control and disarmament," a Soviet editor was quick to reply that the Soviet Union had always sought "disarmament" and had always opposed "arms control." Of course the USSR has accepted a number of "limitation" measures that have had no arms reduction features, and has itself proposed some of these. Such measures are usually described in Soviet documents simply as measures "to reduce tension." Because they do involve some limitations on weapons, however, it seems appropriate to categorize them as "arms control."

When the distinction is required in this study, "disarmament" is used to refer to measures envisaging the reduction or elimination of armaments or armed forces, and "arms control" or "arms limitation" are meant to refer to measures envisaging other kinds of limitations.[3] A study could probably be written in which such terms were invariably used with precision, but it is doubtful if any but the most determined readers would suffer through to the end. Consequently, the practice employed here is to intersperse the terms freely except when it is important to distinguish between measures contemplating reductions of various degrees, i.e., "disarmament," and other kinds of limitations, i.e., "arms control."

This terminological laxity does not require conceptual looseness. In particular, "arms control" as used in this study does not encompass

---

[2] Part of the difficulty is linguistic. In Russian, the word "control" (*kontrol'*) has the connotation of *post facto* verification and rectification, an audit that includes but goes beyond the purely fiscal. As applied to measures such as a ban on tests of nuclear weapons, for example, the phrase "arms control" reflects the broader English meaning of the word "control" but has little significance in Russian.

[3] In ACDA's *Glossary of Arms Control and Disarmament Terms,* prepared by Robert W. Lambert (Washington, D.C.: United States Arms Control and Disarmament Agency, 1967), "disarmament" is defined as one form of "arms control," the latter being used to refer to any "formal or informal international action placing limitations on armed forces, armaments, and military expenditures." In addition, however, arms control "in a broad sense" is said to include "steps to produce a peaceful international environment conducive to such measures" (i.e., measures of limitation).

either measures of control by national leaders over their own military forces or interstate agreements that impose no limitations on national arms policies. The well-known American measures to insure against employment of nuclear weapons except on presidential order are examples of the first. The "hot-lines" established by agreement between Moscow and Washington, Moscow and Paris, and Moscow and London are examples of the second. Naturally, measures of this type may have crucial importance in averting war, especially "war by accident." They are not, however, arms control measures of the kind discussed in this book.

1

TRENDS OF SOVIET POLICY, 1964–1968

Soviet developments since the ouster of Khrushchev in October, 1964, defy any simple characterization. There have been periods in Soviet history when the main course of movement was more or less clear at the time. This was true, for example, of the NEP years beginning in the early 1920's, of the period of repression beginning in the mid-1930's, and of the years immediately following World War II when Soviet policy hardened noticeably with respect to foreign and domestic affairs alike. At other times, developments were more obscure, and the significant course markers had to be charted retrospectively, as important corners were turned. Thus, it was only in 1956–1957 that it was possible to gauge with some accuracy the impact of Stalin's death on Soviet politics. Likewise, it was only in October, 1964, that it became possible to see that Khrushchev, in the immediately preceding years, had been riding toward a fall. In 1968 it was still uncertain where the post-Khrushchev regime led by Brezhnev was heading, and it is therefore hazardous to separate the crucial from the accidental in the history of Soviet affairs for 1964–1968.

The only startling event in the Brezhnev era was its beginning. When Nikita's collaborators and protégés conspired to remove Khrushchev, they brought off a peaceable ouster of a ruler unparalleled in Russian or Soviet history. As drama it was a wonderful opener, but it raised the question of what was possible for an encore. There was no answer, for all the boldness was spent. Caution became the watchword, as the new chiefs began to wrestle both with the persistent problems that had plagued their predecessors, and with the new problems that life thrust before them.

Of course, the ouster of Khrushchev involved more than merely sending the man into obscurity, unharmed but unsung. Repercussions continued to be felt over succeeding months, certainly through the period terminating at the XXIII Congress of the Communist Party of the Soviet Union (CPSU) in March–April, 1966. In this period, many Khrushchevian innovations of policies and institutions were swept

6

away, and many of the doctrinal formulas contaminated by association with Khrushchev were replaced by a series of new guidelines. The successors restored much that had been familiar in the Soviet pattern of rule from Stalin's day. They could be described as bent on a "return to normalcy," if normalcy had meaning in the context of a Soviet history filled with *Sturm und Drang*. Yet to describe these men as "conservatives" or "reactionaries" would be misleading, since they also showed themselves as cautious reformers in many areas, and they continued to uphold many of the policies and doctrines introduced under Khrushchev.[1]

TOWARD A NEW STYLE OF NATIONAL LEADERSHIP

The same leaders who had been Khrushchev's principal colleagues in the Party Presidium and Secretariat remained in power after October, 1964—minus Khrushchev. This minus had major effects on the style of rule, on administrative reorganizations, and on certain areas of policy making. But the coup had surprisingly little effect on personnel. There were only minor Khrushchev-linked dismissals from or additions to the Party Politburo and Secretariat, of which most members are national officials. At the level of the Central Committee (where a majority are regional officials), four out of every five members chosen in 1961 were re-elected in April, 1966. This aftermath suggested that, when the tide turned against the ebullient boss, not only did his supporters abandon the cause, but also that those who inspired the overthrow found reason to demote very few of the officials who owed their rise to Khrushchev. Although the composition of the ruling groups remained generally unchanged, there was a good deal of reshuffling of specific assignments, often in connection with organizational shake-ups.

Liberating themselves from Khrushchev's overweening influence, the successors reaffirmed the principle of collective leadership and, more important, took steps to give it continuing meaning. This was collective leadership of the oligarchic and largely self-perpetuating group

---

[1] The post-Khrushchev regime has repeatedly reaffirmed the "general line" worked out at the xx and xxii Party Congresses (of 1956 and 1961). It has thus endorsed both criticism of the cult of personality and Khrushchev's doctrinal modifications regarding the possibilities of avoiding war and of peaceful transition to socialism. The Party Program of 1961 is still referred to approvingly and prescribed for study. The new leaders apparently looked askance at one of the ideological novelties incorporated into that Program, that describing the Communist Party as a "Party of the whole people." Characteristically, however, they have allowed the formula to lapse without declaring it erroneous. Khrushchev's parallel formula on the "whole-people's state" has been retained. Brezhnev, for example, used the latter in his speech on November 3, 1967, on the 50th anniversary of the October Revolution (*Pravda*, November 4, 1967).

of 24 leaders in the Politburo and Secretariat, not that of the more than 350 members and candidate-members of the Central Committee (regarded formally as the highest organ of collective leadership in the Party, and therefore in the country). Although the top leaders paid more deference to the Central Committee (CC) than had been Khrushchev's custom, they took pains to guard the decision-making prerogatives of the Politburo and Secretariat. It may be, as some foreign observers believe, that a system of oligarchic dominance is so fragile that it must eventually give way either to a restored rule by one man or to a broader democratization of the decision-making process. For the moment, however, the post-Khrushchev leaders seem to be managing without concentrating or dispersing authority. Thus, General Secretary Leonid I. Brezhnev does not appear to have achieved a position of power significantly greater than was implicit in his election as top leader of the Party in October, 1964. Nor has the Central Committee of the CPSU or any other Soviet leadership group of broader scope than the Politburo benefited from any creeping democratization.

The new style of leadership does not relate solely to the prerogatives of the men at the top (as against the Party chief, on the one hand, and larger elite groups, on the other). It involves different emphases in the approach to programs and decisions. The criticism aimed at Khrushchev was not so much that his decisions were wrong because he had made them, but that he had made wrong decisions under the sway of "subjectivism," "voluntarism," and impulsiveness. He had misjudged the objective possibilities of situations, addicted as he was to "leaping before looking" and to "bombast." The collective process was to insure objectivity, the single quality on which the new leadership placed greatest stress. Sobriety, caution, careful preparation: these were the qualities most in evidence. On the negative side, collective decisions encourage postponement of hard choices instead of quick response, and delays and vacillation have been evident on occasion since 1964. Compromises necessary to overcome persistent differences within the leadership may be more political than rational, illustrated in the last four years by the balancing of slaps at the liberal and conservative intelligentsia.

The image the current leaders of the USSR present to the world is not inspiring, and a public conditioned to personalized politics finds little but a grey blur on the Soviet political landscape. For better or for worse, this is likely to be the case as long as collective leadership lasts. Group rule necessarily brings an impersonality to the political process. No one has found a formula for building a stirring imagery around a committee; and group prose is notoriously dull, as committee reports painfully attest.

The other side of the coin is that group decision making may be wiser than that of an individual. Particularly in the Soviet Union, where the top command is subject to almost no control or criticism from below, collective decision making performs an indispensable function. It serves as a means of taking into account the opinions of officials with the different experiences and different preoccupations that result from a variety of functional assignments. Certainly it is premature to conclude that the disappearance of the Stalin and Khrushchev types of individually dominant leaders has meant that a putative age of geniuses has given way to an age of mediocrities. However blurred their image, the present leaders, with some notorious lapses, have dealt with the problems and opportunities confronting the country in a fashion at least as wise as that of their predecessors. This is not boundless praise, but it needs to be said in a period when the cult of individual leader—not confined to the USSR—threatens to warp judgment on the Soviet record in 1964–1968.

RETURN TO TRADITIONAL ORGANIZATIONS

In two major areas, Khrushchev's organizational novelties were abandoned and structures familiar from the era of Stalin (and even of Lenin) were restored in the first year after Khrushchev. The division of most oblast and lower Party and soviet organs into separate agricultural and industrial hierarchies was abolished in the month following Khrushchev's ouster, at the November, 1964, Plenum of the Central Committee. Apparently the leaders were unanimous in abominating this two-year-old experiment, to which many had been cool from the start. They probably shared the objective sought by Khrushchev in this bifurcation—to make the Party more skillful in injecting its weight into specialized economic administration. The advantages expected from this form of specialization, notably in promoting the economic expertise of Party managers, were gained at a heavy price. The rural-urban split further complicated an administrative system already made complex by overlap of authority and loose definition of competence. It also fuzzed one of the Party's principal roles: the function of coordinating at all territorial levels activities of all institutions including Party, government, soviet, and trade unions. The abolition of the industrial-rural setup in the provinces led to the dismantling of the changed structures (introduced under Khrushchev) at central Party headquarters in Moscow: these were staff sections organized to take account of the separate industrial and rural organs in the provinces; the coordinating bureaus, which added a new layer between the Politburo and Secretariat and the specialized departments of the Central Committee, and the cc Buro for the RSFSR.[2]

---

[2] The Central Committee Buro for the RSFSR was not abolished, formally at least, until the xxiii Party Congress, March 29–April 8, 1966.

The other major area of restoration involved economic management. Some industrial production ministries were re-established in March, 1965, and there was a general return to the ministerial system of organizing production and distribution after the September, 1965, cc Plenum. The regional economic councils, in existence since 1957, were liquidated at this time, as was the superstructure of economic coordinating councils at Union-Republic and USSR levels (begun after 1957). The re-emergence of ministries as the agencies responsible for economic administration meant a restoration of a system emphasizing specialization of commodity or service, as against a system emphasizing geographical propinquity.

The restoration of the ministerial system cannot be understood primarily in terms of the preferences of the new leaders for a more centralized form of economic administration, although the reconstituted government bureaucracy was only slightly less centralized than that of the Stalin era. A main motive appeared to be the conviction of the leaders that economic advances, particularly the introduction of new technology, could be promoted more easily through a system grouping industrial and other enterprises on the basis of product rather than of place. Since centralization was only an incidental objective, it was not inconsistent for the September, 1965, measures to combine re-establishment of economic ministries with the launching of an economic reform in which individual enterprises were given greater autonomy in organizing production, in purchasing materials and selling products, and in managing their labor force. Basic goals set by the central authorities and articulated in yearly and longer-term plans were to continue to give direction to economic activities. But the reform contemplated a greater use of "market discipline" and of economic incentives, including rewards based on enterprise profits, as instruments to guide production and distribution of goods. Reliance on administrative commands for this purpose declined.

A third institution to be affected by the sweeping-out of Khrushchev's innovations was the Committee of Party-State Control of the cc cpsu and the USSR Council of Ministers. In December, 1965, it was renamed the USSR Committee of People's Control; the change of its title reflected the abandonment of Khrushchev's plan to make the organization a potent one, drawing strength from its links to both the Party and government hierarchies, on the model of a predecessor agency inspired by Lenin. Henceforward it was to be a purely governmental organ, comparable in many ways to the control agency of the period from the 1930's through the 1950's, with continued use of volunteers from the public to give it a popular flavor.[3]

[3] The reduction of the status of the control function was made clear in the ap-

With the reunification of Party organs in oblast and smaller areas (and of the corresponding soviets in these regions), the abolition of economic councils in favor of ministries, and the elimination of the joint Party-state feature from the control organization, the only significant organizational reform from Khrushchev's period remaining in effect concerned control of agricultural machinery. The machinery had been sold to collective farms in 1957, when the Machine Tractor Stations (MTS) were disbanded. Prior to this change, proposed in Stalin's time and resolutely condemned by him, the MTS functioned with the dual purpose of enforcing state control of agricultural operations and as one means of extracting agricultural products from collective farms. Although the supply, maintenance, and use of farm machinery continued to present serious problems after 1964, and an occasional voice was raised in praise of the old system, the post-Khrushchev leaders avoided reverting to the past in this particular domain.

MILITARY POWER, ECONOMIC GROWTH, AND WELFARE

Because criticism of Khrushchev after his fall centered on his mode of leadership, and because the most thorough of the post-October changes swept away his organizational innovations, it has been appropriate that the developments discussed in the preceding sections concerned procedures rather more than content, organizational structures rather than substantive policies. Brezhnev and his colleagues were far from issuing wholesale condemnations of the many changes introduced into Soviet policy in the decade after Stalin's death, either in domestic or foreign affairs. The problem that seemed most acute in October, 1964, was that of overcoming the serious lag of Soviet economic growth in Khrushchev's last years; indeed, economic difficulties must have contributed greatly to his colleagues' resolution to get rid of him. The urgency they felt in restoring high rates of growth, however, had to be tempered by a realization that they were committed to other objectives, particularly in regard to military prowess and civilian welfare, which limited their freedom to place an absolute priority on measures to speed growth. In Soviet thought, neither military nor welfare expenditures are growth inducing. Yet the Soviet leaders, perhaps responding to pressure from the defense establishment, and certainly fortified in their inclination by the international situation, allocated

---

pointment of P. V. Kovanov as the new chief. He was only a candidate-member of the Central Committee at the time of his appointment, although he was promoted to full membership in April, 1966. He replaced A. N. Shelepin, who had been throughout the existence of the former agency a Party Secretary of the CC CPSU and a Deputy Chairman of the USSR Council of Members (and a full member of the Politburo from November, 1964).

scarce resources to a program of rapid expansion and improvement of Soviet strategic forces. They have appeared to reject the idea, sometimes attributed to Khrushchev, that the USSR needed only a "minimum deterrent" posture based principally on a limited quantity of ICBMs, i.e., that it did not need to equal the United States in strategic power. The build-up of ICBM forces, the initiation of ABM deployment, naval expansion, and heavy investment in military research and development indicate the attention lavished since 1964 on building Soviet military power. The announced defense budget has been increased by substantial amounts over the last three years, with a 15 per cent increase in 1967.

At the same time, the regime has enacted a number of welfare measures affecting minimum wages, pensions, taxes, and hours of work. These measures have principally benefited low-paid workers and peasants, apparently with the aim of reducing the large differential between earners of high and low income in the USSR. Only two weeks after the Party CC Plenum in September, 1967, decreed a series of welfare measures, the USSR Supreme Soviet met in October and voted for both a large increase in overt military spending for 1968 and for a 1968 economic plan calling for a more rapid rise in the production of industrial consumers' goods than of producers' goods. The reversal of the usual Soviet priorities in the 1968 plan was clearly designed as exceptional (if it is realized in fact). But the economic plan for 1966–1970 (approved in preliminary form in 1966 but never enacted in final form) envisaged a narrowing of the gap between growth rates of producers' and consumers' goods, a trend that has materialized in the last few years and has been repeatedly endorsed by Brezhnev, Kosygin, and other Soviet spokesmen.

Sobriety was evident in the targets incorporated into the 1966–1970 plan. The leaders said nothing more about economically overtaking America by 1970—a promise embalmed in the cold type of the 1961 Party Program—nor about the simultaneous introduction of free distribution of certain goods, in anticipation of the transition from "socialism" to "communism." The rates of growth projected in that five-year plan were less than those ostensibly achieved in most earlier years. In agriculture, to be sure, the generally poor record of plan fulfillment in the past makes the projected growth rate seem overly optimistic, particularly for a country whose agriculture is subject to the vagaries of fluctuating climatic conditions and other natural hindrances. In industry, the targets seem feasible, and only the poor performance of the early years of this decade casts doubt on the likelihood of fulfillment.

The approach to agricultural problems differed greatly from that regarding industry. The management reorganization and economic reform in industry were indicative of the leadership's conviction that more goods, and more suitable goods, could be squeezed out of the existing industrial plant and resources by altering lines of control and by adjusting incentives. In agriculture, the stress was less on administrative reorganization and more on altering the distribution of resources. The latter involved betterment of the farmers' terms of trade and the channeling of increased investment to collective and state farms. Such investment decisions met resistance, particularly after agricultural performance improved. Both Leonid I. Brezhnev and Dimitri S. Poliansky complained of bureaucratic opposition to measures benefiting agriculture.[4] (The Party chief, despite his general responsibilities, continued as the regime's principal spokesman on agriculture, and Poliansky served as the highest Party and government official with specific responsibilities in regard to agriculture.)

IDEOLOGICAL TIGHTENING-UP

Ideological problems continued to be troublesome in the USSR. The militant attacks on Stalin to which Khrushchev periodically had resorted went out of vogue, although the post-Khrushchev leaders also avoided the fulsome praise of Stalin in which Khrushchev had indulged on occasion. "De-Stalinization" apparently ceased to be a major factor dividing the top leaders: the issue no longer played the instrumental role that had made attacks on Stalin useful to Khrushchev in undermining rivals and in promoting reforms.[*] The new leaders wanted to hear nothing more about the "Stalin problem." Stalin was buried; let him stay buried.[5] The "cult of personality" was still mentioned (if less often), but descriptions of 1934–1953 as "the period of the cult of personality" were no longer permitted. Modest acknowledgments of Stalin's contributions were voiced by Brezhnev on two ceremonial occasions in 1965, and Stalin's role as leader of the

[4] See Brezhnev's speech to the Central Committee on September 29, 1965, in *Pravda*, September 30, 1965; and Poliansky's speech at Pavlovsk, reported in *Pravda*, March 3, 1967, and his article in *Kommunist*, No. 15 (October, 1967), 15–31.

[*] Some participants in the project disagree with this judgment. They believe that de-Stalinization continues to be a major issue dividing the top leaders, with the "conservatives" seeking to stop all criticism of Stalin or even to restore him to honored status and the "reformers" seeking to continue attacks on Stalin in order to promote reform and "modernization" of the Soviet system.

[5] This attitude had been criticized by Khrushchev in a speech of June 21, 1963, to a CC plenum. He said that opposition to discussing Stalin's "personality cult" came not only from those implicated in the crimes but also from those who "reasoned like Philistines": "Stalin was dead, many of his victims were dead, the Soviet state was advancing, why stir things up?" Plenum of the CC CPSU, June 18–21, 1963, *Stenograficheskii otchet* (Moscow: Politizdat, 1964), 279–80.

Soviet Union in World War II came to be depicted more favorably. But no restoration of Stalin to hero-status was attempted.

The post-1964 leaders were insistent on the portrayal of Soviet development as a great success story, and the 50th anniversary of Soviet power, in 1967, found them pulling out all the stops. Only the barest acknowledgment of "the bitterness of losses, temporary failures, and mistakes" shaded the accounts of progress. The enforcement of optimism dictated not only restrictions on criticism of Stalin but also the silencing of writers given to darker moods about Soviet reality, such as Alexander Solzhenitsyn. He had been able, in 1962, to publish *One Day in the Life of Ivan Denisovich* (the first novel about Soviet forced labor camps) and subsequently a few other stories noticeably lacking in the *partiinost* (Party spirit) prescribed for artists and writers. But even under Khrushchev, in April, 1964, *Pravda* had given a basically negative appraisal of Solzhenitsyn's work by rejecting his candidacy for a Lenin prize; and he was allowed to publish nothing after that. Literature about forced labor camps and purges almost, but not quite, disappeared. There were said to be no "forbidden topics," but there were clearly forbidden ways of treating these topics.[6]

This kind of official pressure resulted not only in the censor's ban on Solzhenitsyn and some other authors, but involved use of criminal prosecutions against a number of intellectuals. The most important case involved the trial and sentencing to hard labor (in February, 1966) of Andrei Siniavsky and Iulii Daniel. These two authors had succeeded in publishing abroad, under pseudonyms, satires and other works critical of Soviet life. Other dissidents brought to trial were less well-known than Siniavsky and Daniel, and the charges brought against them involved less strictly literary offenses than those imputed to these two authors. Nevertheless, the willingness of the regime to resort to such measures of repression indicated the disquiet felt over dissident behavior. This disquiet was aggravated by the fact that a good many scientists and other intellectuals protested the use of criminal sanctions and the cavalier treatment of the defendants in the courtrooms and in the communications media.

The regime's nervousness over the evidences of dissent and the willingness of individuals to resist police and public pressure was un-

---

[6] Almost simultaneously with the XXIII Party Congress, a book was published on life in Soviet forced labor camps: Boris Diakov, *Povest o perezhitom* (Moscow: Sovetskaia Rossiia, 1966). Diakov was incarcerated in the postwar campaign against "cosmopolitans." Iuri Zhukov's *Liudi 30-kh godov* (Moscow: Sovetskaia Rossiia, 1966) includes a discussion of the prewar purge (esp. pp. 281–311). Both Diakov and Zhukov portray the purges as aberrant phenomena, unrepresentative of the "Party," which remained true to its humanist vocation. For all that, Diakov's is a searing account of camp life.

doubtedly tied in with the trend of events in Eastern European countries—in Poland, Yugoslavia, and most of all Czechoslovakia, where an intra-Party opposition successfully dislodged the Novotny regime in early 1968, and the liberalization accompanying the house-cleaning threatened to undermine the Communist Party's monopoly of power. The Soviet leaders made evident their concern, applying both political and military pressure in Eastern Europe to deter the Czechs and the Slovaks from going too far. Certainly the rapid crumbling of the old order in Czechoslovakia was an important factor in Moscow's decision to call a Central Committee Plenum in April, 1968. On February 16, Brezhnev told the Leningrad oblast Party conference that the next plenum would take up agricultural problems. Instead, the April meeting focused on ideological trends and called for stepping up of efforts against imperialist subversion and "bourgeois ideology." Brezhnev, Kosygin, and others who took part in this campaign, directed some attention to "leftist revisionists," such as Mao, but showed that they were most worried about "right-wing" deviations, such as doubts regarding the Communist Party's monopoly of power, ideas of the convergence of socialism and capitalism, and youthful challenges to the wisdom of the "fathers." [7] But the USSR no longer possessed the kind of influence in other Eastern European states to suppress dissidence without a show of force, and thus resorted to an armed occupation of Czechoslovakia in August, 1968. The full consequences of this act are not yet apparent, but it promised to alter expectations about the future of developments within the Soviet Union, in Soviet-East European relations, and in relations of the USSR with Western states.

PATIENT MANEUVER ON THE INTERNATIONAL FRONT

The only *open* change in Soviet foreign policy directly linked to the 1964 leadership shake-up was the temporary cessation of attacks on Mao and the Chinese Communists. This decision implied a criticism of Khrushchev's violent and personal polemics. Although the CPSU did not resume full-scale denunciations of Chinese behavior for two years, the Soviet leaders quickly made it clear (above all to the Chinese, who sent a delegation headed by Premier Chou En-lai to Moscow in early November, 1964) that they were not prepared to yield

[7] See the mid-February speeches of Kosygin (*Sovetskaia Belorussiia* [Minsk] February 15, 1968) and Brezhnev (*Leningradskaia pravda*, February 16, 1968); Brezhnev's speech on March 29 to the Moscow City Party Conference (*Pravda*, March 30, 1968), and Party Secretary Demichev's address on June 19 to an all-union conference of university social science officials (*Izvestiia*, June 20, 1968).

much for a *rapprochement*.[8] The Chinese conclusion that Nikita's
successors wanted to continue "Khrushchevism without Khrushchev"
was not far from the mark. In fact, in foreign policy generally, the
years since Khrushchev's departure saw no shift of policy of the scope
registered after Stalin's death. Nevertheless, post-1964 trends have
revealed a somewhat changed outlook on the means of advancing
Soviet interests.*

In foreign policy, it is particularly difficult to single out the novel
elements introduced by the post-Khrushchev leaders. Changes on
the international scene initiated abroad required new Soviet responses
or invited new Soviet initiatives. This is most apparent in Soviet relations with the United States. The leaders have adopted a more intransigent line toward America, and abandoned the idea that "sober
forces" are firmly in control of American policy. "American imperialism" has become a much more central target for propaganda attacks.
But Khrushchev's ouster preceded by only a few months the start of
systematic American bombing of North Vietnam, which would have
forced *any* Soviet leader to take a harsher line toward United States
official policy. Despite assurances from Washington of the limited
nature of American aims in Vietnam, sometimes depicted in U.S.
statements as anti-Chinese but never as anti-Soviet, the Soviet leaders
probably considered that the enlarged American commitment in Vietnam betrayed an increased willingness to use military power against
Communist and "national-liberation" forces. The Kremlin leaders also
saw the Vietnam struggle as an opportunity, for it presented an issue
on which they could seek to mobilize Communist and radical-nationalist forces under Soviet leadership and to find common cause
with disenchanted "bourgeois" regimes.

Whatever their cries of rage against American policy, the Kremlin
leaders burned no bridges to Washington. In many areas, they followed a policy of business-as-usual, although they preferred to skip any
displays of hand-holding. The fact that the Soviet Union negotiated

---

[8] Brezhnev is quoted as having told Chou En-lai in November, 1964, "that since
the October Plenum of the CPSU Central Committee, new favorable possibilities
have appeared to overcome gradually the difficulties that have developed in the
relations between our Parties." See the version printed in *Die Welt* (Hamburg),
March 21, 1966, of a letter sent by the CPSU to other Communist parties in early
1966. (A partial translation appeared in *The New York Times*, March 24, 1966.)
For a Chinese account of relations with the CPSU in late 1964 and early 1965, see
the editorial articles of *Jen Min Jih Pao* (Peking) and *Hung Chi* (Peking) of March
22, 1965, reprinted in English in *Peking Review*, VIII, No. 13 (March 26, 1965),
10–21.

* Some participants in the study consider that developments subsequent to Khrushchev's ouster brought about a major shift in the foreign policy perceptions, objectives, and programs of the Soviet leaders.

two arms control agreements with the United States against a din of exploding bombs indicated that the Soviet leaders believed that the war in Vietnam could probably be limited in scope and not become the opening engagement of World War III.

In some aspects of Soviet policy toward the "West," the Brezhnev group seems to have adopted an approach different from Khrushchev's. They have avoided any Soviet political-military initiatives comparable to Khrushchev's 1958–1961 campaign to change the status of Berlin, or his attempt in 1962 to install missiles in Cuba. These Soviet moves had tended to enliven prospects for a heady military confrontation, and to consolidate Western military alliances under American leadership. His Berlin and Cuban moves notwithstanding, however, Khrushchev in his last years in office seemed obsessed by the desire to work out some arrangement with the United States. This obsession was not shared by his successors, who have shown less interest in approaches to the United States and much more in trying to isolate the United States. They have patiently cultivated bilateral relations with allies of the U.S. in Europe and Asia. In Europe, much Soviet effort since 1964 has gone into promoting a new "European security" system designed to reduce American influence on the continent. Only the Federal Republic of Germany has been largely excluded from Soviet blandishments. In fact, the adoption in 1966 by the West German coalition government of a more flexible approach toward Communist-led states excited Soviet fears for the stability of the new order in East Germany and Eastern Europe, and the USSR energetically sought to thwart Bonn's initiatives.

In dealing with the underdeveloped countries of Africa, Asia, and Latin America, the USSR continued after 1964 to apply the tactics adopted in the mid-1950's. The USSR sought to move these states— many newly independent—toward a "leftward" and pro-Soviet orientation by channeling to them political-economic and military assistance. Much of this aid went to radical nationalist regimes, although India was also a prominent recipient. Compared to the Khrushchev period, this assistance tended to be even more concentrated on Arab countries, with a decline of Soviet commitments elsewhere. In part, this geographical concentration resulted from the demonstrated fragility of Communist-leaning regimes in other areas, as the downfall of the Sukarno regime in Indonesia and of Nkrumah's in Ghana showed. In part, however, the USSR focused on the Middle East because of its greater capabilities to display a military presence in the area. This potential, of course, was underlined in connection with the Arab-Israeli conflict in the summer of 1967. Despite the rout of the Soviet-equipped forces of the UAR and Syria (as well as those of Jordan) in the June war, the USSR began a speedy re-equipment of these forces, while counseling the Arabs against incautious moves toward Israel. The USSR took hard losses in the Middle Eastern imbroglio, but a year after the cease-fire it seemed that the position of the Soviet Union in the area was at least as strong as it had been prior to the conflict: the USSR had established itself as the only great power to give political and military support to the embattled Arabs; internal repercussions of the defeat, especially in the UAR, strengthened pro-Soviet elements in the Arab states; and states supplied militarily by the USSR regained a military position vis-à-vis Israel comparable to that existing before the June war began.

CONSOLIDATION OF THE PRO-MOSCOW MAJORITY IN THE WORLD COMMUNIST MOVEMENT

In the Communist world, the Soviet Union also made some gains in the period 1964–1968, particularly in repelling Chinese ambitions for leadership and influence. The Soviet leaders benefited from un-witting Chinese "assistance," for Chinese mistakes abroad and turmoil at home redounded to Soviet advantage. Just as the Soviet leaders sought in their approach to the Western states to isolate the United States, so they maneuvered to isolate the Chinese Communists within the world Communist movement and to isolate the Chinese People's Republic on the international scene. They were successful in improv-ing their relations with the two Asian Communist neighbors of China, North Vietnam and North Korea, which moved from a pro-Peking stance to a more neutral position within the divided Communist camp. But Moscow could not persuade either Hanoi or Pyongyang to take part in the preparations for a new world conference of Com-munist and Workers' Parties, an unwillingness shared by other Asian Communist parties.

The Soviet tactics after 1964 in dealing with the fragmented world Communist movement continued generally along the lines laid out in the Khrushchev period, although the successors hesitated before each new step giving formal recognition to the split. In pushing for a new world conference of Communists, the Soviet leaders had to reckon with the possibility that this effort would further divide rather than unify the movement. Apparently they calculated, however, that a greater danger lay in the absence of any kind of multilateral organization and of any agreed up-to-date statement of the majority Communist line. Only time would tell whether the Soviet leaders were right in their belief that the consolidation of the pro-Moscow majority in the movement could be achieved without deepening Mos-cow's differences with the neutralist elements in the Communist fold. The occupation of Czechoslovakia dealt another blow to prospects for

Soviet success in unifying a large majority of foreign Communist parties behind the leadership of the CPSU, for the move was criticized not only by several ruling parties but by the most important Western European Communist parties.

CONCLUSION

It is not easy to sort out what all these developments portend for arms control and other international agreements. The current hard-line in the Soviet Union, with calls for vigilance and combativeness against bourgeois ideology, the Soviet initiative for a world Communist conference, with the "struggle against imperialism" as the single topic on the agenda, and the rough treatment of Czechoslovakia, are unlikely to create an atmosphere propitious for any major deals with the United States and the West. The same cautiousness of the present ruling group that leads it to shy away from heady military confrontations with the United States, also makes it nervous about trends toward ideological coexistence, trends noted in the Soviet Union and even more in Eastern Europe. Czechoslovakia, in the spring of 1968, demonstrated once again that powerful currents for change lay just below the surface, threatening to sweep away the new order so laboriously installed. Whatever satisfaction the Soviet rulers derived from the evidence that such currents could also erupt in advanced Western countries did not mitigate their apprehensions about Communist instability. Only slightly less agitating to the Kremlin crowd were the national "deviations" that have continued to flourish among Communist states and movements, notably in Rumania. The Soviet leaders knew from experience that negotiations with the Western states on armaments questions provided occasions if not causes for accentuation of these differences among Communist ruling groups. They had seen it happen with the proposals, which remained only talk, about general and complete disarmament; in more acute form, with the nuclear weapons test-ban treaty; and once more, with the nonproliferation treaty. Communist-ruled countries were among the most prominent states refusing to approve these two treaties.

Against these negative factors must be placed other developments more favorable to the working out of East-West political arrangements, including possibly some to limit armaments. Prospects have improved for a halt to the escalation of the war in Vietnam and even for a negotiated end to that war. If this occurs, it would certainly remove the most critical and immediate issue shadowing American-Soviet relations. Although unrelated to that war, even the build-up of Soviet strategic nuclear forces to something nearer parity with those of the United States may work in the end to make feasible limitations on nuclear weapons and delivery vehicles that would otherwise be unthinkable.

Within the Communist world movement, the USSR has incentives not only to display itself bristling with revolutionary vigilance against the "imperialists," but also in other modes and models of conduct: to make the Soviet policy mode of coexistence between Communist and Western states yield practical results; and to transform the Soviet Union into that beckoning example of socialism in action that has been so often promised and so often postponed. Much of the Soviet support in the Communist movement comes from parties that rely basically on parliamentary and nonviolent procedures, and have made gains as the Cold War has become less intense. Czechoslovakia in 1968 was a cold shower for such movements.

It is in this perspective that the four years after Khrushchev must be assessed. Differences in outlook and in assessment of priorities among the current leaders will no doubt continue to manifest themselves. Contradictory trends have to be acknowledged, for the present leadership has left open a whole series of options, upon the choice of which depends much in the fate of the world of the 1970's.

2

THE POST-KHRUSHCHEV LEADERSHIP

The fate of Soviet disarmament policies is related to the kind of men who are in power in the USSR and to their mode of decision making. Decisions regarding arms control and disarmament or, alternatively, those on military forces, armaments, and strategy, often require painful choices on allocation of scarce resources, risks to be run, friends and opponents to be placated or spurned. An analysis of leadership developments since 1964 is thus essential to a study of Soviet activities in, and prospects for agreements on, arms control and disarmament.

Although it is obvious that disarmament issues were not important in the dissatisfaction that led to Khrushchev's ouster, there were changes after October, 1964, in the Soviet approach to disarmament questions, too.[1] Some of these were no doubt responses to alterations in the world environment, but others were more directly owing to the shift in leadership and to the perceptions and values characteristic of the new men in command. There is reason to suppose, moreover, that divisions of both an institutional and a personal nature on arms control and disarmament issues continue to exist within the Soviet elite.

PROFILE OF CURRENT LEADERS

Most of the members of the pre-1964 Party Presidium (as the Politburo was called from 1952 until 1966) and of Khrushchev's Party Secretariat continued to hold their positions after October, 1964.

---

[1] No criticism of Khrushchev's activities on disarmament was included in any of the materials published after his ouster. In fact, there was no criticism concerning foreign relations except for an implied rejection of Khrushchev's tactics in dealing with the Chinese Communists. Khrushchev's inclination to noisy campaigns found expression in foreign as well as domestic policy, and the post-October disparagement of such campaigns might be interpreted as a rejection of hullabaloo about disarmament. There seemed to be no such implication, however, in the Soviet materials.

Although the removal of Khrushchev had repercussions on the distribution of functional posts among the leaders, it resulted in few changes in the composition of the leading group. It is important to remember that the "new" leadership was basically the old leadership minus Khrushchev, since at the Politburo-Secretariat levels the only removals more or less clearly attributable to Khrushchev's downfall involved one candidate-member of the Presidium and three Party Secretaries.[2]

The continuity of leading personnel after 1964 was also reflected in the composition of the Central Committee elected at the xxiii CPSU Congress of March–April, 1966. More than 80 per cent of the members from 1961 still living in 1966 were re-elected—a far higher retention ratio than was true at the two preceding Congresses in 1956 and 1961.[3] The small casualty list resulting from the turnover of October, 1964, was emphasized by the fact that two out of the four victims at the Presidium and Secretariat level retained their Central Committee status when the new Committee was formed in 1966.[4]

Of the present members of the Politburo, only three had served under Stalin in the leading group; Mikhail A. Suslov was a full member of the Party Presidium at the time of Stalin's death; and both Leonid I. Brezhnev, now the Party General Secretary, and Aleksei N. Kosygin, now Chairman of the USSR Council of Ministers, were can-

---

[2] Party Secretary V. I. Poliakov, a Khrushchev protégé with agricultural responsibilities, was removed on November 16, 1964. On December 1, 1964, candidate-member of the Presidium L. N. Yefremov was sent out of Moscow to head the Stavropol krai Party organization. Although provincial chiefs are represented on the Politburo, the Stavropol assignment was below the level entitling the chief to Politburo membership. Yefremov was not actually removed, however, until the xxiii Party Congress (April 8, 1966). Party Secretary V. N. Titov had been in charge of Party organizational affairs in the period of Khrushchev's unpopular experiment with a split agricultural-industrial structure. He was sent in April, 1965, to be Second Secretary of the Kazakh Party organization, and was formally removed as a national Secretary on September 29, 1965. Khrushchev's principal official for ideology in the later years of his rule, Party Secretary L. F. Ilichev, was transferred to a less important post in the Ministry of Foreign Affairs, and was dropped from the Secretariat on March 26, 1965. He was the only one of these four subjected, like Khrushchev, to direct public criticism for activities prior to October, 1964.

[3] The "Extraordinary" xxi Party Congress in 1959 did not elect a new Central Committee or other Party organs. It is, therefore, not relevant in this context. For accounts of leadership change, see Jerry F. Hough, "Reforms in Government and Administration," in *Soviet Politics Since Khrushchev,* eds. Alexander Dall and Thomas B. Larson (Englewood Cliffs, N.J.: Prentice-Hall, Inc., 1968), and Severyn Bialer, "Soviet Leadership: Some Problems of Continuity Structure, and Cohesion," unpublished paper presented at the September, 1966, meeting of the American Political Science Association.

[4] The two were Yefremov and Titov.

didate-members.[5] None of the three had been as closely associated with Stalin as those who became the leading figures of the regime in March, 1953: G. M. Malenkov, V. M. Molotov, N. S. Khrushchev, N. A. Bulganin, and A. I. Mikoyan. In fact, Suslov, Brezhnev, and Kosygin were all dropped from the Presidium when it was reduced in size in March, 1953. Suslov came back in 1955, but Brezhnev and Kosygin regained membership only in the wake of Khrushchev's rise to dominance.[6] The ouster in June, 1957, of Khrushchev's principal opponents and rivals, Malenkov, Molotov, and Kaganovich, provided the opportunity for Brezhnev—who supported Khrushchev—to gain full membership on the Presidium and for Kosygin to become a candidate-member. Most of the other senior leaders of the post-Khrushchev regime entered the Politburo in 1957–1960, including Nikolai V. Podgorny (currently the Chairman of the Presidium of the USSR Supreme Soviet—the third-ranking official post); Andrei P. Kirilenko (now a Party Secretary, probably with specific responsibilities for the RSFSR); and Kirill T. Mazurov and Dimitri S. Poliansky (currently First Deputy Chairmen—under Kosygin—of the USSR Council of Ministers, specializing in industry and agriculture, respectively).[7] The present Politburo also includes as full members Gennadi I. Voronov, government chief for the RSFSR, and Piotr Ye. Shelest, Party chief for the Ukraine, who entered the Politburo in 1961 and 1963 respectively.[8] Finally, the youngest and the oldest of the current Politburo members were added in the period after Khrushchev's fall: Aleksandr N. Shelepin, the only member of the Politburo born after the October Revolution (in 1918), and Arvid Ia. Pelshe, a Latvian, who is almost 70 years old.[9] Pelshe's election in 1966 was probably meant to supply an

[5] The Presidium of 1952–1953 was much larger (with 25 full members and 11 candidate-members) than the predecessor Politburo or than the Presidium and Politburo since 1953. Hence, membership in 1952–1953 did not mean as much in terms of belonging to the inner circle of leaders as in other periods. For Kosygin it reflected, in fact, a drop in fortune, because he had been a candidate-member of the old Politburo in 1946–1948 and a full member from 1948 to 1952.

[6] Suslov's election as a full member of the Presidium occurred at the July, 1955, Plenum of the CPSU Central Committee, when both Malenkov and Molotov were under fire. Brezhnev regained candidate status in 1956 at the xx Party Congress.

[7] Mazurov and Kirilenko also benefited from the June, 1957, events by attaining candidate-membership on the Presidium. Kosygin received full membership in 1960 along with Podgorny and Poliansky (both candidates from 1958). For details, see the charts in Michel Tatu, Le Pouvoir en U.R.S.S. (Paris: Bernard Grasset, 1967), pp. 560, 576, 592.

[8] Shelest became a full member in November, 1964, and Mazurov in March, 1965.

[9] Pelshe's age and Party seniority probably dictated his selection in 1966 as Chairman of the Committee of Party Control. This post has its intricacies, but does not appear to involve the heavy administrative load borne by most of the Politburo members.

Old Bolshevik as a decorative element; but the promotion of Shelepin in November, 1964, had more political significance, to be discussed subsequently.

Since so few casualties and few new faces among Politburo and Secretariat members resulted from the turnover in October, 1964, it is clearly impossible to draw any sharp contrast between the men in the top ranks of the Khrushchev and post-Khrushchev periods. Still, some characteristics of the present leadership should be noted. Fifty years after the Revolution it is hardly surprising that this group does not include anyone who made a name for himself in the period of revolution and civil war. Even if Stalin had not killed so many of the veterans of 1917, if they lived today, they would be in their seventies or eighties.

In several respects, the leaders now in power have a different profile from those of even a decade ago. For example, almost all have had higher education of one kind or another, mostly in engineering and technical production institutes.[10] The last of an older generation of leaders who had little formal schooling, such as Khrushchev, Mikoyan, and Shvernik, left the scene in 1964–1966. All the present leaders learned politics in the rough Stalinist school, and several benefited directly from the opening up of high posts in the purges of the 1930's, when younger men rose quickly over the dead bodies of their predecessors. Kosygin is perhaps the best example. At the age of 35, he became People's Commissar of the Textile Industry in 1939, denouncing in the required manner his predecessors (People's Commissars of Light Industry Liubimov and Shestakov) for their "wrecking" activities.[11] But, as mentioned, the senior men of the present group also benefited from the bloodless victory of Khrushchev over the other members of the old guard in the mid–1950's, when Politburo vacancies occurred for which they were logical candidates.

COLLECTIVITY IN PRACTICE

If the faces of the current leaders were familiar in the period before 1964, the absence of Khrushchev and of any Khrushchev-like successor has made a considerable difference in their mode of operation. The Party leadership decided in October, 1964, not only to elect different

[10] Their specialized training was in the following fields: Brezhnev, metallurgy; Kirilenko, aviation industry; Podgorny, food industry; Poliansky, agriculture; Voronov, mining; Kosygin, textile industry; Shelest, metallurgy; and Mazurov, road transport. The others, Pelshe, Suslov, and Shelepin, were trained in political-economic-history faculties.

[11] Edmund F. Janssens, "The People's Commissariat for Light Industry: A Case Study in Soviet Industrial Administration," unpublished Russian Institute Certificate Essay, Columbia University, 1952.

men as Party and government chiefs (combined from 1958) but henceforward to keep these posts separate.[12] This was only one manifestation of a re-emphasis on collective leadership as against the dominance of a single man.[13] In both Stalin's and in Khrushchev's time, collective leadership was proclaimed as the guiding principle for policy making; the xxii Party Congress in 1961 had added a paragraph to the Party bylaws on the subject.[14] But despite the formally collective structure of the principal Party and government organs, practice subverted theory at the top level. Stalin had shown that an all powerful *vozhd* could get away with murder; Khrushchev proved that he could get his way without murder. Each developed his own kind of personality cult, and these cults testified and contributed to the domination of political life by one man.

It became evident after October, 1964, although no decision on the matter came to light, that measures were in effect against undue personification of the Soviet regime by a single leader. The very separation of the two leading posts diminished the tendency to spotlight one man, but other means were used also. For example, some of the photographs published of Brezhnev addressing meetings were so "collectivist" in their angle that the speaker could scarcely be identified.[15]

[12] See P. A. Rodionov, *Kollektivnost—vysshii printsip partiinogo rukovodstva* (Moscow: Politizdat, 1967), p. 219:
The [October] Plenum freed N. S. Khrushchev from the duties of First Secretary and member of the Presidium of the cc, cpsu, and of Chairman of the Council of Ministers of the USSR, and recognized the inexpedience of further assignment to one person of the duties of First Secretary of the cc and Chairman of the USSR Council of Ministers.

[13] Stalin's dictatorship long antedated his assumption in 1941 of the government post. In contrast, however, Khrushchev's assumption of the government chairmanship in 1958 (he had been First Secretary of the Party since September, 1953) did play a part in increasing his leverage over Soviet political life.

[14] "Collective leadership" in Soviet usage refers to the *fact* that groups rather than individuals are placed at the head of Party, governmental, and other institutions, and to the *principle* that these groups should function by discussion and majority rule rather than be under the thumb of the most important member. Soviet discussions of "collective leadership" are usually not centered on organs such as the cpsu Politburo or Central Committee, or the USSR Council of Ministers, but on the activities of the thousands of councils, committees, and buros that exist at all levels of political life. Both the terms "collective leadership" (*kollektivnoe rukovodstvo*) and "collectivity of leadership" (*kollektivnost rukovodstva*) are used. They have slightly different connotations, the former meaning "leadership which is collective," the latter the "collective quality of leadership." The latter term is employed in the Party bylaws. It might also be noted in this connection that the Central Committee, rather than the Politburo, is regarded as "the highest organ" of collective leadership in the cpsu. For everyday affairs, the highest organ is obviously the Politburo, and not the Central Committee.

[15] E.g., the photograph in *Pravda* of May 9, 1965, of Brezhnev addressing the ceremonial gathering in the Kremlin on the previous day in honor of the 20th anniversary of the end of the war in Europe. When Brezhnev dedicated a statue

The "I" fell out of speeches; and speeches, interviews, and personal messages became less common, or were published less often; tributes to Brezhnev were rare.[16] The most remarkable display underlining the principle of collectivity occurred in the Czech crisis of 1968, when all but two full members of the CPSU Politburo participated in talks at Cierna-nad-Tisou with the entire Presidium of the Czechoslovak Party. (It must be granted, however, that a major purpose of this Soviet move was to exploit differences among the Czech leaders.)

Under Soviet conditions, collective leadership does not imply that the members of the ruling group in the Politburo are equal, except in voting rights. On the contrary, they are vastly unequal both in "prestige" and in power. "Prestige" is used here to refer to the respect accorded an individual apart from that derived from his office. Seniority counts for something in giving prestige, and Brezhnev is, except for Suslov, the present leader with the longest continuous membership on the Politburo, followed by Kosygin.[17] Furthermore, unlike both Suslov and Kosygin, Brezhnev has had in the past two decades the kind of posts that reflect the highest esteem among the Party elite, as a regional Party Secretary with final responsibility for coordinating all activities within an important area of the USSR. Incidentally, the lack of this experience makes Kosygin and Suslov unlikely candidates for the top job even if Brezhnev were to drop dead tomorrow, and makes such colleagues as Podgorny, Poliansky, and Mazurov eligible as possible successors.[18]

---

in Moscow to the 12th century Georgian poet Shota Rustaveli, *Pravda* published (October 26, 1966) a photograph showing the Rustaveli statue and some of the audience but no Brezhnev, an ironic variation on the famous (though apocryphal) anecdote of the statue to Pushkin that showed Stalin reading a book by Pushkin.

[16] Brezhnev and the other leaders have continued to be very active in visiting within the Soviet Union and abroad; it is the publicity about these visits which has diminished. Khrushchev also presented impersonal reports on solemn occasions, but these impersonal expressions have become the rule with the post-Khrushchev leaders, as they were with Stalin in his time. The reports and more important speeches delivered by Brezhnev are repeatedly cited by other authors and speakers, but tributes to the man are rare; a few, however, were registered at the XXIII Party Congress and since.

[17] Although Kosygin became a full member of the Party Presidium at the same time as Podgorny and Poliansky, he antedates them as a candidate-member. Brezhnev, Kosygin, Podgorny, and Suslov are all in the upper age group of the present Politburo (full members).

[18] Suslov did have regional assignments up to 1946, in Rostov, Stavropol, and Vilna, but since that time he has been at central Party headquarters (as a Secretary since 1947) with "staff" responsibilities for ideological and world Communist affairs. Kosygin has been a government administrator in Moscow throughout his career. It is their background as Party chiefs in various provinces that gives Mazurov and Poliansky, for example, the flexibility of movement into different posts at the USSR level, despite the fact that they are currently Kosygin's deputies

Personal prestige aside, the office of General Secretary gives Brezhnev the greatest power leverage.[19] The other full members of the Politburo have assignments giving them widely varying amounts of authority and influence. Some occupy posts directly subordinate to others; some have responsibilities for only a part of the country, others for the USSR as a whole. The ranking of Politburo members is thus affected by familiar bureaucratic and geographical practices (chiefs over Indians, national over regional officials) as well as by the supremacy accorded the Party over governmental and other institutions.[20]

POLITBURO AND CENTRAL COMMITTEE

The coexistence of collective leadership with highly unequal distribution of authority has proved difficult to stabilize, and the period since October, 1964, is too short to demonstrate the long-term viability of group rule over the USSR.* Therefore, a reversion to one-man dominance is possible. It is by no means inevitable, however, because barriers to one-man dominance have been strengthened in the past 15 years.[21] The "oligarchs" of the Politburo are now in a stronger position to prevent the top leader from "free-wheeling."

It may be that a trend will set in toward greater "democratization" of Soviet political life, to open up policy discussions to a broader circle within the elite rather than confining it to the Politburo and Secretariat. There are only a few signs, however, that the present

---

in the government apparatus. Although Podgorny's present post as titular chief of state is not one of great power, it should be remembered that Brezhnev occupied this position in 1960–1964. He regained in 1963 membership on the Party Secretariat, and replaced Khrushchev as First Secretary only three months after he was freed as chief of state.

[19] The title of General Secretary had previously been used only by Stalin. Another term associated with the Stalin era was reintroduced at the same time with the restoration of "Politburo" (in use from 1917 to 1952) for "Presidium" to describe the top leadership group of the Party.

[20] This supremacy of the Party is also a "constitutional" fact, as the principle is written into the current USSR Constitution. In connection with the point about "national over regional officials" it should be noted that the CPSU Politburo includes a number of officials with responsibilities in various republics, mostly among the candidate-members but with RSFSR and Ukrainian officials among the full members.

* Some of the members of the study group look on the present leadership as highly unstable, both in its composition and mode of operation. They stress the post-1964 shifts in assignment affecting most of the Politburo and Secretariat members as well as the evidence of delay and of pulling and hauling in opposed directions. They consider, therefore, that the text minimizes this leadership instability.

[21] See Jerome M. Gilson, "New Factors of Stability in Soviet Collective Leadership," *World Politics*, XIX, No. 4 (July, 1967), 563–81.

leaders want to move in this direction, and it may not be in their interest to do so.[22] (The members may want to be consulted before Brezhnev acts, but not want to consult others down the line.)

A trend toward broadening participation in decision making would affect primarily the status of the CPSU Central Committee. As under Khrushchev, it continues to be called into session regularly, but usually to ratify decisions arrived at beforehand by the Politburo.[23] Soviet spokesmen say that the atmosphere at these meetings is now businesslike, that the discussions are frank, and that the members feel relief because there is no longer a bully boy present to dominate the proceedings. This seems to be true, although there is little evidence that the Central Committee (more than 350 members) spends much time in considering alternative courses of action.[24]

Prior to the XXIII Party Congress in 1966 the Politburo paid a nod to the Central Committee by having the latter approve the two reports prepared in its name for the Congress. Normally, the leaders invoke the name of the Central Committee as authority for their acts without bothering to convene that body. Given the length and complexity of these reports, delivered by Brezhnev and Kosygin, the Central Committee could not discuss them in depth in sessions of a single day each.[25]

A more important role for the Central Committee on foreign policy questions seemed to be shaping up in 1966–1968. The Central Committee was assembled in December, 1966, to discuss Sino-Soviet relations and the world Communist movement, in June, 1967, to discuss the Soviet posture in regard to the Arab-Israeli hostilities, and in

---

[22] See on this point the discussion by Richard Lowenthal in *Soviet Politics Since Khrushchev.*

[23] This was exemplified at the March, 1965, meeting on agriculture, where Brezhnev presented a program worked out in the Presidium: at the December, 1966, Plenum on the Chinese problem and the world Communist movement, following rather than preceding a significant step-up (November, 1966) in Soviet polemics against the Chinese Communists; and at the June, 1967, Plenum, called upon to endorse the Politburo's handling of the Middle East crisis.

[24] One reason for the scantiness of the evidence on Central Committee meetings is that, since October, 1964, a stenographic report has been published for only one plenum, that of March, 1965. From 1958 such reports had been published for all of the plenums of the Khrushchev period (though the transcripts were not complete). G. G. Morekhina, writing in *Voprosy istorii KPSS,* No. 9 (1965), 143–50, said that, "according to a decision of the Central Committee of the CPSU, a multivolume history of the CPSU is to be issued and also stenographic reports of the congresses, conferences, and Central Committee plenums of the CPSU." The multivolume history is underway, but the record of publication of other documents is poorer for the Brezhnev than for the Khrushchev period.

[25] The session on Kosygin's report was held on February 19, 1966, and that on the (Brezhnev) report of the Central Committee on March 26, 1966. See *Pravda,* February 20, March 27, 1966.

July, 1968, to discuss the situation in Czechoslovakia.[26] Although foreign policy had been referred to at earlier Central Committee meetings, such discussions had been somewhat incidental to the main business.[27] The June, 1967, meeting resulted in the expected unanimous endorsement of the Politburo's handling of the crisis in the Middle East. Nevertheless, the occasion was enlivened—according to unofficial reports—when a critical speech was delivered by a "hard-liner," Moscow City Party Secretary Yegorychev, who paid for his contumacy by finding himself out of that job seven days later.[28] And the Politburo may not be as enthusiastic in the future about inviting this kind of discussion of their stewardship of the nation's affairs.

LEADERSHIP SHIFTS AND CONFLICT

The relative stability of membership in the Politburo and Secretariat[29] has not prevented shifts in job assignments affecting a large ma-

[26] For the Plenum of December 12–13, 1966, see *Pravda*, December 13–15; for that of June 20–21, 1967, see *Pravda*, June 21–23; for that of July 17, 1968, see *Pravda*, July 18–19, 1968.

[27] There was some discussion of foreign policy at the July, 1955 Plenum; at the Plenum on ideological work in June, 1963; and at the agricultural Plenum in February, 1964. Stenographic reports are available for the last two meetings. That such reports are not complete was indicated in Khrushchev's speech of June 21, 1963, to the Plenum on ideological questions. Khrushchev referred to the fact that the Party Presidium had assigned Suslov, Andropov, and Ponomarev to report to the meeting on problems with the Chinese and on the proposed line to be taken by the Soviet representatives in the forthcoming meetings with the Chinese delegation (held in July). Although the Plenum approved a resolution on the subject, there is no other indication in the stenographic report that any of the three addressed the meeting. See Plenum of the Central Committee of the CPSU, June 18–21, 1963, *Stenograficheskii otchet* (Moscow: Politizdat, 1964), 255.

[28] *Pravda*, June 28, 1967.

[29] In addition to individuals already mentioned who left the Politburo-Secretariat in or after October, 1964 (Khrushchev, Poliakov, Yefremov, Ilichev, and Titov), there were others dropped or added for reasons probably unrelated to Khrushchev's fall. Frol Kozlov was dropped from the Politburo and Secretariat in November, 1964, two months before he died; A. I. Mikoyan and N. M. Shvernik were dropped at the XXIII Party Congress (both were over 70, and Shvernik had become feeble); Podgorny was dropped from the Secretariat officially at the Congress, because his assignment in December, 1965, to the chairmanship of the Presidium of the USSR Supreme Soviet in place of Mikoyan was incompatible with continued service as a national Party Secretary: Party Secretary A. P. Rudakov died after the XXIII Congress and was replaced by M. S. Solomentsev on December 13, 1966; and Shelepin and Iu. V. Andropov were also dropped from the Secretariat as a result of assignments in May–June, 1967, to incompatible jobs. Andropov was elected a candidate-member of the Politburo and dropped as a Secretary on June 21, 1967, as a result of his assignment in May to head the KGB. Shelepin was officially relieved of his post as Secretary on September 26, 1967, subsequent to

jority of the members. Some of these shifts were incidental to administrative reorganizations, especially those of November, 1964, December, 1965, and April, 1966.[30] The ups and downs of individual leaders need not be discussed here. The rise of Comrade X and the decline of Y are not of great interest unless these comrades stand for different policies, and little is known about the individual policy orientations of the present Politburo members[31]—less, in fact, than was true under Khrushchev.

The fate of Aleksandr Shelepin deserves some mention, however. His elevation to full membership on the Politburo in November, 1964, jumping over the usual candidate stage, seemed to place him in an extremely strong position to promote his own career and his policy preferences, generally thought to be conservative rather than reformist. Shelepin's career reminded observers of Malenkov's in an earlier period: he stayed close to the center of power in Moscow and never held a post in the provinces, unlike most of his colleagues on the Politburo. Fifteen years at the national headquarters of the Komsomol, of which the last six involved the top post, and three years as head of the KGB (Committee of State Security) were enough to suggest a "hard-line" orientation.[32] He entered the Politburo while serving as Chairman of

his election in June as head of Soviet trade unions. Party Secretary P. N. Demichev became a candidate-member of the Politburo in late 1964 and D. F. Ustinov became a secretary and candidate-member of the Politburo in early 1965. Three regional officials were added as Politburo candidates in late 1965 and early 1966.

[30] The transformation of the Committee of Party-State Control into a Committee of People's Control in December, 1965, and the abolition of the CC Buro for the RSFSR in April, 1966, affected the posts assigned Shelepin and Kirilenko.

[31] Kremlinologists rely principally on two kinds of indicators to gauge these orientations. (They rarely have access, except in the aftermath of conflicts resulting in the ouster of important leaders, to direct evidence from Soviet sources on differences among leaders. Palmiro Togliatti's advice to Soviet leaders, that they should make public their individual stands on crucial issues, was published in the Soviet Union, but the leaders never followed the advice. See *Pravda*, September 10, 1964.) These indicators are (1) variations in formulas used by different leaders in their speeches, and (2) different career-lines and posts occupied by the leaders. The first of these is discussed subsequently in this chapter, and at greater length in the chapter by Wolfgang Leonhard in *Soviet Politics Since Khrushchev*. The second approach seeks to deduce policy "slants" from the kind of jobs occupied in the past or present by various leaders. Thus, Kosygin's long identification with the consumers' goods industries is presumed to make him favorable toward international and domestic policies that would permit the USSR to promote the material welfare of its citizens. Officials preoccupied most of their lives with heavy industry, or Party officials accustomed to enforcing ideological orthodoxy, are presumed to favor a "harder" line on foreign and domestic issues.

[32] In 1943 Shelepin, then 25, became a national Secretary of the Komsomol organization, which he headed in 1952–1958. In 1958 he replaced General I. A. Serov as head of the KGB. Almost all the incumbents of this post in the period after Lenin's death, like those of top Party head and chief of the government, have come to a violent end or suffered some disgrace.

the Committee of Party-State Control, which allowed him to have membership simultaneously in the Party Secretariat, and the USSR Council of Ministers (as a Deputy Chairman), as well as the Politburo. In December, 1965, however, the control committee was reorganized and downgraded to the accompaniment of some critical remarks about its work by Brezhnev.[33] This marked a setback for Shelepin, because in Moscow as elsewhere, few officials manage to rise while their organizational bases sink. Subsequent to this, Shelepin was active for a year and a half as a Party Secretary supervising domestic trade and service industries, not precisely the post an ambitious official would select to forward his career.[34] His tenure as a Party Secretary was brought to an end in June, 1967, when he replaced V. V. Grishin as head of the Soviet trade unions.[35] This too was a dubious assignment for a full member of the Politburo, because the post offered little leverage and had usually been filled by a candidate-member.[36] The vacancy resulted from the leaders' decision to place V. V. Grishin in the Moscow City Party post after the set-to at the Central Committee Plenum in June, 1967, led to the removal of Yegorychev, another "hard-liner." There were links between Shelepin and Yegorychev, and also between Shelepin and V. Ye. Semichastny, removed as KGB head in May and exiled to a minor position in the Ukraine. Semichastny had succeeded Shelepin in both the KGB and Komsomol posts, after serving under him as a deputy for eight years at the Komsomol national headquarters. Another Shelepin associate, S. P. Pavlov, also suffered a reverse when he was transferred in June, 1968, from the top Komsomol job to be head of the Union of Sport Societies and Organizations of the USSR. Much is unclear in all these shifts, but certainly Yegorychev and Semichastny departed in some disgrace, and Shelepin's star seems to have waned.

The events of May and June, 1967, offered an example of a certain turmoil in Moscow affecting the top leadership, even if it was unclear precisely which personal and policy issues were at stake. Neither the relative stability of the top group since 1964 nor the persistence of the

[33] *Pravda*, December 7, 1965. Brezhnev's criticism was mild, and was accompanied by much praise for the work of the control organization during its three years of operation under the form instituted by Khrushchev. Nevertheless, the criticism signified some top-level dissatisfaction.

[34] Although other Party Secretaries have specific supervisory responsibilities comparable to those assigned Shelepin, his appeared to be even less important than those of Party Secretaries who are not on the Politburo. See Tatu, pp. 546–52.

[35] Shelepin was appointed Chairman of All-Union Central Council of Trade Unions, July 11, 1967 (*Pravda*, July 12, 1967).

[36] Grishin has been a candidate-member of the Politburo only since 1961, although he had been head of the trade unions from 1956. His predecessor was N. M. Shvernik, who was a candidate-member of the Presidium while serving in the trade union post in 1953–1956, and only subsequently became a full member.

collective mode of leadership presuppose that policy conflicts have
disappeared or diminished in intensity since Khrushchev's ouster. The
low casualty rate among Politburo and Central Committee members
does suggest that Khrushchev found very few supporters when some of
his colleagues initiated the move to oust him. Khrushchev had offended
many interests, and thus leaders of very different orientations could
agree that he had to go.[37] But agreement on this point did not mean
continued agreement on the way of solving the problems left behind.

Despite evidence of conflict, it is still difficult to chart the devisive
issues of the present day and the line-up of opponents on such issues.
This difficulty has perhaps been increased since 1964 by the reduction
of "personal" elements in speeches and an increase in "bureaucratic"
and "collective" elements. Frequently the leaders speak with strong
emphasis on their organizational roles as heads of individual Party
or government bodies, and their speeches emerge from a collective
clearance process that squeezes out personal idiosyncrasies. The well-
deserved reputation for dullness of General Secretary Brezhnev and
other leaders comes not just from their colorless personalities but from
the operation of "collective leadership," which produces speeches
sounding like committee reports. These characteristics were all too
evident at the xxiii Party Congress in 1966. The key statements were
assigned to only a few chiefs of the various bureaucracies, who voiced
institutional rather than personal themes. Among the national leaders
on the Presidium and Secretariat only Brezhnev, Kosygin, Podgorny,
and Grishin spoke (as heads of Party, government, soviet, and trade-
union organizations).[38] This pattern contrasted with that of the xxii
Congress in 1961, when every member of the Presidium and Secretariat had a place on the roster of speakers.

ISSUES CONFRONTING THE LEADERSHIP

The cautious approach of the post-Khrushchev leadership to dyna-
mite-laden problems left over from the pre-1964 era—such as that of
de-Stalinization—and to continuing difficulties in foreign policy—how
to deal with Communist China or, alternatively, with the United
States—can be interpreted in contradictory ways. This may be an
"agreed caution" reflecting the values and mood of the dominant leaders. But it could also be that it reflects not agreement but disagreement

[37] For a discussion of this point, see Leonhard, *Soviet Politics Since Khrushchev*.
[38] This does not count Suslov, who merely read an agreed declaration on Vietnam, and Party Secretary I. V. Kapitonov, who read the report of the commission
on credentials. The several members and candidate-members of the Presidium
who have regional responsibilities, with headquarters out of Moscow, all spoke
about their specific republics.

within a Politburo divided between "modernizers" and conservatives, the former flanked by a reformist wing of the elite and the latter by a strongly dogmatic, "neo-Stalinist" faction. From this viewpoint, decisions are seen as compromises reflecting the shifting weight of "modernist" and conservative approaches.[39]

The presence of unresolved conflicts has been strongly suggested by the number of questions on which the regime promised decisions and then failed to carry through.* A new Constitution for the USSR was promised, but a draft has never been published.[40] A final version of the five-year plan for 1966–1970 was never enacted into law, as originally planned; and it is now clear that it will not be published.[41] The decision to convoke a third Congress of Collective Farmers in 1966 and to prepare a new Collective Farm Charter provides an even more telling case, because this was not a left-over from the Khrushchev period (like revision of the Constitution), nor an event tied to a timetable (like the five-year plan). The target date is long past, and little has been heard recently about either the Congress or the new Charter (to replace that of 1935).[42] The ambivalent moves that preceded the Soviet-led

---

[39] Wolfgang Leonhard has suggested that the "modernizing" viewpoint is represented in the Politburo by Kosygin, Podgorny, and Shelest; the conservative viewpoint by Brezhnev, Suslov, and (most of all) Shelepin. See *Soviet Politics Since Khrushchev.*

* Some participants in the study believe that a failure to resolve differences has condemned the present regime to drift and indecision. Other participants considered these "failures to act" of less importance, noting the many issues of domestic and foreign policy on which the leadership was able to respond decisively and even rapidly. The latter viewpoint is upheld elsewhere in this report.

[40] Brezhnev was elected on December 11, 1964, to succeed Khrushchev as head of the commission preparing the new Constitution. There have been occasional references in the Soviet press of work on the draft. There were, also, intimations that the new Constitution would be unveiled to coincide with the celebration of the 50th anniversary of Soviet power in Russia, but this did not occur. *Pravda,* on December 5, 1966 (Constitution Day) referred to "the new Constitution of the USSR, now being worked out, which will crown the glorious half-century course of the country of Soviets." There was no reminder of the new Constitution in either the *Pravda* or *Izvestiia* editorial on Constitution Day one year later.

[41] Gosplan Chairman N. K. Baibakov told the USSR Supreme Soviet on October 10, 1967, that "the drafting of the eighth five-year plan" would be completed after confirmation by the Supreme Soviet of the yearly plans for 1969 and 1970. (*Pravda,* October 11, 1967.) The Politburo and USSR Council of Ministers have already begun work on the ninth five-year plan (for 1971–1975), according to Premier Kosygin (*Sovetskaia Belorussiia,* February 15, 1968).

[42] In March, 1965, the Central Committee approved a decision to convoke the Congress and prepare a new Charter. On January 26, 1966, *Pravda* announced the establishment of a commission under Brezhnev's chairmanship to draft the document. Brezhnev mentioned both the Charter and Farmers' Congress in his report to the XXIII Party Congress. The proposed new Charter was mentioned in an article in *Kommunist,* No. 1 (January, 1968), 55–56.

occupation of Czechoslovakia in August, 1968, may also have been due to conflicts among the Soviet leaders on the gravity of the situation and on appropriate methods of dealing with Czechoslovakia.

In addition to the missing Charter and Congress of Farmers, agricultural problems gave rise to other differences which found overt expression. In his report to the XXIII Party Congress, Brezhnev suggested that a system of elective collective farm organs be set up in the country, headed by a Collective Farm Center of the USSR. Although he asked for the opinion of the delegates on the matter, Brezhnev presented only arguments in its favor. A few Party officials endorsed the suggestion, apparently without great enthusiasm, but the Congress merely referred the question back to the Central Committee.[43] Arguments over allocation of resources to agriculture were alluded to on two occasions by Politburo member D. S. Poliansky (the highest Party official with agricultural responsibilities).[44] He criticized those who thought that agricultural investments could be cut down after the good 1966 harvest year. He named no names, of course, but it seemed clear that he referred to high-level differences, because decisions on competing claims of various sectors have to be made by the Politburo. In a milder way, Brezhnev also complained at the September, 1965, Party Central Committee Plenum of people who wanted to settle accounts at the expense of agriculture.[45]

PRIORITIES IN DEFENSE AND FOREIGN POLICY

The allocations problem became more acute as the USSR sought in the post-Khrushchev period to build up its strategic nuclear forces, and responded to increased American military activities in Vietnam, North and South, by increasing military and economic assistance to Hanoi. There were noticeable differences among the leaders in the summer of 1965 over the priority that could be accorded to internal economic development and to satisfaction of consumer needs, as against that of strengthening Soviet defenses. Podgorny, Kirilenko, and Poliansky tended to view as past the period in which popular welfare had to be sacrificed in favor of more pressing state needs. Suslov and Shelepin, in contrast, spoke more about the dangers of "imperialist attack" and the continuing need for material sacrifices. Brezhnev and Kosygin seemed ambivalent on the issue.[46] As the escala-

---

[43] *The 23rd Congress of the CPSU* (Moscow: Novosti, 1967), pp. 90–91, 296.

[44] For Poliansky's address in Altai krai on March 2, 1967, see *Pravda*, March 3. An article by him on rural affairs appeared in *Kommunist*, No. 15 (October, 1967), 15–31.

[45] *Pravda*, September 30, 1965.

[46] For a discussion of these differences, see Thomas W. Wolfe, *The Soviet Mili-*

tion in Vietnam continued, however, there was a gradual swing toward more emphasis on defense needs, and this was reflected in three successive increases of military allocations in the Soviet budget.

There seem to have been different nuances among the leaders in their appreciation of Soviet foreign policy opportunities and requirements in regard to the post-1965 international scene. None asserted any longer that the United States was in the hands of "sober" forces, although the presence and importance of these elements is still acknowledged.[47] Subtle differences have been registered, however, on the question of the strength of "imperialism," especially the American variety, with Brezhnev, Kosygin, and Podgorny warning against underestimating American power. Others, perhaps inclined to a bolder course of Soviet action, have emphasized the complementary side of standard Soviet doctrine—that American intervention in Vietnam and other areas was a sign of weakness rather than strength.[48]

These differences of expression on foreign policy and on the proper internal response to developments abroad do not show that the leadership has been seriously split into sharply opposed groups. Official statements have provided the main themes on which individuals have been able to introduce their own variations; the effect produced has been a cluster of orthodox views at the center with little outcroppings of unorthodoxy at the edges.

On questions of arms control and disarmament, and on the broader question of the possibility of coming to terms with the United States, there were few public departures from the standard line, which emphasized that the Soviet Union envisaged general disarmament as a desirable goal but saw no hope of its realization in the near future; the immediate task was to organize against American "imperialist aggression." The principal Soviet leaders endorsed various partial measures aiming at arms limitation and "tension reduction," but insisted that "peace is indivisible"; i.e., the United States cannot have good relations with the USSR while continuing to attack a state in the socialist commonwealth.[49]

---

tary Scene: Institutional and Defense Policy Considerations (Santa Monica, Calif.: The RAND Corporation, 1966, RM-4913-PR, processed), 64–69.

[47] For example, Brezhnev said on November 3, 1967: "Lenin taught that in foreign policy both the schemes of imperialist adventurers and the positions of sensible representatives of the bourgeoisie must be taken into account." (*Pravda*, November 4, 1967.)

[48] See the discussion by William Zimmerman in *Soviet Politics Since Khrushchev* of varying formulas in leadership speeches of mid-1966.

[49] Thus, Politburo member A. P. Kirilenko at the Lenin birthday ceremony in 1967: "The U.S. ruling circles . . . declare their desire to improve relations with the Soviet Union. If one is to believe such statements, it appears that they would like to have good relations with one socialist state and at the same time wage a

There was relatively little visible change at the time of the ouster of Khrushchev in 1964 on the specifics of Soviet positions on arms control and disarmament. The new leaders dropped few of the proposals from the Khrushchev repertoire, and added few new proposals to it.[50] When the USSR leaders presented a new list of proposed partial measures in July, 1968, however, they dropped several proposals which they had endorsed in their last previous list, that of December, 1964, and added some not included in the earlier group.

The attitude toward American and other Western proposals changed hardly at all with the replacement of Khrushchev. There was certainly a decline in the attention paid to prospects for general disarmament, and to the use of disarmament symbols in Soviet foreign and domestic propaganda. As noted elsewhere, these changes can be attributed most readily to repercussions of the enlarged war in Vietnam; however, they were also affected by the departure of Khrushchev, an old champion of disarmament initiatives and disarmament propaganda, by the "realism" of his successors, by the impact of American and Chinese policies, and by the adherence to a more collective style of leadership. The latter encourages the search for consensus among the leaders and thus for compromises that give due weight to the claims of the most powerful interest groups in the USSR. The Brezhnev regime has taken pains to conciliate the professional military establishment as one of the most important of these groups. Therefore, in the current mode of decision making, what the military will accept is probably a more determining factor in Soviet disarmament policy than it was under Khrushchev.

DECISION MAKING ON DISARMAMENT

Just how decisions on questions of disarmament and military policy are made in the Soviet Union is not precisely known. The top policy organ, the Politburo, currently includes neither the Minister of For-

---

war against another socialist country. But these hopes are in vain." (*Pravda*, April 23, 1967.) Kosygin told *Life* editors in an interview on January 19, 1968 (*Life*, February 2, 1968) that "in the light of American aggression [in Vietnam] we cannot have normal relations with the U.S. as long as it continues the war."

[50] Some of the old proposals have been referred to very seldom, but most of them seem to still represent Soviet policy. See, *SSSR, SShA i razoruzhenie,* I. S. Glagolev, ed. (Moscow: "Nauka," 1967), pp. 65–103. It appears, however, that the new leaders have dropped the proposal advanced in a Khrushchev message of December 31, 1963, for an international agreement or treaty "on the renunciation by states of the use of force for the solution of territorial disputes or questions of frontiers." United States Arms Control and Disarmament Agency, *Documents on Disarmament 1963* (Washington, D.C.: Government Printing Office, 1964), pp. 654–65; hereinafter cited as *Documents* [*year*]. This was not, of course, a disarmament proposal.

eign Affairs nor the Minister of Defense; historically it has not usually included either of these officials when they were "career" foreign service or military officers.[51] Furthermore, within the Party headquarters of the Central Committee there seems to be no "back-up" organization on foreign or military policy to give General Secretary Brezhnev and other Party officials staff support and position papers independent of those supplied by the ministries.[52] In this respect, the situation differs from that affecting most other areas of Soviet government activity, for which there are usually corresponding supervisory departments at Central Committee headquarters. There are, however, staff organs on disarmament questions in the ministries. It seems probable that the Ministers of Defense and Foreign Affairs (or Deputies) are present at Politburo meetings when important questions involving disarmament policies are scheduled for discussion.[53]

It appears, therefore, that the organization framework for working out disarmament policy is more informal in the USSR than in the United States, and that the arms control interest is not as well-staffed or articulated by officials as highly placed as in the United States, where a separate Arms Control and Disarmament Agency (ACDA) is under the general policy direction of the Secretary of State.[54] Apart from these activities relating to governmental positions on arms con-

[51] The principal exception concerns Marshal G. K. Zhukov, on the Party Presidium as a candidate and later a full member in 1956–1957. Various important Party officials who were Politburo members held the foreign affairs or defense portfolios at one time or another, including Stalin, Molotov, and Voroshilov, the latter for a long period. It is worth noting that the removal of Khrushchev had no apparent repercussions on the Ministers of Foreign Affairs or of Defense: Gromyko and Malinovsky were appointed in 1957, and continued in office after October, 1964. Gromyko remains in office; Malinovsky died on March 31, 1967. He was succeeded by Marshal Andrei A. Grechko, another professional soldier who had been a First Deputy Minister under Malinovsky.

[52] There are departments of the CPSU Central Committee concerned with "Party aspects" of foreign and military affairs. The two most important departments with foreign responsibilities are the International Department (concerned with foreign nonruling Communist parties) and the Department for Relations with Communist and Workers' Parties of Socialist Countries. In the military area the Political Administration of the Soviet Army and Navy functions under the Ministry of Defense but is also regarded as a Department of the Central Committee. There is no evidence that it is involved with general military questions, such as armaments, strategy, and deployment of forces.

[53] Politburo meetings are not announced, and the actual participants are therefore not named. Other Soviet Party and government organs are known to include in their discussions outside officials when this is desired.

[54] For some Soviet comments on ACDA, see *SSSR, SShA i razoruzhenie*, pp. 153–54. The editor, who has visited the United States and talked with American disarmament officials, remarks: "According to American press reports, there are in the Agency people who are actually interested in disarmament problems." [!]

trol and disarmament, there has not developed in the USSR the kind of lively and sophisticated public discussion of disarmament questions that has flourished in the United States. In 1963, the USSR Academy of Sciences founded a Commission for Scientific Problems of Disarmament to coordinate research in this field, carry on relations with foreign scientists on such problems, and initiate scientific conferences and discussions. This commission is attached to the Presidium of the Academy.[55] Up to the present, however, the publications of specialists associated with the Academy's effort on disarmament have not gone much beyond uncritical restatements of the government's official positions on various Soviet and foreign proposals.

[55] *Ibid.*, 113. This book does not mention Soviet government or Party organs concerned with disarmament questions, preferring to dwell on various "public" organizations for the promotion of disarmament and Soviet participation in international nongovernmental discussions, such as the "Pugwash" meetings and the "East-West" round tables.

3

IDEOLOGY AND DECISION MAKING

Like theologians coming back to report that God is dead, some investigators of the Soviet scene have passed down the word: ideology is dead. Or if it is not quite dead, it is dying.

The "erosion of ideology" has importance for the study of Soviet attitudes on disarmament and arms control, because many of the theories and attitudes derived from Marx and Lenin discourage efforts to find common cause with "bourgeois" states. Thus, prospects for Soviet-Western agreements would be considerably brighter if good pragmatic approaches were to drive out bad dogmatic biases in a kind of reverse Gresham's Law.

No one imagines that the Soviet leaders are about to repudiate Marxism-Leninism, or even to employ another vocabulary of discourse on internal and international developments. Conceptually, it provides them with ties to a revolutionary past and offers them intimations of an inevitable future. Likewise, the theory links developments in the Soviet Union to a cause invested with historical grandeur and global sweep.

The present leaders are, of course, basically products of Soviet rule. They accepted Marxism when it was already the ruling ethos of the country, unlike their earlier predecessors—who chose the Marxist way when the "establishment" of the day threatened rather than rewarded adherents of the movement. But the hold of the philosophy is due to much more than habit. Both internally and externally, Marxism serves instrumental purposes as a means of communication, organization, and manipulation. Whatever the ideological fire of the present leaders, they have a strong interest in portraying themselves as guardians of the faith and its true interpreters, particularly in a period when false prophets abound.

Those who profess to see the "end of ideology" believe that the prescriptions of the authoritative books are less decisive than ever on the everyday choices made by the Soviet leadership, and that additional areas will with time be freed in practice from the influence of Marxist-

Leninist doctrine. These observers hold out the prospect that Marxism-Leninism will suffer the fate of some religions: the faithful remain faithful, and the familiar books remain familiar—or almost as familiar —but the operational significance of orthodox doctrine steadily declines. The laity and even the clergy cease to search the texts for answers to new questions posed by an increasingly secularized life.

It is not necessary to discuss here the general question of the role of ideology in modern states, because our concern is not with the erosion of ideology in general but with Marxism-Leninism in the USSR.[1] By Marxism-Leninism is meant very specifically what Marx and especially Lenin said, rather than the currently orthodox doctrines now labeled Marxism-Leninism in the USSR. Hopeless confusion results from a discussion of the "erosion of ideology" in the USSR if ideology is equated to the continually revised explanations and justifications advanced by Soviet rulers for their policies and behavior.

However important in other contexts, an account of recent doctrinal changes or an assessment of current indoctrinational activities is not especially relevant to a discussion of the hold of Marxist-Leninist ideology on Soviet decision makers. None of those who see an "end of ideology" mean by this that the Party regime has given up intensive efforts at molding opinion in the USSR, or that the leaders have ceased to explain decisions and programs in terms drawn from the traditional vocabulary.*

PERMANENCE AND CHANGE

The linkage in "Marxism-Leninism" of two names as widely separated in time and place as those of Marx and Lenin points to a developmental aspect of the Communist movement, to the claim that this "proletarian" revolutionary ideology is not fixed for all time, but is developed and adapted to respond to varied and changing environments. The leading spokesmen have always insisted that Marxism-Leninism is a creative, evolving set of doctrines in which theory guides

---

[1] The literature on the subject is voluminous. Daniel Bell's *The End of Ideology* (rev. ed.) (New York: Collier Books, 1962), made the phrase popular. One of the best discussions of the role of ideology in the USSR appears in a series of articles by Alfred G. Meyer, Alec Nove, P. J. Reddaway, David Joravsky, Morris Bornstein, Henri Chambre, Nigel Harris, Rudolf Schlesinger, and others in *Soviet Studies*, XVII, Nos. 3 and 4, and XIX, No. 1 (January 1966–July 1967). See also, David Dinsmore Comey, "Marxist-Leninist Ideology and Soviet Policy," *Studies in Soviet Thought*, II, No. 4 (December, 1962), 301–20.

* The participants in the project generally accepted the conclusion that ideology has become a less important force in the Soviet Union. Not all used "ideology" to mean the same thing, and several expressed views going well beyond those in the text on the extent and significance of ideological erosion in the USSR.

practice, with practice checking theory, in never-ending reciprocation.[2] Despite this acceptance of the necessity for changes to keep theory in touch with reality, the writings of Marx and particularly of Lenin are unquestionably treated in the USSR as sacred texts. Lenin's complete works appeared recently in a fifth edition of 55 volumes that includes almost every scrap he wrote except for a note on birchbark passed to a schoolmate. They are repeatedly searched for quotations justifying each current policy and propaganda theme. Questions are almost never raised about the validity of any of Lenin's statements or ideas, or about the correctness of any of his political moves. With Stalin in disrepute as an authority (and consequently only rarely quoted), the role of Lenin as the prime source of "Truth" has become even more dominant.

On this level there has been no erosion of Leninist ideology. But honor to the master, and adherence to the orthodox vocabulary do not necessarily mean that the ideology dictates answers to emerging questions. The ideology contains alternative and even contradictory guidelines, as might be expected from a corpus of writings accumulated over almost a century, from Marx in the 1840's to Lenin in the 1920's. Lenin's career included not only the formative and conspiratorial years before the October Revolution, but about five years as active head of the Soviet government and acknowledged leader of the ruling Communist Party. In this period in power, grim reality applied its own shock treatment to expectations nourished in the Russian underground and in the rarefied atmosphere of exile abroad. Incorporating works of both the pre- and postrevolutionary periods, "Leninism" is a storehouse of formulas and precedents accumulated over three decades; "following the leader" thus requires that successors choose among the conflicting precedents and formulas of the classic guides.

In justifying new turns in policy by old dogmas, Soviet leaders frequently have done violence to the spirit of the mentors, although usually some classic writings could be cited in support. Many of the formulas of the present day were introduced into (Soviet) "Marxism" by Lenin or Stalin, including the principle enjoining "peaceful coexistence" between socialist and capitalist states. The process of adaptation was necessary, even if the specific choices of Lenin and Stalin were scarcely inevitable. Leninism underwent a similar process of adaptation. Summarized succinctly but crudely, departures from the dominant spirit of Marxism were dictated by the fact that Communists gained control of a single country, underdeveloped Russia, instead of coming to power more or less simultaneously in the industrial West. Similarly, departures from Leninism were dictated by the inability of

[2] Including, of course, such "dogmatists" as Joseph Stalin and Mao Tse-tung.

Soviet Russia to develop rapidly into a winning example of "socialism," and by the persistence and relative stability of the "capitalist"
system in other parts of the world.

Since Stalin's death, of course, new conditions that have emerged
render questionable or invalid still more of the old prescriptions for
domestic and international policy. This is evident, to take only one
example, with respect to economic development. The "received wisdom" has appeared to hinder rather than help in solving problems
regarding the rate of economic growth and the efficient use of resources.
Marx's hostility to the market economy of capitalism, with its "an-
archy" and cycles of boom and bust, was translated under Stalin to a
faith in central planning as the way of insuring socialist economic
growth. The orthodox doctrines on economics inherited by Stalin's
successors thus militated against the kind of reforms that seemed necessary in the 1950's and 1960's, reforms designed to lessen dependence
on central decision making and to increase the scope of material incentives and profit-loss calculations. It must be granted that the steps
taken since 1964 in the use of market mechanisms have been extremely
cautious. Nevertheless, the economic reforms either bypass or reject
many of the dogmas on economics long held sacred.

PERCEPTIONS OF THE WORLD SCENE

In foreign policy, an area more pertinent to the subject of this book,
a similar discrepancy between old dogma and new conditions strikes
the eye. The discrepancy touches both relations with the capitalist
"enemies" and with Communist "friends." Although Lenin was forced
to make and defend "compromises" in dealing with the "bourgeois"
states of his day,[3] he accepted the notion of an uncompromising hostility in these relations, inevitably leading to violent collisions, until
the exploiting states received a *coup de grace* putting them out of their
miserable existence. Although Lenin stressed the need to utilize conflicts among the "imperialists," he gave little thought to the possibility
that the Soviet Union might eventually find common interests with
bourgeois states going beyond the exchange of commodities. From
Lenin's viewpoint, struggle and war were inevitable. The USSR could
propagandize for peace, but its main objectives were to prevent the
inevitable wars between groups of rival capitalist powers from engulf-
ing the USSR, and to promote the transformation of these wars between nations into civil wars pitting the revolutionary proletariat

---

[3] Lenin's justification of such "compromises" has been emphasized in recent
Soviet writings defending, sometimes against Chinese attacks, concessions made by
the USSR to secure agreements with Western states. See M. I. Trush, "Leninski
podkhod k ispolzovaniiu kompromissov vo vneshnei politike," *Voprosy istorii KPSS*,
No. 6 (1964), 25–33.

against the capitalist rulers. This orientation affected, incidentally, Soviet disarmament policy, which aimed more at showing the inherent warlike character of the bourgeois regimes than at a reconstruction of relationships among all states, including Soviet Russia.[4]

It is significant that after 1953, when Stalin's successors began to activate Soviet foreign diplomatic activities and search for new relationships with both the advanced industrial states and the developing countries, Khrushchev undertook a lightly concealed revision of Lenin's doctrines. Retaining the idea that war was endemic to capitalism, Khrushchev in 1956 asserted that it was not *fatalistically* inevitable, blandly ignoring the decades in which Soviet Marxists had explained that their conception of inevitability had nothing to do with fatalism. The accent was now placed on the noninevitability of war, in contrast to Lenin's emphasis on its inevitability, and to Stalin's postwar (1952) line that a particular war could be postponed if the peace forces were organized, but that war was ultimately inevitable until the peace forces became a revolutionary movement capable of eliminating capitalism. The doctrinal change on war was accompanied by others minimizing the necessity of violence in accomplishing the proletarian revolution, and blurring the sharpness of the division of the world into two opposed camps.

These modifications of doctrine justified the fundamental changes introduced during the first post-Stalin decade into Soviet foreign relations, including relations with nonaligned countries as well as with the United States and its allies. Of most relevance here is the fact that, beginning in 1955, the USSR started to negotiate more seriously on disarmament and to invest more effort in promoting the idea that disarmament was possible even before capitalism was liquidated. Individual measures and clusters of measures were proposed regarding both conventional and nuclear disarmament, of regional and world scope, highlighted by the Soviet presentation of a plan for "general and complete disarmament" (GCD) in 1959.[5]

IF ENEMIES ARE BAD, ARE FRIENDS WORSE?

Marxist-Leninist dogma also conflicted with reality in respect to the relations among Communist-led states and Communist parties. Nothing in the theory passed down from Marx and Lenin took ac-

[4] Walter C. Clemens, Jr., "Lenin on Disarmament," *Slavic Review*, XXIII, No. 3 (September, 1964), 504–25.

[5] See Alexander Dallin and others, *The Soviet Union and Disarmament: An Appraisal of Attitudes and Intentions* (New York: Frederick A. Praeger, Inc., 1965), esp. pp. 120–27, and Lincoln P. Bloomfield, Walter C. Clemens, Jr., and Franklyn Griffiths, *Khrushchev and the Arms Race: Soviet Interest in Arms Control and Disarmament, 1954–1967* (Cambridge, Mass.: The M.I.T. Press, 1966), esp. pp. 138–61.

count of the possibility that socialist states would fall out, a process that began with the expulsion of Yugoslavia from the Cominform in 1948, and took dramatic form in the late 1950's and 1960's with the estrangement of Communist China and the Soviet Union. Repetition of the line that proletarian unity is inherent in the relations between regimes ruling in the name of the "proletariat" and swearing allegiance to the "science" of Marxism-Leninism became most awkward when it appeared that conflict might be not just a sometime thing but a permanent condition. Recently, Soviet authorities have recognized that Communists in different countries could be expected to express different evaluations of domestic and international developments. The Soviet leaders have not yet, however, come to grips with the existence of basic hostility between Communist regimes. The coincidence of a *rapprochement* between the USSR and Western states, on the one hand, and of bitter conflict between the USSR and the Chinese People's Republic (CPR), on the other, sharpened the discrepancy between theoretical expectations and practical results. The discrepancy was flagrant in respect to such issues as the nuclear weapons test ban, on which the USSR concluded an agreement with the U.S. and other Western "bourgeois" states over the strong objections of the comrades in Peking.

It is too early, however, to take for granted that the future of world communism will be one of separate warring churches, each anathematizing and excommunicating the other.* Certainly the Soviet leaders hardly believe this to be the future. They probably do not expect the restoration of the kind of close unity that once prevailed among Communists of different countries, but envisage a loose coalition of Communist parties in which consensus on certain issues is combined with an "agreement to disagree" on others. Divergence among ruling parties is difficult to contain, however, because of the complex intertwining of conflicts between nations or between states, which have little to do with "communism," and of differences on Communist strategy and tactics, which are somewhat accidentally connected with specific countries.

The Soviet leaders probably draw some comfort from the betterment of relations with Yugoslavia after years of conflicts as sharp as those characteristic of the Sino-Soviet quarrel. As to China, the Soviet leaders apparently count on a change of leadership before or after Mao's death to provide the occasion for a Soviet-Chinese *rapprochement* and a subsequent regrouping of the fragmented ranks of the world Communist movement.[6] They may well be disappointed in this

---

* Too early, at any rate, for the author of the report. Some of the participants, in contrast, believe that it is too late to imagine any other outcome.

[6] The current Soviet line, however, is that the anti-Mao forces in China include

expectation. If the conflict continues and becomes worse, the Soviet ideologues will confront a major task in revising doctrines to take account of the failure of proletarian-led states to behave as doctrine prescribed. But the history of the movement has witnessed other such agonizing reappraisals, as in the explaining away of the failure of the industrial proletariat in advanced nations to behave in the manner anticipated by Marx, the failure of the Russian spark to set off world revolution, and the shift of the revolutionary center from developed to less-developed and formerly colonial countries, in which the moving force was not so much class struggle as national collaboration against foreign domination. These challenges have involved not only questions of where and how Communists could come to power, but of the need for Communist parties as the locomotives of history. Cuba showed that a Communist party was not essential for a revolution along Marxist-Leninist lines. In Soviet eyes, China showed that a revolution led by a Communist party (that came to power in 1949) could be derailed.

THE MARGIN OF ORTHODOXY

For the Soviet authorities, the inherited ideology is not dead or dying but had some unfortunate accidents necessitating medical attention: a little surgery here, a little patching up there. In view of these scrapes, will the sphere of ideology be restricted? Actually, the phrase should be "further restricted." Already there has been a gradual shrinkage of the areas of intellectual activity subject to Party rule from central headquarters.

The rule of Party orthodoxy never encompassed all the natural sciences; but under Stalin there were episodic interventions in many of these fields, including physics and chemistry, and especially the biological sciences and psychology. Under Khrushchev, the Party announced a policy of nonintervention regarding disputes in medical sciences, and lessened its interference in other natural sciences.[7] Even in biology, Lysenko no longer enjoyed under Khrushchev the dominating position that he had gained in 1949 through Party endorsement of his theories. He continued in good standing, however, until Khrushchev's successors encouraged or allowed the USSR Academy of Sciences to investigate his operations and issue a devastating report on these late in 1965.[8] Lysenko's influence as a scientist had been

---

both "genuine Marxists" (those favoring unity with the USSR, etc.) and those sympathetic to Mao's "great-power and hegemonistic" course but critical of the methods used to implement this course. See for example, the editorial articles in *Kommunist*, No. 6 (April, 1968), 102–13; and No. 7 (May, 1968), 103–14.

[7] See *The Current Digest of the Soviet Press*, XIV, No. 31 (August 29, 1962), 6.

[8] Published in *Vestnik Akademii Nauk*, No. 11 (November, 1965).

dependent on outside (Party) support, and without this he was nothing. It was significant, however, of the changes brought into Soviet scientific and intellectual life that even after 1965 some of his supporters were able to continue propagating a pro-Lysenko line.

The ideological situation of the social sciences and history is quite different. Unlike the physical and biological sciences, the value of these to the regime lies not—or not as much—in what can be learned and used as a result of studies and research, but in what should be taught through the vast education, information and indoctrination system, as part of the regime's attempt to mold the popular attitudes and behavior, of the youth in schools and of the adult population alike. Even in this area, the post-Stalin Party relaxed its insistence on uniformity, lessened the gap separating "Public Truth" from objective facts, and encouraged greater spontaneity than was usual in earlier years. Nevertheless, a close watch was maintained over the content and direction of research and writing.

Marxism-Leninism retained its monopoly position, and the Party its right to pronounce judgments defining orthodoxy and heterodoxy; however, more attention was paid to empirical research in the social sciences. Within the last decade, and particularly in the last few years, there has been a revival of writing and studies in fields neglected or proscribed under Stalin. Sociology is the prime example of a discipline that disappeared in the 1930's and was resurrected in the 1950's. Social psychology has been recognized as a field of study separate from psychology (long dominated by physiological emphases); statistics and demography became respectable subjects again; and there were (as yet unsuccessful) moves to establish political science as a discipline free from the domination of law studies (particularly constitutional and administrative law).

These innovations would not have been so significant if they had not been accompanied by encouragement of a more empirical approach in these various disciplines. Empirical sociological research has become fashionable in the Soviet Union.[9] Social research bureaus have sprung up everywhere. Sampling techniques have come into favor as a way of reducing the cost of surveys and questionnaires. At the XXIII Party Congress in March–April, 1966, there was a remarkable emphasis on the need to develop the social sciences; and hardly a serious article appears on a social trend or on the efficacy of Party functions without inclusion of references to an empirical investigation.[10] Needless to

[9] Some of the trends in the more "academic" sociology are reflected in the two-volume collection of papers, Sotsiologiia v SSSR (Moscow: "Mysl'," 1966).

[10] For one discussion of empirical research, mostly concerned with economic issues, see V. Shubkin, "O konkretnykh issledovaniiakh sotsial'nykh protsessov," Kommunist, No. 3 (February, 1965), 46–57. The area that has attracted the greatest

say, the topics investigated are confined to a fairly safe list; the methods employed often leave a good deal to be desired (combination of research on religious beliefs with a propaganda campaign for atheism); and the approach is very much that of *applied* research. Furthermore, empirical social research is designed to buttress, and certainly not to supplant, the master science of Marxism-Leninism. Still, there is a difference between writings on political, economic, and social topics that pay some deference to empirically tested hypotheses and those merely expounding authoritative doctrines, illustrating these either by quotations from the classics or by tendentious statistics and examples drawn from a grab-bag of real and fake facts and figures.

REVOLUTIONARY CONFORMISM

A variant of the "decline of ideology" approach among Western observers of the Soviet scene has been expressed in the proposition that radical movements that establish themselves over a long period of time in an environment that escapes their control tend to adjust to that environment by a process of deradicalization. Such movements gain a stake in the existing order that they are loath to lose. Hence they find themselves unable to work for the drastic changes in the environment that were their *raison d'être*. To put it in current terms, such radical movements become part of the "establishment." [11]

This concept was developed in relation to the formerly Marxist Social Democratic Party of Germany, which remained a potent, but always minority group in that country. It was the most prominent Marxist party in the world movement until the war of 1914 stripped away illusions about its dedication to revolution. The German Party had learned to conform to the established order long before it found it expedient to drop its revolutionary rhetoric. In the contrast of revolutionary language and conformist behavior, the Soviet Communists on the international scene bear some likeness to the Social Democrats within Germany. In each case, deradicalization did not mean—at least initially—denial of the goals of the movement, which were strongly reaffirmed, but day-by-day accommodations to the surrounding environment. Applied to the USSR, this theory sees the Communist rulers talking the line of world revolution and increasing adjusting to

---

number of investigations is that of the use of nonworking time. The topic is safe for researchers, and high officials seek guidance from such studies on the best method in which they can recapture from the population on a voluntary basis the hours freed by reduction of the working week. Another area of rather intensive research concerns labor fluidity.

[11] Robert C. Tucker, "The Deradicalization of Marxist Movements," *American Political Science Review*, LXI, No. 2 (June, 1967), 343–58.

their minority position in a world dominated by the "bourgeoisie." They, too, have acquired too valuable a stake in the existing international order to be tempted by hazardous ventures—to gain what? More Chinas? God forbid!

The position of the USSR in the world is quite different, of course, from the position occupied by the Social Democratic Party in Germany. Control of the Russian real estate has enabled Soviet leaders in half a century to alter profoundly the status of Russia and to promote the spread of communism beyond Soviet borders. Consequently, the habituation to living peacefully in a world of entrenched powers has not required of the Russians as complete a renunciation of steps toward the professed revolutionary goals as that required of the German Social Democrats. However, in the eyes of many of their poor relations, such as the Chinese and Cuban clans, the Soviet leaders appear to have betrayed the revolutionary cause, and to have accommodated themselves all too easily to the status quo. Becoming more affluent, the Soviet Union lost much of that hard and hungry look that once made it a revolutionary example worthy of emulation by the poor and powerless.

EROSION OF IDEOLOGY: THE DOMESTIC SCENE

Evidence bearing on the hypothesis that revolutionary ideology is becoming meaningless to the Soviet population is difficult to obtain. Empirical social research in the USSR is not likely to be focused on this topic. Consequently, conclusions must be speculative interpretations of leadership or mass behavior. This behavior is itself ambiguous, because a redoubling of ideological effort can be a sign of the decline of ideological pull. As one analyst of Soviet affairs neatly put it: more is cooked, less is swallowed. (Compared to Stalin's time, however, one might say that less is cooked and less is swallowed.) Ideological guardians complain about the inadequacy of results in indoctrination of the Soviet population, and about the receptivity of Soviet citizens, especially the youth, to bourgeois propaganda introduced in radio broadcasts from abroad or resulting from travel in and out of the USSR. Certainly the lessened isolation of the Soviet population from foreign contacts has created new problems for Soviet leaders in maintaining ideological control.[12]

Resistance to ideological conditioning has existed for a long time, although displays by individuals of unorthodox ideological behavior, like admissions by the regime of difficulties, have occurred more often

---

[12] Former First Secretary Yegorychev of Moscow oblast, for one, has voiced strong apprehensions along this line.

in the freer conditions of post-Stalin society. The decline of ideology as a force capable of moving the population toward desired behavior can be seen in the increased reliance by the regime on material rather than moral incentives, sure testimony to the ineffectiveness of ideological conditioning. The necessity of such material "interestedness" was a favorite theme with Khrushchev. The successors disparage crass references to "goulash communism," but goulash and its equivalents continue to be relied on to elicit desired behavior.[13] Thus, the economic reform has relied on material interest to energize the production of goods and services desired by the regime and, within limits fixed centrally, by the population.

Too sharp a contrast should not be drawn, however, between the present and past proportions of material and moral incentives used to activate the population. Material incentives are an old story in the Soviet economy, including those tying workers' income to production levels and those rewarding enterprises for making profits (a system widely misunderstood in the West). All that it is possible to say is that material interest is called upon to play a greater role at present than in most past periods. The regime now possesses more wherewithal to put content into traditional material incentives, and must rely on such incentives to take over in part the role formerly assigned to force and compulsion on the one hand, and to utopian and idealistic strivings on the other, in disciplining and energizing the population.

EROSION OF IDEOLOGY: FOREIGN POLICY
PERSPECTIVES

In foreign affairs, the extent of *popular* commitment to or alienation from the Marxist-Leninist ideology is a matter of secondary interest compared to the extent of the *ruling group's* similar commitment. In some ultimate sense, the forces motivating the citizenry set limits, of course, to the regime's freedom of action. The people have to pay in sweat and perhaps blood and tears for the material and ideological commitments of the regime abroad. The bills may come high, and the interest in supporting far-off phalanxes of the workers' movement may be slight. But the ultimate time for honoring the checks

[13] The difference is not in the use of material incentives, or even in the importance attributed to these, but in the role of moral incentives. On occasion Khrushchev tended to disparage the role of ideas as a motivating force when the dinner pail was empty. See V. Stepakov (head of the Central Committee's Propaganda Department), "Vyshie idealy i povsednevnye zaboty partii," *Pravda*, May 17, 1965. This article was directed against Khrushchev's "subjectivism," and specifically attacked his conception of communism as a society designed to satisfy only material needs of the population, the "needs of the stomach"—a phrase borrowed from Khrushchev.

drawn on the people's account is distant. There is no effective impact of the population on Soviet foreign policy in any day-to-day sense.

In the context of this study, then, what must interest us is the extent to which the "erosion of ideology" among the ruling group affects the foreign policy objectives and priorities of the regime. The universalism characteristic of Marx and inherited by Lenin—who for a long time thought the Russian Revolution would start a chain reaction abroad—soon gave way to a concentration on preservation and development of the USSR. Ever since Stalin's time, this has been seen as the indispensable Soviet contribution to the world Communist movement. But this objective ruled out neither support for revolution abroad nor deals with "bourgeois" states. The latter had been justified by Lenin (and Stalin) largely in terms of using for Soviet advantage contradictions between imperialist states; Khrushchev's innovation was to find justification for such arrangements apart from any heightening of contradictions.

The dual process of finding points of common interest with Western states and of facing hostile opponents within the camp of socialist states reverses the emphasis derived from Marxist-Leninist ideology. Agreements on arms control and disarmament exemplify the point. The implementation of the nuclear test-ban treaty of 1963 offered clear enough testimony to the fact that the Chinese "comrades" did not have a veto on agreements with the United States and other Western states considered beneficial to the USSR. The negotiations on the test ban, and other arms control questions, tended to disprove, in fact, the idea that Chinese "hard-line" polemics against the Russians would force the latter to be intransigent. Although the Soviet leaders since 1965 have shunned any major gestures of amity toward the United States, they continue to have an interest in demonstrating that their policy of negotiating on international issues with Western states can bring successes.

A striking impact of the ideological component in international relations can be seen in the differences between Soviet-Chinese and Soviet-American relations. The U.S. has remained the central target of hostile Soviet criticism, a target of propaganda that is much greater in volume than that of Soviet output critical of China. In Soviet propaganda concerning disarmament, for example, the United States has always emerged as the principal villain, with West Germany as "Number Two"; Communist China, if mentioned at all, has been chided fairly gently. In contrast, the USSR and the United States have been able to negotiate routinely on a bilateral basis as well as in multilateral meetings in Geneva and New York, and even to agree on a *tête-à-tête* meeting of the two government leaders after the war in Vietnam had escalated to major scale. (It must be acknowledged, however, that the fact of the Glassboro meetings of President Johnson and Premier Kosygin in June, 1967, was very awkward for the Russians, who minimized the significance of the encounter.) Diplomatic negotiations between the Soviet Union and Communist China, by contrast, have been sporadic since 1963, whether on a Party or government level, and have involved no encounters of the top leaders.[14]

This apparent discrepancy has ideological roots. The ideology calls for the closest linking of Marxist-Leninist states, and disharmony raises fundamental questions about the validity of the creed. Such questions are not raised by conflict in Soviet-American relations. Ideology assigns to the imperialists the function of behaving like themselves, i.e., being beastly; therefore, from an ideological standpoint, the United States is doing only what comes naturally. Mere coexistence is not satisfactory for relations among Communist states, because these relations are supposed to be on a higher level (coexistence is defined in the Soviet lexicon as the correct policy for states with *opposed* social systems). Coexistence doctrine justifies the Soviet regime in maintaining active relations and, despite nefarious behavior by the West, even negotiating agreements with the U.S. and other Western states on a hard-boiled business basis, or to keep interstate tensions from erupting into war.

IDEOLOGICAL DECLINE AND WORLD PROSPECTS

To the extent that Marxist-Leninist theory encourages Soviet leaders to view the world as divided on a simple two-camp basis, and to expect little but hostility from "bourgeois" states and little but agreement from "proletarian" states, an erosion of the hold of Marxist-Leninist theory on Soviet policy makers would be a positive factor from the standpoint of progress on arms control. It would allow attention to be centered on those problems of national security and of weapons systems that are essentially "classless." Such a trend would nourish embryonic perceptions of common interests with Western nations.

On the other side of the spectrum, the decline of a simplistic two-

---

[14] The only meetings involving top officials were those in November, 1964, between a delegation headed by Premier Chou En-lai in Moscow, and those in Peking in February, 1965, when Premier Kosygin passed by on his Hanoi trip. Neither side pretended that the results were anything but dismal. Apparently the Soviet leaders proposed to the Chinese at either the November, 1964, meetings in Moscow or the February, 1965, meetings in Peking that a top-level encounter of the leaders (presumably including Brezhnev and Mao Tse-tung) be arranged in either Moscow or Peking. The Chinese rejected the proposal. See *The New York Times*, March 24, 1966, which reprints from *Die Welt*, March 21, 1966, excerpts of a CPSU letter sent to other Communist parties earlier in 1966.

camp approach would encourage Moscow to realize that Communist movements can turn anti-Soviet after attaining power, and thus make Soviet leaders ambivalent about support for such movements. Whether there is such ambivalence is not clear. Compared to leaders in Peking and Havana, the Soviet chiefs have shown restraint on the question of national liberation wars. This seems to have been dictated, however, more by apprehensions that little wars might turn into big ones than by concern over the future orientation of revolutionary movements gaining power over this route. Moscow's restraint has also been affected by the realization that failures of militant groups resorting to premature insurrections would set back the world Communist movement. Whatever the reason, the Soviet leaders have often seemed to be more comfortable with Communist parties addicted to legal forms of political activity than with the more bold and adventurous movements.

In any case, ideological erosion of this kind is likely to make itself felt only over a long period of time, and hence to be of minor importance in calculations of Soviet behavior over the next decade or so. In this period, the Soviet leaders will probably continue to view the United States and other Western nations involved in arms negotiations as basically hostile in their orientation toward the USSR and the "socialist commonwealth," professions of good will notwithstanding. And despite the difficulties experienced by Moscow in relations with Chinese and other comrades in and out of power, the Soviet leaders are likely to regard Communist states and movements as their natural allies.

4

FOREIGN POLICY UNDER
KHRUSHCHEV'S SUCCESSORS

Moscow's policies on arms control and disarmament must be viewed in the context of Soviet foreign policy as a whole. Elsewhere in this study we focus attention on political, economic, and military trends within the post-Khrushchev USSR. The trends considered affect Soviet capabilities for maneuver in the world, and thereby influence choices for and against agreements on arms limitations. Here we look at the attitudes and activities of the Brezhnev-led regime in dealing with the world outside Soviet borders.

PERCEPTIONS OF THE WORLD

Both leadership perceptions of the world and Soviet international behavior underwent changes after 1964. In a study concentrating on post-Khrushchev trends, there is a temptation, however, to exaggerate changes and neglect elements of continuity. Much remained stable in Soviet foreign policy despite Khrushchev's departure. Indeed, many of the staples of current outlook and behavior can be traced back to Stalin's day and even to Lenin's. Brezhnev and his colleagues claim that the greatest contribution of the USSR to the world revolution is in its construction of "socialism" and of foundations of "communism." In this they follow a policy firmly established in the 1920's by Stalin. On this basis, Soviet leaders from Lenin to Brezhnev have been easily able to convince themselves that what is good for the USSR is good for world communism. Although the USSR in fact encouraged and promoted the spread of Communist rule beyond Soviet frontiers, notably in the aftermath of German and Japanese defeats in World War II, Soviet leaders have been unwilling to let such activities impinge on efforts for development within the USSR or seriously endanger the safety of the Soviet state. All this is very old hat. It would not be worth repeating, were it not for the occasional neglect of some of the persistent elements of the Soviet world view.

One such element, particularly relevant to a discussion of arms control and disarmament problems, concerns the value placed on "stability," either broadly as applied to interstate relations or more narrowly in the area of military relationships. In Western discussions, "stability" is often taken as a desired objective, and frequently a similar valuation is attributed to the USSR. No doubt certain kinds of international instability seem threatening to the Soviet leaders, even if these present opportunities for plucking gains out of danger. In the field of armaments, this may also be true, at least to the extent that some changes in military relations and some technical innovations in armaments jeopardize Soviet military standing. But stability in relations among great powers is not highly cherished by the men in the Kremlin, who are more attuned to a vision of movement carrying Soviet socialism toward a dominant political, economic, and military superiority.* American approaches to the Soviet Union in favor of arms control proposals (such as abstention from installation of ABM systems) have sometimes sought to appeal to a mutual interest in avoiding "destabilizing" arms innovations. These are likely, as in the past, to fall upon deaf ears, particularly if they are focused solely on areas of Soviet initiative, and propose to leave unregulated the areas in which the United States is making quantitative and qualitative advances.

In fact, the idea of movement from the dark past to the bright future is central to Marxism. In one form it is embedded in the Communist argument that capitalism at the time of World War I entered a period of "general crisis," a crisis so severe that the patient could never recover, but so prolonged that the "doctors" could never predict when death would come.[1] A second phase of this crisis was said to have coincided with World War II. Each of these war stages was marked by the breakaway from "capitalism" of more countries as "proletarian revolution" spread.

In Khrushchev's time it was announced that a third stage of this crisis had begun in the middle 1950's.[2] This was said to be distinct

---

* Some of the participants in the study consider that stability in political and military relations has a much greater appeal to the Soviet leadership than this text suggests. They believe that preservation of the status quo has become basic in Soviet thought, and that the Soviet leaders have come to realize that, in the military field, any innovations—whether Soviet or Western—redound eventually to the advantage of their opponents, because the USSR is unable to compete effectively with the United States on either a military-technical or military-economic level.

[1] The theory was propounded by Lenin, who emphasized the bloody clash between rival "imperialist" powers (England, France, and Russia against Germany and the Austro-Hungarian Empire) rather than the Revolution in Russia *per se*.

[2] The doctrine found expression in the 1960 Statement of the Communist and Workers' Parties and in the CPSU Program adopted in 1961. The text of the former is reprinted in *The Sino-Soviet Dispute*, eds. G. F. Hudson, Richard Lowenthal, and Roderick MacFarquhar (New York: Frederick A. Praeger, Inc., 1963), pp. 177–

from the two earlier phases in that it did not result from general war, but was similar in that it involved a change in the correlations of forces between capitalism and socialism. According to Soviet authorities, the third phase occurred as a result of three major world developments:

1. The USSR was emerging from military inferiority to the leading "capitalist" country, the United States, by developing a strategic force of nuclear-equipped long-range ballistic missiles;
2. Former dependent people were breaking away from their colonial masters, who were unable to resist the tide of independence;
3. Some of the ex-colonial and newly independent countries were taking initial steps on the road to socialism.

The notion that capitalism has entered a further stage of deterioration is less popular in Moscow today than it was before 1964.[3] Its implied optimism regarding the international scene is not to the taste of the present cautious leaders. They are aware of American military power and of American willingness to use it on a global scale. They are also aware that trends toward "socialism," i.e., toward Soviet-style regimes, have proved fragile in many Afro-Asian countries. Even in Eastern Europe they showed their nervousness over the solidity of the socialist order, despite two decades of Communist rule, when they resorted to force in August, 1968, to repress a trend to liberalization of political life in Czechoslovakia. But their caution in evaluating achievements and prospects (and in shying away from adventures) does not mean that they have rejected the basic notion of inevitable transformation of the world along socialist lines. The goal of the Soviet leaders is not one of stabilizing the correlation of forces with capitalist states, but of shrinking the sphere of "capitalism" and of achieving superiority for the USSR and for Soviet-allied movements.

In adjusting Soviet approaches on foreign affairs since 1964 to changing conditions, the present leaders have not felt it necessary to introduce any changes of doctrine comparable to those articulated by Khrushchev at the xx Party Congress in 1956. In lightly veiled form, Khrushchev then revised Leninist doctrine to insist that interstate wars were no longer fatalistically inevitable, and that under certain cir-

---

205. The Party Program is available in numerous English editions, e.g., Jan F. Triska, *Soviet Communism: Programs and Rules* (San Francisco: Chandler Publishing Co., 1962), pp. 39–40.

[3] For example, it does not seem to have been reasserted in the (Brezhnev) report of the Central Committee to the xxiii Party Congress or the Congress resolution on the Report, nor in the principal Soviet statements dealing with the celebration of the 50th anniversary of the October Revolution. But references to the third stage continue to appear, e.g., *Kommunist*, No. 1 (January, 1967), 118.

cumstances Communist-led revolutions could gain power by peaceful means.[4]

In 1968, war is still treated as preventable, and peaceful rather than violent means of struggle are still emphasized as the best Communist tactic. On the latter issue, in fact, the line-up of forces in the world Communist movement has strengthened tendencies in the USSR to defend those parties oriented toward use of legal methods of political activity against attacks from the "militants" in China, Cuba, and elsewhere. Nevertheless, since 1964 the Soviet leaders have gradually reduced emphasis on doctrines stressing the avoidability of war and the likelihood of peaceful coexistence between states of different social systems.

In his first major speech after he replaced Khrushchev in 1964 as Party Chief, Brezhnev on November 6, 1964, explicitly endorsed the proposition that "world war in present conditions" is not inevitable.[5] Giving the Central Committee report to the XXIII Party Congress on March 29, 1966, Brezhnev used a weaker formula by referring to the viewpoint of the international Communist movement "on the possibility of checking aggressors, of avoiding a new world war." [6] By 1967, however, when Brezhnev delivered the main address on November 3 at the celebration of the 50th anniversary of the October Revolution, he gave no assurances that peace was secure, but rather emphasized that "imperialism has not changed its aggressive nature. It remains . . . a serious threat to the peace and security of all peoples. And we cannot, we have no right, comrades, to forget it." [7]

A parallel development affected coexistence doctrine. The assurance that "peaceful coexistence is the general course of Soviet foreign policy" was often reiterated in the Khrushchev period.[8] Although echoed in the early post-Khrushchev period,[9] the emphasis on peaceful coexistence declined in favor of emphasis in 1965–1968 on the need for a united struggle of Communist and peace-loving forces against imperialism. In the November 3, 1967, speech already cited, Brezhnev's only strong reference to "peaceful coexistence" occurred in a passage devoted to Soviet-European relations. Variations of these Brezhnev emphases have appeared in the speeches of other leaders and in more impersonal Party or government documents. In all these, the Soviet interest in avoiding wars and in peaceful coexistence has

[4] For the pertinent passages, see *The Sino-Soviet Dispute*, pp. 42–46.
[5] *Pravda*, November 7, 1964.
[6] *The 23rd Congress of the CPSU*, p. 49.
[7] *Pravda*, November 4, 1967.
[8] For example, N. V. Podgorny in the October Revolution anniversary speech of 1963 (*Pravda*, November 7, 1963).
[9] In Brezhnev's speech of November 6, 1964, for example. The comparable speeches on November 6 in the next two years, by Politburo members Poliansky and Pelshe, gave much less stress to coexistence.

been reaffirmed, but in less optimistic tones, and in contexts stressing the need for struggle rather than the possibility of accommodation.

THE NEW LEADERS AND THE UNITED STATES

A discussion of Soviet leadership views on coexistence naturally involves attention to Soviet perceptions of the United States, a subject that deserves special discussion. Such a discussion is particularly necessary in the context of a report concerned with Soviet attitudes on disarmament, in view of the central role of Soviet-American agreement or disagreement in determining progress on arms control. Khrushchev's ouster came only a little more than a year after signature of the partial test-ban treaty, when the USSR chose agreement with the United States at the expense of disagreement with China. After the treaty was signed in Moscow, both President Kennedy and Premier Khrushchev warned against any euphoria about détente—a reminder that further agreements on arms measures would not be easy. The point was underlined by Soviet rejection in early 1964 of a series of partial measures proposed by President Johnson not long after his move into the White House. Still, the way seemed clear for serious negotiations as a follow-up to the 1963 treaty, and the endorsement by the new Soviet regime in December, 1964, of a whole group of partial measures familiar from the Khrushchev period suggested that the new administration in Moscow, like the new administration in Washington, would seek to build on the Khrushchev-Kennedy achievement. Other policy shifts in the two capitals darkened the picture. Initially Khrushchev's successors sought to alleviate tensions with the Chinese, and no doubt wanted, at the minimum, to avoid any moves in the disarmament field that would worsen Sino-Soviet relations. President Johnson's decision in February, 1965, to begin systematic bombardment of North Vietnam introduced a new complication into Soviet-American relations, with inevitable effect on prospects for new agreements.

Beginning in 1965, there was a definite hardening of the Soviet line on America. Khrushchev had been drawn to the idea of negotiating arrangements with the United States that would reflect the special Soviet-American responsibilities in the world. As Khrushchev once told the Rumanians: "The Soviet Union and the United States are great world powers. History itself has assigned them such a place. On our two powers depends to a large extent the way in which the international situation will develop in the future—along the road of strengthening peace or along the road of straining relations." [10] Along with this idea of Soviet-American primacy went another Khrushchev

[10] Address of June 21, 1960, to the Rumanian Communist Party Congress; excerpts in *The Sino-Soviet Dispute*, pp. 132–39.

theme, that "sober forces" had the upper hand in the United States. He often varied his delivery with denunciations of the aggressiveness of certain American politicians espousing "ultra" positions in the ruling circles. Nevertheless, Khrushchev seemed convinced that "people of sound mind," i.e., those who sought to avoid ventures leading to war, were "in the majority even among the most deadly enemies of communism."[11]

Even under Khrushchev, some other Soviet officials expressed less confidence in the dominance of "sober forces" in the United States than Khrushchev himself evinced. In the years since his departure, the Soviet leaders have eliminated favorable references to American leaders and etched their portrayals in acid.[12] (They have generally refrained, however, from personal attacks on President Johnson or other American leaders, possibly because an impersonal style of leadership at home encourages the same impersonal treatment of leaders in other countries.) The presence of sane elements in American political life is still acknowledged, but their supremacy is no longer taken for granted.

It is difficult to determine just how much the heightened American involvement in Vietnam contributed to the change in the Soviet views of the United States, because the escalation of the war coincided roughly with the switch in the Kremlin. No matter who was in power, Vietnam would have produced a hardening of Soviet attitudes and a heightening of concern over the possibility of war spreading. In the period between Khrushchev's ouster in October, 1964, and the beginning of systematic American bombing of North Vietnam in February, 1965, the Soviet line on the United States underwent little change. Thus, in November, 1964, Brezhnev interpreted the victory of President Johnson over Senator Goldwater in the American presidential election as convincing evidence that the majority of the American people wanted peace and "were fed up with the 'cold war.' The defeat of the American 'ultra' was a good lesson for all those addicted to reactionary and adventurous policies."[13] The talk heard from Moscow after February, 1965, was quite different.

The hardening in the Soviet line on the United States was accompanied by the appearance of different nuances in the evaluation of the strength of the "imperialists" (read: American imperialists).* None

---

[11] *Ibid.* The emphasis on the control by sober forces varied, of course, with the ups and downs of tension in Soviet-American relations; the quoted remarks are from a speech shortly following the U-2 incident, the abortive summit conference, and the break-up of the Ten-Nation Disarmament discussions.

[12] See the discussion by William Zimmerman, in *Soviet Politics Since Khrushchev.*

[13] *Pravda,* November 7, 1964.

* Some participants in the project believe that differences among the Soviet leaders on foreign policy questions, including policy toward the United States, are more acute than the text implies. They see the leadership as sharply divided over

of the leaders borrowed from Mao Tse-tung the idea that America was a paper tiger whose nuclear teeth should not frighten anyone. But some seemed inclined to stress American capabilities, and others to minimize them. The first attitude implies a low-risk policy of avoiding confrontations; the second, a policy of greater boldness.[14] Whatever the extent of these differences, the basic stand of the new regime was outlined in the (Brezhnev) report of the Central Committee to the xxiii Party Congress and in the Congress's resolution approving the report. Brezhnev said that "the increased aggressiveness of imperialism by no means signifies that there has been a change in the alignment of world forces in its favor." He argued, however, that the threat of war had increased as a result of aggressive acts of American and other imperialists.[15] The Congress's resolution reiterated these themes in concluding that "the balance of forces in the world keeps changing in favor of socialism, the working-class, and the national liberation movement," while internal capitalist contradictions are driving "imperialism" to "greater adventurism," thus adding to the dangers it presents.[16]

The disappearance after 1964 of statements on the dominance of sober forces in the United States was to be expected. At various times Brezhnev, Kosygin and others have explicitly rejected the idea that U.S.-USSR relations could go on as usual despite the American military activities in Vietnam, especially the bombing of North Vietnam.[17] There have even been suggestions that the Soviet Union would not ne-

---

the desirability of seeking arrangements with the United States, and over the dangers for the USSR of opposing the U.S. in situations involving a risk of military collision.

[14] See Zimmerman. He detects a cleavage between the principal leaders (Brezhnev, Kosygin, and Podgorny) and two lesser members of the Politburo (Voronov and Shelepin), based on speeches in June, 1966. The former he identifies with the low-risk orientation and the latter with the high-risk emphasis on American weakness. Voronov's remarks on the subject in his speech of June 3, 1966, were borrowed directly, however (as Voronov himself implied), from documents of the xxiii Party Congress, held two months earlier; and Shelepin's formulation was only a slight embroidery on the standard Party line. Reading the same speeches of June, 1966, Fritz Ermath concluded that Brezhnev, Shelepin, and Kirilenko were strong on the need to bolster Soviet defense efforts, in contrast to Kosygin, Podgorny, Mazurov, Poliansky, Suslov, and Ustinov. ("Has Kosygin Won a Showdown on Defense Spending?" Radio Free Europe, August 5, 1966.)

[15] *The 23rd Congress of the CPSU*, pp. 9, 42–43.

[16] *Ibid.*, 286.

[17] Brezhnev at the xxiii Party Congress, *The 23rd Congress of the CPSU*, p. 45; Party Secretary Demichev (in charge of propaganda and ideological affairs) in the Lenin birthday anniversary speech of April 22, 1965 (*Pravda*, April 23, 1965), and Politburo member A. P. Kirilenko on the same occasion in 1967 (*ibid.*). For Kosygin's views on Soviet-American relations, see an interview of January 19, 1968, in *Life*, February 2, 1968.

gotiate a nonproliferation agreement with the United States while the war in Vietnam continued.[18] In fact, however, negotiations (largely bilateral in nature) on the outer space treaty and on the draft nonproliferation treaty (NPT) were brought to a successful conclusion in 1967 and 1968—patently subsequent to the escalation of the war in Vietnam.*

American involvement in the war in Vietnam, and especially U.S. bombing of North Vietnam, became issues helpful to the USSR in its long-term objectives of isolating both the United States and Communist China. In Soviet propaganda, the United States is attacked much more often and more vehemently than is Communist China. Furthermore, the "disproportion" of material critical of the U.S. compared to that of China has increased significantly in the period after 1964.[19] The United States served as the target of a large-scale Soviet campaign against aggressive interference in Vietnam, and China of a lower-keyed campaign emphasizing Peking's unwillingness to join forces in combating American "aggression." Despite this instrumental use of the Vietnam issue, the USSR seemed more anxious to see the hostilities controlled or stopped than to have them continue in the hope of inflicting on the United States a major military and political defeat. Nevertheless, Soviet diplomatic efforts have been rather passive in regard to Vietnam, because the USSR has sought above all to keep in step with Hanoi. The Soviet leaders have seized, however, upon every

[18] *The New York Times*, July 29, 1965, p. 11, and January 26, 1966, p. 12.

* It is debatable whether the war in Vietnam encouraged the USSR and the United States to come to agreement on arms control and similar issues, or whether these agreements were made in spite of the war. The participants in this project were divided on the question. Those who held to the first view believed that without the war there would have been less incentive for the two states to find areas of agreement. These post-1965 agreements became attractive to the U.S. and the USSR precisely because they promised to slow the drift toward a more serious military confrontation over Vietnam. Proponents of the second view considered that Vietnam had closed opportunities for negotiation of more fundamental agreements, and that the negotiations that survived the war were reminders of what might have been accomplished had Soviet-American relations not worsened.

[19] A study of *Pravda* references to the United States and Communist China in four periods (September 1–10 of 1964 and of 1966, October 23–November 1, 1966, and January 4–13, 1967) showed that in the 1966 and 1967 samples over 95 per cent of the *Pravda* material on the United States was negative, in contrast to the 1964 sample in which half the references were negative and the other half neutral. The volume of anti-Chinese material in the 1966–1967 samples was less than half that in the 1964 sample; the volume of anti-American material doubled and tripled. Thus, in the 1964 sample there were almost twice as many column-inches against Communist China as against the United States, whereas in the 1966–1967 samples there were three and four times as many inches critical of the United States as of Communist China. These changes were heavily affected, of course, by the war in Vietnam, which gave rise to much more "news" than did the "cultural revolution" in China. "*Pravda* as a Mirror of Recent Soviet Policy: The United States and Communist China" (New York: Radio Liberty Committee, Propaganda Analysis 1, 1967).

indication of North Vietnamese willingness to come to a diplomatic settlement to encourage negotiations, whereas China has pushed in the opposite direction. The benefits that the USSR has derived from exploitation of American activities in Vietnam have been accompanied by the great danger of the Soviet Union being sucked increasingly into the hostilities. More direct involvement could, in turn, escalate into a major war involving the United States, Communist China, and the USSR.*

Although the USSR has sought to use the Vietnam war to organize world opposition to the United States, it has also sought to avoid a direct Soviet-American military confrontation over Vietnam. In the early stages of American attacks on North Vietnam, the Soviet authorities tended to play down Soviet military assistance in North Vietnam, which has never included a commitment of combat forces. Although Soviet aid is now more public, the USSR has, by and large, cautiously channeled its military supplies to Vietnam by the overland route through China, despite all the difficulties entailed by this choice, rather than chance the sea-route, with all the risks of a collision involving the United States.[20] In these and other ways, the Soviet leaders have sought to keep options open for the day when more far-reaching arrangements with the United States might be possible or desirable, whether in over-all political relations or on measures for arms control and disarmament.

STRATEGY TOWARD EUROPE AND THE "THIRD WORLD"

In turning away from attempts to bring about in the short term the kind of Soviet-American détente that preoccupied Khrushchev, the new leaders have infused more energy into attempts to woo American allies in Europe and elsewhere. They have avoided pressures that might lead to a closing of ranks in the West, and have sought with great patience and caution to develop bilateral ties with individual European and Asian countries. The USSR has especially wooed France, a natural candidate for attention, given President de Gaulle's orientation away from close ties with the United States. But it has also cultivated relations with Great Britain, Japan, and other advanced industrial

---

* A division of opinion existed among those who participated in the project on whether the Soviet Union was really interested in promoting a negotiated solution to the Vietnam conflict, or considered its interests best served by a continuation of the hostilities.

[20] The Chinese taunted the Soviet leaders for their avoidance of the sea route. See the press conference of Foreign Minister Chen Yi, December 30, 1965 (*Peking Review*, IX, No. 2 [January 7, 1966], 7), and a Chinese Foreign Ministry statement of May 3, 1966 (*Peking Review*, IX, No. 19 [May 6, 1966], 26).

states. This was not true of the Federal Republic of Germany (FRG), which Moscow has sought to confine and isolate along with the United States. In 1967–1968, the USSR made an exceptional approach to West Germany for agreements between the FRG and Warsaw Pact states to renounce the use of force in their relations. The USSR sought to bring about, in connection with this, limitations on West German activities in West Berlin and some acceptance by the Federal Republic of the East German state.[21] But nothing came of the attempt.

With the drift toward an easing of the Cold War and a loosening of hostile alliances, the USSR has tried to encourage in Europe tendencies toward consolidation of the European territorial status quo and toward trans-European arrangements designed to cut America out and keep Russia in. In almost all the measures and procedures suggested by Moscow as palliatives for Europe's ills, a central or subsidiary element has been recognition of the German Democratic Republic (GDR) and of the permanence of the Oder-Neisse frontier of Germany. Soviet spokesmen have focused on West Germany as the great European danger to be combated. This anti-Bonn emphasis runs counter, however, to desires in many of the Eastern European states for stablization of relations with West Germany, an important partner in economic deals; it also prevents the Soviet Union from achieving a rapport with France on European policies. Thus, President de Gaulle has sought close collaboration with the Federal Republic in orienting Europe toward structures and policies independent of the United States. In contrast, the Soviet leaders, who are also interested in reducing American influence in Europe, have sought to isolate West Germany, to make permanent the Federal Republic's current borders, and to limit West German leverage over neighbors east and west.

The European situation is perhaps more fluid today than at any time since the end of World War II. Neither the U.S. nor the USSR has as much control over its allies as was once the case, and consequently the field for maneuver within and across alliance lines has been opened up. Proposals to diminish the military confrontation in Europe form a part of these maneuvers, as in the American initiative to reduce gradually, by tacit or formal understandings, the number of foreign troops in Germany.[22] European arms control proposals appear

---

[21] Exchanges initiated by the USSR took place in 1967–1968. See *The New York Times*, January 17, 1968, and February 3, 18, 1968; *Izvestiia*, July 12–14, 1968.

[22] The United States received NATO backing for a reduction of some 50,000 in the number of American troops stationed in Europe, most of which were to remain committed to NATO while being re-stationed in the United States. American authorities expressed a hope for, but no confidence in, the likelihood of Soviet reciprocation. See the testimony of Secretary of State Rusk, Secretary of Defense McNamara, and Undersecretary of State Katzenbach before Senate Committees on April 26 and

now to have less interest for the Soviet leaders. Since 1964 the USSR has showed most interest in promoting broad politico-military rearrangements rather than arms control as such. The Soviet proposals for dismantling alliance military structures and for a security arrangement covering all Europe are discussed subsequently.

The interest in cutting back American influence, a determinative aim of Soviet policy toward Europe, has also been one among several factors strongly motivating Soviet policy in the underdeveloped countries. The leaders in Moscow have had, however, greater hopes of revolutionary transformations in the Middle East, Africa, and Asia—and perhaps even Latin America—than in the advanced states of Europe. Soviet activities among underdeveloped countries have continued along lines made familiar in the Khrushchev era: military and economic aid and trade agreements, support of movements against colonial and former colonial powers and against the American "imperialists," and close Soviet Party and government ties to radical nationalist regimes. The failure of the Communist coup in Indonesia and the subsequent withering away of Sukarno and the overthrow of Nkrumah in Ghana have already been mentioned as factors producing some decline in the Kremlin's confidence that the choice of a "noncapitalist" route was irreversible.[23] But, even apart from the bittersweet taste left by the Indonesian events—where China's loss was not Moscow's pain—the reverses have been seen by the Soviet leaders as temporary setbacks. Accepting these losses, the USSR has sought above all to hold onto depleted assets and to rebuild for the future.

The post-Khrushchev leaders have continued to value close links with the "revolutionary-democratic parties" of the radical nationalist states.[24] These one-party states of Asia and particularly Africa have no Communist party and sometimes specifically proscribe Communist activities. Partly because of the reverses mentioned above, present Soviet doctrine seems to be more ambivalent than was earlier the case on the prospects of underdeveloped countries evolving toward socialism without a proletariat and a proletarian (i.e., Communist) party. There is

---

May 3, 1967. *United States Troops in Europe*, combined hearings before the U.S. Senate Subcommittee of Foreign Relations and Armed Services Committee, 90th Cong., 1st sess. (Washington, D.C.: Government Printing Office, 1967).

[23] In Indonesia the failure of a coup attempt on September 30, 1965, supported by the Communists, set off the chain of events, which included the mass killing of hundred of thousands of Communists and the banning of the Party. In Ghana, Nkrumah was overthrown, while out of the country, by a coup of February 24, 1966.

[24] At the xxiii Party Congress, for example, eight such parties were represented. They were mostly from Africa, and all five representatives of such parties called upon to address the Congress were from Africa.

less frequent voicing of the theory that the USSR and other Communist states could provide an absentee proletariat for countries too underdeveloped to have their own, and of the accompanying theory that if a
Communist party is not on the scene, the local ruling party—if progressive enough—could be an effective surrogate. Despite these signs
of lessened optimism, the Soviet leaders have little choice but to rely
on these radical nationalist regimes to advance the Communist cause
in the "third world."

The area of the underdeveloped world that has drawn the most
Soviet interest is the Middle East, where the USSR has channeled a
great portion of its "foreign investment." In the period preceding the
1967 outbreak of Arab-Israeli hostilities, the Soviet leaders could look
with satisfaction on leftward shifts in several Arab countries. Partly as
a result of this, the USSR strengthened its ties with almost all the more
nationalist regimes of the area. The war that erupted in June, 1967,
presented a heady assortment of dangers and opportunities, which allowed the new Soviet leaders to show their style of "crisis management." Cautious about any military confrontation that might involve
the USSR, they sought above all an end to the fighting, even on terms
registering the disastrous defeat of their Arab friends. In a posture
quite unlike their diplomatic passivity in the face of the escalating
conflict in Vietnam, the Soviet leaders subsequently launched a major
diplomatic offensive in an unsuccessful attempt to force the Israelis to
disgorge their military gains. If the fighting made them nervous—for
the first time the hot-lines linking Moscow to Paris and to Washington
came into use—the leaders still used the occasion for a demonstration
of Soviet naval power in the Mediterranean. Resupply after the war
of UAR and Syrian forces, which lost much Soviet equipment to the
Israelis, indicates that the USSR is prepared to sink more rubles into
a costly investment. But the USSR benefited from the war, too.[25] Repercussions in the UAR caused by the poor showing of the Arab military forces, for example, promised to lead to changes of a kind that
would be welcome to the Soviet Union. The USSR also stood to gain
from the Arab identification of the United States with the Israeli cause.
Thus, the war and its aftermath increased Arab dependence on the
USSR for both military supplies and diplomatic support.*

In deploying forces in the Mediterranean, the USSR has continued

---

[25] On resupply, see Premier Kosygin's speech in Minsk, February 14, 1968 (*Sovetskaia Belorussiia*, February 15, 1968). For an appreciation of the Soviet position in
the Middle East after the imbroglio of 1967, see the article by Hedrick Smith (based
on Washington sources) in *The New York Times*, January 15, 1968.

* Some participants emphasized Soviet losses in the Middle East as more significant than any gains.

to insist that it does not seek military bases there.[26] But the USSR, having shown the red flag on the Mediterranean during the tense summer of 1967, seems likely to maintain a presence there. For this reason, it is interested in having access to friendly ports. Nor have Soviet activities been limited to states bordering Israel, such as the UAR and Syria. The USSR has also extended military assistance to former French and British possessions, such as Algeria, the Yemen, and the People's Republic of Southern Yemen.[27]

THE NEW LEADERS AND THE WORLD COMMUNIST MOVEMENT

Khrushchev's successors inherited from him a badly split world Communist movement and the enmity of the other great Communist power, China. The specifics of Soviet strategy toward China deserve special treatment later on. Here it must be noted that the divergences among Communists in and out of power are not simply a function of Sino-Soviet differences; they are deeply rooted in conflicting concepts of Communist strategy and tactics, and in differences of national interests. The disunity in the Communist camp could not be overcome, and was not overcome, merely by the application of conciliatory tactics on the part of the post-Khrushchev leaders. These leaders have been able to improve the Soviet position in the Far East, halt any further deterioration of Soviet influence in the world movement, and prevent the collapse of the Soviet position in Eastern Europe. But the Kremlin leaders have often seemed to be like men on a treadmill who have to walk faster in order to stay in the same place.

Moscow can no longer expect unquestioning obedience from other Communist parties, in or out of power. And persuasion has proved insufficient as a method of achieving consensus. The blessing of the cpsu still counts for something, of course, and thus Soviet prestige as the first and foremost Communist state has kept a good many Communists tuned to Radio Moscow. But the attention to national values, which has done much to consolidate the hold of Communist elites on peoples they rule, and has influenced the strategy of nonruling parties toward their clienteles, has also worked against maintenance (or restoration) of unity behind Moscow's leadership.

The Soviet leaders have found that even the economic assistance and

---

[26] Such as Mers-el-Kebir in Algeria, returned by the French to Algeria in January, 1968. *Le Monde, Sélection Hebdomadaire*, XXI, No. 1007 (February 1–7, 1968).

[27] See A. Lavrishchev, "The Soviet Union and the Developing Countries," *International Affairs* (Moscow), No. 1 (January, 1968), 59–65.

military protection they can offer are not sufficient to keep other Communist regimes in line. This was demonstrated by Cuba—dependent on the USSR for economic support and vulnerable to economic and military pressure from the United States. Yet Castro still felt free to show his defiance of the USSR (as well as China).[28] In Europe, where the USSR heads multilateral military-political and economic alliances (the Warsaw Treaty Organization and the Council of Economic Mutual Assistance), the Soviet leaders have had to deal with a deviationist Rumania and a wayward Czechoslovakia, and accept the fact that joint action depends on bargaining among the alliance partners.

Rumania had defiantly asserted its intention to follow an independent course well before Khrushchev's departure, as its famous declaration of April 22, 1964, testified.[29] The conflict extended to an increasingly wider range of issues after 1964. Economic differences had long played a role, for Rumania opposed Soviet-sponsored moves to treat Eastern Europe as a single economic entity, and thereby to increase specialization in production among the various countries. Since Rumania was one of the least developed of these states, the leaders feared that "division of labor" would condemn Rumania to perpetuation of an economy centering on agricultural and raw materials production at the expense of Rumanian ambitions for industrialization.

In other fields as well, the USSR has encountered Rumanian recalcitrance. The 20th anniversary of the Rumanian-Soviet treaty of friendship, cooperation, and mutual assistance, in February, 1968, passed without conclusion of a replacement treaty, although one was agreed upon subsequently.[30] Soviet dominance of the military organization of the Warsaw Pact has aroused resistance from Bucharest, which wants changes in the command arrangements, including rotation of the post of Commander-in-Chief.[31] Rumania has for a long time played a very special role in disputes between Communist China

---

[28] Some of the Cuban differences with the Soviet leadership stemmed from differences over strategy in Latin America, where the USSR sought to improve relations with regimes in power and tended to favor established Communist parties, largely preoccupied with parliamentary politics, over militant groups seeking to overthrow bourgeois governments. Cuban disaffection with Moscow was revealed in many ways, including the sending of a low-level representative to the Moscow celebrations of 50 years of Soviet rule, and the refusal to take part in the Budapest consultative meeting of February 26–March 5, 1968. Of the Communist parties which sent representatives to Moscow in March, 1965, for a preliminary meeting, Cuba was the only one which refused to go along with Soviet preparations in 1967–1968 for a new world conference.

[29] See *The New York Times,* April 27, 1964.

[30] *The New York Times,* February 4, 1968. See Foreign Minister Gromyko's address to the USSR Supreme Soviet, June 27, 1968 (*Pravda,* June 28, 1968).

[31] *The New York Times,* March 7, 1968.

and the Soviet Union, in seeking to maintain a certain distance from both sides and to stay clear of moves to organize parties sympathetic to Moscow in a unity movement openly or covertly oriented against the Chinese.

But divergences have spread from questions involving Rumania's specific economic and military interests, and the Rumanian viewpoint on the world Communist movement, to other foreign policy issues. Thus, the USSR was unable to prevent Rumania from accepting in early 1967 the West German offer to re-establish diplomatic relations.[32] In 1967 too, when the Arab-Israeli conflict broke out, the Rumanians adopted a more neutral and less pro-Arab position than the USSR and other Communists of Eastern Europe, including the Yugoslavs.[33] Finally, the USSR found the Rumanians making trouble in arms control and disarmament negotiations. At the Geneva discussions in the ENDC, Rumanian representatives showed their unhappiness with the draft of the nonproliferation treaty that the USSR had negotiated with the United States. Part of their negativism stemmed from the Rumanian stand for more equal status of the states allied in the Warsaw Pact. However, they also repeated many of the objections expressed by nonaligned states, particularly on the omission of security guarantees for the countries not possessing nuclear weapons, and of any requirements on the nuclear weapons states to reduce their armaments.[34] At the Sofia meeting of the WTO Political Consultative Committee, March 6–7, 1968, Rumania did not sign the declaration in support of the nonproliferation treaty. However, the Rumanians voted in favor of a U.N. General Assembly resolution approving the treaty three months later, and signed the treaty promptly on July 1, 1968.

The evolution of events in Czechoslovakia after Novotny's ouster in January, 1968, caused an alarm in the Kremlin that had not been aroused by Rumanian displays of independence. The Soviet leaders saw there what appeared to them as the disintegration of Communist rule and not just the aberrations of Communist rulers. Finding in the summer of 1968 that ideological, political, and military pressures were insufficient to brake or reverse the trend toward "liberalization," they finally resorted to joint military intervention with other Warsaw Pact allies, some of whom had probably urged the step.

Because of this special nature of the situation in Czechoslovakia, the Kremlin departed from the policy of avoiding polemics with Communist regimes that maintained at least superficially friendly relations

---

[32] *Ibid.*, February 1, 1967.
[33] *Ibid.*, June 24, 1967.
[34] See, for example, the speech to the ENDC on February 6, 1968, by Rumanian representative Nicolae Ecobescu, as transmitted by Bucharest AGERPRES.

with the USSR. This rule—largely observed in regard to Rumania
and Cuba, for example—made the Soviet leaders hold their tongues
while they pushed ahead with their projects, sometimes lowering their
sights in order to carry along dissidents, and sometimes going ahead
without full unanimity.[35] They managed to increase the Warsaw Pact's
military importance after years of a rather shadowy existence. They
benefited from the fact that most of the regimes of Eastern Europe
have had enough common interests with the USSR, or felt enough in-
security about their capability of handling internal or foreign enemies,
to value close ties to Moscow. Prior to the invasion of Czechoslovakia,
the leaders of the USSR seemed to be learning to operate within an
alliance system that in many aspects began to resemble conventional
alliances found elsewhere in the world, with limitations of scope, play
of national politics, and decisions through compromises, rather than
the rigidly unified bloc arrangement of the days when Moscow's wishes
became law for its allies.*

As one tactic of bolstering Soviet leadership in the world Communist movement, both Khrushchev and his successors reverted to the
idea of assembling another world conference along the lines of those
held in Moscow in 1957 and 1960. A new conference will clearly have
to serve a purpose different from that of its predecessors. Sufficient desire for unity, and particularly for a façade of unity, existed even in
1960—when the movement was already strife-ridden—for agreement
on a common statement by the Chinese, Soviet, and other Communists. Neither Khrushchev nor his successors could have been under
any illusions after 1963 that the Chinese (or the Albanians) would
take part in another such meeting. Chinese opposition was only one,
and probably not the most important, cause for the postponement of
a preparatory meeting; the meeting was scheduled, while Khrushchev
was in power, to take place in December, 1964, but was delayed by the
successors until March, 1965, and attended by delegates from only 19
of 26 parties invited.[36] After temporizing for more than a year, Soviet

[35] An example of the latter practice was furnished by the meetings of the Eastern
European Communist leaders on the Middle East crisis of June, 1967 (*Pravda*, June
10, 1967), where the joint stand received Tito's assent for Yugoslavia but not Ceau-
sescu's for Rumania.

* A dimmer view of Soviet prospects in regard to other Communist regimes in
Europe is held by some of the participants in the project. They believe that the
Soviet leaders face a dilemma in dealing with the Eastern European regimes:
whether they put on or relax pressure for conformity, the Soviet interests suffer;
and Soviet support for some countries worsens the standing of the USSR with
others.

[36] For the declaration issued by this group of parties, see *Sino-Soviet Relations,
1964–1965,* William E. Griffith (Cambridge, Mass.: The M.I.T. Press, 1967), pp. 393–
95.

leaders and their supporters in the movement began to say in late 1966 that "conditions were ripening" for such a meeting.[37] The "dress rehearsal" for the world conference was finally announced November 25, 1967, and took place in Budapest, February 26–March 5, 1968.[38] This meeting, like the Moscow meeting in March, 1965, was "consultative," but differed from that of 1965 in that all Communist parties present at the 1960 conference were eligible to attend. (This excluded the Yugoslavs.) Sixty-six parties were represented (two by observers); however, the absentees included not only the Chinese and Albanians but also the North Vietnamese, North Koreans, and Cubans among the ruling parties, as well as the Yugoslavs. The Rumanians wavered before finally deciding to go, but then walked out before the meeting was over.[39]

In pushing for another world conference, originally scheduled to take place in Moscow in November–December, 1968, but postponed in the aftermath of the Czech affair, the Soviet leaders seemed to have concluded that the obvious disadvantages of such a conference were outweighed by the advantages. The Budapest preliminary gathering and the intended full conference later in 1968 were certain to highlight and perhaps to sharpen divisions in the movement. Prospects for the conference, for it to be held and still more for its "success" if held, darkened after the Soviet invasion of Czechoslovakia. About half the ruling parties and some other important parties (mostly Asian) were already set to boycott such a meeting; and many of the parties which had agreed to attend were critical of the occupation of Czechoslovakia. The convocation of a new world conference had appealed to Moscow as a means of establishing an up-to-date platform lending international authority to the views of the majority in the world Communist movement. Simultaneously, it was seen by the Soviet leaders as a way of instituting an organizational device they could use to maintain their position of primacy. At the time of the Budapest meeting, the word from Moscow and capitals sympathetic to the Soviet position emphasized that they "understood" why some parties chose not to participate. In taking this line, Moscow sought to distinguish the reticence of absentees from the blunt rejection by Peking and Tirana. The USSR thus pursued somewhat contradictory goals—seek-

---

[37] The renewal of the campaign for a new world conference occurred at a Bulgarian Party Congress, when Bulgarian Party chief Zhivkov gave the word on November 15, 1966, with Brezhnev seconding the motion.

[38] *Pravda*, November 25, 1967.

[39] The Rumanians objected to criticism of their position voiced by the Syrian Communists at the meeting, but a more fundamental reason seemed to be their realization that the USSR had decided to go ahead promptly with a world conference (*The New York Times*, March 1, 1968).

ing to give great weight to the conference it inspired, and at the same time trying to avoid drawing a line between parties that did and did not attend.

COMMUNIST CHINA AND
POST-KHRUSHCHEV SOVIET POLICY

Initially, Khrushchev's successors apparently had hopes of bettering Soviet relations with the Chinese Communists without making fundamental concessions. They put a stop to polemics, considering that Khrushchev's bitter and personal attacks on Mao Tse-tung and the Chinese leaders had been unproductive. In fact, the only foreign policy shift ever publicly attributed to the October, 1964, Plenum was this change in tactics toward China.[40] Besides halting public attacks on the Chinese and postponing the preparatory meeting for a world conference of Communist parties, the CPSU also proposed to the Chinese that the top leaders of the two parties should meet either in Peking or Moscow.[41] The Chinese turned this down.

Although the Chinese initially reciprocated by suspending their own polemics, Premier Chou En-lai and other delegates who were in Moscow November 5–13, 1964, found that the successors had repudiated only Khrushchev and not "Khrushchevism," i.e., the CPSU line worked out at the XX and XXII Party Congresses in 1956 and 1961. According to a Chinese authority, the new Soviet leaders

explicitly stated that there was not a shade of difference between themselves and Khrushchev on the question of the international Communist movement and in their attitude towards China. . . . These new leaders of the CPSU had to oust Khrushchev, not because they had any difference of principle with him, but because Khrushchev had become too odious and had been too stupid in some of his practices, and because Khrushchev himself had become a serious obstacle to the carrying out of Khrushchev revisionism.[42]

[40] The communiqué on the October Plenum made no mention of this shift, but a link has been consistently drawn in Soviet commentary between the October Plenum and the cessation of polemics. It was alluded to in the (secret) letter sent in January, 1966, by the CPSU to other Communist parties. *The New York Times,* March 24, 1966, published excerpts from the CPSU letter, which first appeared in *Die Welt,* March 21, 1966.
[41] The postponement was announced in Moscow on December 12, 1964. The Soviet letter of November 24, 1964 to the Chinese Party about the postponement was never published in the USSR, but was published in *Jen Min Jih Pao,* March 20, 1965. See reference above, note 41, to Soviet letter of January, 1966.
[42] Editorial article in *Jen Min Jih Pao* and *Hung Chi,* March 22, 1965; reprinted in *Sino-Soviet Relations, 1964–1965,* pp. 407–18.

It very soon became clear, therefore, that neither the USSR nor China was prepared to alter its position sufficiently to bring about a *rapprochement*. The succeeding years only deepened the differences and the hostility between the two powers. Nevertheless, the change of Kremlin leadership did affect the conduct of Sino-Soviet relations in 1965–1968, i.e., even after the short moratorium on polemics was forgotten. Brezhnev and his colleagues seized upon the American bombing of North Vietnam to change the focus of the dispute to the practical issue of aid to North Vietnam. They proposed in April, 1965, a conference of representatives from the Soviet Union, China, and North Vietnam to coordinate Communist aid to the threatened regime in Hanoi.[43] The Soviet leaders then used Chinese rejection of this and other forms of joint assistance as a handy issue with which to work against the Chinese in the world Communist movement.

In spite of new issues in dispute and Chinese public attacks, the Soviet leaders refrained for a long time from open attacks on the Chinese. The first comprehensive Soviet attack on the foreign and international policies of Mao and his group in the post-Khrushchev period was published in a *Pravda* editorial article on November 27, 1966, more than two years after Khrushchev's ouster.[44] This Soviet reversion to polemics followed the Plenum of the Chinese Party's Central Committee, August 1–12, 1966. This meeting was regarded by Moscow as crucial not because of the attacks on the Soviet leaders (these were already frequent) but because the Chinese Communist Party formally called for a line of demarcation, both politically and organizationally, between the Chinese and their Soviet opponents.[45] The November, 1966, *Pravda* blast at the Chinese prepared the way for a plenum of the CPSU Central Committee on December 12–13, 1966. On the basis of a report by Brezhnev, that plenum discussed Soviet tactics in regard to the Chinese and to disunity in the Communist movement.[46] The Soviet leaders preferred to have the Soviet line expounded through impersonal Party documents, government notes, and newspaper editorials. In their own speeches, Brezhnev, Kosygin, and other leaders were restrained in their comments on Chinese behavior and in their references to Chairman Mao, usually speaking in tones of sadness rather than anger.[47]

---

[43] This secret letter was dated April 3, 1966, and was followed by another on April 17 criticizing the Chinese rejection.

[44] *Pravda* published on November 28, 1965, an editorial article critical of divisive acts of the Chinese, but it was restrained in tone and content.

[45] *Peking Review*, IX, No. 34 (August 19, 1966), 7.

[46] *Pravda*, December 13–15, 1966.

[47] "Mao and his group" became the standard formula used in Soviet leadership communications, and was rarely if ever amplified.

As the quarrel deepened in 1965–1966, there was a change both in the mode of discussion and in the issues raised. The open letters exchanged frequently in Khrushchev's time implied the existence, despite the differences, of some common ground in the search for appropriate strategies. From October, 1964, through February, 1966, the CPSU continued to send letters to the Chinese. Keeping to its ban on open polemics, the CPSU published none of these.[48] Nor did it publish a letter sent to other parties in January, 1966, criticizing Chinese attitudes and behavior.[49] From 1966 onward, the Soviet Party leaders apparently no longer addressed communications directly to the Chinese, now regarded as beyond the pale.

As Vietnam policy questions became more urgent, many of the old issues lost some of their former importance. These included the role of "peaceful coexistence" in Communist strategy, the inevitability or noninevitability of war, the dominant characteristic of the present age, and the role of violence in the Communist struggle for power. The post-Khrushchev leaders saw their task not as outarguing the Chinese leaders, but as outmaneuvering Chinese Communists in the world movement, and Communist China in Asian and world politics.

Most of these maneuvers were directed toward confining and isolating the Chinese. Aided considerably by Chinese mishaps and mistakes in 1965–1967, the Kremlin moved with considerable skill to achieve a number of successes. These were particularly evident in Asia, where Moscow benefited from a shift in the ruling groups in North Vietnam and North Korea toward a more neutral as against a pro-Peking position, and a similar shift in the Japanese Communist Party. Nevertheless, the Moscow leaders were not able to bring around most of the Asian Communist parties to support of the Soviet line in the world Communist movement. On the level of interstate relations, the USSR managed to better its relations with Japan, important in any long-term containment of China, and to improve its standing with Pakistan without worsening its position vis-à-vis India.[50]

Outside Asia the direct influence of China was much less important in the Communist movement and in interstate relations. Here, too, the Chinese suffered setbacks, notably in attempts to win friends and gain

[48] In addition to the secret letters of November 24, 1964, April 3 and 17, 1965, already mentioned, the CPSU sent a letter on November 28, 1965, probably along the lines of Pravda's editorial article of the same date, entitled "The International Duty of Communists of All Countries." (See reference to this letter in Pravda, November 27, 1966.) Finally, on February 24, 1966, the CPSU addressed to the Chinese Communist Party a letter inviting the Chinese to send representatives to the XXIII Congress.

[49] The letter that appeared in Die Welt of March 21, 1966; excerpted in The New York Times, March 24, 1966.

[50] For a discussion of Soviet handling of the China problem after October, 1964, see Lowenthal in Soviet Politics Since Khrushchev.

influence among the states of Africa, a continent sparsely endowed with Communist parties. The Soviet leaders could not, however, overcome recurrent dissension among and within various Communist parties, several of which had splintered into hostile fragments. Moscow's problem in trying to restore order and unity to the movement outside of Asia stemmed less from Chinese activities than from the fact that in many countries Communist and near-Communist groups were attracted to a militancy of which Peking was a better exemplar than Moscow.

The Soviet leaders appear to have given up earlier expectations of a negotiated solution to the issues separating them from the Chinese. The turmoil in China associated with "the great proletarian cultural revolution," and the continued Chinese acknowledgment that dissident leaders remain in office, probably encourage the Kremlin to believe that new persons may come to power in China—before or after Mao's death—who may be more tractable than the present leaders in Peking. But the Soviet leaders probably do not count on such a change, and do not assume that Mao's successors will reject his "great-power chauvinism" and his ambitions for "hegemony" in the Communist movement; i.e., post-Mao China will still be a rival and opponent in interstate and inter-Party affairs. In any case, the Soviet authorities realize that the former close alliance cannot be restored even if the extreme hostilities subside. Their maneuvers to contain and isolate China in the Communist movement and in the world of states seem to be based on a perspective of long-term estrangement. If the prediction they read is one of foul weather ahead, however, the Brezhnev-Kosygin-Podgorny group seem to expect that the struggle will be confined to the political plane, and will not soon involve a clash of arms. They have, therefore, concentrated on precautionary measures designed to deal with a long-term Chinese threat rather than an imminent military challenge.[51]

THE SINO-SOVIET CONFLICT AND DISARMAMENT PROBLEMS

Disarmament issues have lost a good deal of their importance in Soviet-Chinese differences since 1964. In the Khrushchev period, both Soviet sponsorship of "general and complete disarmament" and Soviet agreement to the partial test-ban treaty occasioned bitter polemics. With the test ban an accomplished fact, and with GCD no longer prop-

---

[51] There have been rumors, it is true, of Soviet transfers of troops from Europe to the Far East, but these seem to be unsubstantiated. This is not to say that the USSR expects to have no trouble with border incidents involving the Chinese. Many of these have been alleged by both sides. See Thomas W. Wolfe in *Soviet Politics Since Khrushchev*.

agated with zest by the Soviet leadership, there has been less to argue about in the area of arms control and disarmament. Differences on issues in this area have not disappeared, as Chinese attacks on the proposed treaty banning nuclear proliferation have shown, but other differences have overshadowed them.

Despite this diminished impact, some of the post-1964 developments concerning disarmament and Sino-Soviet relations are of interest. Thus, the post-Khrushchev leaders have seemed to try to avoid steps damaging to Chinese ambitions for great-power status. In agreeing to a test ban in 1963, Khrushchev placed Communist China in a dilemma. Acceptance of the agreement would have meant a renunciation by China of the possibility of its development into an independent, first-class military power, and would have forced China into permanent dependence on the USSR's nuclear "umbrella." In rejecting the agreement and asserting China's claims to great-power status, the Peking leaders were forced to break with the USSR on a major international issue, which they did.

Since that time, no issue of comparable scope has been presented to China, for the USSR has not proposed or accepted measures infringing on Chinese claims. This applies in particular to the most important disarmament negotiations in which the Brezhnev leadership has engaged, those leading to the nonproliferation treaty. China's continued development of a nuclear arsenal would not be hindered even if it were to adhere to the agreement. Under the treaty terms, China falls into the privileged class of nuclear-weapon powers, whose military advances in the nuclear field are subject to no restriction, and whose civilian (peaceful) programs for the use of nuclear energy are subject to no foreign scrutiny or control.

The nonproliferation treaty, it is true, would restrict Communist China from passing on nuclear weapons or "know-how" to non-nuclear states. It is not at all clear that China intends to do this, however, even when its production of nuclear weapons becomes more advanced.[52] In any case, it appears likely that the overwhelming majority of states will sign a nonproliferation treaty, thus removing them as potential customers even if China wants to be a supplier. In addition, the states with the greatest potential for developing nuclear weapons (including India, Japan, Sweden, Israel, and others) are not likely to be beneficiaries of any Chinese aid. The Communist states—in addition to China—that refused to sign the 1963 test-ban treaty (Albania, North Korea, North Vietnam, and Cuba), and thus displayed their

[52] See remarks by Vice-Premier Chen Yi of the CPR, September 29, 1965, in *Documents 1965*, p. 463. Note that Secretary of State Rusk said on March 25, 1966, that "possibly even Peiping" agreed that it was not a good thing to see the proliferation of nuclear weapons. See *Documents 1966*, p. 174.

antipathy to Soviet-American sponsored restrictions on weapons development, have little capacity to equip themselves with modern weapons systems.[53]

China's opposition to the nonproliferation treaty seems to be based not on any hindrance the treaty would impose on Chinese development or transfer of nuclear weapons, but on other considerations. To Peking it looks like another deal between Soviet "revisionists," who are said to be even worse than Khrushchev, and the American and other "imperialists."[54] More specifically, Peking sees the nonproliferation treaty as an attempt by the status quo powers to justify their possession of nuclear weapons and to establish the principle that the spread of nuclear weapons to additional states is something to be deplored—and prohibited. In contrast, Chinese spokesmen claim that the more "peace-loving" states acquire nuclear weapons, the better for the world. By "peace-loving," Peking means revolutionary states, and specifically, Afro-Asian countries.[55]

If Khrushchev's successors have avoided negotiation of any arms control agreement damaging to Chinese interests in developing the kind of military establishment held in esteem by all the great powers, they have also been careful in other ways to avoid the appearance of thwarting China. The Soviet Union has shied away from international condemnation of China's program to develop a nuclear arsenal. It thus took pains to separate itself from the mild strictures aimed at Communist China in a U.N. Disarmament Commission resolution of June 15, 1965, which included a statement "deploring . . . that nuclear weapons tests have taken place. . . ."[56] The day before passage of the resolution, Soviet representative Tsarapkin objected to this "censure" of the People's Republic of China. According to Tsarapkin, "it is not for the Disarmament Commission or for any other United Nations organ either directly or indirectly, openly or in a veiled manner, to comment on the position of, and even less to condemn [China]."[57] (Soviet scruples were subsequently somewhat relaxed; at the U.N. General Assembly session in the fall of 1966, the USSR approved a December 5 res-

[53] Probably the decision of the nonsignatory Communist states was little affected by any intention to carry out a nuclear weapons test program, but was a gesture to Peking, or more generally a sign of discontent with Soviet-American collaboration.

[54] The successors were said to be even worse than Khrushchev in that they masked more cleverly the same "revisionist" approach that Khrushchev had represented.

[55] Chen Yi, in *Documents 1965*, p. 463, and interview of Premier Chou En-lai with a correspondent of Karachi *Dawn*, April 10, 1966, in *Documents 1966*, p. 211; and an article in *Jen Min Jih Pao* on disarmament, June 20, 1966, in *Documents 1966*, p. 359.

[56] *Documents 1965*, pp. 260–61. The USSR abstained in the vote on this resolution.

[57] *Ibid.*, pp. 254–55. Tsarapkin even described as anti-Chinese the appeal of the U.N. Disarmament Commission for all states to adhere to the test-ban treaty.

olution that urged "all countries" to adhere to the 1963 treaty and noted "with great concern" the fact that some states had not adhered to the treaty.) [58]

The USSR supported the Chinese proposal reiterated in October, 1964, for a world disarmament conference,[59] and was active in securing the backing of the U.N. Disarmament Commission, June 11, 1965,[60] and of the U.N. General Assembly, November 29, 1965,[61] for convocation of such a conference. Communist China was expected to be the principal participant outside U.N. ranks. The Chinese rejected participation, however, and the conference was never held.[62] The plan approved in the U.N. organs differed somewhat from that suggested by the Chinese, who had called for a "world summit conference." The Chinese rejection did not refer to such differences, however, and it seemed that Peking had changed its position on the utility of such a meeting.

It may be that the absence from Soviet disarmament activities since 1964 of any moves potentially infringing on Chinese national ambitions can be explained by considerations having nothing to do with

---

[58] Even in 1965, at the session of the U.N. General Assembly in the fall, the USSR endorsed language in a resolution of December 3 on suspension of nuclear weapons tests calling upon all countries to "respect the spirit and provisions" of the 1963 treaty. For other reasons, however, the USSR abstained, in the vote (*ibid.*, pp. 551, 623–24). In 1966 the USSR voted for the resolution quoted in the text (*Documents 1966*, pp. 764–65, 802–3).

[59] The idea of a world disarmament conference (i.e., including China) had been discussed long before the Chinese exploded their first atomic device, and the Cairo (second) conference of heads of nonaligned countries had called for such a world meeting on disarmament in a declaration of October 10, 1964, i.e., prior to the Chinese explosion (*Documents 1964*, p. 445). In response to the Chinese proposal for a world summit conference on disarmament, advanced at the time of the first atomic explosion, Foreign Minister Gromyko told the U.N. General Assembly on December 7 that the Soviet government endorsed both the Cairo and Peking proposals. In a letter of December 28 to Premier Chou En-lai, Premier Kosygin said that the Soviet government was in "complete agreement" with the Chinese proposal. In fact, however, in most of these and subsequent statements the USSR placed more stress on the Cairo variant than on that of Peking (with its summit feature) (*ibid.*, pp. 503, 532–33).

[60] *Documents 1965*, pp. 195–96, for statement on May 24, 1965, of Soviet representative Federenko, and p. 253 for resolution accepted by Disarmament Commission. The discussions and recommendation centered on the Cairo and not the Peking proposal.

[61] Address by Foreign Minister Gromyko to the U.N. General Assembly, September 24, 1965 (*ibid.*, p. 436); for text of resolution voted by General Assembly, see *ibid.*, p. 585.

[62] See Premier Chou En-lai's interview given to Pakistani Dawn, April 10, 1966, *Documents 1966*, pp. 210–11; and the editorial article in *Jen Min Jih Pao*, June 20, 1966, *Documents 1966*, pp. 358–59.

China. Thus, the concentration on the nonproliferation problem after 1964 was largely dictated by the fact that there were no prospects for serious East-West negotiations on arms reduction. (In most areas, except on proposals to ban all nuclear weapons tests, the United States and the USSR disagreed even on objectives to be sought.) Furthermore, Soviet negotiators have continued over the past years to advance on occasion a proposal—part of their GCD plan—for retention of a Soviet-American "nuclear umbrella" while other states were being entirely divested of their striking forces. Although never the subject of serious negotiations, the "umbrella" proposal could have had little appeal in Peking. Agreement on such a measure would have cut across Chinese national objectives and relegated China to a position of dependence on Soviet power; the similarity to the situation involving the test ban is apparent.

Despite these caveats, there may have been a "pro-China" element in Soviet disarmament behavior since 1964 in the sense that the Soviet leaders sought to distinguish between the disarmament policies of the Chinese leadership and the interests of China as a great power in any arms control arrangements. If true, such Soviet deference can be explained by the calculation of the Kremlin that chances of a *rapprochement* with China under some post-Mao regime might be improved if the USSR avoided acts likely to be interpreted by the Chinese elite as anti-Chinese and not merely anti-Mao.

To Moscow policy makers who are involved in disarmament questions, China presents an important problem apart from its articulation of divergent policies on disarmament. China represents an increasingly significant military power which must be taken into account in the substance of disarmament negotiations. October, 1964, marked the first of a series of six successful nuclear explosions carried out in China in 1964–1967. The rapidity of Chinese development was indicated by the successful explosion of a multimegaton thermonuclear device on June 17, 1967, in China's sixth test.[63] Communist China had moved in 32 months from mastery of atomic technology to mastery of thermonuclear technology. It jumped ahead of France to become the fourth-ranking thermonuclear power in the world. Although the thermonuclear device of June, 1966, was apparently dropped from an airplane, in an earlier test (the fourth, October 27, 1966) the Chinese exploded

---

[63] See *The New York Times*, June 18, 1967, for Chinese and U.S. AEC statements on Chinese test. Official briefings by American intelligence and military authorities on Chinese nuclear progress through July, 1967, are reflected in the report, *Impact of Chinese Communist Nuclear Weapons Progress on United States National Security*, Joint Committee on Atomic Energy, 90th Cong., 1st sess. (Washington, D.C.: Government Printing Office, 1967).

a fission device carried by a short-range guided missile. Because of this nuclear and missile progress, American authorities expect China to have an ICBM and an appropriate thermonuclear warhead in the 1970–1972 period.[64]

These Chinese military developments are certain to affect disarmament negotiations. For a long time it has been recognized that Chinese conventional forces were so substantial that China's participation would be essential for any general disarmament agreement to be acceptable to the other great powers. Chinese nuclear development and initial work on strategic missiles show that even agreements confined to advanced weapons and delivery systems may become dependent on Chinese acquiescence if such agreements are to involve important inhibitions on participating powers.

The Chinese factor might in time jeopardize even the viability of the 1963 test-ban treaty, although this possibility seems very distant. The 1963 treaty is the only arms control agreement in effect from which China gains a significant military advantage as a nonsignatory in comparison to the signatory states. The partial test ban closed off for the latter states certain types of technological advance, or made such advance more costly. But even this treaty placed no barriers at all on the growth of stockpiles of nuclear weapons based on the technology of 1963 as improved in underground testing from that time to the present. Despite the enormous Soviet and American superiority in nuclear weapons over China, probably the rather mild yearning in the U.S. and USSR for extension of the partial ban to cover underground tests will be affected adversely by Chinese nuclear developments.[65] These Chinese strides already seem to have influenced the American decision of 1967 to install a thin ABM system, and thus in turn to have affected the chances of any Soviet-American agreement covering anti-ballistic and other missile systems.[66]

No doubt the saving grace for possible future Soviet-Western accords ignoring China is a time factor. The American and Soviet military establishments are so well endowed with advanced weapons systems that certain partial measures limiting these might still be feasible without China's participation. The Chinese determination and capa-

[64] See *Impact of Chinese Communist Nuclear Weapons Progress*, p. 3.

[65] Despite Secretary Rusk's intimation of October 18, 1964 (*Documents 1964*, p. 457) that the United States might not be willing to accept a comprehensive test ban if the Chinese did not participate, since that time both the United States and the USSR have reaffirmed their desire for such a ban, and have not made agreement conditional on Chinese adherence.

[66] The anti-Chinese rationale was heavily stressed in Secretary McNamara's San Francisco speech of September 18, 1967, but the anti-Soviet capabilities of the proposed system received more attention in the *Life* interview with McNamara, September 29, 1967.

bility to equip itself, at great sacrifice, with a formidable military establishment is no longer in doubt. For both Moscow and Washington, therefore, the time seems to be approaching when, if China does not participate in agreements on arms control and arms reductions, these agreements will be impossible.

5

ARMS AND THE ECONOMY

On no other facet of prospects for disarmament is there as much agreement as on the beneficial effects for Soviet economic development that would result from any substantial measures of disarmament. Yet prospects of economic betterment appear to play a relatively small role in determining Soviet decisions on armament and disarmament questions.*

The nations which are big spenders on arms naturally would have the most to gain from massive reductions in armed forces and armament budgets.[1] This is particularly true of the Soviet Union, for the USSR is a big spender whose resources are insufficient to maintain without great exertion and sacrifice a military establishment on a level competitive with its strongest opponent, and sufficient to give firm backing to Soviet foreign policy. The prospect of easing the tautness of the economy or satisfying consumer needs by cutting the arms budget undeniably has an appeal to Soviet decision makers. Naturally, it has more appeal to some than to others, because of their varying respon-

---

* In the opinion of some participants in this study, this chapter underestimates the weight of economic incentives in (1) restraining Soviet decisions toward vigorous competition in armaments; and (2) making agreed arms limitation measures attractive to the Soviet leadership. These particpants believe, for example, that the Soviet leaders will shy away from a decision to install an ABM system for the USSR as a whole, because of the cost, and will look with favor upon an agreement to prevent ABM competition. In other areas of arms rivalry, also, these experts think that economic considerations will be an important and possibly decisive factor affecting Soviet decisions on armament and disarmament policy.

[1] World-wide military expenditures in 1965 were close to $140 billion, according to estimates prepared for the United States Arms Control and Disarmament Agency, and they may have risen in 1966 to $155–160 billion. About 84 per cent of these 1965 expenditures were made by members of NATO and the Warsaw Pact; together the United States and the Soviet Union accounted for almost two thirds of the total spending. In contrast, total foreign aid to developing countries in 1965 amounted to about 1/20th of world-wide military expenditures. See *Worldwide Military Expenditures and Related Data, 1965,* a report prepared by the Economics Bureau of the United States Arms Control and Disarmament Agency (Washington, D.C.: U.S. Arms Control and Disarmament Agency, 1967, Research Report 67-6, processed).

sibilities in administration of the country. In the domestic tug-of-war over allocation of resources some sectors of the economy are more likely than others to benefit from arms reductions and to suffer from increases in military spending.

Whatever the differences in their positions, Soviet leaders as a group are well-trained to resist acceptance of disarmament measures whose attraction is mainly economic. They are not in danger of being thrown out of office by dissatisfied electors, unhappy with leaders who sacrifice the material interests of citizens as consumers by giving first priority to defense needs. Economic considerations are introduced by another route. In deciding on military allocations, the leaders must take account of the requirements of the economy as a whole. In order to maintain a rapid rate of economic expansion, they may have to restrict output of final military products, which are just as "unproductive" as any consumers' goods, in order to advance output of means of production.[2] They must also make sure that the population (i.e., the present and potential labor force) has access to the physical and educational conditions for efficient work. Under present conditions at least—given the stress on material incentives—this requires due attention to the satisfaction of popular needs going well beyond subsistence levels. When all this is said, however, the choices are made in a social order in which the people as a whole have very little direct influence on national decisions.

Given the scale of the Soviet economy in the late 1960's, the Politburo has considerable leeway in making allocations among the competing claims and claimants.* Although it is doubtful that any single influence dominates these decisions, they are influenced heavily by the level of international tensions and the changing military capabilities of the USSR's probable military opponents. Theoretically at least, measures of arms limitation could both reduce international tensions and lessen the level of competitive military establishments, thus allowing the Soviet Union to devote fewer resources to military efforts. (The word "theoretically" deserves stress, because none of the arms control measures so far realized has offered many direct economic benefits.) The USSR has repeatedly rejected measures proposed by the United States on production and deployment of armaments

[2] Unproductive in the sense that they do not augment capabilities for producing additional goods and services. See V. Ia. Aboltin, in *SSSR, SShA i razoruzhenie,* p. 183; and Morris Bornstein, "Economic Factors in Soviet Attitudes Toward Arms Control," in *Disarmament and World Economic Interdependence,* ed. Emile Benoit (New York: Columbia University Press, 1967), pp. 60–85.

* Some participants in this study believe that economic growth has not made the allocations problem confronting Soviet leaders any easier today than it was years ago, when the total economy was much smaller, because pressures from rival claimants have increased along with the increase in production.

and vehicles—measures that would have allowed substantial economic benefits to the Soviet Union. They were rejected because they would have either perpetuated Soviet military inferiority or involved a diminution of Soviet security through installation of foreign military observers on Soviet soil. Impulses to better welfare standards have been stronger in the post-Stalin period than earlier, but there is little evidence that economic benefits have become significant in persuading Moscow to accept disarmament or arms control measures considered disadvantageous militarily for the Soviet Union.[3]

THE DEFENSE EFFORT OF THE USSR

How much the USSR spends for military purposes is not known. (Even if detailed yearly budgetary allocations were made public, it would still be hard to determine whether or not to classify certain expenditures as "military," e.g., certain kinds of industrial investment, training, research and development, and space activities.[4] But no such details are published.) A single sum is published each year in the USSR budget under the heading of "defense," but this figure almost certainly does not include many expenditures that would be regarded as military under any definition.

The overt allocations for recent years are given in Table 1.

TABLE 1—DEFENSE ALLOCATIONS IN USSR BUDGET FOR 1955–1968 [5]
(IN BILLIONS OF RUBLES)

1955	10.7	. .	1962	12.7
1956	9.7	. .	1963	13.9
1957	9.1	. .	1964	13.3
1958	9.4	. .	1965	12.8
1959	9.4	. .	1966	13.4
1960	9.3	. .	1967	14.5
1961	11.6	. .	1968	16.7

[3] The Soviet attitude toward such measures is discussed in Chapter 8.

[4] Studies of Soviet defense spending by Western scholars arrive at varying estimates, in part because of differences in classification of items. See Abraham S. Becker, *Soviet Military Outlays Since 1955* (Santa Monica, Calif.: The RAND Corporation, 1964, RM-3886-PR, processed), pp. 12–13; J. G. Godaire, "The Claim of the Soviet Military Establishment," *Dimensions of Soviet Economic Power*. Joint Economic Committee, 87th Cong., 2d sess. (Washington, D.C.: Government Printing Office, 1962), pp. 33–46; Timothy Sosnovy, "The Soviet Military Budget," *Foreign Affairs*, XLII, No. 3 (April, 1964), 487–94.

[5] Table compiled from: Becker, *Narodnoc Khoziaistvo SSSR i 1964 godu* (Moscow: "Statistika," 1965), hereinafter cited as *Narkhoz* [year]; *Pravda*, December 20, 1966, and October 13, 1967.

To the extent that these announced figures approximate the actual totals for military spending, they show that there was a downward trend until 1957, a leveling through 1960, then an upward swing in 1961 to a high in 1963. Appropriations for the two succeeding years were modestly lower. They then advanced each year in 1966–1968, with the largest increase (15 per cent) for the 1968 calendar year. The 1961 turning point coincided, of course, with the Kennedy Administration's increase in military spending for U.S. strategic forces and U.S. ground forces in Europe, the latter largely in response to the threatened confrontation over Berlin. The Soviet increase announced in 1965 followed the inauguration by the United States in February, 1965, of systematic bombing of North Vietnam and the U.S. commitment of large number of troops to combat in South Vietnam. The recent Soviet increases thus paralleled, at a lower level, the increases in American military spending.

The military allocation figures announced in Soviet budgets probably do not always follow the trend of "total military spending," however the latter is defined. Most foreign analysts who have studied Soviet military financing believe that the overt appropriations cover certain definite categories of spending (notably military pay and subsistence, operations and maintenance, and some procurement), and that other expenditures, e.g., for military research and development and for investment in the armament industry, are included in other budgetary categories.

Actual reductions in overt appropriations might occur simultaneously with increases in the hidden categories of spending, or vice versa. For the years since 1964, however, there is no reason to doubt that announced increases in budgetary allocations to defense reflect real increases in total military spending. Thus, budgetary expenditures for "science"—which include military-oriented activities—have also been rising, with an 11 per cent increase stated for 1968. Furthermore, a stepped-up growth in defense industry is suggested by data on Soviet machinery output. The official Soviet index for total machinery production (including defense) shows no slackening in 1966–1967, whereas an index (composed by American experts) of civilian machinery output in the USSR shows a decline of 1½ percentage points in the rate of increase.[6]

Various Western studies covering the past two decades have provided some estimates of total Soviet military allocations in relation to announced expenditures. In a 1962 study, J. G. Godaire concluded that actual Soviet defense and space allocations in 1960–1962 may

[6] *Soviet Economic Performance: 1966–67*, Joint Economic Committee, 90th Cong., 2d sess. (Washington, D.C.: Government Printing Office, 1968), p. 21; hereinafter cited as *Soviet Performance: 1966–67*.

have exceeded announced expenditures by 30 to 60 per cent.[7] A more
detailed study in 1964 by Abraham S. Becker, covering military outlays for 1955–1962, concluded that total outlays in 1960 may have
exceeded announced figures by 23 per cent on one set of assumptions
and 55 per cent on another. Becker's comparable range for 1961 of
total military expenditures to published budgetary allocations was
57 to 91 per cent and for 1962 was 48 to 85 per cent.[8] Morris Bornstein, in a more recent article, came to the conclusion that total military outlays were at least 50 per cent and perhaps as much as 100 per
cent above the sums mentioned in the budget.[9]

These attempts to present more or less realistic estimates of military spending are of interest in several ways. In particular, such estimates permit calculations of the defense burden borne by the USSR,
that is, the portion of total goods and services used for military purposes. Stanley Cohn calculated that in 1964 about 11.3 per cent of
Soviet gross national product (GNP) went to the military sector. This
was the highest proportion among any of the advanced industrial
countries, although only slightly in excess of the 1963 proportion in
the United States (10.8 per cent). Such West European countries as
the United Kingdom, France, and the Federal Republic of Germany
devoted significantly less (5 to 7 per cent of their GNP) to military
establishments.[10]

Other studies have suggested both higher and lower figures for the
USSR. Morris Bornstein arrived at a figure of 15 per cent for 1964.[11]
In contrast, the ACDA compilation of figures on world-wide military
spending in 1965 estimated Soviet military outlays in rubles at 7 to 8
per cent of GNP, almost the same as the U.S. ratio of 7.6 per cent.[12]
Although this figure was based on "estimates made by Western analysts" of Soviet military spending, details on the method of arriving
at the percentage were not indicated.

Even if the USSR devotes to military activities about the same

[7] Godaire, pp. 38–42. The "possible total" is for defense and space allocations
combined. The estimates were arrived at by adding to the published defense sum
amounts derived from other budget categories: science, the national economy residual, and the general budgetary residual. Godaire's estimates posit an increasing gap
between total and announced figures.

[8] Becker, p. 36. The percentages are calculated from the absolute numbers in the
table prepared by Becker.

[9] Bornstein, p. 69.

[10] Stanley Cohn, "Soviet Growth Retardation: Trends in Resource Availability
and Efficiency," in New Directions in the Soviet Economy. Joint Economic Committee, 89th Cong., 2d sess. (Washington, D.C.: Government Printing Office, 1960), II-A,
106. Cohn's calculations were based on extrapolations from the Becker study mentioned above.

[11] Bornstein, p. 70.

[12] Worldwide Military Expenditures, 1965, pp. 8, 12.

proportion of its total output as does the United States, this weighs more heavily on the Soviet than on the American economy.[13] Despite its smaller population, the United States annually produces approximately double the GNP of the USSR,[14] and can thus afford with less strain to spend a tenth on military affairs. In comparison to the industrialized countries of East and West Europe, where the national income *per capita* is closer to the Soviet level,[15] the USSR devotes a markedly higher proportion of its output to military activities.

MILITARY SPENDING AND ECONOMIC GROWTH

There is no need to labor the point that arms expenditures constitute a drag on the Soviet economy. The fact is well recognized in statements of Soviet authorities, however much they may minimize and obscure the exact proportion of the burden. In spending for arms and armies, nations buy (or hope to buy) protection for their homeland and capabilities for influence abroad, but at the cost of foregoing or slowing consumer satisfaction and economic progress. The most recent Soviet treatise on disarmament argues that development of military production over a prolonged period at a faster rate than production for the civilian economy is impossible, because it would lead to a reduction and eventually a cessation of the accumulation of capital for development of production. According to the Soviet author: "Military production is basically lost to social production, for it is intended to be destroyed or to be preserved only until it loses its efficacy. Military production thus has a nonproductive, parasitical character." [16]

How heavily the burden weighs—and how attractive, therefore, is the prospect of some relief through major reductions in military spending—depends in large part on the rapidity of economic growth. Over the past half century, the Soviet Union has narrowed substantially the gap separating it from the United States in economic power, despite

[13] Soviet sources assert that the Soviet Union spends a considerably smaller portion of its national income on defense than does the United States. Thus, *Narkhoz 1965*, p. 781, claims that in 1965 the USSR spent only 6.6 per cent of its national income for military activities, in comparison to almost 15 per cent for the United States. These figures use the announced military appropriations in the Soviet and American budgets and employ national income estimates for both countries based on the Soviet concept of material product, i.e., they exclude most services.

[14] *Soviet Performance: 1966–67*, p. 8, places the USSR GNP at 47 per cent of U.S. GNP in 1967. *Narkhoz 1965* claims that Soviet national income in 1965 was 62 per cent of the U.S. in equivalent prices and 53 per cent of the U.S. at the official exchange rate, both ratios based on the Soviet concept of national income.

[15] See *Worldwide Military Expenditures, 1965*, p. 8.

[16] V. Ia. Aboltin in "Conclusions" to *SSSR, SShA i razoruzhenie*, p. 183. Aboltin is writing, of course, about capitalist economies.

heavy losses sustained in wars during that period. Were this not so, the United States would not need to be concerned about the USSR as a rival on the world scene.

But Soviet hopes of rapidly overtaking the United States in economic power were dimmed in the first half of the 1960's, when the American economy did better than anticipated and the Soviet economy did worse. Undoubtedly the poor performance of Soviet agriculture in the early 1960's, and the far from brilliant performance of Soviet industry, helped spur the "dump Khrushchev" movement. With Khrushchev out, the new leaders stopped referring to the overambitious projections of the 1961 Party Program on equaling and surpassing the United States by 1970 and 1980. This does not mean that they have renounced the objective of overtaking and surpassing the United States, or think it incapable of realization; but they certainly became more aware of the difficulties they faced, and of the considerable time that would be required to accomplish this goal.

Compared to 1964, the Soviet competitive position in 1968 has improved. Although the vagaries of agriculture, which provides a much larger contribution to Soviet GNP than to that of the United States, continue to exercise a marked influence on yearly rates of growth in the USSR's total product, the Soviet Union has apparently overcome the slump registered in the early 1960's. Table 2 presents a calculation of Soviet growth in 1961–1967 in gross national product, with comparable data for the United States.

TABLE 2—COMPARATIVE GROWTH RATE OF GROSS NATIONAL PRODUCT[17]
(ANNUAL PERCENTAGE INCREASES)

	1961	1962	1963	1964	1965	1966	1967 (prelim.)
USSR	7.0	4.2	2.8	7.9	6.2	7.1	4.3
United States	1.9	6.6	4.0	5.3	5.9	5.8	2.6

[17] Soviet Performance: 1966–67, p. 12.

Over this period the Soviet rate of growth exceeded that of the United States in five of the seven years, and in all the years beginning with 1964 and the advent of a new regime in the USSR. Since this was a period of exceptionally rapid American economic growth, and included some equally remarkable years of poor Soviet performance, the USSR did little to "catch up" with the United States, as Table 3, carried back to the 1950's, illustrates.

The record of industrial performance is much less affected by agricultural developments than is the GNP, and offers a more relevant,

TABLE 3—COMPARATIVE GROSS NATIONAL PRODUCT[18]
(IN DOLLAR VALUES AT MARKET PRICES)

		1950	1955	1961	1965	1966	1967
USSR	billions of dollars	132	185	272	330	357	372
United States		414	508	575	711	743	762
USSR GNP as percentage of United States		31.9	36.4	47.3	46.4	48.0	48.8

[18] *Ibid.*, p. 16.

although still crude, measure of Soviet economic development in the area most pertinent to decision-making on armament and disarmament questions. Industrial production in the USSR grew at an average annual rate of 7.5 per cent in the 1960's, and civilian industrial production by 1967 had increased 55 per cent over that of 1961, as compared to 37 per cent for GNP.[19] If comparative statistics on Soviet and American GNP and gross industrial output were placed on a *per capita* basis, they would show, of course, a much greater disparity in favor of the United States than do the national totals. Such *per capita* comparisons are relevant in many contexts, but they are less important in a study concerned with relations among states, each of which functions as a single aggregate on the world scene.

ECONOMIC REFORM MEASURES

Whatever the future trends, the leaders who took charge of the USSR in 1964 were certainly worried over the slowdown of economic development. This concern was reflected in the adoption—sometimes after a period of experimentation—of reforms and reorganizations designed to improve the qualitative and quantitative performance of the economy. Giving up the administrative system sponsored by Khrushchev in 1957, which stressed regional links between enterprises, his successors returned in 1965 to the former ministerial system. This stressed grouping of enterprises by commodity branches rather than by geographic location; it also involved the restoration of a more openly centralized control from Moscow than had existed in the prior period of the regional economic councils. The authorities were motivated in this return to the "tried and true" pattern by several considerations, including a belief that the ministerial system, with a specialized headquarters for each branch of industry, was

[19] *Ibid.*, pp. 19–23.

better suited than a regional organization to introduce technical innovations into the production process.

This reorganization of government administration was not the only, and perhaps not the most important, change introduced by the Brezhnev-Kosygin leadership. After years of relatively free discussion of alternative measures of economic reform, in September, 1965, the post-Khrushchev leaders announced a program of reforms centering on the management of enterprises. This placed more emphasis on economic levers and less on administrative decisions in guiding factory managers and other industrial and trade officials. Central planning remained of course, and the basic decisions on the direction and speed of economic development were still to reflect leadership preferences rather than those of consumers. But producers were given more autonomy thanks to the reduction in the number of centrally imposed standards to which they had to conform, with a further reduction suggested as likely in the future. Initially only the better-run enterprises were transformed to the new system. It was supposed to be extended to most enterprises by the end of 1968, as key personnel were retrained and the "bugs" in the system eliminated. This gradualness was also meant to characterize the introduction of revised wholesale prices, a necessary accompaniment to the increased use of economic levers in guiding enterprise decisions.

In 1964, agriculture presented urgent problems to the new leaders, and thus engaged top-level attention even before the industrial reform was taken up.[20] The CPSU Central Committee in March, 1965, ratified a program presented on behalf of the Politburo by Party General Secretary Brezhnev. This program centered more on improvement of farmers' terms of trade than on administrative reorganization. Prices were raised on agricultural products sold to the state and lowered modestly on industrial goods sold to farmers. Delivery quotas for grain were fixed for a five-year period ending in 1970, with strict injunctions against any increases before the terminal date. Substantially increased investment was to be channeled to agriculture, particularly to increase the supply of agricultural machinery to collective farms (which had noticeably slowed after 1958).[21] There were other steps taken to improve agricultural prospects, including a long-term program of irrigation and reclamation outlined at the May, 1966, Central Committee Plenum. Some of Khrushchev's pet ideas were renounced, such as his condemnation of the use of arable land for grasses and fallow, and his

[20] Even by Soviet statistics, the rate of agricultural growth had declined from 5.9 per cent annually in 1956–1960 to 2.4 per cent in 1961–1965 (*Narkhoz 1965*, p. 258).
[21] Plenum of the Central Committee of the CPSU, March 24–26, 1965, *Stenograficheskii otchet* (Moscow: Politizdat, 1965).

encouragement of the maximum expansion of acreage devoted to corn. There was talk of a basic administrative reorganization of collective farms, through the institution of a nationwide elective system tying all the farms together under a Collective Farm Center. So far, however, this has not come to pass.[22]

Underlying the reforms in both agriculture and industry has been the idea that individual and enterprise incentives, if buttressed materially, could be harnessed to the cause of bringing about more efficient use of the large stock of plant, equipment, and resources, and the increasingly skilled labor force. The expected increase in efficiency was seen both as a means of providing at a given level a more satisfactory output of goods and services, and as a means of quickening economic expansion.

Despite increased military expenditures in most of the years since Khrushchev's departure, the new leaders have repeatedly reaffirmed their intention to increase production of consumers' goods to eliminate the traditional lag of their rate of growth behind that of producers' goods. Some progress along this line has occurred. According to Soviet indices, the production of industrial producers' goods increased by an average of 9.6 per cent annually in 1961–1965, as against 6.4 per cent for industrial consumers' goods. In 1966, the comparable rates were 9 and 7 per cent; and in 1967 the difference was narrowed to 10.2 and 9 per cent. The plan for 1968 even called for a greater expansion of consumers' goods than of producers' goods—8.6 per cent for the former and 7.9 per cent for the latter.[23] In view of the Soviet commitment to rapid growth and of the threatening international scene, this shift of priority was remarkable, even though the faster growth of consumers' goods production (if actually realized) was intended to be exceptional. Long-term plans for improvement of welfare and living standards were dependent, however, on attainment of rather ambitious goals in agriculture.[24] The latter was called upon to provide an increasing volume not only of foods for retail trade but also of foodstuffs and raw materials for light industry. The spotty record of Soviet agricultural development in the past suggested that realization of these goals could not be counted upon.

[22] The subject was mentioned by Brezhnev and some other speakers at the XXIII Party Congress in March–April, 1966; subsequently it all but disappeared from discussion.

[23] For 1959–1965, see Brezhnev speech in *Leningradskaia pravda*, February 16, 1968; for 1966 and 1967, see reports of Central Statistical Administration, *Izvestiia*, January 29, 1967, and January 25, 1968; for 1968 plan, see speech by Gosplan Chief Baibakov, *Pravda*, October 11, 1967.

[24] See the article by Alec Nove, "Economic Policy and Economic Trends," in *Soviet Politics Since Khrushchev*.

MILITARY NEEDS AND POPULAR WELFARE

Although they may seek to improve living standards, the Soviet leaders are not prepared to cut back either investment for future growth or military spending in order to satisfy welfare demands of the population. Premier Kosygin, the regime's principal spokesman on general economic plans, could not have been more explicit on this point in an address in February, 1968. After mentioning that about one quarter of Soviet national income went into "accumulation" (i.e., investment and reserves) and three quarters into consumption, he stated:

> The people's standard of living could rise more quickly if the portion of the income going toward state accumulation were reduced. I think that everyone . . . would say that it is impossible to do this since we would hinder the development of our entire economy in this case. We could not reduce that portion of the national income which goes for the country's defense needs, either. What is more, in 1968 we even have had to increase these expenditures somewhat, a move which was evoked by a certain complication of the international situation. So, the only way to raise the people's standard of living is to increase the entire national income, including the segment going into consumption.[25]

Soviet leaders have always been willing to allow the population to "postpone" improvements in housing and consumption in order to maintain or improve military strength. Thus, World War II ended with the USSR in a severely weakened economic state, although strong militarily by virtue of the absence of any state in Europe or Asia capable of challenging Soviet power. Yet Stalin to 1953 and his successors since then put a high priority on maintaining large Soviet military forces and seeking to equip them with technologically sophisticated weapons systems on a par with those of the United States. Competition in the military area was more important to the USSR than rivalry in other areas. The resources needed for this program had to be squeezed out of a taut economy, but the leadership was confident that the civilian consequences of military priority were manageable.

There were constraints on Soviet military competition, however, which stemmed from factors other than welfare needs. Thus, the expressed intention of the Soviet leaders to devote "everything necessary" to defense should not be taken too literally. Military "needs"

[25] Speech of February 14, 1968, in *Sovetskaia Belorussiia*, February 15, 1968.

are neither unchanging nor independent of over-all Soviet capabilities. The priority of defense allocation does not mean that "what the military want, the military get." In the 1930's and earlier, the Soviet leadership had to keep a tight rein on defense expenditures in order not to waste away for "nonproductive" military purposes resources needed to achieve speedy industrialization. Even in the postwar world, the USSR accepted something far less than strategic parity with the U.S. Undoubtedly the size and shape of the Soviet economy influenced specific decisions along this line, as in the less-than-expected build-up of long-range bombers in the early 1950's and icbms after 1957, when the USSR lost its early developmental lead and had to be content to become a poor second behind the United States.

What this means is that the need to foster economic growth may constrain military procurements, but that welfare programs have only marginal effects. A slow rate of growth forces tough decisions on the leadership; a fast rate eases the options. Nevertheless, in Khrushchev's last years in office—a period of slow economic growth—decisions with large price tags were taken to build up various elements of Soviet strategic power, including the development of an anti-ballistic missile system. There was simultaneously a cutback on new housing and other measures affecting the welfare of citizens as consumers.

The definition of Soviet military needs is ultimately a task of the political leadership, whose decisions are not necessarily those proposed by professional military leaders. In this case, political expediency is the mother of necessity. Particularly in the allocation of resources, the political leaders have to weigh military uses against other claims on Soviet resources. Details of the Soviet budget-making process are not known, but it is apparent that in the past, at least, some of the military services, such as the Soviet Navy and theater ground forces, have discreetly but clearly voiced objections to reductions in allocations to their services and to measures reducing the total military budget by cutting the size of the forces in uniform. Individual service spokesmen have also rejected doctrines disparaging the value of the services' contribution to national defense.[26]

The greater freedom of public expression in the post-Stalin period enabled various military spokesmen and periodicals to publicize in only slightly nuanced form their claims on resources and manpower and their demand to participate in the making of decisions having important military consequences. In Khrushchev's heyday, however, his authority was so great that he was able to express, occasionally in

[26] Thomas W. Wolfe, *The Soviet Military Scene: Institutional and Defense Policy Considerations,* pp. 54–56.

radical terms, and sometimes to carry out, ideas and policies on military allocations that went against the interests of the Soviet military establishment or individual services.[27]

It appears that the Brezhnev-Kosygin-Podgorny regime pursues a more "conventional" policy in this area. Since Khrushchev's ouster, the new leadership has not instituted any major measures seemingly deleterious to the interests of a particular military service or to the armed forces as a whole. We do not know, of course, how military requests for procurement, force levels, installations, and research and development have been treated. It seems, however, on the basis of the continued and rapid expansion of Soviet ICBMs, the installation of ABMs, and the increase of naval power that the leaders are making even more effort to overcome the Soviet strategic lag behind the U.S. —an effort that must have responded to preoccupations of the professional military chiefs.[28]

ECONOMIC INCENTIVES FOR DISARMAMENT MEASURES

For reasons discussed elsewhere, prospects are slight indeed for the realization of "general and complete disarmament," which would release vast economic resources for alternative uses in such big-spending countries as the USSR and the United States. In the latest Soviet works on disarmament, the most realistic authors dismiss the possibility of agreed GCD in any near term, and consider only partial measures as having any likelihood of success.[29] This judgment appears to be valid, and thus there seems little point in discussing the economic consequences of general disarmament. However, some consideration needs to be given to the economic effect of various partial measures, both those realized and those proposed.

The economic impact of such partial measures varies, depending on the specific proposal, from nil to moderate. Obviously, proposed agreements to cut military budgets by fixed percentages would be economically beneficial in releasing resources for other uses. If the explicit military budget did not include all expenses related to military efforts, however, such an agreement might simply result in a shift of items from open to hidden categories. Whatever other considerations may also have militated against acceptance, the existence of such a possibility has made Soviet proposals of this type unacceptable to the United States.

[27] Thomas W. Wolfe, *Soviet Strategy at the Crossroads* (Cambridge, Mass.: Harvard University Press, 1964), pp. 30–37.
[28] See Chapter 6.
[29] *SSSR, SShA i razoruzhenie*, p. 177.

Proposals for reciprocal reductions in U.S. and Soviet (or NATO and WTO) forces stationed in Germany and other European countries have aroused more interest, and implementation of such plans might reduce military costs of the affected powers. The USSR has repeatedly proposed such reductions and withdrawals, often in support of Polish initiatives. Ironically, in recent years the Soviet authorities appear to have lost interest in modest reciprocal cuts of forces in Germany, just as U.S. interest has quickened.[30] Even if realized, the reduction of forces in this area might coincide with expansions in other regions, and thus have little economic effect.

The possibility of Soviet-American negotiations to "halt the missile race" requires some words on the role of economic incentives in spurring the two sides to come to an agreement limiting these expensive weapons. Although other considerations were involved, the American proposal of early 1967 for talks on averting competitive installation of ABM systems was influenced by the unhappy prospect of the U.S. committing itself to spend anywhere from five to forty billion dollars on ABMs in a period when the defense budget was already swollen by allocation of large funds to carry on the war in Vietnam. On the Soviet side, if the enormous expense of building an ambitious anti-missile system weighed heavily on the minds of the Soviet leaders, they betrayed little evidence of such concern as the "negotiations about negotiations" proceeded intermittently in 1967–1968. The Soviet insistence that the talks concern offensive as well as defensive missiles made it evident that the USSR would not "buy" a moratorium limited to ABM missiles. If past experience was any guide, neither would it accept an agreement that froze missile deployment as of a given date, at least not if the Soviet Union then possessed a strategic force markedly inferior to the American. Both in the Khrushchev period and under his successors, the USSR was repeatedly offered such a "freeze," with its enticing economic benefits, and just as often it turned it down. (The "freeze" proposed by the United States included not only offensive and defensive missiles but also all other "strategic nuclear weapons vehicles," i.e., bombers and missile-equipped submarines.)[31] Prior to mid-1968, the USSR has advanced no proposal of its own in this field except in the context of a plan for GCD. The provisions on missiles in the Soviet GCD plan, and especially the amended version, which contemplated retention by the United States and the Soviet Union of a "nuclear umbrella" of land-based missiles, suggested that the USSR would be interested in a separate arms limitation measure in the missile field only (1) if it involved very substantial reductions,

---

[30] See Chapter 11.
[31] See Chapter 9.

and (2) if it brought about an equalization of Soviet and American forces.

Certainly any agreed limitation on missile deployment—and particularly any reductions in missile forces—would have an economic appeal to the Soviet leaders. Such agreements would do more than merely reduce defense spending by *x* number of rubles. Unlike, for example, possible agreement on reductions in the forces stationed in Central Europe, reductions of requirements for offensive and defensive missiles would free for the civilian economy highly trained technicians and sophisticated production facilities, which are in very short supply in the USSR.[32] But the attractiveness of this prospect does not mean that an arrangement can be worked out. With the USSR having begun installation of an ABM system around Moscow, and being in the throes of a major program to build up its strategic offensive forces, and the United States having decided late in 1967 on installation of at least a limited ABM system, the odds would seem to favor a spiraling upward, rather than downward, of competition in sophisticated weapons systems.

A look at the arms control agreements successfully negotiated thus far offers little reassurance that economically beneficial accords can be brought to fruition. It is ironic that the treaties already concluded are among those with the least economic impact on the great powers. The outer-space agreements signed in 1963 and 1967 may have reduced slightly Soviet and American drives toward certain types of military utilization of space, and thus have had a minor economic effect. The only activities specifically banned, however, were the orbiting of satellites loaded with weapons of mass destruction, and the deployment of military installations on planets other than Earth. The agreements left untouched a wide field in which the space powers could spend freely, including military reconnaissance and communications satellites. No restrictions were imposed, of course, on ICBMs and other missiles designed to pass through outer space, and the agreements did not prohibit development (as against deployment) of orbital vehicles (like the Soviet FOBS) intended to be armed with nuclear warheads.

As to the agreement in 1963 to ban nuclear weapons tests in three environments, it is not altogether clear that the agreement has reduced military expenditures. Although some devices cannot be tested underground, both the U.S. and the USSR have increased greatly their programs of testing underground, i.e., in an environment making tests much more expensive than the atmospheric and shallow tests formerly predominant in both countries. Furthermore, even for untestable weap-

[32] See the discussion on this point in Bornstein, pp. 61, 66–67.

ons, the United States and probably the Soviet Union have maintained weapons laboratories in a state of readiness. This would permit quick resumption of atmospheric testing if national authorities should so decide.[33]

The nuclear nonproliferation treaty could have substantial economic consequences for the non-nuclear countries which accept the treaty's ban on acquisition or development of nuclear arsenals. Acceptance of the treaty would remove the temptation for certain states to follow the French example in building nuclear forces of marginal utility at great expense. For the USSR, the United States, and other nuclear weapons states, however, the direct budgetary effects of the treaty will be close to nil, because they are prohibited merely from disseminating nuclear weapons or know-how to non-nuclear states. There were few prospects that they would do this, even in the absence of a nonproliferation treaty.

CONCLUSION

The conclusion would seem to be that agreements that could deflate military budgets seem unlikely to be realized and that agreements that *have* been realized or appear negotiable have small economic significance for the great powers. A conclusion stated this way may be too pessimistic. Arms build-ups and arms reductions are usually not correlated directly with the failure or success of disarmament negotiations, but with increase or decrease of interstate tensions. The history of the postwar world has seen cyclical—or spiraling—movements in Soviet and American military spending which could not be explained in terms of the achievements or failures of arms control negotiations. Even if agreements such as the 1963 test ban and the 1968 treaty on nonproliferation of nuclear weapons have no direct effect on weapons expenditures, they undoubtedly contribute to changing evaluations by the big spending nations of their opponents' intentions and of the likelihood of armed conflict. Such atmospheric changes do influence arms spending in Eastern and Western capitals. No doubt, the "arms race" has a momentum of its own, as the powers respond to changes in the military capabilities of probable opponents and take advan-

---

[33] The United States program to maintain readiness for resumption of atmospheric tests is well-known, because this was one of four conditions insisted upon by the U.S. Joint Chiefs of Staff as necessary for their endorsement of the partial test-ban treaty in 1963. President Kennedy agreed to the four conditions, partly in order to facilitate Senate ratification of the treaty. On recent activities concerning these safeguards, see the speech in the Senate by Senator Henry M. Jackson, November 30, 1967 (*Congressional Record*, LXIII, No. 195, S17415–S17417).

tage of technological innovations. Agreements on arms control and other measures testify, however, to the presence of certain shared interests and to the possibility that conflicts of interest can be reconciled without war. In this way they may brake, gently or strongly, the military preparations of the great powers.

6

SOVIET MILITARY POWER
AND DISARMAMENT ISSUES

Any consideration of Soviet attitudes on arms control and disarmament must give weight to Soviet military capabilities and intentions, the structure of forces, and the purposes these forces serve. Changes over the past half century have altered the status of the Soviet military services, their professional skill, the quantity and sophistication of their equipment, and their political reliability. As a consequence of changes in military capabilities, the political leaders of the Soviet Union now have available to them a wide range of options with respect to the means of promoting Soviet influence and protecting Soviet power. But they face difficult choices in balancing domestic and foreign commitments, and in finding suitable ways of combining military and political means to accomplish national objectives.

Among such choices are those on possible international agreements for mutual limitations on military activities. Decisions on arms control or arms reductions form part of the spectrum containing decisions on levels and deployment of military forces, on arms production, and on the development of new weapons systems. All these present alternative ways of gaining security and influence. Like state leaders elsewhere, Soviet leaders have been very conservative in preferring to rely on unilateral, non-negotiated decisions on armed forces rather than to accept the kind of arms control agreements that could be negotiated with rivals. But free competition in armaments has been both costly in resources and unproductive of the security that was sought by nations such as the Soviet Union and the United States. Consequently, representatives of these suspicious states have been pulled back to seemingly endless negotiations on disarmament.

Because none of the agreements so far realized has placed severe restrictions on the military activities of the USSR and other participating states, the Soviet leaders have been able to maintain their armed forces and armaments at levels they have considered necessary, within the economic and technological capabilities of the country. The kind of military establishment that has been built up in the USSR and the purposes it is meant to serve are subjects to which we now turn. Needless to say, since the subject goes far beyond the scope of this report, the development of Soviet military power and strategy can be touched on only in summary form.

*   *   *

No single formula can characterize in a succinct sentence the purposes that the Soviet military establishment is designed to serve. These purposes run the gamut from protection of the Soviet regime at home to promotion of Soviet influence in the world at large. Control of powerful forces of nuclear destruction is the *sine qua non* for claims to great-power status in the latter half of the twentieth century, and the Soviet leaders have used their possession of such weapons to create an aura of invincibility about the USSR. Despite a substantial augmentation of its military punch, the USSR has remained throughout the postwar period in a largely defensive military posture.[1] The realm to be protected has been extended, however, with the spread of Communist rule and of Soviet influence. In addition to the USSR itself, its allies in the Warsaw Pact come within the perimeter that Soviet forces are bound to defend in case of attack. The situation is less clear with China (despite the mutual defense pact) and with outlying members of the "socialist commonwealth." Soviet capabilities have been insufficient to project military power at a distance from USSR borders, particularly overseas; this is one reason, among others, that Soviet "assurances" of assistance to such states as Cuba and North Vietnam have not been translated into formal treaties. The "defense" commitments, if any, of the USSR to friendly states of the "third world" are still more cloudy. Blessed in Soviet ideology as virtuous because they have chosen the "noncapitalist" road of development, with "socialism" as their destination, they have also been blessed with Soviet armaments. But Moscow has shown few signs of being ready or able to protect these states against foreign foes by using its own military forces.

Beyond defense of this rather uncertain realm, the use of Soviet military force to aid in the expansion of Communist rule, or to promote other changes desired by the USSR in the external environment, involves still more imponderables. An opportunity comparable to that presented by the Red Army's advance westward at the end of World War II has not recurred, of course, and Khrushchev had to abandon his attempt of 1958–1962 to bring about, under the shield of Soviet military power, a change in the German situation. The post-1964 leadership has been particularly careful to avoid unsettling initiatives of this kind.

[1] For a more detailed discussion of this point see *The Soviet Union and Disarmament*, pp. 96–103.

There are, no doubt, still differences among political and military leaders on the extent to which it is feasible to employ Soviet military power in crisis situations, as on other questions pertaining to the Soviet military establishment. The impersonal and collective quality of the present regime tends, however, to obscure public expression of such differences. Although the spectrum of discourse has shifted toward a harder line on America, for example, making obsolete old differences on the dominance of "sober" forces in American leadership, variations have reappeared in the evaluation of U.S. power. These involve nuances between those who tend to minimize American power and those who emphasize it—all variations on the standard theme that "aggressive" behavior on the part of the United States in Vietnam and elsewhere does not indicate a shift in the correlation of forces in favor of "imperialism," but that the military and economic might wielded by the United States must be taken fully into account.[2]

The discussion that follows considers the military situation and Soviet policies in three areas: strategic nuclear forces, theater (or general purpose) forces in Europe, and conventional forces for operations distant from the USSR. Even if somewhat arbitrary, this division facilitates discussion of current Soviet military capabilities and programs in the light of the various political-military objectives sought by the USSR and in relation to arms control and disarmament prospects.

Comparisons with the United States have a justified place in this discussion. Nevertheless, the military forces of the USSR serve various national purposes, some of which are related vaguely, if at all, to great-power rivalries and interactions. The interaction between the USSR and the United States in strategic nuclear forces is very great. It also affects the level and type of other forces deployed by the two states and their allies elsewhere, especially in Europe. Both countries, however, but particularly the United States, maintain other "general-purpose forces" (ground, air, and naval) at levels and in postures that are largely unrelated to activities of the rival state. Both the United States and the USSR must take China into account in their deployment of forces; but they do this in different ways. In addition, each has more or less farflung interests to protect or promote, and seeks a capability for influencing by display or use of military force the outcome of intrastate and interstate conflicts in various regions.

STRATEGIC NUCLEAR FORCES

The bipolar element in the development of Soviet and American strategic nuclear forces has been dominant in the entire postwar period and is likely to remain crucial in the next decade. This kind of

[2] See Chapter 4.

strategic interaction between the two states is almost wholly a phe-
nomenon of the postwar years. It may be lessened in the future if
Communist China acquires significant long-range military power, or
if, even apart from the Chinese factor, the Soviet Union and the
United States are able to enlarge their small base of shared interests.[3]
The reciprocation resulted from political and military developments
dating back to World War II. Having fought as uneasy allies against
common enemies, the United States and the Soviet Union assumed
new world roles as a result of the eclipse in defeat of Germany and
Japan and the eclipse in victory of Great Britain and France.

Even this political situation *might* not have been enough to place
the United States and the USSR in a bipolar strategic confrontation
had not the war spurred developments in military technology: the
appearance of long-range bombers showed that nations could not be
guarded from attack by ground or naval forces alone; the atom bombs
exploded by the United States over Hiroshima and Nagasaki showed
what enormous destructive power could be concentrated in small airborne packages. The Soviet Union thereby became vulnerable to attack from the United States; and as these American technological
achievements gave rise to "socialist competition," the United States
in turn became vulnerable to attack from the Soviet Union. This
mutual vulnerability was heightened by their parallel development
in the early 1950's of thermonuclear weapons, and in the late 1950's
of more rapid and less vulnerable carriers in the form of long-range
guided missiles.

(This mutual vulnerability is real enough, but perceptions of vulnerability are reinforced in both societies by certain groups which
profit from danger. Their power, prestige, and influence depend on
the continued existence of arms competition. The higher the level of
international tension, the easier it is to keep the arms race booming.
But even apart from such tension, the process of mutual interaction
creates its own momentum. Among the superpowers at least, an innovation by one state can be matched by another, and an opponent's
advance in weaponry simplifies the decision making process in a rival
state by giving definition and focus to the problem.)

It is this vulnerability that creates the basis for strategic deterrence:
the prospect of suffering great destruction if a state assaults or gravely
damages a rival serves as a powerful restraint against imprudent conduct. But under conditions of mutual vulnerability the prospect of
inviting such destruction also warns statesmen against imprudent deterrence, i.e., against primary reliance on nuclear weapons to prevent

---

[3] Although the motivation is not entirely clear, the September, 1967, U.S. decision
to begin installation of a "thin" ABM system was justified by Secretary McNamara
principally in terms of possible future Chinese capabilities (*The New York Times*,
September 19, 1967).

inimical moves below a threshold at which very high stakes are involved.[4] The possession by both the Soviet and American forces of relatively invulnerable nuclear strategic forces has prevented casual use of nuclear weapons in "policing" international relations. It thus re-emphasized the importance of conventionally equipped military forces.

For some time these implications about nuclear and conventional forces did not sink in. The diminution in frequency of hints and threats of resort to nuclear weapons in international conflicts testifies, however, to an appreciation of the first point.[5] The Cuban missile crisis of 1962 was a clear demonstration of the second point: having overwhelming conventional superiority in the area, the United States could comfortably handle the situation without resort to nuclear weapons. By doing so, it placed on the USSR the onus of choosing or rejecting a nuclear confrontation.[6]

In the competitive development of strategic nuclear forces, the USSR has always lagged behind the United States. Unlike American authorities, Soviet officials do not publish any figures on Soviet strength in nuclear weapons and in ICBMs and other delivery vehicles (and rarely publish any hard statistics on military forces generally). Khrushchev in his time, and Brezhnev more recently, have claimed that Soviet strength was greater than that attributed to the USSR by American authorities.[7] In recent years, Soviet spokesmen have tended

[4] In the speech mentioned in the preceding note, Secretary McNamara pointed out that even the American nuclear monopoly in the early postwar period had not sufficed to deter either Soviet pressures against Berlin or support of North Korea in the Korean war, and that American superiority has not deterred the USSR from giving aid to North Vietnam.

[5] There were suggestions by American officials of the possible use of nuclear weapons in the Korean and Indochinese wars, and by the USSR during the hostilities over Suez—i.e., all in the 1950's. They have been virtually absent from the recent fighting in Vietnam and from the Arab-Israeli war of June, 1967. The latter may be explained, however, by the fact that no great power was directly involved in 1967.

[6] President Kennedy's address of October 22, 1962, stated:

It shall be the policy of this nation to regard any nuclear missile launched from Cuba against any nation in the Western Hemisphere as an attack by the Soviet Union on the United States, requiring a full retaliatory response upon the Soviet Union. (*Documents 1962*, II, p. 970.)

[7] Among other examples from Khrushchev, see Norman Cousins' report in *Saturday Review*, November 7, 1964, of an interview with Khrushchev on April 12, 1963. The latter referred to statistics in an advertisement about American superiority in "killing power" and said: "Your figures are all wrong. We're not that far behind."

Brezhnev told graduates of Soviet military academies on July 3, 1965:

Here and there abroad there continue to be noises about the supposedly achieved superiority of the United States over the USSR in the strategic weapons field. This campaign is carried on not only by the press; high officials in

to make general claims of superiority rather than specifically claiming superiority in ICBMs and similar strategic weapons systems.[8] Frequently they have retreated behind the formula that the Soviet Union has "sufficient means" to deal "a crushing blow" to any attacker. This proposition, admitted by American officials, is consistent with a certain degree of strategic inferiority, and thus does not directly rebut American claims of superiority. Thus, former Secretary of Defense McNamara, while claiming a substantial U.S. superiority in strategic forces, has said that "neither the Soviet Union nor the United States can now attack the other, even by complete surprise, without suffering massive damage in retaliation." *

---

the U.S. government take part in it. . . . Everyone knows that our strength does not need advertisements and lengthy evidence. But it is necessary to note that the figures and calculations cited in the West regarding the nuclear-missile forces of the Soviet Union do not indicate knowledge on the part of the compilers, and, in particular, of the intelligence services of imperialist states. . . . There is hardly any need to cite concrete data on the quantity of intercontinental and orbital missiles possessed by the Soviet Union. I can only say this: they are sufficient, fully sufficient, to finish once and for all with any aggressor or any group of aggressors. (*Pravda*, July 4, 1965.)

A year later on July 1, 1966, he returned to the same theme before a similar audience, disparaging specifically the intelligence from "spy-satellites" and other sources on the number of missiles and submarines in Soviet possession. Now he claimed not only that the "armed forces" of the USSR had superiority over those of "imperialist" states, but also that the USSR had superiority in the latest kinds of military hardware (*Pravda*, July 2, 1966).

Authoritative Western estimates are provided by the Institute for Strategic Studies in London in its annual publication, *The Military Balance*.

[8] See, e.g., Col.-Gen. M. Povaly, "The Doctrine of the Aggressor and International Gendarme: The Strategic Concepts of Imperialism," *Krasnaia zvezda*, March 16, 1968.

* A word needs to be said about the complexity of calculations of superiority-inferiority or of "parity." (The latter term is used not in the dictionary sense of equivalence, but to mean "rough equality.") A calculation of the strategic nuclear forces available for a duel between the United States and the USSR has to reduce to a common measure such factors as (1) numbers and yields of nuclear warheads and (2) numbers and lift-capacity of vehicles capable of placing these warheads on enemy targets: ICBMs, missile-launching submarines, and heavy bombers. Other vehicles, such as medium bombers, have marginal offensive capabilities for such a long range duel, and these must be added to or excluded from the calculation. This strategic equation must also include defensive weapons systems, because these are capable of degrading attack forces—clearly in the case of anti-aircraft defense, but also to a limited degree with antimissile defenses. The absence of any one simple measure of strategic capabilities is illustrated by the fact that data on numbers of ICBMs and long-range bombers must be taken in conjunction with the fact that Soviet ICBMs can carry heavier loads than the American Minuteman, whereas American heavy bombers can carry larger loads than Soviet long-range bombers. The possible use of these long-range aircraft in a stand-off role (firing missiles from outside defense

In fact, Soviet writers on disarmament questions have implicitly recognized Soviet inferiority in strategic nuclear forces. One writer argued, for example, that the proposals for a percentage reduction of armaments—such as the American GCD plan—are formulated to allow the Western powers to have more than enough means for an armed attack at any stage of disarmament. Even if this were true, reduction by equal percentages would seem to be disadvantageous to the Soviet Union only if the latter were militarily inferior and expected to overcome this inferiority through unilateral armament measures.[9]

A similar recognition appears in the most recent (1967) Soviet volume on disarmament, in a chapter by the well-known disarmament expert, I. S. Glagolev. Referring to American proposals (in the GCD plan) for equal reductions of delivery vehicles and for transfer to international control of equal quantities of fissionable materials, Glagolev said that this would mean either a perpetuation or an increase of the existing U.S. strategic superiority. Without mentioning Defense Secretary McNamara by name, he cited the Secretary's claim that the United States had three or four times more long-range delivery vehicles than were in Soviet possession. As to fissionable materials, Glagolev alluded to the fact that the United States began production of these earlier and possessed a greater economic potential than the USSR, and cited a hypothetical figure of a two-to-one American superiority in such stocks. Although Glagolev's text is peppered with reminders that he is referring to American claims, and he modestly refuses to judge "which state in actuality disposes of the greater quantity of nuclear weapons and delivery vehicles," the argument against these proposals has no meaning unless the Soviet stocks of nuclear weapons and of delivery vehicles are inferior in fact and not merely in hypothesis.[10]

Contrary to expectations in the United States, the Soviet Union never attempted to develop, in the period when bombers flourished, a strategic bombing force approaching the strength of the American fleet of B-47s and B-52s. Although in the next stage of the arms race

---

perimeters) introduces another element of complexity into any analysis of relative strength.

These and similar complexities are conceptual, in that they would exist even if reliable data were freely available on all the relevant factors. In real life, of course, many of the data on Soviet and U.S. forces are unavailable, and calculations must be based, for one side at least and, in works such as this, for both sides, on incomplete data and estimates of uncertain reliability. Nevertheless, for purposes of a disarmament study, sufficient data are available to establish gross magnitudes and relationships of military forces.

[9] O. Grinyov, "Soviet Efforts for Disarmament," *International Affairs* (Moscow), No. 12 (December, 1967), 63–69.

[10] *SSSR, SShA i razoruzhenie*, pp. 159–60.

it successfully tested an ICBM in 1957 before the United States, the USSR let its developmental lead slip in the ensuing production and deployment phases. In the latter years of Khrushchev's tenure it seemed to most Western observers that the USSR would content itself even in the ICBM field with a force greatly inferior to that deployed in the United States.[11] Probably Khrushchev himself was not satisfied to have merely a "minimum deterrent" force, i.e., the minimum number of offensive weapons that would be sufficient under any circumstances to deal a destructive blow to U.S. territory. At any rate, it seems clear that his successors are committed to overcoming the Soviet lag behind the United States in ICBMS.

At the time of Khrushchev's departure, the USSR had about 200 ICBM launchers, most of these in "soft" sites and therefore highly vulnerable to counterblows. The number has more than tripled since then, we are told, and the augmentation has been accompanied by hardening of the emplacements. Table 4 indicates the most recently published U.S. estimates of Soviet strategic strength in missiles and bombers, as of October 1, 1967, with official data on comparable U.S. systems.[12]

TABLE 4—STRATEGIC WEAPONS SYSTEMS

	United States	USSR
ICBM Launchers	1054	720
Submarine Ballistic Missile Launchers	656	30
Intercontinental Bombers	697	155

According to Department of Defense data, the American superiority is even greater than these comparisons indicate, because the number of separate warheads that could be delivered by these various carriers is about 4500 for the United States, as against 1000 for the USSR.

[11] Secretary McNamara was quoted in *U.S. News and World Report,* April 12, 1965, as saying that the Soviet leaders "have decided that they have lost the quantitative race, and they are not seeking to engage us in that contest."

[12] McNamara's statement on *The Fiscal Year 1969–73 Defense Program and the 1969 Defense Budget,* January, 1968, p. 54; hereinafter cited as *McNamara Posture Statement, 1968.* The U.S. figures are from mid-1967. The estimates for the USSR exclude ICBM test-range launchers, MRBMS and IRBMS, launchers on diesel submarines, launchers for cruise (air-breathing) missiles, and medium-range bombers. Except for the first group, the vehicles listed are designed for other targets than the United States. There is a controversy about the proper classification of medium bombers because these could possibly be used against American targets. See *The Changing Strategic Military Balance: U.S.A. vs. U.S.S.R.,* report prepared by the American Security Council for the House Committee on Armed Services, 90th Cong., 1st sess. (Washington, D.C.: Government Printing Office, 1967), pp. 79–83. This report treats Soviet medium bombers as part of the Soviet intercontinental strategic force.

The greater U.S. advantage in warheads is apparently a function of the greater carrying capacity of American long-range bombers.[13] On the other hand, Robert McNamara has admitted that Soviet warheads contain more explosive power and therefore comparisons in megatonnage would show a smaller Soviet inferiority.[14]

The strong element of interaction in Soviet-American development of strategic nuclear forces has not meant that responses have always been symmetrical. The USSR has shown a predilection for defensive weapons systems that is not characteristic of American behavior. Thus, in the period when bombers constituted the main element of U.S. strategic attack forces, the USSR devoted more effort to constructing strong air defenses than to matching America in bombers.[15] The continued attention to Soviet defenses against bomber attacks is well illustrated by the recent deployment of the so-called Tallin system over the northwestern approaches to the USSR and other areas. Although some doubts persist, this system is now judged by most American intelligence specialists to be intended for defense against aircraft rather than against ballistic missiles.[16] In general, the Pentagon expects the USSR to continue improving its air defenses so as to have in the mid-1970's a much more advanced anti-aircraft defense system than it has today.[17] Although the same pattern of emphasizing defense rather than offense was not repeated with missiles, it is significant that the USSR has begun the installation of an ABM system (around Moscow), in spite of the great expense that would be entailed in a nationwide system, and in spite of doubts about its efficacy.[18]

[13] Although subsequently reduced, American heavy bombers at one time carried as much as 23-megaton bombs. Jerome B. Wiesner and Herbert F. York, "National Security and the Nuclear-Test Ban," Scientific American, CCXI, No. 4 (October, 1964), 1–8.

[14] See McNamara's comments on megatonnage in an interview in Life, September 12, 1967, and The Changing Strategic Military Balance: U.S.A. vs. U.S.S.R., pp. 29–30 and pp. 46–52. McNamara argues that the number of separately targeted warheads is the significant figure because most targets can be destroyed by a single one-megaton warhead, and hence no advantage is gained by sending over a 20-megaton weapon. In fact, the USSR is now moving in the direction of smaller warheads.

[15] McNamara Posture Statement, 1968, p. 65.

[16] Ibid., p. 55. McNamara's formula that "the majority of our intelligence community" does not believe that the system has "any significant ABM capability" is another way of stating that some service(s) do so believe.

[17] Ibid., p. 71.

[18] The doubts have been expressed in the United States. There are, however, variations in Soviet statements on the USSR's capabilities of knocking out incoming missiles, with the frequent addition of the word "some." McNamara's argument was that even if an ABM system overcame significant technical difficulties (e.g., in distinguishing real missiles from decoys), the other side could still swamp the ABM defense by adding missiles. For the purposes of deterrence, this would be cheaper than building an ABM system.

One reason for the greater proportionate effort devoted to defense measures in the USSR as compared to the United States concerns differing evaluations of the likelihood of nuclear war. The belief in the efficacy of deterrence appears to be stronger among American authorities than among Soviet. Effective defense measures contribute to deterrence, especially by the protection they afford to offensive forces, but this contribution is only indirect: they cannot hurt the enemy's homeland or threaten enemy forces until the latter attacks. Thus, defensive weapons systems are more directly relevant to carrying on war than to deterring an opponent.[19] Believing that such a war can break out (i.e., that deterrence can fail), the Soviet authorities seek to insure that the USSR survives an initial nuclear exchange sufficiently to fight another day.

In the post-Khrushchev period, it should be noted, Soviet leaders have gravitated toward a more somber view of the possibility of general war than was characteristic prior to 1964. Although even now a full-scale nuclear war seems—on balance—to be considered unlikely by the USSR,[20] the commitment of large American forces to the war in Vietnam, and the attacks on North Vietnam, a state in the "socialist commonwealth," have apparently led Brezhnev and his colleagues to the conclusion that the United States *is* willing to risk a showdown with the USSR in contesting control even of areas distant from American bases of power.

In line with this sober evaluation, some military authors in the USSR have reasserted the idea that victory in a thermonuclear war is possible. They thus reject the notion current earlier that *any* nuclear war would be so devastating for all participants that distinctions between victors and vanquished would lose meaning. In a 1965 article, for example, Lt. Col. Yevgeni I. Rybkin took to task the well-known Soviet writer, General Nikolai Talensky, for spreading the "fatalistic" doctrine that it was no longer possible to find acceptable forms of nuclear war. Not only could a state be victorious, Colonel Rybkin wrote, but it could minimize damage to itself, either by defeating the enemy

---

[19] In contrast to Secretary McNamara, the U.S. Joint Chiefs of Staff have favored installation of an ABM system against USSR ICBMs. This is partly because they, like their Soviet counterparts, have less faith in deterrence and are interested in capabilities for fighting if deterrence fails. In addition, however, they believe the USSR could not compete with the U.S. in the ABM field, for technical and economic reasons. See the statement of General Earle G. Wheeler, Chairman of the Joint Chiefs of Staff, in the hearings on the 1968 defense budget, January 27, 1967. U.S. Senate Committee on Armed Services and the Subcommittee on Department of Defense of the Committee on Appropriations, *Military Procurement Authorizations for the Fiscal Year 1968.* 90th Cong., 1st sess. (Washington, D.C.: Government Printing Office, 1967), p. 296; and *The New York Times,* October 16, 1967.

[20] Wolfe, in *Soviet Politics After Khrushchev.*

quickly or by creating new means of countering the enemy's nuclear blows—perhaps a reference to ABM defense.[21] In another article Lt. Col. V. Bondarenko in 1966 stressed that the key to superiority and thus to victory lay in technological breakthroughs resulting from R & D efforts. Innovations in weapons could, he urged, alter the "correlation of forces" within a short period of time.[22]

In these two articles, the immense costs for both sides of a nuclear war were recognized, and talk about ways of achieving "victory" does not necessarily indicate increased Soviet willingness to pursue dangerous courses of action. The articles probably reflect, in part, concern in Soviet military circles over the problem of morale, a consideration to which Rybkin specifically alludes. If nuclear war is considered possible, a doctrine that there will be no difference in the fate of victors and vanquished is hardly calculated to inspire the necessary will to fight, even to fight a war of defense. If the international situation becomes still more tense, and Soviet expectations that a major conflict is brewing increase, Soviet writings will probably express more vigorously the idea that the USSR will emerge victorious from such a war, and will minimize emphasis on its terrible consequences for all participating nations.

Disarmament Questions From its position of superiority in strategic nuclear forces, the United States has repeatedly proposed to the USSR that it opt out of competition for parity or superiority in this area. These proposals have involved atomic and thermonuclear weapons or the vehicles designed to carry these to targets. They include, among others, the Baruch plan of 1946 for "internationalization" of "all phases of the development and use of atomic energy"; President Eisenhower's proposal of January 12, 1958, to stop the development of weapons using outer space, i.e., ballistic missiles; the American outline (1962) of a treaty for general and complete disarmament— which contemplates percentage reductions in strategic forces, and the U.S. proposal of 1964 for a "freeze" on levels of nuclear strategic delivery vehicles. The USSR showed no interest in any of these. By contrast, it advanced proposals that aimed at the immediate liquidation of American superiority. These included separate proposals for the elimination of foreign military bases (none of the Soviet military es-

---

[21] *Kommunist vooruzhennykh sil,* No. 17 (September, 1965), 50–56. This article is discussed in Wolfe, *supra,* and in Roman Kolkowicz, *The Soviet Military and the Communist Party* (Princeton, N.J.: Princeton University Press, 1967), pp. 304–5.

[22] *Kommunist vooruzhennykh sil,* No. 17 (September, 1966), 7–14. The article is discussed in Wolfe, *supra,* and also in a paper (to which a translation of the Soviet article is appended) by Benjamin S. Lambeth, *The Argument for Superiority: A New Voice in the Soviet Strategic Debate* (Washington, D.C.: Institute for Defense Analyses, 1967, N-419 [R], processed).

tablishments in Eastern Europe are called bases) and of all bombing aircraft, as well as the Soviet plan for "general and complete disarmament"—which contemplates elimination, or reduction to equal and small numbers, of nuclear weapons and delivery systems. The United States showed no interest in any of these proposals.[23]

The stalemate regarding proposals for limitations on strategic weapons systems has meant that competition in both production and deployment of armaments and vehicles and in technological innovation has remained unchecked. A word needs to be said about the latter, on which the Soviet leaders appear to rest a good many hopes. These hopes spring in part from a belief that "socialism" is more favorable than "capitalism" to the introduction of technological innovations. Soviet officials were no doubt fortified in this belief by the experience of the USSR in rapidly overcoming the 1945 American lead in mastery of nuclear weapons technology and in developing an ICBM faster than the United States. The two strategic weapons areas where the USSR has appeared to be concentrating technological efforts recently have been ABM systems and the use of satellites as vehicles from which to discharge nuclear warheads into orbit.[24] Although the effectiveness of these defensive and offensive weapons systems has been minimized by Secretary McNamara and other American officials, the inauguration of ABM systems may at least spur an arms race in a new field.

The U.S. build-up of ICBMs reached in 1967 the quantitative level (1054, mostly solid-fuel Minutemen in hardened installations) fixed several years earlier as the desired number; this, however, did not mean that the American authorities intended to remain passive while the Soviet Union built up its offensive missiles to this or a higher level.

[23] For a discussion of some of these proposals, see Chapter 9.

[24] Soviet authorities have often mentioned USSR capabilities in the ABM field. They have not referred, however, to the FOBS system. They have often alluded to, and have displayed, what purported to be "orbital" missiles. Secretary McNamara announced on November 2, 1967, that the USSR might have in 1968 an operational capability of using a "fractional orbital bombardment system." In contrast to ICBMs, launched on a ballistic trajectory to a height of 800 miles, FOBS involves a satellite launched on a low orbital trajectory about 100 miles above the earth. The satellite could then release a nuclear warhead from this orbit, "generally"—according to McNamara—before completion of the first full orbit. The system would have the advantage for the USSR of reducing the warning time to the U.S. through BMEWS (Ballistic Missile Early Warning System). This system covers only the northern approaches of the United States, and a FOBS satellite could avoid BMEWS entirely on a southerly approach. McNamara indicated that the accuracy and payload would be less than those of ICBMs and that the U.S. would not develop a comparable system —the idea had been considered and rejected earlier. Although McNamara minimized the significance of FOBS, he indicated subsequently that the United States had decided to review its entire defense system and was developing a satellite-borne missile warning system with capabilities against FOBS. See *McNamara Posture Statement, 1968*, pp. 55, 73–74.

In addition to other improvements planned for both land-based and submarine-based ballistic missiles, the United States has been programming the introduction of multiple warheads for these launchers, called MIRV in the Minuteman III version and Poseidon (replacing Polaris) in the submarine version. These "multiple, individually targeted reentry vehicles" would allow a many-fold increase in the number of targets that could be programmed into a single launch.[25] Provided that the USSR did not follow suit,[26] the American superiority in long-range striking power would thus be restored to the dimensions that existed before the rapid Soviet deployment of ICBMs in 1964–1967.

There is a question, of course, about the meaningfulness of attaining or maintaining strategic nuclear superiority. In January, 1968, Secretary McNamara reiterated that what really mattered was the fact that "neither the Soviet Union nor the United States can now attack the other, even by complete surprise, without suffering massive damage in retaliation." In other words, each side has a "second-strike capability" of absorbing a nuclear blow and giving back as good as given. According to McNamara,

> In terms of numbers of separately targetable, survivable, accurate, reliable warheads, our strategic forces are superior to those of the Soviet Union. But . . . in terms of national security, such "superiority" is of little significance. For even with that "superiority," or indeed with any "superiority" realistically attainable, the blunt, inescapable fact remains that the Soviet Union could still effectively destroy the United States, even after absorbing the full weight of an American first strike.[27]

The logical conclusion that would seem to flow from these words is that neither side should worry about inferiority as long as it possesses an assured deterrent force, but this is not the conclusion that American policy has implemented. The Secretary of Defense has accompanied remarks on the relative insignificance of nuclear superiority with expressions of American determination to maintain it, and he has stated that "any disarmament treaty or agreement or procedure that

[25] In contrast, equipping Minuteman ICBMs with MIRVs would not add to the number of "counterforce" targets requiring attention by the USSR in any nuclear exchange. It might be noted here that MIRV deployment, particularly if the USSR developed a comparable system, would degrade the capabilities of reconnaissance satellites to provide information on the strategic nuclear forces of the opposing sides.

[26] According to *The New York Times* report on September 10, 1967, a classified report circulating in U.S. government circles claimed that the Soviet Union was giving top priority to development of multiple warheads for its ICBMs. Apparently Soviet authorities have made no claims about this development.

[27] *McNamara Posture Statement, 1968*, pp. 45–46, 52.

we participate in must be one in which we maintain . . . our favorable differential balance of power." [28] American proposals have faithfully reflected this point of view.

Soviet disarmament proposals reflect a comparable interest in the balance of military power, more specifically, in improving the Soviet position vis-à-vis the United States. This rationale is not expressed openly, of course, in Soviet statements. In fact, Soviet discussions of the military balance are clouded by the failure to publish specific data and by assertion of vague and general claims to superiority which assign great weight to factors that cannot be quantitatively evaluated. Against the Chinese the Soviet writers argue the importance of weapons and equipment, but against the Americans they stress the advantages that the Soviet armed forces derive from their social base, that is, from a socialist society. Such a society is said to produce not only better weapons and better organization but also better fighting men.[29] When such immeasurable factors are ground into comparisons, claims of military superiority tend to be rather opaque.

From Soviet writers and from Soviet behavior, however, it seems clear that superiority in all realms, including that of strategic nuclear weapons systems, is a value cherished by the Soviet political and military leadership, and a value worth great investment of effort. On the other hand, although Soviet disarmament proposals are designed to improve the Soviet military position and degrade that of the United States, they generally tend to propose Soviet-American equality as a

[28] Secretary McNamara at the Senate hearings on military procurement in 1964; quoted in Jeremy J. Stone, *Strategic Persuasion: Arms Limitations Through Dialogue* (New York: Columbia University Press, 1967), p. 137.

[29] Soviet military writers disparage the emphasis placed by the Chinese on "man over weapons." The variation in Soviet approach is explainable by the great superiority of the USSR over Communist China in military hardware, and by the inferiority of the USSR to the United States in this area. The problem of how much weight should be attached to nonmaterial factors has long been troublesome to the Soviet Union. It is interesting to note that in a secret conference of January 13, 1941, bringing together the Politburo and the top military command, Joseph Stalin dismissed as unrealistic (though perhaps useful for propaganda purposes) Marshal K. A. Meretskov's calculation that, in a defensive posture, a single Red Army division could repulse two or three German divisions, and that, for an offensive, only one and a half Soviet divisions were necessary to overcome a German division. According to a participant in the conference, Stalin said at the end of the meeting that the war would be a war of motors, and would be won by the side having the greatest number of such motors in its forces and in reserve. General M. I. Kazakov, *Nad kartoi bylykh srazhenii* (Moscow: Voenizdat, 1965), pp. 61–67. Recently a Soviet admiral tried to explain to a reader of *Krasnaia zvezda* how "the objective law of the correlation of forces among belligerent sides is concretely measured." He said that this could be expressed in a very simple formula: "In war it is the stronger who is victorious." At least he admitted that "at first glance" this sounded trivial. Rear Admiral V. Andreev, in *Krasnaia zvezda*, December 13, 1967.

goal (if often at radically diminished levels of military effort). This is not inconsistent with the search for superiority, in view of the Soviet leaders' belief that nonquantitative factors (basically organization and morale) give an advantage to the USSR over America.

Whether or not Soviet behavior in world affairs would change if the USSR attained parity with (or superiority over) the United States in strategic nuclear military power is a difficult question. No doubt the responsible Soviet officials would sleep a little easier at night, and perhaps they would wake up with bold schemes designed to exploit the changed correlation of forces in the world. Probably, however, the marginal difference in their freedom of action would be small, because they would still be aware of the great risks inherent in any political or military moves seriously threatening vital interests of rivals and opponents.* It can hardly be doubted, however, that the Soviet regime would seek to exploit its "reputation for power" or military prestige —if this could be demonstrated—by encouraging rulers and peoples throughout the world to look on the USSR as an ascending, and the United States as a descending, force in world affairs.

Questions of strategic superiority-inferiority have played a large part in producing the stalemate on significant agreements affecting strategic nuclear weapons systems; however, they have not been the subject of direct negotiations in connection with disarmament discussions, and they are not likely to be in the future. Rather, they have lain just below the surface of the overt discussions: the American proposals did not baldly demand a recognition of American superiority; nor did Soviet proposals openly assert that their aim was to eliminate this superiority.

If the USSR were to achieve a position of real equality (or a position that both sides believed to be one of equality), whether through American willingness or because events forced this on the United States, some of the current American and Soviet arms control proposals on nuclear weapons systems might become negotiable. The "freezes" and percentage reductions characterizing the American approach, and the limitations and reductions to equal numbers characterizing the Soviet approach, would then have different implications. There is nothing to suggest, however, that strategic parity is likely in the near future, and therefore the disparity of military power is likely to continue to block agreements on strategic arms limitations.[30]

---

* Some of the members of the group felt strongly that such a change in power relations would encourage "adventures" by the Soviet leaders, who would be overly impressed by the change in strategic ratios and would unduly minimize the willingness of the United States to exert its deterrent power against Soviet "forward" moves.

[30] Even if the superiority question were out of the way, major problems would remain in reconciling differences between U.S. and Soviet disarmament postures.

THEATER FORCES IN EUROPE

We have considered some of the elements determining Soviet policy on strategic nuclear forces and on agreed limitations affecting such forces. A shift of focus to nonstrategic forces is not a shift of attention from nuclear to conventional forces, because American and Soviet forces (and the forces of at least some of their allies) in Europe and elsewhere are equipped to fight with nuclear as well as conventional weapons. The difference is that a strategic missile duel between the United States and the USSR would require the use of nuclear weapons, whereas the resort to such weapons in limited conflicts is becoming less and less probable.[31] In consequence, the deployment of ground, naval, and air forces capable of operating with conventional arms alone retains its importance for all situations except that of a possible U.S.-USSR duel at long range.

Because of this requirement for general-purpose forces, the USSR has maintained throughout the postwar period a large standing army. Conceivably it might have done this even if the situation in Europe had not been tense; keeping an army of millions is an old Russian tradition. In any case, Europe remained tense, and continues to present the most likely battleground for hostilities involving the Soviet Union, although Soviet authorities repeat incessantly that their forces are ready to repel any assault from North or South, East or West.[32]

After an initial postwar demobilization, which brought the strength of Soviet armed forces down to less than 3 million, the armed forces were increased to over 5 million men in the early 1950's as a result of the Korean War and the NATO build-up in Western Europe. There

---

They differ, for example, on inspection requirements and on preferences for radical or minimal shifts in levels of forces and armaments. Soviet representatives frequently dismiss arms control proposals on the ground that they do not go far enough toward disarmament, but their opposition frequently seems to be based on other unspoken considerations. The USSR has actually accepted and even proposed measures having no direct "disarmament" features.

[31] Of course, the United States in particular, but also the USSR, retain bombers in their strategic forces, and these—unlike missiles—have dual capabilities for conventional (HE) and nuclear bombs.

[32] The change referred to is not in the deployment of Soviet armed forces, which have always been dispersed to take care of threats along any frontier, but in the advertisement of defense capabilities for "all azimuths." Thus, Brezhnev declared at the November 3, 1967 meeting celebrating the 50th anniversary of the October Revolution: "From wherever . . . an infringement [on the security of the Soviet country or on its allies] might come, from the north or from the south, from the west or from the east, the aggressor will be met with all the shattering might of our valiant armed forces." (*Pravda,* November 4, 1967.)

was then a reduction in the last half of the 1950's to 3 plus millions, a level which has apparently been maintained with little change. This total is perhaps somewhat smaller than the present (1968) U.S. total of over 3.5 million.[33] Direct comparisons are not especially in point, however, because the force levels are affected by other factors than Soviet-American rivalry. Thus, the expansion of American forces to provide over half a million men for operations in South Vietnam was clearly irrelevant to Soviet force levels.

There would be a point in considering armed force totals if general disarmament were being discussed in even a half-serious way. Both Soviet and American plans for general disarmament contemplate fixed maxima for United States and USSR armed forces as well as for those of other nations. The plans in their latest variants call for a first-stage reduction to equal numbers for both countries: under the American proposal to 2.1 million, and under the Soviet proposal to 1.9 million.[34] The Soviet-proposed figure includes civilian employees of the military establishments; in the United States, these alone currently number 1.25 million persons.[35] (The corresponding Soviet total is unknown.) But agreements to reduce total armed forces are not very promising.

Soviet armed force deployments in Eastern Europe invite special attention. The strength and deployment of Soviet forces in Europe are strongly influenced by the confrontation with American and other NATO forces, although even these Soviet forces serve or have served various purposes—some of which do not remotely involve the United States. Apart from the general protection of frontiers, the Soviet forces were placed in Eastern Europe to insure the maintenance of Soviet control in territories acquired or reacquired as a result of World War II, and to insure the preservation of the new "socialist" order in Eastern Europe against any attempts to re-establish non-Communist regimes. Thus, the Red Army played an essential part in the "communization" of Eastern European countries in the late 1940's, and in preserving Communist rule in Hungary when revolt broke out in 1956. Soviet forces were again employed in Czechoslovakia in August, 1968, in an effort to block what the Kremlin saw as a disintegration of Communist control of the country. In contrast to these instances in which Communist rule seemed to be in jeopardy, Soviet armed forces have not been used against Communist regimes in Eastern Europe which

[33] For the period through 1962, see Godaire, p. 37. For current estimates, see *The Military Balance: 1967–1968* and preceding annual issues. The 1967 total of regular Soviet forces is estimated there at 3,220,000 men. The current U.S. total is in *McNamara Posture Statement, 1968*, p. 186.

[34] *Documents 1965*, pp. 85, 116.

[35] *McNamara Posture Statement, 1968*, p. 185.

gravitated toward courses of action independent of, and sometimes hostile to, the USSR. Cases in point are provided by Yugoslavia, Albania, and Rumania.[36]

At present, the USSR maintains large forces in East Germany (about 20 divisions) and much smaller forces in Poland (two divisions) and Hungary (four divisions). The stationing of these forces obviously has some bearing on internal developments in these countries, and probably has residual significance for Eastern Europe in general; but the primary mission of these forces—especially the northern group in East Germany and Poland—is to give the USSR and its Warsaw Pact allies offensive and defensive capabilities against American and other NATO forces in West Germany and elsewhere in Western Europe. In other words, the equipment and dispositions of Soviet forces go far beyond what would be necessary for purposes of maintaining Communist internal rule. Nuclear weapons, for example, are apparently well-integrated into the armaments of these troops and aircraft, in anticipation of a possible conflict between Warsaw Pact and NATO forces involving the use of at least "tactical" nuclear weapons.[37]

According to the latest U.S. estimates, the opposing Soviet-led and American-led forces in Europe are of approximately equal strength: 900,000 NATO troops in continental Europe, and 960,000 WTO troops. Each side also has thousands of tactical aircraft positioned in Europe, but the specific numbers of these are less significant than those of ground troops, because reinforcements from distant bases could be made even more rapidly than in the case of troops.[38] The USSR has a fleet of some 800 medium bombers/tankers (mostly TU-16), which would be available for attacks on European targets, and in addition has about 750 MRBMs and IRBMs which could cover targets such as airfields in Western Europe.[39] The missiles would be relevant, of course, only in case of nuclear hostilities.

[36] Soviet forces had been withdrawn from Rumania in 1958. In 1956, after quelling the Hungarian revolt, the USSR suggested the possibility of withdrawing its forces from Hungary, Poland, and Rumania, but did so only from the last named. See *National Communism and Popular Revolt in Eastern Europe,* ed. Paul Zinner (New York: Columbia University Press, 1956), pp. 487–88.

[37] Soviet military spokesmen often refer to the nuclear weapons in possession of ground forces and other units, in addition to those of the strategic forces. See, e.g., General I. G. Pavlovsky, Commander-in-Chief of Ground Forces, in *Pravda,* January 20, 1968. Marshal A. A. Grechko, Minister of Defense, in the principal speech at the February 23, 1968, meeting celebrating the 50th anniversary of the Soviet Army and Navy, declared: "The Soviet armed forces are capable of successfully waging military operations under all conditions—on the ground, in the air, or at sea, by day or night, with or without nuclear weapons." (*Pravda,* February 24, 1968.)

[38] *McNamara Posture Statement, 1968,* p. 80.

[39] *The Military Balance 1967–1968,* pp. 5–9.

This reference to Soviet weapons trained on Western Europe and usable only with nuclear warheads is a forcible reminder of the link between the European theater confrontation considered here and the Soviet-American strategic confrontation discussed earlier. Prior to development of Soviet long-range striking power (essentially in ICBMs) the Soviet Union could have "hit" the United States only by invading or striking American-allied countries in Europe; therefore, Western Europe was conceived by Soviet strategists as a kind of hostage for American "good behavior." The situation changed with the development of Soviet capabilities for a direct missile attack on American cities and other targets. The capabilities for nuclear attacks on European targets continue, however, to seem useful to the USSR as a supplement to its long-range forces.[40]

Despite the continued flow into the European theater of nuclear weapons,[41] observers on both sides are far less convinced today than earlier that any hostilities in Europe would inevitably become nuclear and that any use of tactical nuclear weapons would result in a full-scale nuclear war entailing attacks on the USSR and the United States. Particularly in the post-Khrushchev period, some Soviet military leaders have suggested the possibility of a non-nuclear war in Europe, or a war in which only tactical nuclear weapons were used. Most Soviet discussions of the issue continue to imply, however, that a limited war in Europe is likely to escalate into a general nuclear war.[42]

Disarmament Questions Certain of the various arms control and disarmament proposals that have been discussed would have a significant impact on the European military scene.

Some possibility exists that Soviet and Western troops can be thinned out in Europe through unilateral but reciprocal reductions, or through a more formal agreement. The Soviet leaders have often proposed measures to eliminate or reduce foreign troops, and have supported Polish proposals envisaging limitations on the deployment of nuclear weapons in "Central Europe," i.e., Germany (both parts), Czechoslo-

---

[40] Trends toward loosening of NATO ties may affect this situation, because the hostage role assigned to American allies in Europe by the USSR probably serves to reinforce military ties between Western Europe and the United States.

[41] No figures are published on Soviet nuclear stocks at home or abroad, and few on American. It is interesting to note, however, that since 1961 a substantial increase of American conventional capabilities in Europe has been paralleled by an almost doubling of American nuclear weapons in Europe (*McNamara Posture Statement, 1968*, p. 94). Although not relating specifically to Europe, a recent discussion of economic factors in the Soviet defense effort stressed the importance of reserves and stocks of nuclear weapons available at the beginning of hostilities. Col. G. Kravchenko, in *Krasnaia zvezda*, December 8, 1967.

[42] See Wolfe in *Soviet Politics After Khrushchev*.

vakia, and Poland. In different variants, these have called for a "freeze" on existent levels of such weapons, or for reductions, or for complete elimination. While shying away from any denuclearization, the United States (with NATO approval) has reduced by about 50,000 its troop strength in Europe in 1967–1968. Some hopes were expressed by American officials that this reduction could evoke a reciprocal response from the Soviet Union; and on a more general plane, President Johnson has expressed interest—again with NATO endorsement—in the exploration of possibilities for mutual thinning out of NATO and WTO forces. Although the Soviet Union was once eager for such reductions, there has been no response to either the American expression of interest or the unilateral U.S. initiative. It may be that the Soviet leaders consider that mutual reductions would contribute to the American war effort in Vietnam by reducing pressures on military manpower and by easing U.S. balance-of-payment difficulties. In addition, such "collusion with the American imperialists" would make the USSR still more vulnerable to attacks from the Chinese, who have already charged that the USSR has remained quiet in Europe in order to aid the United States. Although American officials have implied that such mutual reductions would be most likely to occur through unilateral moves, if reciprocation occurs at all, it is not clear that the Soviet leaders would prefer this procedure—if, indeed, they are still interested in reductions, which is doubtful. The negotiations on, and conclusion of, a more formal agreement would appear to offer them some political opportunities, and would presumably lend an air of permanence to arrangements that otherwise might not last very long.[43]

A variety of other Europe-oriented proposals with arms control components have been advanced, mostly by the USSR, which would affect the NATO and WTO military establishments. These are discussed elsewhere in the report, as their political aims and consequences are as important as their military aspects. They include proposals for "measures against surprise attack," for a treaty of nonaggression between NATO and WTO states for disestablishment of the NATO and Warsaw Pact's military organizations in anticipation of the liquidation of these military alliances, and for withdrawal of foreign troops from European countries in which they are stationed. None of these proposals was mentioned in the latest Soviet memorandum (July 1, 1968) on partial measures. The omission made evident the lessening of Soviet interest in European-centered measures of arms limitation.

One proposal that, on its face, is not directed to Europe deserves a word here. This is the proposal for a (declaratory) ban on the use of nuclear weapons, or, in another version, on the "first use" of such weapons. An agreement of this kind would not necessarily affect military establishments, in Europe or elsewhere, but its importance is largely European. The proposal has received a good deal of support, including some in the United States, but the American government has always strongly rejected the idea. This is largely because of the declared NATO and American policy of using nuclear weapons (even first, if necessary) in case of a Soviet-led offensive that could not be stopped by conventionally equipped forces.

Continuing to insist that it opposes such declaratory bans, the United States has nevertheless become more "flexible" in its approach to this question. Thus, the United States voted for a U.N. resolution regarding African "denuclearization" despite the fact that it contained a provision calling on all states not to use nuclear weapons against African states renouncing possession of such weapons.[44] On May 25, 1966, in the Warsaw talks between American and Communist Chinese ambassadors, the United States indicated that it might agree to a ban on the use of nuclear weapons (which the Chinese have often endorsed) provided that China would adhere to the nuclear test-ban treaty.[45] Recently the United States signed a protocol to the Latin American denuclearization agreement, which contains in Article 3 a pledge on nonuse. In announcing on February 14, 1968, that the United States would sign the protocol, President Johnson mentioned specifically that it "calls upon the powers possessing nuclear weapons . . . not to use or threaten to use nuclear weapons against the Latin American states party to the treaty." A corollary American declaration indicated, however, that the U.S. did not consider itself bound by the literal terms of the non-use clause.[46]

Clearly, these steps involving Africa, China, and Latin America do not indicate a changed U.S. position on a general ban that would include Europe. But the situation in Western Europe has also changed as a result of diminished fears of Soviet aggression, of the build-up of NATO conventional forces to a level at which they could presumably hold their own with Warsaw Pact forces if a conflict broke out, and of

---

[44] The U.S. did object, however, to the clause of the resolution regarding a pledge of non-use of nuclear weapons.

[45] See *Documents 1966*, p. 355.

[46] *Department of State Bulletin*, LVIII, No. 1497 (March 4, 1968), 313–14. The United States indicated that it would not be bound by the pledge if a (signatory) Latin American state received assistance from a nuclear weapons state in "an armed attack" (i.e., even with conventional weapons). In other words, were Cuba to become a party to the treaty, the United States would feel free to use nuclear weapons against Cuba if the latter received even non-nuclear assistance from the Soviet Union in a conflict. See the U.S. statement made public at the time of signature of the Protocol, in *Department of State Bulletin*, LVIII, No. 1505 (April 29, 1968), 554–56.

the dissemination of nuclear weapons among Soviet forces (and possibly those of their Warsaw Pact allies) so that first use of nuclear weapons in a European conflict would bring fewer advantages to the United States and NATO than were once expected.

LONG-RANGE CONVENTIONAL CAPABILITIES

A third area of military power that invites attention concerns conventionally equipped forces capable of operating at considerable distances from Soviet borders. Relatively strong in strategic nuclear and European theater forces, the USSR is weak in capabilities for projecting its power on a world scale. Khrushchev's acceptance of the American demand for the withdrawal of IRBMs from Cuba was an implicit recognition that the Soviet Union had almost no means of protecting its "interests" in Cuba or of protecting Cuba, a friendly socialist state, from its northern neighbor: "almost no means" except, that is, resort to the very same ICBMs whose insufficient numbers were to have been supplemented by IRBMS in Cuba. The avoidance by the USSR of the sea route for shipments of military supplies to North Vietnam also testifies to the absence of a Soviet force capable of insuring communications with, and protection of, another member of the "socialist commonwealth."

The USSR has, it is true, substantial naval forces, including about 20 cruisers and over 100 destroyers, some equipped to launch guided missiles, but these and other surface ships are apparently intended to protect the sea approaches to the USSR itself, as are the land based bombers and fighters of Soviet naval aviation.[47] The very large fleet of some 330 conventionally powered and 50 nuclear powered submarines could do damage to enemy shipping and offer some challenge to American naval supremacy in a war at sea;[48] but this capability is relevant chiefly to a full-scale war between the U.S. and USSR. It does not contribute much to the Soviet capabilities for use of conventional military power at a distance from the Soviet borders under consideration here. The Soviet Union does have, of course, airborne troops (about seven divisions, totaling some 50,000 men). About half of these could be lifted simultaneously, but only over short or medium ranges.[49]

Some steps have been taken to improve the USSR's capabilities for distant operations. In 1964 marines were re-established in the Soviet naval service to provide a ship-based infantry for overseas operations, and marine units were prominent in the November, 1967, parade in

[47] See *The Military Balance 1967–1968*, pp. 5–9.
[48] *McNamara Posture Statement, 1968*, p. 85.
[49] See *The Military Balance 1967–1968*, pp. 6–7.

Moscow celebrating 50 years of Soviet power. The USSR has also constructed one helicopter carrier, the *Moskva*, and has another on the ways. In contrast, however, the USSR has built no aircraft carriers, and has given no sign of an intent to build any. It lacks, therefore, the mobile attack forces provided for the United States by 15 attack carriers.

In connection with the Middle East crisis of 1967, the USSR made a point of displaying its military power in the Mediterranean area and augmenting its patrol fleet to about 45 ships. The augmentation included, perhaps significantly, amphibious landing craft. These naval forces demonstrated capability for refueling and resupplying at sea, a necessity in view of the lack of Soviet naval bases outside the USSR. Soviet naval vessels and bombers also paid calls to friendly Arab countries. In the Mediterranean and elsewhere, Soviet naval and air units became more aggressive in their tactics in regard to American vessels on patrol. Despite all this activity (in an area relatively close to the USSR), the Soviet capabilities remain small for operations in the Mediterranean. It follows, then, that potential Soviet ability to support friendly regimes or movements at still greater distances from the USSR is even less.

Furthermore, it is not completely clear that Soviet leaders intend to develop substantial forces for such purposes. Since surface warships would probably be the central element in such forces, the question in part concerns the goals sought by the USSR in its recent naval build-up, a question currently in dispute among Western observers. Some believe that the build-up is part of an effort to challenge American naval supremacy on the major oceans. Others consider the motivation merely one of showing the Soviet flag, particularly in the "third world," and of thus offering some rivalry to the United States in such displays.[50]

Both Brezhnev and Kosygin have publicly demonstrated their interest in the Soviet naval forces, visiting surface and submarine vessels, and praising their level of equipment and training.[51] None of the lead-

[50] See *The New York Times,* March 30–31, 1968, on speech by U.S. Secretary of the Navy Paul R. Ignatius, and on controversy over a book by Commander Robert W. Herrick. The Ignatius speech and the Herrick book tend to minimize Soviet naval objectives, as did Secretary McNamara in his *Posture Statement, 1968*: "The increased levels of Soviet naval activity in the Mediterranean appear to be primarily diplomatic gestures aimed at recouping political losses. . . ." (p. 9). For a different view, from U.S. naval officers, see *The New York Times,* January 24, 1968. (For a discussion of these issues, see Thomas W. Wolfe, *The Soviet Quest for More Globally Mobile Military Power* [Santa Monica, Calif.: The RAND Corporation, December, 1967, RM-5554-PR, processed].)

[51] The two visited Northern Fleet installations at Murmansk and Arkhangelsk on the Barents and White Seas on May 31–June 3, 1967 (*Izvestiia,* June 6, 1967).

ers, certainly, has disparaged surface warships as Khrushchev did in his time.[52] The top Soviet admirals have recently been emphasizing that the Soviet Navy "has gone out into the oceans," referring to the Atlantic, Pacific, and Indian oceans and to the Mediterranean Sea.[53] Frequently such references to distant operations place the latter in the context of training missions, although some mention a rather vague "protection of Soviet state interests." [54] Soviet spokesmen tend to avoid, however, even general comparisons (of the type that are not uncommon regarding nuclear missile forces) of Soviet and American naval power.

A further improvement of Soviet naval and other capabilities for distant military operations may be designed for something less than a broad challenge to American naval supremacy and for something more than a mere gesture of showing the Soviet flag. In some sense, the USSR aspires to be the protector of the entire "socialist common-wealth" and of the radical-nationalist states of the Middle East, Africa, and Asia.[55] Moscow cannot fortify their pro-Soviet leanings unless it can provide military support in time of trouble (as well as political, economic, and military assistance). Soviet incentives *to be able* to render such direct military support (not necessarily to provide it immediately) have probably increased since Khrushchev's time. For the leaders now in power appear to have a better awareness than did Khrushchev of the limited political-military utility of strategic nuclear forces. Given their general outlook on the world configuration of friends and foes, this realization is likely to encourage them to continue development of long-range conventional capabilities. An increase of Soviet capabilities to render such direct support would probably supplement,

[52] *Soviet Strategy at the Crossroads*, pp. 44, 183.

[53] Interviews with Fleet Admiral of the Soviet Union S. G. Gorshkov, Commander-in-Chief of the Soviet Navy, in *Sovetskii voin*, No. 24, December, 1967, 2–3; and *Pravda*, February 14, 1968.

[54] Creation of military capabilities, in the Soviet Union, as elsewhere, can precede as well as follow formulation of doctrines on the need for, and use of, these capabilities. In the *Sovetskii voin* interview previously mentioned, Admiral Gorshkov indicates the way this happens: "New weapons and technical equipment have expanded the circle of tasks carried out by the [Soviet] Navy. In turn, it is necessary to create fundamentally new classes of ships to accomplish these tasks."

[55] Except for its Warsaw Pact allies, Soviet authorities avoid hard-and-fast commitments of direct armed support to friendly (Communist and non-Communist) states. No recent statement has come to the author's attention comparable to the statement on the fifth anniversary of the Warsaw Pact:

> The Soviet government has frequently stated that the borders of all its true friends—the socialist countries—will be defended by the Soviet Union exactly as if they were its own borders. This is how we understand proletarian internationalism and this is how all the peoples of the socialist countries understand it. (A. Lukovets, *Pravda*, May 14, 1960).

The context made this pledge less sweeping than a literal reading would imply.

rather than replace, Moscow's principal program to alter the distribution of military power in the "third world," that is, through the shipment of substantial quantities of arms to Arab and other radical-nationalist regimes and the training of sizeable contingents of military specialists from these countries.[56]

Disarmament Questions Although some, probably modest, arrangements for arms limitations can conceivably be negotiated regarding strategic nuclear forces and European theater forces, such agreements appear even less likely in the area under discussion (except for the nonproliferation treaty). One reason for this is the great disparity between Soviet and American capabilities for distant operations. Some Soviet "arms control" plans were patently designed to affect the military situation in the "third world" to the detriment of the United States, such as the suggested ban on all foreign military bases. Most of these proposals have no prospect of being negotiated. An exception concerns steps toward the "denuclearization" of Africa and Latin America, supported in general by both the U.S. and the USSR. Possibly other areas might be "denuclearized," too, although the Near East does not seem a very promising candidate at the moment, despite Soviet and American endorsement.

There have been suggestions from American and other sources for some limitation on arms shipments to regions such as the Middle East, where hostilities are a constant danger and where arms are eagerly sought. The USSR did not respond to suggestions by President Johnson and Secretary Rusk just after the Arab-Israeli war that nations supplying arms to Middle Eastern countries should register their shipments with the U.N. and should exercise restraint in the supply of arms, to avoid a dangerous arms race. The USSR urged in November, 1967 (in presenting a resolution to the U.N. Security Council) that all states "undertake measures restricting a useless and ruinous arms race" in the Middle East, and reiterated its interest in regional disarmament measures for the Middle East in the proposals advanced on July 1, 1968. A precondition was emphasized, however, in the demand for the return to Arab states of all territory taken by Israel in the war of June, 1967. Despite these gestures, the Soviet Union committed itself in 1967 to resupply the Syrian and UAR forces, battered by the Israelis in the June war.[57] The Soviet Union has also been using military supplies and

---

[56] *The Military Balance 1967–1968*, p. 53; *The New York Times*, September 5, 1967.

[57] *Ibid.*, January 15, 1968. On February 14, 1968, Premier Kosygin said in a speech at Minsk that the USSR had taken "important measures to restore the military potential of the United Arab Republic and Syria and to strengthen their defense." *Sovetskaia Belorussiia*, February 15, 1968.

other assistance to encourage an "anti-imperialist" stance, and an orientation toward Moscow, on the part of other Arab states not directly involved in the conflict with Israel.[58] Short of actual limitations on arms shipments, a U.N. system of registration and publicity for all arms shipments from one state to another was proposed by Malta to the U.N. General Assembly, but received support from neither the United States nor the Soviet Union.

SOVIET POLICY AND CHINESE MILITARY POWER

Not all Soviet military preoccupations have concerned the United States and its allies. Soviet military policy and Soviet disarmament policy alike have had to take account of the antagonism to the USSR and its leaders manifested by the Chinese Communists, and of the prospective emergence of a Chinese military capability, potentially threatening to the Soviet Union. Chinese progress in 1964–1968 in the development of atomic and thermonuclear weapons and of missiles was not enough to present a significant military threat to the integrity of the USSR. There was enough drumbeating, however, about alleged Chinese aspirations to take (or take back) territory presently held by the USSR, and enough skirmishing along the Sino-Soviet border, to force on Moscow a serious consideration of the Chinese potential. However, there has been no evidence of any large-scale Soviet redeployment or build-up to meet the Chinese threat, which looms larger for the future than for the present.[59]

The Sino-Soviet issues are discussed elsewhere, but the impact of Chinese military developments on Soviet military and disarmament policies must be noted here. Under the terms of the partial test-ban treaty, Soviet testing of new weapons was restricted; Communist China as a nonsigner could go ahead with atmospheric tests. Nevertheless the USSR was far ahead of China in sophisticated weapons systems, and neither the partial test ban nor any other agreement hampered Soviet production and stockpiling of nuclear weapons, or development and production of delivery vehicles.

The situation is somewhat different in regard to conventional forces. Given the long and disputed Sino-Soviet border, China's 2.3 million troops give her some limited capabilities against Soviet territory, which

[58] Most Soviet military assistance agreements concluded since 1966 have been with Arab and Middle Eastern countries; the USSR promptly exchanged military visits with the new "People's Republic of Southern Yemen," characterized by Moscow as the "fourth" Arab country (after Algeria, the UAR, and Syria) to have chosen the "noncapitalist" road of development.

[59] Thomas W. Wolfe, *Evolution of Soviet Military Policy* (Santa Monica, Calif.: The RAND Corporation, 1968, P-3773, processed), 28–30.

would be significant in the event of any future negotiation of a general disarmament agreement. The Chinese Communist antipathy to the Soviet leadership and disinclination to participate in disarmament negotiations has probably helped, therefore, to cool Soviet interest in promoting GCD. Chinese adherence will become increasingly necessary if any measures affecting total military strength are to be acceptable to the Soviet Union (and probably to the United States as well, despite the lesser vulnerability of American territory to possible Chinese attacks).

Reference to Chinese military capabilities provides an occasion for mention of Soviet attitudes toward the "Chinese threat." The more or less simultaneous occurrence of Soviet disagreements with China and of agreements with America was not fortuitous: the Soviet leaders had to be willing to disregard a loud Chinese "No!" in order to conclude such agreements with the U.S. as the test ban and the nonproliferation treaty. Probably, also, Soviet leaders are worried about the rise of Chinese military power, and they may even be inclined, because of a faith in the efficacy of Communist rule, to exaggerate the rapidity of future Chinese military development.

This does not mean, however, that the leaders of the USSR are inclined to join forces with the United States against a present or future Chinese menace, as some Western observers appear to believe. Agreements with the United States in spite of Peking's disapproval are one thing; agreements with the United States against China are quite another.[60] As noted elsewhere, since 1964, Soviet propaganda against "American imperialism" has become much more extensive and virulent than polemics against the Chinese.[61] Furthermore, in discussions by Soviet leaders of menacing forces on the world scene, the Chinese are usually placed in an entirely different spectrum from the Americans. The United States is cast in the role of world aggressor, menacing both Communist and non-Communist states; Communist China, as a trouble-maker in the Communist camp, blocking unified resistance to American "aggressive" actions. When the two are compared (as, for instance, by Premier Kosygin), the United States is portrayed as the principal villain and China as a minor villain; but such treatment is usually eschewed.[62]

Such propaganda treatment is of course not a conclusive indicator of Soviet estimates, because the USSR has other reasons for singling

[60] There may be occasions—for example, in tensions between China and India —when Soviet and American interests will be somewhat parallel.

[61] See Chapter 4, note 20.

[62] For a typical presentation, see the speech of Politburo member and Party Secretary A. P. Kirilenko, April 22, 1967 (*Pravda,* April 23, 1967). For Kosygin's speech of March 6, 1967, see *ibid.,* March 7, 1967.

out the American "menace" and for treating Chinese foreign activities in a separate context. But it appears to be indicative of a general Soviet approach tending to place in different frameworks and perspectives the struggle against Communist China and the struggle against the United States. The "Chinese menace" to Soviet state interests would have to become much more threatening to start the Kremlin leaders thinking of actively making common cause with Washington against Peking.

7

DISARMAMENT NEGOTIATIONS AND SOVIET POLICY: FAILURES AND SUCCESSES

This chapter, and the three that follow, survey the record of disarmament negotiations involving the Soviet Union both with respect to proposals for modest or radical arms reductions, and proposals for limited measures of arms control. Within this latter area, negotiations have resulted in four agreements involving limitations on the deployment or development of nuclear weapons. After discussion of the four areas in which these agreements have been achieved, consideration is given to other areas of disarmament negotiations. These involve a variety of proposals, none of which has yet come to agreement, for general or regional limitations on conventional or nuclear military forces and equipment.

This examination of the record is designed to elucidate the pattern of successes and failures in negotiating arms control and disarmament agreements. (Whereas virtually all the agreed and proposed measures look to multilateral participation, the discussion centers on the roles of the USSR and the United States. Agreement between these two states has usually been decisive for forward movement in arms control, and disagreement between them has almost invariably meant stagnation.)

The record of the seemingly interminable negotiations on disarmament can be portrayed as one of futility and failure. It can also be depicted as one marked by bright successes, promising others to come. In the older sense of "disarmament"—referring to agreements to reduce or abolish military forces or weapons systems, to curtail military spending, and to curb the arms race—progress has been nil. In regard to "arms control"—referring to other kinds of agreed limitations on military activities—there has been significant progress. The key to success in advancing arms control was discovered in the transfer of attention from major weapons competition to peripheral issues and potential problems. Four major arms agreements have been negotiated in the past decade. In 1959 the United States and the USSR joined with other powers in agreeing not to establish military installations in Ant-

arctica; in 1963 they agreed to stop all but underground tests of nuclear weapons; in 1967 they pledged not to send weapons of mass
destruction into orbit around the earth; and in 1968 they agreed on
a treaty prohibiting transfers of nuclear weapons to other states. These
accords are discussed at greater length below.

To recognize the fact that these four agreements did not slow down
the competitive build-up of major weapons systems is not to deny the
magnitude of the achievements. The problems successfully dealt with
in these agreements were significant, even if they were not all matters
of the first urgency. The barring of some potential areas of arms competition was second in importance only to the task of curbing the actual arms race. Furthermore, these agreements bettered the atmosphere
of political relations among the signatory states, encouraged the recognition of certain shared interests among opponents, and sparked some
optimism that more central issues, too, might eventually yield to negotiated solution.

INSTRUMENTAL USES OF DISARMAMENT PROPAGANDA

Before reviewing the successes and failures in negotiating disarmament agreements, it is well to note that attainment of agreements is
not the only objective of disarmament campaigns, and such agreements may not be an immediate objective at all. Naturally, states
advancing proposals for arms control or disarmament are usually
perfectly willing to have them accepted.[1] Most proposals, however,
are so clearly weighted in favor of the sponsors that acceptance is
scarcely expected. Campaigns in favor of proposals of this type offer a
means for a state to display its good will and peaceful intentions, and
to use the predictable rejection by opponents as a way of portraying
their belligerence and unwillingness to disarm. In this kind of political
struggle among rival states, the typical proposals combine asymmetrical
distribution of advantages (to the sponsors) and disadvantages (to the
respondents) with a degree of plausibility that gives them resonance in
the public opinion of interested countries.

---

[1] There have been a few instances of rejection by sponsors of proposals accepted by opponents. In its May 10, 1955, proposals the USSR accepted *elements* of
a plan advanced earlier by the U.S. and other Western states, but the U.S. subsequently withdrew its earlier proposals (*Documents 1945–1959*, I, pp. 456–67, 513).
After years of promoting proposals to condemn "war propaganda," the USSR
rejected on May 29, 1962, a declaration against war propaganda that had been
agreed to, *ad referendum*, four days earlier by the Soviet and other representatives
at the ENDC (*Documents 1962*, II, pp. 545–52).

Certainly the USSR found disarmament campaigns useful even if they resulted in no serious negotiations and no agreed measures. This was evident in Khrushchev's campaign for "general and complete disarmament." [2] But it also pertains to more limited proposals. The Soviet campaign for proposals envisaging the liquidation of foreign military bases was clearly designed to embarrass the United States and activate sentiment against American bases in areas where these are located, rather than to bring about American agreement to a general withdrawal. The USSR utilized aircraft accidents involving loss of U.S. nuclear weapons over Spanish waters and on the territory of Greenland to promote a ban on flights beyond national borders of nuclear-armed aircraft. Since the Soviet authorities could hardly have expected the U.S. to agree to an international ban on such flights, the campaign was designed to play upon fears of a nuclear catastrophe in these and other countries, and thus put pressure on the United States to change its policies.

The examples just cited are extreme cases in the sense that they involved proposals of clearly unilateral impact, since the USSR professes to have no foreign bases and apparently does not send nuclear bombers on patrol outside its borders. (Consequently, even if the United States were prepared to abandon such activities, it would have no incentive to tie its hands by negotiating international prohibitions, since there would be no Soviet *quid pro quo*.) Most disarmament proposals are not as obviously weighted in favor of the sponsors: they gain in plausibility if they require "sacrifices" from sponsors as well as opponents. Nevertheless, national policy makers usually make sure that their disarmament proposals advance national security interests; and in a world of hostile powers, this means that such proposals envisage arrangements of greater benefit to sponsors than to opponents.

The political struggle carried on around disarmament proposals involves both professional disarmament negotiators and large numbers of people in various countries. As to the former, the USSR has sought forums organized in such a way that they emphasize the support for Soviet positions. Over the past decade it has insisted on a forum in which the USSR had an equal position with the United States, whether this was in bilateral negotiations or in an organ including an equal

[2] GCD was a favorite theme for Khrushchev between 1959 and 1964. Although diplomatic negotiations never approached any agreement on general disarmament in this period, there were at least more serious discussions than in the period after Khrushchev's ouster. The acceptance by the United States of the goal of "general and complete disarmament" removed some of the Soviet advantage in portraying itself as the sole exponent of a "world without arms," although Soviet propaganda used American rejection of the USSR's plan for GCD as evidence that the American commitment was not serious.

number of Soviet and American allies.[3] In the period 1964–1968, the principal forum for disarmament discussions has continued to be the Eighteen-Nation Disarmament Committee (established in 1961) with five Warsaw Pact and five NATO states, plus six nonaligned.[4] Soviet insistence on parity had very little to do with actual negotiation of agreements, because any significant agreements require the unanimous consent of the interested great powers, and majority votes are meaningless if the minority includes the USSR or the United States. But parity enabled the Soviet Union to improve the public image of the support given to Soviet positions.

The principal exception to Soviet insistence on parity involved discussions before world forums, that is, before all U.N. members. In 1965 the USSR demanded that the U.N. Disarmament Commission (of all member states) be called into session, instead of reconvening the ENDC, as the United States would have preferred.[5] But this exception to parity requirements showed the interest of the USSR in seeking to galvanize world support for its proposals, and had little to do with the achievement of negotiated agreements. At this session of the Disarmament Commission (held in New York, April 26–June 16, 1965), the USSR shifted attention from the question of nonproliferation of nuclear weapons, the principal topic before the ENDC in 1964–1968, to two other proposals. The Soviet authorities calculated that proposals to ban foreign military bases and to prohibit the use of nuclear weapons would gain support from the nonaligned states, which bulk

[3] In 1954–1957 most disarmament negotiations occurred in the U.N. Disarmament Subcommittee, where the USSR dealt with four NATO states: the United States, the United Kingdom, France, and Canada. The parent body, the U.N. Disarmament Commission, had originally been created in 1952, with membership consisting of the permanent and temporary members of the U.N. Security Council, plus Canada. Both the UNDC and the Subcommittee in this make-up became inactive in 1957, because the USSR refused to participate any longer. The Disarmament Commission was enlarged in 1957 to 25 members, but the USSR considered the group of 25 to be weighted against the "socialist countries." In 1958 the U.N. Disarmament Commission was broadened—with Soviet agreement—to include all members of the U.N. It met once in 1959 and three times in 1960, the only meetings between 1957 and 1965 (Documents 1945–1959, I, pp. 337–39; II, pp. 916–17, 1216–17). The USSR first attained parity in 1958–1959, especially when the Ten-Nation Committee on Disarmament was established by the United Nations in 1959. It had been agreed to at the "Big Four" Foreign Ministers' meeting in Geneva (ibid., pp. 1441–43).

[4] Documents 1961, pp. 741–42; Documents 1962, pp. 577–81. The ENDC began to function on March 14, 1962. France has never participated, so only 17 nations have been represented. Of the eight "nonaligned" members, the two Latin American states, Brazil and Mexico, are allied to the U.S. in the Organization of American States.

[5] Documents 1965, pp. 30–31.

so large in the current U.N. membership.[6] Despite its search for world-wide support, the USSR failed to gain endorsement of the UNDC for either of the measures, and accepted a return to the Geneva negotiations of the ENDC.[7]

It should be noted that Soviet authorities do not draw a sharp distinction between "serious disarmament negotiations" and "disarmament propaganda." They do not appear to think of these as alternatives between which they are forced to choose. They advance proposals to which they do not expect immediate agreement, but calculate that a campaign in their behalf will be worthwhile for other reasons. But they also see propaganda campaigns as means of bringing to bear world pressure, including popular pressure in the homelands of their negotiating "partners," upon governments resisting Soviet proposals. On disarmament, as on other international questions, the Soviet leaders consider "open diplomacy" (i.e., exchanges involving public statements of rival positions) as a technique of bringing their opponents around.[8] This kind of "open diplomacy" dates back to the earliest days of the Soviet regime. The techniques have changed over the past half century, but the practice is still considered useful to the Soviet cause. Soviet authorities claim that open diplomacy is the rule in negotiations between "socialist" countries, but say that secret diplomacy still has to be resorted to on occasion in their relations with the "imperialist" powers.[9] In fact, the opposite is nearer the mark. Secrecy pervades the relations within the socialist camp, because the USSR has little interest in bringing popular pressure to bear upon more-or-less friendly allies. In contrast, "open diplomacy" is more useful in relations with "capitalist" states, because the USSR has every interest in counterposing people to government in these countries.

[6] The drafts of the two Soviet resolutions are in *ibid.*, pp. 206–8.

[7] *Ibid.*, pp. 260–62.

[8] See A. Kovalev, "Sovetskaia diplomatiia—instrument borby za uprochenie mira," *Kommunist*, No. 18 (December, 1964), 92–101. An unpublished study by the present author on the treatment in Soviet historical accounts of postwar negotiations that led to some kind of agreements (such as the ending of the Berlin blockade, the Korean truce, the Austrian State Treaty) showed that Soviet authors placed major emphasis on the external pressures forcing the "imperialists" to concessions. They gave less stress to Soviet skill in negotiations *per se*, although Communist "patience" and willingness to introduce compromise proposals were said to have contributed to the resolution of differences.

[9] Kovalev claims that the Soviet method of open diplomacy and of the use of propaganda forced opponents to imitate Soviet practice. According to him, the sphere of secret diplomacy is being generally reduced, and in Soviet practice is now limited primarily to relations with the "imperialist" states.

DISCUSSIONS ON GENERAL DISARMAMENT
PROPOSALS

While it would be an exaggeration to say that there were ever serious negotiations of the disparate Soviet and American plans for general
and complete disarmament, discussions of GCD before disarmament
forums and elsewhere have become more rare and desultory since
1964 than they had been in the period of Khrushchev's hegemony.
Since Khrushchev's departure, nothing basically new has been introduced into either the American or Soviet GCD plans. The occasional
discussions of GCD in the ENDC have centered on the U.S. plan of 1962,
only slightly amended later, and on the Soviet plan of 1959, modified
by 1962–1963 amendments.[10] The latter provided for retention by
the U.S. and USSR of a "nuclear umbrella" (equal numbers of ICBMs)
until the end of the disarmament process. Neither the revised Soviet
plan nor the latest version of the American proposal for GCD has been
acceptable to the other side as a "basis for negotiation," and in 1964–
1968 the two principally interested powers did not move a step nearer
agreement.

In view of this situation, there seems to be little need to discuss
here the contrasting features of the Soviet and American GCD proposals. Although each uses the words, "general and complete disarmament," to describe its goal, the terminally disarmed world looks very
different in the two plans.[11] There are major differences, also, in the
steps proposed for movement to the final stages of disarmament. One
of these differences is so basic that it deserves to be singled out, for
it reflects a difference between Soviet and American disarmament approaches affecting many partial measures as well as GCD. Contrary to
what might be thought, this crucial question is not that of control and
inspection. (No doubt differences on verification needs and procedures
might block an agreement for GCD even if the plans were otherwise
reconcilable. Such apprehensions, however, are founded more on the
history of Soviet resistance to inspection than on the control clauses in
the USSR's GCD proposal.)

The crucial difference in the GCD proposals concerns the military

[10] For the latest revised version of the USSR draft treaty on GCD, dated April 28,
1965, see *Documents 1965*, pp. 77–102. The latest U.S. version of its plan is in
ibid., pp. 111–40.

[11] The American plan envisages, terminally, the creation of an international
peacekeeping force of considerable military potential, possibly equipped with
nuclear weapons. The Soviet GCD plan envisages nothing comparable to this military force. Terminally, under this plan, the "International Disarmament Organization" would have control of the "police (militia)" forces of the various states.

relations of the major powers in the course of disarmament. The American plan calls for the progressive reduction by equal percentage cuts of Soviet and American nuclear and conventional armaments and vehicles; the Soviet plan specifies reduction to zero, or to a fixed number of Soviet and American armaments and vehicles, beginning with nuclear weapons systems. The American plan is thus based on the idea of *perpetuating the force ratios* of the pre-GCD period as disarmament progresses; the Soviet plan, on the idea of *changing force ratios* to equality (usually zero) in the step-by-step dismantling of nuclear and then other armaments and vehicles. Although this general subject is one to which we must return, it can be said here that this difference of approach has been more important than differences on control in preventing any progress on general disarmament.

Moscow's interest in "general and complete disarmament," even as a propaganda theme, has noticeably lessened since 1964. GCD is now mentioned only in passing by Soviet leaders in their speeches. In the report of the Central Committee to the XXIII Communist Party Congress, General Secretary Brezhnev, on March 29, 1966, referred once to "general and complete disarmament" as a distant objective, but did not list it among the more immediate foreign policy goals for which the Party would strive.[12] At the ceremony in Moscow on November 3, 1967, celebrating the 50th anniversary of Soviet power, Brezhnev reiterated the USSR's commitment to "general and complete disarmament" as a goal.[13] Since October, 1964, however, neither Brezhnev nor any other Soviet leader has focused major attention on the Soviet plan for GCD, or fought hard to bring about international negotiations on general disarmament plans. Appeals for general disarmament continue to figure in the addresses of Soviet representatives to the U.N. General Assembly and other broadly representative gatherings. The major Soviet drive in such meetings, however, has been focused on various partial measures rather than general disarmament. Even at the 1965 U.N. Disarmament Commission session in New York, the first since 1960, the USSR made no attempt to push its GCD plan, although the presence of representatives from all U.N. states provided a tempting occasion.

This decline in attention to far-reaching disarmament plans can be explained by several developments, but most of all by the war in Vietnam. The commitment of large American forces in South Vietnam,

[12] *The 23rd Congress of the* CPSU, pp. 54–57.
[13] *Pravda*, November 4, 1967. GCD as a goal of Soviet policy appeared in each set of May Day and November 7 slogans of recent years until the fall of 1967. It did not appear in either the slogans for November 7, 1967 (*ibid.*, October 15, 1967) or for May Day, 1968 (*ibid.*, April 17, 1968). However, the total number of slogans was drastically cut for these latter occasions.

and the American bombing of North Vietnam, would have made it inexpedient for any Soviet regime to talk a great deal about general and complete disarmament. The Chinese, for one thing, could have exploited Soviet talk and maneuvers regarding disarmament as a betrayal of the revolutionary need to fight the "imperialists" with guns in hand. Apart from Peking, however, the Soviet leaders themselves saw American behavior in Vietnam as indicative of a growing tendency of the U.S. to throw its military power into anti-Communist struggles.[14] Talk in sober terms began to be heard about the possibility of a new war involving the Soviet Union.[15] The leaders of the USSR were prepared, it is true, to conclude new "arms control" agreements with the United States even after February, 1965, when routine American bombing of North Vietnam started. But for the Soviet leaders to promote general and complete disarmament in the face of these daily attacks was something else again. Speeches glorifying disarmament possibilities did not create the mood music that the Kremlin leaders thought appropriate.

In addition to the Vietnam events, the growth of Chinese strategic power and Peking's negativism regarding disarmament negotiations probably helped cool Soviet interest in GCD.

Furthermore, it seems likely that the current Soviet phlegmatism— or realism—about GCD owes a good deal to the change of leadership in 1964, i.e., both to the character of the new directors and to the very fact of a more collective style of leadership. In a way, GCD was Khrushchev's pet idea. The present leaders have shown, on disarmament as on other matters, a penchant for cautiously explored steps and an aversion to bold initiatives. This orientation is in line with their criticism of the Khrushchev regime for impulsive and "harebrained schemes." In addition, collective decision making tends to give such groups as the professional military more leverage on national policies. In the absence of a single dominant leader, policies emerge from a bargaining process in which the important support groups of the regime seek to protect their competing interests. The process may not result in *immobilisme,* but it hardly encourages the search for radical shifts in power relationships. Radical disarmament measures would substantially alter the economic and political status of various social groups, most of all the military, a group which the

[14] See Brezhnev's report to the XXIII Party Congress, *The 23rd Congress of the* CPSU, pp. 9, 42–57; and his speech to the Leningrad oblast Party conference on February 16, 1968 (*Leningradskaia pravda,* February 16, 1968). Soviet spokesmen frequently refer to American and other "imperialist" attempts to "export counter-revolution."

[15] See Brezhnev's speech to the XV All-Union Komsomol Congress, in *Pravda,* May 18, 1966.

Brezhnev regime has taken pains to conciliate. Such effects would materialize only if disarmament measures were executed, and not merely proposed; but the groups concerned are probably loath to see such proposals seriously promoted and discussed. Even proposals, if pushed strongly enough, have ideological consequences in catering to or disparaging diverse groups of the elite and the general population, in fortifying certain expectations and weakening others.

To the extent that these considerations are valid, even the ending of the war in Vietnam may not lead to a prompt upsurge of official Soviet interest in radical disarmament proposals. Although some constraints on such efforts would be lifted, there are others that have inhibited the post-Khrushchev regime from seriously concentrating on GCD. Moreover, the intervening experience will have colored the leaders' attitude toward GCD. Even if full acknowledgment is made of the instrumental uses of disarmament propaganda as a means of berating opponents and glorifying Soviet devotion to peace, the pre-1964 Soviet focus on GCD reflected Khrushchev's optimism about the course of history, a quality now much less evident. In his peculiar way, Khrushchev was an idealist, whereas the present leaders accept the reality of a more complex world, take fewer chances, and are not as sure that all change will redound to their advantage.

AGREEMENTS ON PARTIAL MEASURES OF ARMS CONTROL

Unlike negotiations regarding general disarmament, those on partial measures of arms control have registered some successes. These softened the image of disarmament negotiations as an activity characterized by endless talk that never produced results. Four agreements involving some limitations on military activities have been concluded in the past decade, two in the Khrushchev era and two under his successors. The first of these was the Antarctic Treaty concluded in 1959 by 12 states, including the USSR and the United States.[16] Although the treaty was significant in many ways, it is perhaps the least important of the four agreements from the standpoint of arms control. The treaty prohibited all military activity in Antarctica, non-nuclear as well as nuclear, and banned all nuclear explosions, even for peaceful purposes. The right of free "unilateral" inspection by any signatory state of any Antarctic installation was established as the means of checking on compliance with the treaty. In January, 1964, and again in February–March, 1967, the United States utilized its inspection rights under the agreement and published reports indicating that it

[16] Text in *Documents 1945–1959*, II, pp. 1550–56.

found no violations of the arms control or other provisions of the treaty.[17] Since no problem relating to Antarctica or the treaty reappeared in disarmament discussions, the subject does not enter into the scope of the present work on the period since 1964.

The other three subjects giving rise to agreements have continued to be under negotiation in the post-Khrushchev period. These include the banning of nuclear weapons tests, restrictions on the use of outer space for military purposes, and prohibition of the dissemination of nuclear weapons. On both nuclear weapons tests and outer space, important steps were taken in Khrushchev's time; and the 1963 partial test-ban treaty in particular must be regarded as the most significant agreement yet recorded in either disarmament negotiations or postwar political relations between the USSR and the United States. Because nuclear weapons testing has remained on the agenda of arms control discussions since 1964, the subject is treated in more detail in the next chapter. In that chapter consideration is also given to outer space and nonproliferation, the subject of the two arms control treaties concluded in the period since 1964. An agreement restricting certain military uses of outer space was reached between the Soviet and American authorities in 1963, but this agreement was transcended by a treaty on the subject negotiated in 1966 and signed in January, 1967.

Nonproliferation of nuclear weapons has been the central subject of disarmament negotiations in 1964–1968, with both Soviet and American attention directed, with few deviations, toward achievement of some kind of agreement.[18] This parallelism of attention to the same disarmament topic was not always evident in the past, and it contributed to the final resolution of differences. Even so, the negotiations were long and difficult, and it seemed for a long period that Soviet objections to the proposed NATO multilateral force (MLF) would block any agreement. After abandonment of the project, however, the United States and the USSR were able to find common language for all but one section of a draft treaty, made public in August, 1967. They finally agreed on a

[17] For the report of the U.S. inspection in January, 1964, see *Documents 1964*, pp. 195–203. For details of the most recent inspection—February–March, 1967— see *Documents 1967*, pp. 283–90. The American utilization in 1964 of the formal inspection rights under the 1959 treaty was discussed critically in *SSSR, SShA i razoruzhenie*, where the editor (I. S. Glagolev) wrote that the inspection trip "was superfluous; foreign scientists live for long periods at the Antarctic stations of various states; all of the work has an open character, and no supplementary inspection is necessary." (p. 145).

[18] A survey of Soviet official documents and public statements in 1964–1967 showed that nonproliferation was given much more attention than any other disarmament measure, and was described as the most urgent measure. See Alan C. Lopez, "Priorities in Soviet Policy on Arms Control and Disarmament, 1964–1967," an unpublished paper prepared for this study.

complete draft—including the disputed inspection clause—in January, 1968. This was later supplemented by a U.S.-U.K.-USSR agreement (not included in the treaty) on a "security guarantee" to non-nuclear weapons states.

These four agreements, the Antarctic Treaty of 1959, the partial test-ban treaty of 1963, the outer-space treaty of 1967, and the 1968 treaty prohibiting proliferation of nuclear weapons, are considered here as the successful achievements in arms control. The list of Soviet-American arms control agreements could be expanded if agreements of only transitory significance were to be included, such as the parallel but unilateral moratoriums on nuclear weapons tests in 1958–1959,[19] and the mutually agreed announcement in April, 1964, of unilateral reductions in the production of fissionable materials for weapons.[20] It could be further extended if agreements were included which imposed no limitations on national policies, such as the agreement in 1963 to establish a "hot-line" between Moscow and Washington,[21] and the 1961 agreement on basic principles of "general and complete disarmament," endorsed by the U.N. General Assembly on December 20, 1961.[22] In contrast to these agreements, which are excluded from subsequent discussion of arms control achievements, the four treaties considered here as successfully negotiated measures of arms control placed certain limitations of indefinite duration on the military policies of the signatory states.

THE PRINCIPLES OF SUCCESS
IN ARMS CONTROL NEGOTIATIONS

The agreements achieved in four areas of arms control provide a guide to the kind of measures that may have the best prospects in the future; and this is because the four treaties have certain common characteristics. Although they are discussed in more detail in the succeeding chapter, some anticipatory conclusions can be drawn here as to the characteristics that made them acceptable to the rival and often hostile powers. It is these characteristics that distinguish the successfully negotiated partial measures of arms control from both the ambitious plans for general disarmament, already mentioned, and from a number of other proposed partial measures, most of which contemplated reductions of armaments.

[19] *Documents 1945–1959*, II, pp. 978–80, 1142–43, 1200–1, 1221, 1439–41, 1590–91.
[20] Texts of announcements in *Documents 1964*, pp. 4, 165–71.
[21] *Documents 1963*, pp. 236–38.
[22] *Documents 1961*, pp. 741–42.

*All four agreements involve matters secondary to the "big issues"
of the threat of nuclear war and of a spiraling arms race.* The single
regional agreement, on Antarctica, and the quasi-regional outer-space
treaty concern areas with only transient human habitation and of
uncertain military value for the stationing of weapons or military
personnel. The partial test-ban treaty and the nonproliferation treaty
deal with advanced weapons on a more general basis, but impose no
limits on the great powers' activities in producing, deploying, and
preparing for the use of nuclear weapons. Three of the four treaties
prohibit activities in which the powers have never engaged and in
which they might never have engaged, regardless of whether or not a
formal ban existed. In making such agreements, the Soviet Union and
the U.S. accepted few "sacrifices" in terms of stopping activities to
which they had grown accustomed (with the exception of the search
for improved nuclear weapons technology, restricted or made more
expensive by the test ban). A different way of putting the last point
is to note that *these agreements involved, for the most part, renunciation of activities in which neither of the great powers had important
vested interests.*

Another characteristic of the agreements is that they involve no
system of international inspection intruding on the territory of the
USSR or of the other nuclear powers. Observance of the partial test-
ban treaty and the outer-space treaty was to be controlled by *national*
inspection systems. The Antarctic Treaty involved freedom of national inspection by any party to the treaty regarding the activities of
any other party. This satisfied the United States because it established
inspection as a necessary ingredient of an "arms control" arrangement
in which other means of verification were insufficient. It was acceptable to the USSR because the area was far from Soviet territory and
from Soviet military installations, and it offered the USSR an opportunity to display its supposed willingness to support inspection of
"disarmament" (in this case, nonarmament), as against inspection of
"armaments." The nonproliferation treaty provided for an international inspection system, but this did not extend to the states possessing nuclear weapons.

Finally, and most important, *the four agreements permitted the
continuation, almost undisturbed, of the strategic military programs
of the two major military rivals, the U.S. and the USSR.* The accords
were presumably acceptable to the USSR because they did not freeze
militarily or sanctify legally the strategic superiority of the United
States. The same agreements were acceptable to the United States
because they did not cut into the American superiority in strategic
nuclear weapons and delivery systems. In fact, only one of the four

agreements, the partial test-ban treaty, had significant effects on activities-in-being. The 1963 treaty did place certain barriers before technological advances in the design of nuclear weapons. But the technological plateau was set at the high level of 1963, representing a decade of advances after thermonuclear weapons came into being, and allowing further advances through underground testing.

As long as these Soviet-American discrepancies in military capabilities and military programs exist, they will continue to impede any significant agreements for arms stabilization or arms reductions.[23] It may be, of course, that the evolution of Soviet and American military capabilities—or changes in their viewpoints on their relations of military power—will in time alter their attitudes on disarmament measures affecting the size and strength of their military establishments. Thus, these "lessons from the past" need not be interpreted as iron laws to which future agreements must conform. The concentration in the four achieved treaties on relatively peripheral and potentially troublesome problems helps explain why they were negotiable; it does not preclude a movement toward more central and contentious issues. The fact that none of the four agreements provided for an international inspection system functioning on great-power territory facilitated USSR acceptance; this circumstance does not mean that agreements involving international inspection on Soviet soil (and elsewhere) cannot be concluded at some future point. None of the four treaties involved arms reductions, and the USSR has been most adamant against intrusion of foreign inspectors on its soil under agree-

---

[23] The 1961 "Agreed Principles for Disarmament Negotiations" offer little evidence that the two sides agree on the relation between disarmament measures and ratios of military force. The relevant principle, the fifth, is susceptible to different interpretations. It states: "All measures for general and complete disarmament should be so balanced as to ensure [1] that at no stage of the realization of the treaty should any state or group of states be able to obtain a military advantage, and [2] that security should be equally provided to all." The principle relates to GCD, but it has often been cited as a standard for separate partial arms control measures as well. American officials interpret the principle to mean that any arms control measure should not upset the ratio of military forces in existence, the correlation of forces, be it one of parity or of superiority-inferiority. Soviet spokesmen interpret the principle to mean that a disarmament measure should result in the absence of military advantage, or superiority, for any state, even if a superior-inferior relation existed prior to the disarmament measures. The U.S. proposals for equal percentage cuts of various weapons or delivery vehicles possessed in unequal quantities, or for the "freezing" of unequal existing forces, illustrate the American understanding of the principle. Proposals from the USSR for reductions of unequal quantities of bombers to zero levels, or (in its GCD plan) for elimination of all strategic delivery vehicles except for small and equal numbers of missiles, illustrate the Soviet interpretation. The "Joint Statement of Agreed Principles" was dated September 20, 1961, and is in *ibid.*, pp. 439–42.

ments devoid of any arms reduction features. Finally, even the great concern of the U.S. and the USSR about the impact of arms control and arms reduction measures on their military capabilities toward each other need not prevent future arms limitation agreements reducing levels of competition and confrontation in both conventional and nuclear forces.

8

ADVANCES IN NUCLEAR ARMS CONTROL

Of the four subjects on which arms control agreements between the USSR and the United States have been achieved, all except Antarctica continued to be under negotiation in the period since 1964. Post-Khrushchev developments regarding negotiations on nuclear weapons testing, military use of outer space, and proliferation of nuclear weapons are the topic of this chapter. To simplify the presentation, however, the earlier (1963) agreements to ban all except underground nuclear weapons tests and to ban the stationing of nuclear weapons in orbit are noted in connection with the post-1964 developments in these fields. Nuclear weapons testing continued on the agenda in 1964–1968, but attempts failed to go beyond the epochal treaty of 1963 ruling out for signatories tests in three environments. In the second area, however, that of outer space, the treaty signed in 1967 extended the scope of the more informal agreement reached in 1963. The third area on which progress has been made is that of nonproliferation of nuclear weapons, the only new arms control measure on which the United States and the USSR have been able to agree in the post-Khrushchev period.

NUCLEAR WEAPONS TEST BAN

The agreement in July, 1963, on a three-environment ban (in the atmosphere, under water, and in outer space) on tests of nuclear weapons* was not only the first major agreement in the arms control field but probably outranks in importance all other arms control achievements.[1] First, it was the only agreement that required the

---

* To be precise, the treaty banned all nuclear explosions—not merely weapons tests—in the three environments, and also banned underground tests or explosions that caused radioactive debris to pass outside national territory.

[1] Text in *Documents 1963*, pp. 291–93. The long history of negotiations on cessation of nuclear weapons testing is discussed by Bernhard G. Bechhoefer, *Postwar Negotiations for Arms Control* (Washington, D.C.: Brookings Institution, 1961). See also, U.S. Senate, Committee on Foreign Relations, Hearings on Nuclear Test-

nuclear powers to reduce some form of on-going military activities, namely, the free testing of weapons in all environments. Second, the treaty was almost equivalent to a nonproliferation treaty for the non-nuclear states signing the agreement. Renunciation of all except underground tests foreclosed for them any practical possibility of developing their own nuclear arsenals, and the nuclear powers showed little inclination to share their weapons wealth. Signature of the treaty by France and the CPR would have meant a similar renunciation of the active programs of those nations to develop atomic and thermonuclear weapons. For this reason, these two powers refused to sign the treaty, as did certain other countries—for motivations that were largely political.

The test ban involved no reductions in armaments; it was rather a partial "freeze" of technology. Usually the USSR has objected to freezes of this kind, but the long advocacy by Soviet authorities of a comprehensive atomic weapons test ban showed that they did not think that a test cessation would place them at a disadvantage in the production of advanced nuclear devices.[2] Initially, they did appear to regard a *partial* ban as disadvantageous to the Soviet Union, apparently because of the greater U.S. experience in underground testing, and the greater financial ability of the U.S. to afford testing in a costly medium. (The USSR may also have resisted the exemption for underground testing because the Soviet leadership thought—perhaps rightly, as it turned out—that acceptance of a three-environment ban would leave them with no leverage to exert in favor of a comprehensive ban.) Consequently, before an agreement could be concluded in 1963,[3] the Soviet leaders had to reverse their earlier rejection of a test ban excluding underground tests.

The conclusion of the three-environment test-ban treaty proved to be no stimulation to achievement of a comprehensive test ban. Both the Soviet Union and the United States stepped up underground

---

Ban Treaty, 88th Cong., 1st sess. August 12–27, 1963 (Washington, D.C.: Government Printing Office, 1963); and V. A. Zorin, ed., *Bor'ba Sovetskogo Soiuza za razoruzhenie 1946–1960 gg.* (Moscow: IMO, 1961).

[2] The USSR was the first of the nuclear powers to accept, in 1955, the idea of a test ban separate from other disarmament measures. India had proposed this in 1954. *Documents 1945–1959*, I, pp. 408–13, 571. See also, *SSSR, SShA i razoruzhenie,* p. 68.

[3] See the letter of Premier Khrushchev of April 23, 1959, rejecting President Eisenhower's proposal of April 13, 1959. Khrushchev called it a "dishonest deal." *Documents 1945–1959*, II, pp. 1392–93, 1396–98. President Kennedy in 1961 again proposed a ban on tests in the atmosphere; and in 1962 the United States (with the United Kingdom) presented a draft treaty to ban tests in the three environments. *Documents 1961*, p. 351, and *Documents 1962*, II, pp. 804–7. These proposals were also rejected by the USSR.

testing of nuclear devices. In the following years, even the less experienced USSR mounted a substantial program, rivaling that of the United States. In October, 1966, the Soviet Union set off at Novaia Zemlia what was described as the largest underground nuclear explosion ever carried out.[4]

On the detection side, American scientists and technicians made progress in developing scientific means to detect and identify underground tests at a considerable distance, and American negotiators suggested that the advance of knowledge would permit monitoring of an underground test ban with a less ambitious international inspection arrangement than had been considered possible prior to 1963.[5]

The U.S. insisted, however, that some international inspection was still necessary. American firmness on inspection was met by an equally dogged Soviet rejection of any proposal that would entail other than national means of verification. The USSR refused to engage in any technical discussions of the adequacy of the improved technical means of distinguishing between natural and artificially produced earth tremors.[6] The USSR and most other Communist states even abstained from voting on a U.N. General Assembly resolution of 1965 urging cessation of all nuclear weapons tests and increased efforts to reach a complete test ban, because the resolution urged the ENDC to continue "work . . . on arrangements to ban effectively all nuclear weapons tests in all environments." The Soviet representative regarded this phrasing as favorable to U.S. claims that inspection was necessary to police a full test ban.[7]

Although the USSR did not push hard to bring about a comprehensive test ban, it responded favorably to a UAR proposal of August 17, 1965, reminiscent of earlier proposals by the Soviet Union and other states. The suggestion to combine a formal treaty ban on large underground nuclear weapons tests (above a magnitude of 4.75 on

---

[4] *The New York Times,* October 28, 1966.

[5] See the statement by ACDA Director William C. Foster to the ENDC on September 2, 1965, in *Documents 1965,* pp. 384–90; and of ACDA Deputy Director Adrian Fisher on April 4, 1966, in *Documents 1966,* pp. 190–99.

[6] For example, at the ENDC on August 25, 1966. *Ibid.,* p. 601.

[7] This was the resolution passed on December 3, 1965. (*Documents 1965,* pp. 623–24.) The Fifth Annual ACDA Report of January 19, 1966 (*Ibid.,* p. 645), attributes the Soviet abstention to a reference in the resolution to "the improved possibilities for international cooperation in the field of seismic detection." In his comments of November 26 on the resolution, Ambassador Tsarapkin did not refer to this clause, however, but alluded to the passage implying the need for "some new type of arrangements." (*Ibid.,* p. 55.) The USSR has not been averse to steps taken, on the urging of Sweden, toward formation of a voluntary "detection club" of nonnuclear states to exchange seismic data relating to possible underground tests. (*Ibid.,* pp. 390–93 and *Documents 1966,* p. 438.) The United States also supports this effort.

the Richter scale) with a moratorium on all other tests took account of the fact that the difficulty of discriminating between atomic and natural seismic disturbances varies inversely with the size of the disturbance.[8] (Even in highly seismic areas, few large seismic shocks occur, and natural shocks produce wave patterns different from those produced by atomic blasts.)

The Egyptian proposal was rejected by the United States, which considered that national means of verification provided inadequate assurances that the agreement would be observed. American representatives also argued that such a moratorium would almost certainly remove all incentives for negotiating a comprehensive treaty extending the same kind of legal prohibition to underground as to other tests. Finally, American spokesmen argued against a moratorium on the ground that the Soviet Union had broken such a moratorium in September, 1961, when it resumed atmospheric testing after a three-year period of absention.[9]

In an effort to find a way out of the impasse between the United States and the Soviet Union on the need for on-site inspections, pro-

[8] Documents 1965, pp. 345, 395–97.

[9] Ibid., pp. 406–8. No atomic weapons tests were known to have been conducted by the USSR or by the United States from 1958 to 1961. A tacit suspension was thus in effect. The only "formal" moratoriums, however, had been a series of unilateral but reciprocal declarations of Premier Khrushchev and President Eisenhower in 1958–1959. President Eisenhower, on December 29, 1959, released the United States from its self-imposed moratorium, saying that "we consider ourselves free to resume nuclear weapons testing." He added, however, that the U.S. would give advance notice before resuming tests. (Documents 1945–1959, II, pp. 1590–91.) On several occasions subsequent to this announcement, Premier Khrushchev stated that the USSR would not be the first to begin tests again, a promise that was not recalled when the USSR broke the de facto moratorium and, almost without warning, resumed testing in the fall of 1961. Thus, on January 14, 1960, after the Eisenhower declaration of December, Khrushchev said that "the Soviet government . . . will continue to abide by its pledge not to renew experimental nuclear explosions . . . if the Western powers do not start testing atomic and hydrogen weapons." (Documents 1960, pp. 5–6.) This "pledge" referred to a Soviet statement on August 29, 1959, that "the Council of Ministers of the USSR has resolved: not to resume nuclear tests in the Soviet Union if the Western powers do not resume the testing of atomic and hydrogen weapons. Only in case of resumption by them of nuclear weapons tests will the Soviet Union be free from this pledge." (Documents 1945–1959, II, pp. 1440–41.)

The U.S. argument implying that there existed in 1961 an agreed moratorium comparable to that proposed in the UAR plan, and that the USSR had broken such an agreement, seems singularly unpersuasive. Insofar as reciprocal obligations to refrain from testing existed, they were extinguished in 1959, and all that the USSR broke in 1961 was its earlier promises not to be the first to resume testing. Even in the period of the reciprocal moratoriums in 1958–1959, the informality of the exchanges was such that they added up to a kind of international agreement very different from that implied in the UAR proposal.

posals have been advanced for a challenge-and-response system of checking adherence to a comprehensive test-ban treaty. Under this procedure, seismic or other data suggesting the occurrence of a suspicious event would be brought to the attention of the government of the country involved. If successive exchanges of data did not remove doubts about the nature of the event, the troubled adversary would ask, or be invited, to make an on-site inspection. If still not satisfied, the questioning government would have to decide whether or not the situation called for the final step of withdrawal from the treaty. This would be subject, presumably, to requirements similar to those of the 1963 treaty. The latter requires three months' advance notice and a decision by the withdrawing state "that extraordinary events, related to the subject matter of this treaty, have jeopardized the supreme interests" of the country.

The Swedish representatives were the best-known proponents of the plan, which Mrs. Myrdal discussed in considerable detail at the ENDC on March 10, 1966. She pointedly recalled that, four years earlier, the Soviet representatives had endorsed a somewhat similar plan submitted by representatives of the eight nonaligned countries represented on the ENDC.[10] But on August 25, Soviet representative Roshchin flatly rejected the suggestion, saying that it was "absolutely unacceptable to the Soviet Union, as it is aimed at pushing through in a disguised form the idea of international inspection." [11]

The United States was also cool to the proposal, on the grounds that such challenges and responses would be more likely to make a test-ban treaty into a source of dissension than into a force for good relations.[12] But the American rejection was not nearly as categoric as that of the Soviet Union—a curious change from the 1962 pattern.[13] Then the American representatives insisted that on site inspections must be "obligatory," and the Soviet representative endorsed the formula of "on-site inspection by invitation." [14] The reversal of the

[10] *Documents 1966,* pp. 130–39.

[11] *Ibid.,* p. 601.

[12] See the discussion by ACDA Deputy Director Fisher on April 4, 1966, in *ibid.,* pp. 194–99.

[13] American representatives showed some interest in a trial of the challenge method for a limited period, during which there would be a moratorium on underground tests. This had been discussed at the Scarborough (Ontario) meeting in June, 1966, of the International Assembly on Nuclear Weapons. (*Ibid.,* pp. 370–76.) For later comments in Washington and Geneva by ACDA Deputy Director Fisher, who attended the Scarborough meeting, see *ibid.,* pp. 381–85, 513–15.

[14] See *Documents 1962,* I, pp. 334–36 for the memorandum of the eight "nonaligned" nations; II, pp. 773–76, for U.S. Representative Arthur H. Dean's statement; and II, pp. 776–88 for the statement of Soviet representative V. V. Kuznetsov.

Soviet position on this matter testifies to the general hardening in the Soviet attitude since the 1963 test-ban treaty, especially toward foreign inspection.

Unlike most of the other proposals touching on nuclear matters, a comprehensive test ban is favored in principle by both the United States and the USSR. Even so, the two have taken opposed stands on the sticky question of inspection. The confinement of U.S. and USSR tests to the underground environment has itself diminished popular pressure for a comprehensive test ban—the "danger" of tests was more dramatically perceived by the world in the poisonous clouds of radioactive debris loosed into the atmosphere than in any refinement of nuclear weapons destined for stockpiles. Furthermore, there are pressures in the United States and possibly also in the USSR for the resumption of atmospheric tests.[15] These may become stronger if tests above ground become necessary to perfect ABM systems, whose deployment has been programmed in both countries.

Although they have excited little public attention, minor violations of the test-ban treaty have occurred and have given rise to diplomatic exchanges. In both the United States and the USSR, a number of underground tests have vented, presumably by accident, releasing radioactive debris into the atmosphere. It appears, however, that only with the Soviet venting did the debris pass beyond national frontiers, in violation of the standard set forth in the treaty.[16] Venting is likely to recur as both states strive to carry out large-magnitude underground tests, tests that prior to 1963 would have been performed in the atmosphere.

It scarcely needs to be pointed out that these "violations" of the 1963 treaty do not present the kind of problem that might be involved in policing a comprehensive ban. Under the latter, the very act of testing would be illegal, and hence evidence suggesting a violation would directly raise the question of the violator's intentions regarding continuation of the agreement. As against this yes-or-no situation, the apparent violations of the 1963 treaty have concerned permissible underground tests. Venting results from difficulties encountered in engineering perfectly legal tests so that they fall within the limits that the

---

[15] Although the "American Security Council," with its large representation from the "military-industrial complex," has favored resumption of tests, support for this has been sparse even among Congressmen normally most favorable to a military build-up. Presumably this is because the AEC has indicated that the restriction of testing underground has not proved as detrimental to ABM and other weapons developments as had been anticipated. See the speech of Senator Henry M. Jackson of November 30, 1967. There has not been any public demand in the USSR for resumption of tests, but the voicing of such a demand would be most unusual.

[16] The only prolonged diplomatic exchanges on possible violation of the treaty occurred in connection with venting from the Soviet test of January 15, 1965 (*Documents 1965*, pp. 4–5, 9–10).

given structure can contain underground. In fact, the 1963 treaty does not establish any precise standard for measuring the amount of radioactivity that, if discovered outside national borders, would be sufficient to constitute a violation.[17]

OUTER-SPACE TREATY

The outer-space treaty, negotiated in 1966 and signed in January, 1967, was obviously of less interest to Soviet leaders than many other measures in the field of arms control and disarmament; it has never been extensively exploited for propaganda purposes. The treaty extended a Soviet-American space agreement of 1963, embodied in two U.N. General Assembly resolutions.[18] The first of these, passed on October 17, 1963, was of most importance in regard to arms control, because it called upon all states to refrain from orbiting weapons of mass destruction. The 1963 accord had become possible when the USSR dropped its earlier insistence on banning all military activity in space, and the United States abandoned its original demand for inspection of space launches.[19] Neither the 1963 resolution nor the 1967 treaty outlawed the orbiting of reconnaissance vehicles ("spy satellites"), the orbiting of communications satellites, or various other actual and potential uses of outer space for military purposes. The treaty went beyond the 1963 agreement, however, in several respects. Most significant for arms control was the additional prohibition on military installations of any kind on other planets (i.e., military installations of earthly powers; the other planets may have their own!). The treaty also had important elements outside the field of arms control.

[17] The treaty prohibits, in Article I, nuclear explosions in the atmosphere beyond its limits, including outer space, as well as under water or "in any other environment if such explosion causes radioactive debris to be present outside the territorial limits of the State under whose jurisdiction or control such explosion is conducted." The United States Atomic Energy Commission, in announcing the venting from the Soviet test of January 15, 1965, said that "the amounts of radioactivity measured to date will not produce measurable exposures to persons."

[18] *Documents 1963*, pp. 523, 535–38, 644–46. The United States preferred to put the accord on orbiting weapons in the form of a U.N. resolution accompanied by separate U.S. and USSR declarations rather than in treaty form, which would have required Senate approval. See the comments in *SSSR, SShA i razoruzhenie*, pp. 144–45. For a Soviet discussion, see I. I. Cheprov, "Dogovor o kosmose: pobeda sovetskoi diplomatii," *Sovetskoe gosudarstvo i pravo*, No. 4 (1967), 48–56.

[19] Early exchanges regarding outer space are represented in *Documents 1945–1959*, II, pp. 901–2, a U.S. statement regarding inspection; *Documents 1962*, I, p. 193, a U.S. statement on advance notification regarding space launches; II, p. 872, a Soviet statement regarding a ban on use of satellites for intelligence purposes; II, pp. 1121–22, a U.S. statement on the absence of "workable dividing-line between military and nonmilitary uses of space"; and II, pp. 1178–79, another U.S. statement regarding principles governing the use of outer space.

Thus, it ruled against claims of national (earthly) sovereignty over other planets, and it included provisions regarding astronauts and space vehicles landing on the territory of other states.[20]

From the standpoint of arms control, the 1967 treaty represented an advance over the 1963 agreement primarily in the more binding character of the inhibitions placed on orbiting of nuclear weapons and other instruments of mass destruction.[21] But the 1963 and 1967 agreements prohibited little and permitted much in the military utilization of outer space. These agreements were acceptable to the Soviet Union and the United States because neither had decided on the deployment of the widely discussed terror weapon—armed satellites constantly orbiting the earth and ready to launch nuclear weapons at any moment. The Soviet Union has, however, developed weapons that use the orbital trajectory of space satellites rather than the ballistic trajectory of ICBMs and their shorter-range relatives. Soviet civilian and military leaders have referred to orbital rockets in the armory of the USSR, and models of these have been displayed in military parades.[22] And after a series of Soviet re-entry tests of space satellites in 1966–1967,[23] Secretary McNamara on November 3, 1967, announced that the USSR had developed a new space-oriented weapons system.

[20] A further "Agreement on the Rescue of Astronauts, the Return of Astronauts, and the Return of Objects Launched Into Outer Space" was negotiated by the United States, the USSR, and other powers, in late 1967, and unanimously endorsed by the UNGA on December 19. For the text, see *Department of State Bulletin*, LVIII, No. 1490 (January 15, 1968), 86–87.

[21] The UNGA resolution of October 17, 1963, referred to "expressions . . . of intention" by the U.S. and the USSR not to station in outer space nuclear or other weapons of mass destruction, and "solemnly" called upon all states to avoid such stationing. The treaty *bound* the signatories not to place such weapons in orbit. It should be noted, however, that in one respect the treaty did not go as far as the 1963 agreement. The latter included, in addition to the clause calling upon states not to station weapons of mass destruction in outer space, a supplementary clause asking states "to refrain from causing, encouraging or in any way participating in the conduct of the foregoing activities." (*Documents 1963*, p. 538.) This language was apparently intended to discourage development of, and preparations for use of, orbiting vehicles capable of being loaded with mass-destruction weapons. No similar clause appears in the 1967 treaty.

[22] Premier Khrushchev said on March 16, 1962, that Soviet scientists had developed an ICBM that "they" called "global" because it could "fly around the world in any direction and deal a blow at any set target." (*Documents 1962*, I, p. 152.) Brezhnev and other leaders, including military officials, have frequently referred to Soviet possession of "intercontinental and orbital rockets." See *Pravda*, July 4, 1965, and *The New York Times*, November 19, 1967. As to the 1965 displays, see *Pravda*, November 8, 1965.

[23] See *Review of the Soviet Space Program with Comparative United States Data*, a report prepared for the House Committee on Science and Astronautics, by Charles S. Sheldon, II, 90th Cong., 1st sess. (Washington, D.C.: Government Printing Office, 1967), pp. 41–43, 68, 137.

This is the fractional orbital bombardment system, which employs satellites as vehicles to carry nuclear warheads and release them on targets, normally before completing a single orbit.[24] McNamara minimized the weapons system as inaccurate and inefficient, and said that it could be countered.

Although undoubtedly designed to carry "weapons of mass destruction," these Soviet vehicles do not seem to fall under the treaty ban. They are not intended for continuous circuiting of the globe, and presumably would not be equipped with nuclear warheads until the authorities made a decision to use them against enemy targets. On the day of such a decision, violations of the space treaty would be among the least of mankind's worries. Nevertheless, the Soviet development showed that the outer-space treaty, as in fact its precise wording suggests, by no means guarantees the peaceful use of outer space but merely restricts certain specific military uses.

NONPROLIFERATION OF NUCLEAR WEAPONS

From the first mastery of atomic weapons technology in 1945, the atomic powers have been concerned over the development of nuclear weapons by additional countries. As the first possessor, the United States sought to head off Soviet development after 1945. Probably the U.S. would not have succeeded even if it had offered a proposition more attractive to the USSR than the Baruch plan.[25] In any case, the USSR pursued its own program and successfully exploded an atomic device in 1949. This was followed in 1953 by the first Soviet test of a thermonuclear device. In roughly the same period (1952–1954), the United States made its first tests of thermonuclear devices. The United Kingdom successfully tested an atomic device in 1952, and a thermonuclear device in 1957. Despite continued efforts to halt development, the list of nuclear weapons states lengthened as France exploded an atomic device in 1960 and Communist China did the same in 1964.

Although unrest over proliferation was especially strong in possessor countries, anxious to preserve their special position, similar anxi-

---

[24] *The New York Times*, November 4, 1967. Apparently the only specific Soviet reference to McNamara's announcement was in a comment by Alexander Boiko in the English-language *Moscow News*, No. 46 (November 25–December 2), 1967. Boiko denounced speculation on Soviet use of space in violation of the space treaty as "fabrication."

[25] The Baruch plan, in brief, envisaged the creation of a supra-national authority that would have exclusive control of all atomic energy facilities everywhere, with unlimited rights of inspection, and with an enforcement authority unrestricted by any veto. The United States promised to turn over gradually its atomic weapons after an effective system of control began to function. See *Documents 1945–1959*, I, pp. 7–16, 25–42, 44–47.

eties were vivid in other countries as well. The feeling became wide-spread, but not universal, that the dangers of a nuclear war occurring would multiply with the addition of more and more states to the ranks of possessors.

Long before negotiations on a nonproliferation treaty became serious, it was clear to all that such a treaty could not be justified as a barrier to Chinese nuclear ambitions. Certainly this was confirmed by 1963, when the CPR rejected the partial test-ban treaty. The CPR then made plain its intention to develop an arsenal of nuclear weapons and its refusal to sign any agreement hindering its program.[26] The explosion of Communist China's first atomic device in October, 1964, and rapid follow-up tests, showed that China had not only the will but the capability to build a nuclear arsenal.[27]

In fact, Soviet authorities never justified the nonproliferation treaty as a barrier to Chinese ambitions, but have primarily stressed the dangers of West German "access" to nuclear weapons. Throughout the early negotiations on nonproliferation—before and after Khrushchev's ouster—the most important issue dividing the USSR and the U.S. related to the proposed creation by a group of NATO countries of a multilateral nuclear force (MLF), envisaged as a sea-borne strategic force equipped with nuclear weapons. Because the United States was to participate in the MLF as the principal supplier of nuclear wherewithal, its assent was necessary before the weapons could be used. The Federal Republic of Germany was the most important non-nuclear power involved in the planning of the force; and, supported by the United States, which awakened and guided its interest, West Germany became the most ardent champion of the MLF.

In its earlier treaty drafts, the U.S. proposed wording that would have legitimized the MLF, insisting that the projected arrangement did not constitute proliferation, since the weapons involved would not

---

[26] A statement of August 15, 1963, issued by the CPR government, declared:

> As far back as June 20, 1959, when there was not yet the slightest sign of a treaty on stopping nuclear tests, the Soviet government unilaterally tore up the agreement on new technology for national defense concluded between China and the Soviet Union on October 15, 1957, and refused to provide China with a sample of an atomic bomb and technical data concerning its manufacture.

The document also said that the Chinese had requested the Soviet government in 1962–1963 not to "infringe on China's sovereign rights and act for China in assuming an obligation to refrain from manufacturing nuclear weapons." Text in *The Sino-Soviet Rift*, William E. Griffith (Cambridge, Mass.: The M.I.T. Press, 1964), p. 351.

[27] See *Impact of Chinese Communist Nuclear Weapons Progress*, which has a brief summary of Chinese nuclear developments.

be transferred to the national control of any other state. There would thus be no addition to the number of countries possessing national control over nuclear weapons. Soviet spokesmen insisted with equal doggedness that they would never sign an agreement allowing the slightest "crack" through which the German "revanchists" could get access to nuclear weapons.[28]

Independently of Soviet and East European opposition, the prospect of an MLF never aroused much enthusiasm among most NATO governments, either on military or on political grounds. Conceived as a device to integrate the Western alliance and to sublimate into harmless channels European ambitions for a nuclear role, MLF proved in fact to have divisive effects within the alliance. One reason for this was that the orientation for or against an MLF emphasized the so-called Washington-Bonn axis within NATO. Eventually, therefore, the United States drew back from the MLF idea, forcing a similar retreat on the part of West Germany. The project was allowed to disappear from Western planning, although as a target of Soviet propaganda it had a rather long after-life.[29] With the disappearance of these plans, the way was cleared for American agreement on a treaty draft, satisfactory to the USSR, with more categoric language regarding the transfer of nuclear weapons.[30]

Occasionally Soviet authorities have referred to the increased danger of a world in which a large number of countries possess nuclear weapons—the "Nth-country" problem.[31] This has been a subordinate theme, however, rather uncongenial to Soviet Marxist patterns of thought. Moscow recognized that nuclear weapons were in some sense "classless"—if exploded, they would leave good Communists just as

[28] See, for example, the statement by Soviet representative Semion K. Tsarapkin to the ENDC on March 3, 1966, in *Documents 1966*, pp. 84–96.

[29] Even after MLF was no longer a live issue, the USSR continued to pick up West German criticism of the nonproliferation treaty for example, on the inspection issue), in order to portray the Federal Republic as the main stumbling block, interpreting any signs of objection or lack of enthusiasm in Bonn as evidence that the West Germans sought to block the treaty in order to get their hands on nuclear weapons. As a result of this propaganda policy, the USSR took relatively little note in its output of the objections voiced by India and other states.

[30] The United States submitted amended language on March 21, 1966, which prohibited the transfer of nuclear weapons not only to the "national control" of other states but also "into the control of any association" of such states. It also amended another article to forbid actions "which would cause an increase in the total number of States and associations of States having control of nuclear weapons." (*Documents 1966*, pp. 159–68.) In the wording finally agreed upon by the United States and the USSR, there was a flat prohibition of the "transfer to any recipient whatsoever of nuclear weapons . . . or control over such weapons . . . directly or indirectly . . ." (*The New York Times*, August 25, 1967.)

[31] Radio broadcast from Moscow, S. Buranov commentator, February 3, 1968.

dead as bad capitalists.[32] But from this the Soviet leaders did not conclude that it was a matter of indifference whether "socialist" or capitalist states came into possession of nuclear weapons. Soviet spokesmen argued, as in the 1963 polemics with the Chinese, two basic themes: (1) Soviet nuclear power protected other "socialist" states; and (2) in order to prevent West Germany and other capitalist states from coming into possession of nuclear weapons, it was necessary to prevent all additional states, even socialist states, from acquiring such arms.[33]

After the MLF problem was disposed of, another problem loomed in 1967 to threaten progress on the nonproliferation treaty. This concerned the system of verification and inspection designed to make sure that the states without nuclear weapons remained so, that is, confined themselves to "peaceful" uses of atomic energy. Although the USSR initially showed little interest in a verification requirement, it came to insist that if there was to be inspection, this should be performed by the International Atomic Energy Agency (IAEA). The Federal Republic of Germany and certain other states belonging to the European Economic Community (EEC) sought to have the verification of peaceful uses handled by Euratom, the atomic energy agency of "the Six." But the USSR insisted that the IAEA (to which the USSR and other Communist-ruled countries belonged) should inspect atomic activities in the FRG and other non-nuclear states of the European Economic Community on the same basis as other states subject to control under the proposed treaty. The United States supported the idea of a gradual transfer of verification from Euratom to the Vienna-based IAEA.[34]

The line-up of states on the inspection issue presented some anomalies, if considered in the light of the history of negotiations on disarmament projects involving international inspection. Fear of espionage (in this case, industrial rather than military) contributed to West German and some other West European resistance to inspection by rival powers, just as Soviet resistance to inspection had been motivated by fear of military espionage. Furthermore, in seeking to retain Euratom authority, the FRG and some other EEC members favored something closer to the "self-inspection" that had characterized Soviet approaches to earlier control issues. Euratom included only closely allied states, all members of NATO, in contrast to the much more broadly representative IAEA, which included Communist, Western, and nonaligned nations.

This inspection issue did not involve the vital interests of either the

---

[32] The Soviet "Open Letter," July 14, 1963; English translation in *The Sino-Soviet Rift,* p. 299.

[33] Soviet government statement of September 21, 1963; English translation in *The Sino-Soviet Rift,* pp. 426–61.

[34] *The New York Times,* February 23, 1967, p. 11.

USSR or the United States, for both were to be free from inspection.[35] Therefore, it aroused neither Soviet apprehensions about on-site inspection within the USSR, nor American striving to have an international inspection system function on Soviet soil. U.S.-USSR differences on this issue were resolved in a formula providing that the IAEA safeguards system would be applied to all states on the basis of negotiations between the IAEA and individual countries or groups of countries. A transitional period—which could be as long as two years—was envisaged between the coming into force of the NPT and of the verification agreements negotiated with the IAEA.[36]

Although reconciliation of the MLF and the verification issues removed the major blocks to Soviet-American agreement, other issues regarding the treaty caused some of the non-nuclear states to regard it with mixed feelings. These doubts affected various American allies, including the Federal Republic of Germany, Rumania (an ally of the USSR), and a number of nonaligned states, especially India.

By mid-1968, when the NPT was opened to signature, it seemed obvious that the treaty would gain fewer adherents than the test-ban treaty. France and China again made known their refusal to participate, although the reasons were far less clear than in the case of the test-ban treaty. As nuclear states their own development of nuclear arsenals would not be hindered by the nondissemination treaty, and there were no indications that either France or the CPR intended to pass on nuclear weapons or technical assistance to other countries. Their positions on proliferation differed, however. France has declared that nuclear proliferation is a danger.[37] In contrast, Chinese representatives have stressed the good that would come from further disintegration of the "Soviet-American nuclear monopoly" and from possession of nuclear weapons by revolutionary Afro-Asian states.[38]

Unlike the test-ban treaty, which established equal prohibitions on all signatory powers (however unequal their effects), the nonproliferation treaty gave formal recognition to the existence of two classes of states—those that had developed nuclear weapons (as of January 1, 1967) and those that had not. The only restriction placed on the former was the ban on the transfer of such weapons or of nuclear "know-how"; the others pledged themselves neither to acquire nor develop such weapons. Because inspection of peaceful uses was relevant

[35] The United States was willing, however, as the USSR was not, to allow IAEA inspection of its own peaceful nuclear activities. See President Johnson's statement of December 2, 1967, *The New York Times*, December 3, 1967.

[36] For the text, see *The New York Times*, January 19, 1968.

[37] See the joint French-Soviet communiqué, signed in Moscow by Presidents de Gaulle and Podgorny on June 30, 1966. *Pravda*, July 1, 1966.

[38] See *Documents 1965*, p. 463, and *Documents 1966*, p. 359.

only to the states forbidden to develop a nuclear arsenal, these were to be subject to a safeguards system covering all their nuclear activities, to be administered by an agency that included the nuclear powers. The non-nuclear states were also forbidden to carry out any nuclear explosions, even for peaceful purposes, but were to entrust these to states already possessing nuclear weapons.[39]

It was the lack of progress in the nonproliferation agreement toward any nuclear "disarmament" or toward slowing the pace of nuclear stock-piling that galled a number of the non-nuclear nations. It was primarily this feature that led India to abstain from the U.N. General Assembly's endorsement of the treaty in June, 1968, and presaged an Indian refusal to sign the treaty. On this issue, however, the USSR and the U.S. stood together. Both professed their willingness to accept disarmament measures (their own proposals), and both professed to see the ban on proliferation as merely a step toward more far-reaching measures of actual disarmament. The two states agreed, however, that it was not justifiable to postpone or abandon a nonproliferation treaty by making the agreement depend on settlement of disarmament issues. Soviet and American representatives consistently argued that proliferation would harm the non-nuclear nations. First, as additional states came into possession of nuclear weapons, the security of their neighbors and rivals would decline. Second, the further spread of weapons would spiral into an expensive pursuit of both weapons and vehicles.

Considerations such as these had appeal to many of the non-nuclear nations. Some of those with aspirations for recognition as great powers, or with capabilities for the development of nuclear weapons, resisted the blandishments. Their representatives asserted that states were being asked, in permanently renouncing nuclear ambitions, to give up much; on the other hand, the states in possession of nuclear weapons were asked to give up very little—and certainly none of their armaments. By signing the treaty, the non-nuclears would even give up one of their few means of pressing nuclear states toward arms reductions.[40]

The initial failure of the treaty sponsors to envisage arrangements improving the security prospects of non-nuclear states also bothered

[39] This provision, supported by both the United States and the USSR, was regarded by some non-nuclear states as potentially damaging to their programs for peaceful uses of atomic energy.

[40] It was probably this consideration that led a number of the non-nuclear states to support an Italian proposal for a moratorium under which the non-nuclear states would pledge not to manufacture or receive nuclear weapons during a limited period (*Documents 1965*, pp. 289, 411–18). India proposed a two-stage treaty in which the nuclear powers would first undertake obligations regarding nondissemination and arms reductions before the non-nuclear states accepted any obligations not to fabricate or receive nuclear weapons (*ibid.*, p. 338).

some of the latter, especially nonaligned and neutral nations. India forcefully and repeatedly expressed concern on this score, pointing to Chinese development of nuclear armaments, and arguing that a nonproliferation agreement should inhibit "vertical proliferation" (inside the nuclear club) as well as "horizontal proliferation" (to non-nuclear states). In a message from Premier Kosygin to the ENDC on February 1, 1966, the USSR proposed an arrangement purporting to deal with the security issue. Kosygin suggested that the treaty include a pledge by the nuclear weapons states that they would not use nuclear weapons against signatory states which banned the presence on their soil of nuclear weapons, i.e., those of other states.[41] As submitted to the ENDC on June 23, 1966, the suggested clause was to read as follows:

> The parties to the treaty possessing nuclear weapons undertake not to use nuclear weapons and not to threaten the use of such weapons against states which do not possess nuclear weapons and in whose territory, territorial waters and air space there are no foreign nuclear weapons.[42]

The wording suggested that states which were parties to the agreement could continue to allow their allies to deploy nuclear weapons on their soil; but as a price for their hospitality they would remain perfectly "legitimate" targets for nuclear blows in case of war.

The USSR sought to use this proposal to kill two birds with one stone: to discourage deployment of nuclear weapons in foreign countries, and to elicit from nuclear powers pledges of non-use. It was, thus, an adaptation to the nonproliferation treaty of two earlier Soviet proposals of broader scope. One was for an international convention prohibiting the use (or first use) of nuclear weapons; the other for an agreement prohibiting deployment, temporary or permanent, of nuclear weapons in foreign countries. Both were aimed at American military policy, which justified use (including first use) of nuclear weapons in a "defensive" war, and which justified world-wide deployment of nuclear weapons under American control. Acceptance of the Kosygin provision within the treaty framework would have established, in addition to the division between nuclear and non-nuclear states, a secondary distinction between non-nuclear states "legally" immune from nuclear blows in case of war and those "legally" targetable.

The Kosygin proposal attracted the support of many nonaligned states, and received something of an endorsement in a U.N. resolution of November 16, 1966.[43] However, it was rejected by the United States

---

[41] *Documents 1966*, pp. 9–13.
[42] *Ibid.*, p. 367.
[43] *Ibid.*, pp. 748–50. The resolution merely called on the ENDC "to consider urgently the proposal that the nuclear weapons powers should give an assurance that

and various other Western powers, and the proposal was not included in the agreed drafts of the treaty submitted by the USSR and United States in 1967–1968.

Whatever the merits of the Kosygin security clause, it did not meet the concerns of a nonaligned state such as India, and for other reasons did not appeal to most of America's allies. For Indian observation of the Kosygin arrangement would have meant only that, in case of war, the USSR and the United States would not use nuclear weapons against India. But India's fear centered on Communist China, which scorned the treaty and whose assurances would probably have meant little to India in any event. Even for states unconcerned about China, the arrangement offered no reliable guarantee against nuclear attack in case of war. This was particularly true of states allied militarily to the United States or the Soviet Union, which could hardly expect to be safe from attack if their territories were useful to, or used by, a nuclear belligerent, even if the latter stationed no nuclear weapons on such territory.

In the course of negotiations on the NPT, representatives of the United States spoke positively about a multilateral security arrangement connected with the United Nations.[44] The U.S. offered no proposal on security arrangements for incorporation in the treaty, however, and simply promised American assistance on a unilateral basis. The basic U.S. position was outlined in a speech of President Johnson on October 18, 1964, following the first Chinese Communist atomic weapon test. The President declared: "The nations that do not seek national nuclear weapons can be sure that, if they need our strong support against some threat of nuclear blackmail, then they will have it." [45] This declaration became the standard U.S. reply to calls for security guarantees. A unilateral approach to a security guarantee did not fully meet, of course, the needs of nonaligned countries which were anxious to avoid dependence on one or another great power.

As a result of negotiations outside the ENDC discussions, the United States, the Soviet Union, and the United Kingdom announced in Geneva on March 7, 1968, their agreement on the text of a draft U.N. Security Council resolution aimed to dispel the worries "of certain

---

they will not use, or threaten to use, nuclear weapons against non-nuclear weapons states without nuclear weapons on their territories, and any other proposals that have been or may be made for the solution of this problem. . . ." By singling out the Kosygin formula, however, the resolution gave it a certain standing, particularly since there were no other proposals for dealing with the problem within the context of the treaty. This paragraph was adopted by a vote of 98–0, in which the United States abstained, along with Spain, Cameroon, and France.

[44] *Documents 1965*, p. 434; *Documents 1966*, pp. 6, 393, 668.
[45] *Documents 1964*, p. 468.

states" over the absence of security guarantees in the U.S.-USSR treaty draft.[46] The resolution, passed in June, 1968, called for prompt action on the part of the Security Council in case of "aggression with nuclear weapons." It reaffirmed the "inherent right, recognized under Article 51 of the Charter, of individual and collective self-defense" prior to Security Council action, if a member state was attacked. It also endorsed the pledge of certain states to provide assistance "in accordance with the Charter" to any non-nuclear weapons state signing the NPT, in the event that the latter became a victim of "aggression"—or was the "object of a threat of aggression"—involving nuclear weapons. The resolution was accompanied by separate declarations of intent to act in accordance with the Security Council decision by the U.S., the Soviet Union, and Great Britain.

The Security Council posture statement on response to nuclear aggression modifies neither the nonproliferation treaty nor Security Council procedures. The well-known difficulties that have slowed or prevented Security Council action in dealing with international crises are not removed; and the resolution changes in no way the competence of states to take unilateral or joint military action in a crisis. They have done this in the past and could do so in the future, under the terms of Article 51 of the Charter. Nonetheless, the joint resolution reflects a further shift in Soviet and American expectations about the possibilities of future collaboration. In one sense, it harks back to the original governing concept of the Security Council—a presupposition that there would be sufficient unity among the great powers (or sufficient indifference on their parts) to allow the Security Council to operate effectively except when the permanent members' immediate interests were at stake. In the postwar world, however, the great powers permanently represented on the U.N. Security Council displayed neither unity nor indifference, for the USSR and the United States headed opposed alliance systems and sought to influence events everywhere in the world. Usually this resulted in a blockage of Security Council action.

The proposed resolution by no means assures future Soviet-American collaboration in the Security Council, but the very fact that these often antagonistic great powers have underlined their will to agree is significant. The tripartite announcement is particularly relevant to the position of Communist China, the only nuclear weapons state that currently lacks a seat on the U.N. Security Council, and thus the only such state incapable of preventing Security Council action through the veto power accorded permanent members.

Although falling far short of any guarantee, the procedure suggested

[46] Text in *The New York Times*, March 8, 1968.

by the United States, the USSR, and the United Kingdom has a multilateral quality that makes it acceptable to the nonaligned states, and raises hopes for effective assistance from the superpowers in case of crisis. The tripartite proposal has a number of advantages over the earlier Soviet and American suggestions on the security protection of non-nuclear states. Thus, it is more relevant to the needs of non-nuclear countries than the Kosygin proposal, which appeared to be directed against the United States rather than in favor of the non-nuclear weapons states. Likewise, it seems more relevant to the political orientation of the nonaligned states than was the "Johnson formula," which contemplated that these states would base their security in dependence on American military power.

For some states, however, and groups within states, the proposal for joint action in the Security Council by rival alliance leaders may be less welcome. Those finding comfort in the preservation of close military alliances, and in the maintenance of a sharp line of demarcation between rival political systems, are not likely to applaud the step. As with the nonproliferation treaty itself, the security procedure implies that the rival great powers have an interest in acting together, even at the expense of their allies. This community of interest was expressed in the NPT in the form of a grouping that separated the powerful from the less powerful states, a line cutting across alliance ties. The Security Council procedure implies that the rival great powers and rival alliance leaders will find a common position on other political-military issues. The Soviet-American accord may thus contribute to a further loosening of alliance structures.

9

PROPOSALS FOR
NUCLEAR ARMS CONTROL

Two trends have characterized Soviet and American efforts over the past decade in respect to nuclear weapons systems. The major efforts of both countries have gone into strenuous competition for technological and numerical superiority, each trying to outdo the other in amassing tremendous forces of destruction. Simultaneously, however, they have remained in virtually uninterrupted negotiation on various measures for control of nuclear armaments, and have even agreed to four measures instituting limitations on nuclear weapons. The achievements were modest, particularly if compared to the continuous augmentation in quantity and quality of their strategic nuclear forces. But the modest limitations on which they agreed gave nourishment to hopes for the eventual feasibility of other, more ambitious steps, designed to reduce the chances of nuclear war or to reduce the economic and psychic costs of the nuclear arms race.

Although radical disarmament steps were still proposed and sometimes discussed in disarmament forums, by the 1960's little was heard of earlier proposals to do away completely with nuclear weapons. "Ban the bomb" measures thus reappeared only in the context of plans for "general and complete disarmament," whose improbability seemed obvious to all but the most determined believers in a "world without arms." True, a Chinese proposal "to prohibit and destroy" nuclear weapons met Soviet approval. This was advanced by the CPR in the aftermath of the first Chinese atomic test in October, 1964, and called for "a summit conference of all the countries of the world" to accomplish this objective.[1] It was clear, however, that the Soviet leaders approved this proposal only because they could not afford to turn it down. They expected nothing to come of it, and they were right. Furthermore, they apparently decided that even its exploitation would yield them no returns, and hence invested little effort in promotion of the idea.

[1] Letter of December 28, 1964, from Premier Kosygin to Premier Chou En-lai in *Documents 1964*, pp. 532–33.

157

The variety of separate measures bearing on nuclear weapons discussed at disarmament sessions in recent years form the subject of this chapter. The measures involve approaches to restrict production of fissionable materials for use in weapons (a U.S. proposal) and of delivery vehicles (also a U.S. proposal), to limit geographical deployment of nuclear weapons (a Soviet proposal), and to ban the use of nuclear weapons. Although all these proposals originated before October, 1964, they have continued to be discussed in 1964–1968.

PROPOSALS ON NUCLEAR WEAPONS STOCKS

In the period between signature of the test-ban treaty in 1963 and Khrushchev's ouster in 1964, there seemed to be some prospect of movement on partial measures affecting Soviet and American armaments, either by reciprocation of unilateral steps or by formal agreements. Several American initiatives sought to take advantage of the test-ban precedent by finding other areas of agreement.

One approach to a slowdown in the nuclear arms race was suggested in an American proposal of January, 1964, for a "verified agreement to halt all production of fissionable materials for weapons use." Short of this step, President Johnson suggested an interim measure that would have allowed a reduction of this production, to be achieved "through both sides closing comparable production facilities on a plant-by-plant basis, with mutual inspection." [2] The USSR rejected both proposals, but agreement was subsequently reached for simultaneous announcement, on April 20, 1964, by the United States and the USSR of unilateral reductions in production of fissionable materials for nuclear weapons. This is the only "agreement" ever achieved touching fissionable materials.

The April announcement of a U.S. cut in production came on top of a 25 per cent cut in uranium production decreed in January, 1964, with total reductions to bring about within four years a 20 per cent reduction in the production of plutonium and a 40 per cent reduction in the production of enriched uranium.[3] Premier Khrushchev announced on the same day in April, 1964, that the USSR was stopping construction of two new plutonium-producing atomic reactors. He said that the Soviet Union would "reduce substantially the production of uranium-235 for nuclear weapons" over the next few years. The British Prime Minister, Sir Alec Douglas Home, made a similar promise for his country.

---

[2] Message from President Johnson to the ENDC, January 21, 1964; *ibid.*, p. 9.
[3] Address by President Johnson; *ibid.*, pp. 165–66.

The U.S. frankly admitted that it was adjusting production to military needs. The USSR was somewhat less frank, although in his statement Premier Khrushchev indicated that "the present correlation of nuclear power in the world arena" permitted the reduction, "without in any way weakening the defensive capacity of the Soviet Union and the solidity of the nuclear missile shield which reliably safeguards the security of all the countries of the socialist community." [4]

Soviet discussions of the parallel U.S.-USSR reductions noted the benefits of this "agreement" as an illustration of the "policy of mutual example"; Soviet writers, however, claimed that the United States was simply taking out of production some outmoded plants at Savannah River and Hanford because it already had superfluous stocks of enriched uranium. American sources in turn later made known the existence of evidence that the USSR had not actually reduced its output of fissionable materials after the April declaration of intent.[5]

In rejecting the proposal for a complete halt in production of fissionable materials for military purposes, the USSR stated that this would be realizable only within the context of an agreement for general disarmament. The Soviet rejection made much of the proposed control over the cessation of production, which was considered objectionable because the measure involved no major "disarmament." [6] Undoubtedly a major unspoken consideration was the Soviet belief that U.S. stocks of fissionable materials far exceeded those of the Soviet Union.

Although the American proposal to stop all production of fissionable materials for weapons involved a "freeze" rather than a reduction of nuclear weapons, an accompanying American proposal went further in the direction of arms reduction. If production were halted, the United States would agree to the transfer of quantities of weapons-grade uranium-235 to peaceful uses. The U.S. originally called for transfers of equal amounts of enriched uranium to civilian uses, but subsequently offered a ratio of three-to-two between U.S. and Soviet transfers, mentioning 60,000 (U.S.) and 40,000 (USSR) kilograms of U-235. Further strengthening the "disarmament" aspect of the proposal, Ambassador Goldberg suggested, in an address to the U.N. General Assembly on September 23, 1965, that the U-235 to be given over to peaceful uses be taken from existing American and Soviet nuclear

---

[4] *Ibid.*, pp. 166–68.

[5] For a Soviet comment see *SSSR, SShA, i razoruzhenie*, pp. 150–51. According to Senator Henry M. Jackson, the Atomic Energy Commission late in 1965 reported that it had "no evidence" that the USSR had cut back its production of fissionable materials as promised on April 20, 1964 (*The New York Times*, November 25, 1965).

[6] Statement to the ENDC by Soviet representative Tsarapkin, August 13, 1964, in *Documents 1964*, pp. 339–41.

weapons. "Several thousands" of these would have to be destroyed, it was said, to obtain the required quantities of U-235.[7]

Like the production cut-off, a transfer along these lines was rejected by Soviet representatives. In addition to the extensive inspection required to police any transfer, additional inspection would have been necessary to make sure that the uranium came from nuclear weapons. The control features, therefore, raised familiar Soviet objections. More important, however, the Soviet authorities probably believed that the U.S. superiority in nuclear stockpiles was greater than three-to-two, and that therefore a reduction at this ratio would have increased American superiority.[8] The September, 1965, modifications by the United States made it more difficult for Soviet representatives to argue that the proposed measure involved no arms reduction.[9] Nevertheless, the USSR did not relax its opposition. In its memorandum of July 1, 1968, the Soviet Government proposed that talks be opened "on an end to the manufacture of nuclear weapons, the reduction of their stockpiles, and the subsequent total ban on and liquidation of nuclear weapons under appropriate international control." The wording suggested a rapid and complete abolition of nuclear stocks rather than the curb on production and gradual reduction characteristic of the American approach.

NUCLEAR DELIVERY VEHICLES

The impasse over measures aimed at nuclear weapons as such, and the difficulty in the 1960's of even imagining a world in which all

[7] *Documents 1965*, pp. 433–36. The mention of "several thousands" is from a statement at the UNGA by ACDA Director William C. Foster, October 27, 1965; *ibid.*, pp. 507–8.

[8] *SSSR, SShA, i razoruzhenie*, p. 160:

Transfer under international control by the U.S. and the Soviet Union of equal or nearly equal quantities of fissionable materials would have meant, from the point of view of U.S. leaders, acquisition of a military advantage at the expense of the security of the Soviet Union. In the opinion of these leaders, the United States, having begun the production of nuclear weapons before the USSR and controlling a greater economic potential than the USSR, had produced more fissionable materials than the Soviet Union. . . . Suppose, for example, that the U.S. produced 200 tons and the USSR only 100 tons of fissionable materials, then the transfer of 50 tons of these materials by the Soviet Union and the same quantity by the U.S. would have increased the coefficient of superiority of the United States from two to three times—not a small difference!

[9] The argument that a measure is unacceptable because it involves no "disarmament," i.e., arms reduction, has been used rather inconsistently by Soviet spokesmen. The USSR has in fact proposed or agreed to several measures regarding armaments with no arms reduction features.

nuclear weapons had been destroyed, gave impetus to the search for other approaches. One of these called for the limitation, reduction in number, or destruction, of delivery vehicles designed to carry nuclear weapons to their targets. The delivery vehicle approach had for some time been central to French thinking on disarmament, but it also entered into proposals advanced by the Soviet Union and the United States. (Both the American and Soviet plans for "general and complete disarmament" incorporated provisions aimed at delivery vehicles, but this chapter is concerned only with separable measures.)

The most important proposal on strategic nuclear delivery vehicles was a measure suggested by the United States on January 21, 1964, for a verified "freeze" on the numbers and character of such vehicles in Soviet and American military forces.[10] Production would not be completely cut off, because limited replacements were envisaged on a one-for-one basis. The idea was to keep the "parks" of strategic vehicles from either deteriorating or expanding. Anti-ballistic missile systems were to be specifically included, along with offensive missiles and bombers. Had this measure been accepted and implemented, it would have brought to a halt the steady build-up of offensive missile systems, and would have prevented installation of ABM systems.

Soviet negotiators never consented to consider this proposal seriously. Their arguments centered on the claim that the "freeze" was not in any way "disarmament." [11] According to Soviet spokesmen, the proposed halt in expansion of delivery systems was motivated by the American desire to reduce military expenditures, since the United States already had more than enough delivery vehicles to reach all its contemplated targets. Soviet representatives attacked the proposal also on the familiar ground that the inspection required to authenticate observance of the "freeze" meant acquisition by foreign intelligence of information on Soviet military forces, i.e., "control over armaments" rather than "control over disarmament."

Although the measure would not have increased American superiority in nuclear weapons delivery capabilities, it would have stabilized a fairly high level of superiority for the United States. From the Soviet point of view, the "freeze" would have "legalized" the disparity by an international agreement placing a seal of permanence on the USSR's recognition of its own inferiority. A suggestion was advanced by the

[10] Message from President Johnson to the ENDC, in *Documents 1964*, pp. 7–9. The proposal was spelled out in a statement by ACDA Director Foster to the ENDC on January 31, 1964 (*ibid.*, pp. 17–21); in a statement by Adrian S. Fisher on April 16 (*ibid.*, pp. 157–62); by Clare H. Timberlake on August 27 (*ibid.*, pp. 367–73) and in a statement by Fisher on August 2, 1966 (*Documents 1966*, pp. 490–95).

[11] USSR Foreign Minister Andrei Gromyko dismissed the proposal in an interview published in *Izvestiia*, March 2, 1964. Ten days later, Ambassador Tsarapkin discussed it in a similar vein at the ENDC. See *Documents 1964*, pp. 88–95.

U.S. that progress on "stabilization" would lead the United States to "explore the possibility" of reductions in the number of these vehicles, but this did not elicit any Soviet interest. Soviet authorities obviously preferred an untrammeled competition in offensive and defensive missiles to stabilization of the sort proposed.

As on the subject of fissionable materials, the Soviet Union initially presented no proposals of its own regarding nuclear delivery vehicles. It must be noted that the Soviet proposal for a "nuclear umbrella" was a constituent part of the USSR's revised plan for "general and complete disarmament," and was inseparable from this plan. The "nuclear umbrella" was to consist of "a strictly limited number" of missiles (ICBM, ABM, and SAM), which would be retained by the United States and the Soviet Union until the final stage of the disarmament process. According to the Soviet plan, these missiles were the only vehicles to be saved from the destruction contemplated in the early phases of general disarmament. They were to be land-based (i.e., excluding submarine-launched missiles) and confined to American or Soviet soil (i.e., not allowed at foreign bases). Presumably the numbers for the USSR and the United States were to be equal, and reduction to equal numbers would thus deprive the U.S. of the very strategic superiority the U.S., in its proposal of a "freeze" on delivery vehicles, sought to preserve.[12]

In connection with the signature of the nonproliferation treaty on July 1, 1968, however, the USSR indicated willingness to agree upon "the limitation and subsequent reduction of strategic means of delivery of strategic nuclear weapons." The Soviet proposal called for "the destruction of the entire arsenal of means of strategic delivery, and, in any case, the reduction of this arsenal to the absolute minimum, with the retention, and this only temporarily, of only a strictly limited quantity of such means." [13] As with the comparable proposal on nuclear weapons stocks, this vehicle proposal was described so briefly that it was unclear whether or not there was any narrowing of the Soviet-American differences. It sounded very much like an amended version of the Soviet GCD provisions on vehicles with the "umbrella" feature broadened to permit temporary retention of some bombers and submarines as well as missiles. If so, the new proposal did not go far to meet American emphasis on curbing development and production of strategic vehicles while initiating very gradual reductions.

---

[12] The proposal advanced in 1962 was modified in 1963 to lengthen, until the final (third) stage of the disarmament process, the period in which the Soviet Union and the United States could retain their "nuclear umbrella." For the latest version (April 28, 1965) of the Soviet GCD draft incorporating the umbrella proposal, see *Documents 1965*, pp. 77–101.

[13] *The New York Times*, July 2, 1968.

A rather special problem is presented by the anti-ballistic missiles, designed for use in defense against attacking missiles. Both the United States and the Soviet Union have for years devoted great effort and resources to research and development of ABM systems. American concern over Soviet development of such a system is long standing, and was reflected in the "freeze" proposal discussed above. ACDA Director William C. Foster told the Eighteen-Nation Disarmament Committee on January 31, 1964, that "a freeze on strategic delivery systems without a freeze on anti-missile systems would be destabilizing and therefore unacceptable." [14] Concern in the United States over Soviet ABM advances heightened in 1966, as evidence accumulated that the USSR had begun installation around Moscow of an ABM system designed to knock out attacking U.S. missiles.[15]

American authorities, reluctant to add to a military budget already swollen by expenditures for the war in Vietnam, and reluctant to begin a competitive race in a new field of armaments, proposed to the USSR in late 1966 and early 1967 that conversations be held on the subject.[16] Although the USSR agreed in principle to discussions, provided offensive missile systems as well as defensive ones were included, Premier Kosygin and other Soviet spokesmen rejected the proposition that Soviet defensive measures were "destabilizing." [17] Their arguments

---

[14] *Documents 1964*, p. 20.

[15] Secretary McNamara confirmed initial deployment by the USSR of an ABM system in a news conference on November 10, 1966. (*The New York Times*, November 11, 1966.) He was quoted in a *Life* interview (September 29, 1967) as saying that the system around Moscow was not yet operational and that another (so-called Tallin) system, covering the northwestern approaches to the USSR, might have some ABM capability. When McNamara presented his final "Posture Statement" to the U.S. Senate Armed Services Committee on February 1, 1968, he reported that a majority of the Washington "intelligence community" believed that the Tallin system had no significant ABM capability.

[16] President Johnson expressed hopes for a freeze on ABM deployment in his January, 1967, State of the Union message. (*The New York Times*, January 11, 1967.) Just before the possibility of talks was explored by Ambassador Llewellyn Thompson in Moscow with Premier Kosygin (February 18, 1967), President Johnson said:

It is my belief that the United States and the Soviet Union have reached a watershed in the dispiriting history of our arms competition. Decisions may be made on both sides which will trigger another upward spiral. The paradox is that this should be happening at a time when there is abundant evidence that our mutual antagonism is beginning to ease.

The President and Secretary McNamara also discussed the ABM question with Premier Kosygin at Glassboro in June, 1967.

[17] Kosygin commented on the ABM issue at a press conference in London on February 10, 1967. He distinguished between defensive weapons systems, which prevent the destruction of people, and offensive systems, which can destroy cities and whole states (*Izvestiia*, February 11, 1967; *The New York Times*, February 11, 1967).

were consistent with the traditional Soviet military posture, in which weapons of defense have always played a far larger role and received a greater relative proportion of military allocations than in the United States.

In Soviet thinking, the fact that an ABM system—unlike ICBMs—cannot be used to threaten any other country, but can serve only to defend a nation against attack, means that ABMs would reduce the danger of nuclear war. There was no echo in the USSR of a major anti-ABM argument often voiced in the United States: that an ABM system constructed on the basis of present technology would be ineffective and could be overwhelmed by additional numbers of attack missiles, particularly those equipped with multiple warheads and improved guidance.[18] Nor did Soviet strategists respond to the U.S. contention that ABM installations, to the extent that they were effective, would lessen each side's confidence in its capacity to deter the enemy. From this viewpoint, ABM installations would increase incentives for a pre-emptive attack by reducing confidence in mutual deterrence.[19]

Some of the Soviet-American differences of viewpoint on ABMs have probably been a function of differences in judgments regarding the likelihood of nuclear war, a possibility rated greater by the USSR than by the United States. Although some U.S. strategists emphasize that the absence of ABMs promotes deterrence, the USSR prefers to emphasize that ABM defenses would aid a country to reduce destruction and casualties if deterrence failed, i.e., if a war broke out involving strategic nuclear weapons.[20]

In September, 1967, Secretary of Defense McNamara announced plans to install a "light" ABM system in the United States, citing a pos-

[18] For the McNamara version of this argument, see his speech at San Francisco (*The New York Times*, September 19, 1967), and the interview in *Life*, September 29, 1967. In his press conference in London, Premier Kosygin made a thinly veiled attack on McNamara's cost-effectiveness calculations (that it was cheaper to add new offensive missiles to overwhelm ABM defenses than to build such defenses), by saying that an ABM system might be more expensive but that it was also more humane.

[19] "Pre-emption" is the "defensive" tactic of nullifying or reducing the effectiveness of an imminent enemy attack by a "counter" blow struck in advance. One theory justifying a large build-up of well-protected offensive weapons is that it averts the temptation for this kind of "advance retaliation," since the sufficiency and relative security of offensive forces enable a country to accept an enemy attack before launching a second strike.

[20] This is one reason, but not the only reason, for the U.S. Joint Chiefs of Staff tendency to favor installation of an ABM system in the United States. They also believe that both technical and economic considerations would prevent the USSR from initiating or countering an ambitious American program of ABM deployment. See remarks by General Earle G. Wheeler, January 26, 1967, in *Military Procurement Authorization for Fiscal Year 1968*, p. 296.

sible future Communist Chinese (rather than a Soviet) threat to the
United States as the determining consideration. Even a large-scale deployment of an ABM system by the U.S. could not, according to
McNamara, prevent a major Soviet attack from wreaking heavy destruction and loss of life in the U.S.; but even a thin deployment of
ABMs could protect the United States against significant losses from a
Chinese attack. It was acknowledged that the "anti-Chinese" system
would have, in addition, some capability of protecting American
missile bases from a Soviet attack, thus enhancing American capabilities for a retaliatory strike against the USSR.[21]

Despite the Soviet view of the innocuous nature of defenses as compared with offenses, the USSR's agreement in principle, in February,
1967, to talks covering all strategic missile systems indicated awareness
of the uncertainties posed by the build-up of strategic arms. The
prospects for negotiations over nuclear delivery systems brightened in
mid-1968, when the USSR and the United States agreed to begin substantive discussions on the problem. Whether there was a sufficient
change in either the American or the Soviet position to provide a basis
for agreement was not immediately clear. In its 1964 proposal, the
United States had put emphasis on the "freeze" aspects, although it
suggested that some reduction might also be arranged. By mid-1968,
the only clear suggestion of a U.S. modification of its position concerned requirements for international inspection. American officials
let it be known that foreign inspection might not be necessary to police
an agreement for a freeze or for modest reductions.[22] In the Soviet memorandum of July 1, 1968, the USSR manifested a willingness to accept
"limitations" but put more stress on the need for "subsequent reduction" of strategic delivery vehicles.[23]

No one knows, of course, how much of the Soviet opposition to the
1964 American "freeze" proposals has been directed against the objectives of the measures, and how much came in response to the inspection requirements. Most of the proposals have envisaged substantial
degrees of foreign inspection. In recent years, the United States has
scaled down its inspection requirements as it has become satisfied that
national means of verification give sufficient assurance of compliance.
Observational satellites and other means of collecting intelligence have
provided this increased assurance. Nevertheless, some activities cannot

---

[21] The decision to construct a "thin" ABM system was announced by Secretary
McNamara in a speech at San Francisco (*The New York Times*, September 19,
1967), and discussed by him with more emphasis on considerations pertaining to
the USSR in the *Life* interview, September 29, 1967.

[22] Address by Paul C. Warnke, Assistant Secretary of Defense for International
Security Affairs, October 6, 1967 (*Documents 1967*, pp. 454–59).

[23] *The New York Times*, July 2, 1968.

be gauged with much certainty by unilateral means of verification, and some recent weapons innovations, in particular, are likely to prove resistant to detection by existing intelligence techniques. Mobile launchers for ICBMs, to take an example, complicate intelligence problems in the strategic missile field, as do multiple warheads on either stationary or mobile missiles.[24]

Even apart from the problem of inspection, all U.S. missile proposals have collided with a fundamental principle of Soviet policy on arms and disarmament—preservation of opportunity for the Soviet Union ultimately to equal or surpass the United States in significant weapons systems. This principle has never been violated in any of the partial measures to which the USSR has so far acceded.

It may be, of course, that Soviet-American calculations of superiority-inferiority will diminish in importance as a limiting factor on arms control and disarmament agreements. This could occur if parity became a fact, or if both sides became convinced that strategic superiority was not essential to security. But neither of these conditions seems to be in the offing.

Doubts about the importance of military superiority in strategic nuclear forces have been expressed in the United States, and may exert some influence in the USSR. Certainly it is not easy to calculate the effect of this kind of superiority on either military or political confrontations. It can be argued (as Secretary McNamara has done) that the significant military factor is the possession of a secure force of "deterrence," and not the question of whether this force is greater or smaller than that of the major opponent. On the political side, it is clearly difficult to translate strategic military superiority into political gains. The difficulty of assessment of the superiority-inferiority factors stems partially from the great inhibitions that have prevented use of nuclear weapons since 1945: they can be produced, perfected, accumulated, displayed, discussed, and brandished in time of crisis; but detonation against an enemy is something else again.

These doubts about the value of strategic superiority are merely doubts, however, and they have by no means paralyzed the drive for nuclear dominance of the political and military leaders of the superpowers. It seems probable, in fact, that in both the USSR and the United States, the strategic equation will play a major role for a long time in determining the acceptability of arms control and disarmament proposals touching nuclear stockpiles and strategic weapons vehicles.*

---

[24] Soviet military authorities have often referred to their development of mobile, land-based ICBMs. See, for example, the remarks of the late Marshal Malinovsky at the XXIII Party Congress, on April 1, 1966 (*Stenograficheskii otchet* [Moscow: Politizdat, 1966], I, p. 411).

* Among the participants in the study there were differing views of the prob-

ATOM-FREE ZONES

Over the years, the Soviet Union has introduced numerous suggestions for "atomic-free zones." The latter are sometimes called "denuclearized zones," particularly if nuclear weapons have been stationed or
tested in the area. Such proposals contemplate agreements putting a
region off limits for nuclear weapons or weapons testing, whether controlled by local or extraregional powers. In practice, however, almost
all the proposals seek to prevent states outside the region from stationing nuclear weapons in the zone. In this approach to the control of nuclear weapons, Soviet authorities have been as forward as they have
been reticent about proposals touching fissionable materials and delivery vehicles. Although no new zone has been proposed since 1964,
and old proposals have been given little more than routine exploitation, most of the proposals advanced by the Soviet Union over more
than a decade remain in good standing. A proposed Pacific Ocean
basin atom-free zone is given little attention, however, perhaps because it touches Communist Chinese sensibilities.[25]

There is now an area of overlap in Soviet and American policies
on atom-free zones. The United States has accepted the desirability of
agreements on such zones in Latin America, Africa, and the Near
East, and these areas are also on the much longer Soviet list of regions
proposed for denuclearization. The three listed zones are of less interest,
however, to Soviet authorities than some others, for the Soviet leaders are interested primarily in the denuclearization of regions where
nuclear weapons are heavily concentrated. Their enthusiasm is mild
indeed for denuclearization of places without permanent inhabitants
(Antarctica) or without deployed nuclear weapons (such as Latin America and Africa). Of course, atom-free zones even for these areas can
serve some Soviet policy interests. The USSR has always favored measures to "blacken" nuclear weapons, and zonal agreements can serve
this end, since they respond to apprehensions about the stationing
and use of such weapons. Soviet authorities probably also see some
advantage in the prevention of possible future basing of nuclear weapons in areas now free of them.

---

able impact on Soviet behavior of attainment of parity in strategic nuclear weapons. Many believe that attainment of parity or better would embolden the Soviet
authorities to run more risks in situations involving the possibility of military
confrontations. Some consider that the attainment of parity would have little effect on overt Soviet behavior.

[25] The Pacific proposal is discussed briefly in *SSSR, SShA, i razoruzhenie*, pp.
86–87, with no reference to China. In contrast, the Pacific zone was not mentioned
in the list of proposed zones in the December 7, 1964, post-Khrushchev package of
separate measures (*Documents 1964*, p. 514).

The successful negotiations among Latin American states for a treaty fixing the atom-free status of the area has owed little to Soviet blessing, and in fact the Cuban problem has caused difficulties for the USSR in regard to this zone. The Cuban government, which did not participate in the negotiations, sought (with the support of the USSR) to extend the atom-free principle to American dependencies in the Caribbean and to bring about through the treaty the return of Guantánamo Base from American to Cuban control. The United States successfully opposed any link between the treaty and the Guantánamo issue. The treaty signed in 1967, however, includes all U.S. territory within the limits of the Latin American denuclearized zone, except for the "continental part." [26] Consequently, the United States did not sign protocol I signifying adherence to the treaty by outside states with Latin American possessions. When the U.N. General Assembly passed a resolution late in 1967 endorsing the treaty, the USSR abstained. The Soviet representative criticized the treaty for failing to prohibit nuclear explosions for peaceful purposes and to restrict transport of nuclear weapons through the zone, and also objected to the inclusion of large areas of the Atlantic and Pacific Oceans in the nuclear-free zone. He indicated that the Soviet decision on adherence to Protocol II—addressed to nuclear weapons states—would depend principally on the position taken by the United States, whose attitude toward the treaty obligations he found unsatisfactory.

Although the African states have not negotiated any convention establishing the African continent as permanently atom-free, they have repeatedly secured recognition by the U.N. General Assembly of Africa as a denuclearized area. The problem is somewhat simpler in regard to Africa than for most other suggested zones (even Latin America), because there are no nuclear-equipped countries in Africa and no independent states in Africa allied militarily to either the United States or the USSR.[27] The USSR has strongly backed U.N.

[26] For the text of the treaty, signed February 14, 1967, see U.N. General Assembly document A/C. 1/946, October 3, 1967, "Treaty for the Prohibition of Nuclear Weapons in Latin America." The United States, on February 13, 1967, declared that it understood the treaty to forbid at the present time peaceful nuclear explosions (as well as weapons tests). On February 14, 1968, President Johnson announced that the U.S. would sign treaty protocol II, which requests nuclear weapons states to respect the denuclearized status of Latin America "and not to use or threaten to use nuclear weapons against the Latin American states party to the treaty." (*Department of State Bulletin*, LVIII, No. 1497 [March 4, 1968], 313–14.) President Johnson also reiterated the American understanding that the treaty prohibited the "acquisition of nuclear explosive devices for peaceful purposes," and that it did not interfere with the "transit rights" of the United States within the treaty zone.

[27] This is subject to slight exceptions. The Portuguese have territories in Africa and ties to the United States through NATO, and there are military ties between France and the United Kingdom and certain African states.

resolutions on an atom-free Africa, and seized the chance to incorporate into them a favorite Soviet proposal for a "use" ban. The General Assembly resolution of December 3, 1965,[28] thus included a call to "all states to refrain from the use, or the threat of use, of nuclear weapons on the African continent." The United States voted for the resolution, but it objected to this provision, as it has objected to almost all agreements containing a declaratory ban on the employment of nuclear weapons.[29]

Prospects are dim for an atom-free zone in the Near East, despite indications that both the Soviet Union and the United States might support a movement in this direction. From 1958 on, the USSR repeatedly proposed the "Near and Middle East" as an "atom-free and rocket-free" zone; the proposal was repeated in the post-Khrushchev collection of partial measures suggested by the USSR, in December, 1964. For the United States, Vice-President Humphrey announced in a speech of February 17, 1965, to the *Pacem in Terris* conference in New York that the U.S. deemed an atom-free zone in the Near East acceptable.[30] It is not clear that the Soviet and American authorities envisage the same group of countries or the same conditions for such a zone; and the idea has evidently not been explored in Soviet-American negotiations. What does seem clear is that even if there were no Soviet-American differences, the present hostility in Arab-Israeli relations would probably remove any possibility of movement toward an atom-free zone in the Near East, at least in the next few years.

Most earlier Soviet and Soviet-allied proposals on denuclearization concerned Europe, with suggested regions specified as (1) Central Europe, (2) the Baltic Sea and Scandinavia, (3) the Balkans and the Adriatic Sea, and (4) the Mediterranean. All these proposals were diametrically opposed to American and NATO policy, because they would have resulted in a weakening of the American forces deployed in NATO and other allied countries. Since 1964 the USSR has not invested great effort in behalf of the proposals formerly at the center of attentions—those concerning "Central Europe," i.e., Germany (East and West), Czechoslovakia, and Poland. The well-known Rapacki plan (named after the Polish Foreign Minister) called for the denuclearization, in stages, of Central Europe; and the subsequent and more modest Gomulka plan called for a "freeze" of nuclear weapons in the same area, to be policed by observation groups from the NATO and Warsaw Pact countries.[31] Although the substantive provi-

[28] *Documents 1965*, pp. 624–26.

[29] ACDA Director Foster told the UNGA on December 1, 1965: "It is the concept of pledges of non-use which we find unsound, in general, and not its application to Africa." (*Ibid.*, p. 598.)

[30] *Department of State Bulletin*, LII, No. 1341 (March 8, 1965), 329.

[31] The Rapacki Plan exists in several variants. See *Documents 1962*, I, pp. 201–5. The Gomulka proposal was advanced by the Polish First Secretary on Decem-

sions embodied in certain of these plans, especially in the Gomulka proposal, might have interested Western countries, they all involved the thorny question of a divided Germany. Through its membership in the Warsaw Treaty Organization, the German Democratic Republic was to be a "subject" of any such arrangement as well as a participant in its negotiation and administration. The effectuation of any such proposal would thus have brought about dealings with the GDR on a level so far avoided by the Western powers.

Meanwhile, however, the European situation has become more fluid, and in the new political structure that is emerging, some zonal plans involving nuclear arms may become negotiable. Even the stumbling block of a divided Germany may become less formidable a barrier to movement toward arrangements desirable on other grounds. Europe offers at least one advantage, by contrast with proposals for worldwide agreements on limitations of Soviet and American power, namely, that both sides seem prepared to accept "parity" as the basis for arrangements between Western-allied and Soviet-allied forces.

BAN ON USE OF NUCLEAR WEAPONS

Although the Soviet Union has dropped serious propagation of proposals to "abolish" nuclear weapons, it has continued to support proposals for an international agreement banning the "use" of nuclear weapons or reciprocal pledges to forswear the first use of such weapons.[32] An adaptation to African conditions of the proposed ban on use of nuclear weapons appeared, as mentioned, in the 1965 U.N. resolution recognizing Africa as an atom-free zone; and a similar adaptation to the nonproliferation treaty was suggested by Premier Kosygin in his proposal of February 1, 1966.[33]

Proposals by the Soviet Union for a convention banning the use of nuclear weapons have been promoted since Stalin's time, when atomic weapons first appeared. Unchanged in substance, they have been pushed with some vigor in 1964–1968, although more often in large public forums (such as those representing all U.N. member states) than

---

ber 28, 1963. (*Documents 1963*, pp. 651–52.) The formal Polish government expression of the Gomulka proposal appeared in a memorandum of February 24, 1965. (*Documents 1964*, pp. 53–55.)

[32] For recent official statements of the Soviet position, see the speech by Soviet representative Roshchin to the ENDC, July 7, 1966 (*Documents 1966*, pp. 429–35), the Soviet draft—submitted to the UNGA on September 22, 1967—of a convention prohibiting use of nuclear weapons (*Documents 1967*, pp. 420–21), and a speech by USSR representative V. V. Kuznetsov on November 20, 1967 (*ibid.*, pp. 579–85). A partial account of the history of the proposal is included in *SSSR, SShA, i razoruzhenie*, pp. 65–68.

[33] Message to the ENDC, *Documents 1966*, pp. 9–13.

in smaller negotiating bodies (such as the Eighteen-Nation Disarmament Committee). In all these gatherings, the proposals have encountered the determined opposition of the United States and many of its allies.

A proposal for a conference to formulate a convention against the use of nuclear weapons has received considerable support in the U.N. General Assembly since 1961, when the UNGA endorsed a declaration that the use of nuclear weapons was contrary "to the spirit, letter, and aims of the United Nations . . ." and that any state using nuclear weapons "is to be considered as violating the charter of the U.N., or acting contrary to the laws of humanity, and as committing a crime against mankind and civilization." [34]

When the U.N. Disarmament Commission (comprising representatives of all U.N. members) met in New York in 1965, one of the two Soviet-proposed resolutions provided that a conference be called before July, 1966, to work out a convention banning the use of nuclear weapons. All states, not just U.N. members, were to be invited—a clear enough reference to the Chinese People's Republic, the newest atomic power and the only such state outside the U.N. The Soviet draft also called on nuclear states to declare, prior to the conference, that they would not be the "first" to use these weapons. (Soviet proposals containing a renunciation of "first use" dated back to 1955 and, in a different form, to 1953.) In the face of American and other opposition sufficient to bring about a defeat, the USSR did not put its resolution to a vote at the New York meeting. However, at the session of the U.N. General Assembly in the fall of 1966, a resolution on the subject sponsored by five nonaligned states (India, Nigeria, Ethiopia, the United Arab Republic, and Yugoslavia) was passed by the General Assembly by a vote of 80–0, with 23 abstentions (including the United States).[35] The resolution asserted "that the signing of a convention on the prohibition of the use of nuclear and thermonuclear weapons would greatly facilitate negotiations on general and complete disarmament. . . ." The "world disarmament conference" that was supposed to work out this convention never met, however. In the U.N. General Assembly session of the fall of 1967, the USSR presented on September 27 a draft convention to prohibit the use of nuclear weapons. A resolution endorsing such a convention was subsequently approved by the General Assembly, with the United States, Cuba, and 27 other states abstaining.

As this account suggests, there has been a growth of support for these proposals from states which are not only unequipped with nuclear

[34] *Documents 1961*, pp. 648–50.
[35] The text of the resolution, passed on December 5, is in *Documents 1966*, pp. 803–4.

weapons but also nonaligned, i.e., unprotected by any nuclear-equipped ally. Like most other arms control proposals, however, their realization can be blocked by the United States or any other nuclear power, for a convention against use would be meaningless if it did not have the general support of the powers possessing nuclear weapons.

It might be noted here that the Soviet and Chinese positions on first use differ slightly, since Communist China has stated categorically that it will not be the "first" to use nuclear weapons, whereas the Soviet Union makes its willingness to accept such a pledge dependent on reciprocity from other nuclear states.[36] The difference is not too surprising in view of the fact that China is much more poorly equipped with such weapons than the Soviet Union, and therefore the initiation of their use by China would involve something close to a death-wish.

A convention "prohibiting" the use, or first use, of nuclear weapons would not, of course, remove a single nuclear weapon from any military force or stockpile of armaments. It would not, therefore, be a measure of "disarmament." Any state could continue to deploy its weapons as its strategy dictated, add to its nuclear arsenals, and continue preparations for nuclear warfare, either limited or general.

The U.S. has consistently rejected such proposals because of their disharmony with more or less openly declared U.S. strategic plans to initiate the use of nuclear weapons, particularly in Europe, if conventional forces should prove insufficient to contain a serious threat to the security of the United States or its allies.

This reason has usually been only hinted at in public statements by American representatives at disarmament negotiations,[37] who have

---

[36] Thus, Premier Kosygin in the February 1, 1966, message to the ENDC: "The Soviet Union is prepared to assume immediately an obligation not to be the first to use nuclear weapons, provided that the other nuclear powers do likewise." (Text in *Documents 1966*, p. 11.) Compare the message of Premier Chou En-lai to various heads of government, October 17, 1964: "The Chinese government solemnly declares that at no time and in no circumstances will China be the first to use nuclear weapons." (*Documents 1964*, p. 455.)

[37] Proposals of this type have been much discussed in international disarmament meetings, including the U.N. General Assembly sessions considering arms control and disarmament questions. For a recent statement of the United States position against such an agreement, see the remarks of Adrian S. Fisher to the General Assembly on November 20, 1967, in *Documents 1967*, pp. 585–92.

The issues are also discussed in: Robert C. Tucker, Klaus Knorr, Richard A. Falk, and Hedley Bull, *Proposal for No First Use of Nuclear Weapons: Pros and Cons* (Princeton, N.J.: Center of International Studies, Research Memorandum No. 28, 1963, processed); Richard A. Falk, Robert C. Tucker, and Oran R. Young, *On Minimizing the Use of Nuclear Weapons* (Princeton, N.J.: Center of International Studies, Research Memorandum No. 23, 1966, processed); Herman Kahn, *On Escalation* (New York: Frederick A. Praeger, Inc., 1965), pp. 102–133; Herman Kahn and Carl Dibble, "Criteria for Long-Range Nuclear Control Policies," *California Law Review*, LV, May, 1967), 473–92; Bernard T. Feld, "A Pledge: No First Use," *Bulle-*

argued that no weapons are condemned in the U.N. Charter, where a distinction is drawn between aggressive and defensive use of force, not between legitimate and illegitimate weapons. The charter was drawn up, of course, before atomic weapons were known. It is frequently argued, also, that any ban on use of nuclear weapons would be void of meaning because it could not prevent the use of such weapons *in extremis*. It would inhibit only the more restrained party. The primary effect of a "use" ban would probably be to discourage the brandishing of nuclear weapons in crisis situations (a practice resorted to on occasion by the USSR as well as other powers). This might benefit "crisis management" a little, but Washington fears that it might also have the negative effect of reducing subjective fears of nuclear war when the objective possibility of such war had not been reduced at all.

Nevertheless, the inhibitions on use of nuclear weapons have grown in the years since Hiroshima and Nagasaki. Even the best-equipped and most secure nuclear weapons power, the United States, has drawn back from introducing nuclear weapons into such conflicts as the Korean War, the Indochinese War ending in 1954, and the present conflict in Vietnam. There is still no agreement on the desirability of moving from this inhibition in practice to a prohibition in law. But the likelihood of an agreement against use of nuclear weapons has increased as nuclear weapons have proliferated among five great powers.

---

tin of the Atomic Scientists, XXIII, No. 5 (May, 1967), 46–48; and, Carl H. Amme, Jr., *NATO Without France* (Stanford, Calif.: The Hoover Institution on War, Peace, and Revolution, 1967), pp. 109–14.

10

ARMS CONTROL PROPOSALS
AFFECTING BOTH CONVENTIONAL
AND NUCLEAR FORCES

Of the partial arms control measures successfully negotiated, only the Antarctic and outer-space treaties have touched conventional as well as nuclear weapons. And the nonmilitarization of an icy area at the South Pole and planets on which no human being has ever set foot is clearly of minor significance in the confrontation of the great powers. Most of the partial measures discussed in disarmament forums have centered on nuclear weapons and delivery systems; yet three kinds of proposals that have been directed to military establishments and military forces are relevant to both nuclear and conventional war.

The first type includes proposals, by the U.S. and the USSR, for bomber bonfires; the second consists of Soviet proposals for agreed limitations on, or reductions of, military budgets; and the third involves proposals, also Soviet in origin, for the elimination of foreign military bases and the withdrawal or reduction of troops stationed abroad. None of these proposals is of post-1964 origin. In fact, if venerable old age elicited signs of honor in disarmament assemblies, the Soviet budgetary and foreign bases proposals would be among the most respected of all those maintained in the repertory.

BOMBER BONFIRES

At one time the idea of reciprocal destruction of bombing aircraft seemed to offer a promising field for agreement. In the 1960's, both the USSR and the United States began to rely primarily on missiles rather than manned aircraft as the vehicles to carry nuclear weapons to the enemy's homeland if war erupted between the two states. Planned and agreed reductions under a disarmament label could thus ride ahead of inevitable unilateral reductions resulting from the obsolescence of bombing aircraft. Bombers to this day remain, however, an important part of American and, to a lesser extent, Soviet capabilities for strategic nuclear warfare—probably more so than had been expected a few years ago.[1] Unlike guided missiles, moreover, even bombers designed for delivery of nuclear weapons continue to be of great importance for conventional warfare.

The USSR periodically repeated an earlier proposal for the destruction of all bombing aircraft.[2] The only modification introduced in the course of discussions was a proviso that powers dependent on bombing aircraft for defense—i.e., those lacking missiles—should be allowed to retain bombers longer than those possessing missiles. Soviet representatives agreed to discuss the details of their proposal only if there was agreement "in principle" to the destruction of all bombers.[3]

Rejecting the Soviet plan, the U.S. countered with another proposal, which in turn received a cold Soviet response. On March 19, 1964, the U.S. suggested that the U.S. and the USSR progressively destroy an equal number of medium-range bombs (American B-47's and Soviet TU-16's) over a two-year period—a reduction of about 500 each.[4] Apparently the Soviet authorities expected the U.S. to get rid of its B-47's in any case, and in fact the retirement of the planes has removed the proposal from the agenda. The shelving of the idea was made complete when the USSR dropped from its July 1, 1968 list of desirable measures its own proposal to destroy all bombing aircraft.

Even if the demand for bombers were to diminish further in the strategic planning for nuclear war, this trend would not necessarily better the chances of agreement on a general bonfire of all manned bombers. For the United States, the interest in maintenance of "conventional options" on a worldwide basis has left a very large role to bombers in preparing for non-nuclear hostilities, as Vietnam attests daily. In addition, for a variety of reasons, bombers occupy a more important role in American than in Soviet planning for a possible nuclear duel. One reason is that superiority in heavily loaded long-range bombers enables the United States to avoid a "megatonnage

---

[1] The fact that the USSR is constructing a new defense system, the "Tallin" system, now believed to be primarily or entirely anti-aircraft rather than antimissile, testifies to the Soviet belief in the continued importance of bombers in the strategic equation. Whatever their disadvantages, bombers can carry a greater quantity of nuclear explosives than missiles; they are more flexible in tactics; if airborne, they are less vulnerable to surprise attack, and so forth.

[2] The proposal was included in the set of separate measures advanced by the USSR in a memorandum of January 28, 1964, and repeated in the comparable memorandum circulated by the USSR on December 7, 1964 (*Documents 1964*, p. 16).

[3] Ambassador Tsarapkin to the ENDC, April 2, 1964, and July 16, 1964, in *ibid.*, pp. 139, 284–88.

[4] *Ibid.*, pp. 101–5. The phasing out of service of B-47's made the 1964 proposal less relevant in subsequent years. American negotiators shifted their attention to the broader 1964 proposal on freezing levels and characteristics of all strategic nuclear delivery vehicles.

gap."[5] (Although the Soviet Union has fewer ICBMs than the U.S. has Minutemen, the payload capacity of the American missiles is smaller.) For this and other reasons, the U.S. has not foreclosed the possibility of "follow-on" bombers to replace those now in the strategic nuclear forces (B-52's and B-58's) and under production (FB-111's).

The wide disparity in military needs and perspectives between the U.S. and the USSR made it unlikely that an agreement for reciprocal bomber destruction could be worked out. Prospects of an agreement in this area would be improved if unilateral plans for replacement of obsolescent types became sufficiently parallel, a condition that has not yet existed. Such measures would have to avoid the asymmetry that prevented serious negotiation on either the U.S. or the Soviet bomber proposals. Both of these proposals struck at the heart of the opponents' concepts of strategy and of disarmament. Thus, the U.S. proposal for destruction of equal numbers of Soviet and American medium-range bombers was unacceptable to Soviet authorities because it would have perpetuated and even increased U.S. superiority in strategic nuclear delivery vehicles. The contrasting USSR proposal to destroy all bombers would have eliminated far more American than Soviet vehicles. This would have reduced the general superiority of the U.S. in strategic delivery vehicles, particularly since destruction of bombers would have increased the importance of ballistic missiles, in which Soviet inferiority was less pronounced. Even more important, perhaps, the Soviet proposal would have reduced American capabilities for applying air power to far-flung military operations of non-nuclear character—operations of a kind which the USSR has generally avoided.

LIMITATIONS ON MILITARY SPENDING

Although routinely re-endorsed by Soviet authorities, proposals by the USSR for agreed limits on military budgets have received relatively little emphasis since 1964. Such proposals were advanced by the USSR repeatedly after Stalin's death: reduction by one third (1954), by 15 per cent (1956), by 10–15 per cent (1958), a "freeze" at the January 1, 1961, level (1960). The later proposals envisaged smaller

---

[5] There is controversy about the significance of comparisons of the total weight of destructive power that can be delivered against an opponent. Although he asserts American superiority even in this area, Robert McNamara has disparaged the importance of megatonnage comparisons and emphasized the greater importance of numbers of individual warheads that can be delivered on targets. See his San Francisco address, September 18, 1967 (*The New York Times,* September 19, 1967), and interview in *Life,* September 29, 1967. A report prepared by the American Security Council, a private organization, for the House of Representatives Committee on Armed Services, *The Changing Strategic Military Balance: U.S.A. vs. U.S.S.R.,* emphasizes the significance of megatonnage.

cuts because they were not part of a general disarmament plan. The post-Khrushchev regime included in its December, 1964, list of desirable partial measures a proposal for a 10–15 per cent reduction, thus repeating the goal set in the last Khrushchev list of partial measures, that of January, 1964. The July 1, 1968, list of measures proposed by the USSR made no reference to military budget cuts. There have never been, in any case, serious negotiations regarding these proposals.[6]

Cool to such budget reduction proposals, American officials have countered with a suggestion that there be technical discussions of what is included in military budgets of various countries.[7] Such discussions were acceptable to the USSR only if the United States would agree in principle to the reductions. Although the Soviet proposals were not clear, presumably they contemplated a one-time reduction, and any subsequent controls or reductions would have to be renegotiated.

Discussions of the possibility, or desirability, of agreed limits on, or reduction in, military spending are often clouded by a failure to distinguish between two problems. One concerns the adequacy of available information on military spending;[8] the other, the desirability of a state tying its military spending to an internationally agreed ceiling. The spotlight thrown on the first question tends to leave obscure the second, equally difficult, question. To make the point sharply: the Soviet proposal for a budget cut or budget ceiling could hardly have been accepted by the United States after 1964, even if the American authorities had known as much about Soviet military spending as the Soviet authorities knew.

In fact, of course, this information was not available. Almost nothing is published in the Soviet Union to explain what its military budget item includes and excludes. In contrast, the U.S. publishes a fairly detailed annual breakdown of expenditures for specific military and quasi-military services and programs. Thus, it is possible for Soviet authorities to have a far greater confidence that they have access to the facts on American military spending than the United States has about Soviet military spending.[9]

It is most improbable, therefore, that the U.S. would ever agree to an arrangement pairing trends in American defense spending with Soviet budgetary allocations while the USSR continued to publish

[6] See the discussion in *SSSR, SShA i razoruzhenie*, pp. 91–94. The Soviet proposal of January, 1964, was discussed by ACDA Deputy Director Adrian S. Fisher at the ENDC on April 9, 1964. See *Documents 1964*, pp. 152–57.

[7] Secretary of State Rusk, December 1, 1965, in *Documents 1965*, pp. 596–97.

[8] Apart from the question of information on Soviet military spending, there is a real question about the appropriateness of classifying various expenditures as military. This conceptual difficulty would not be as serious, however, if information were available on specific programs.

[9] See Chapter 5 above.

only one-line, one-sum accounts of its military expenditures. It may be that the USSR would also reject such a pairing if it involved total military expenditures and not merely those assigned to a budget category publicly labeled "military." An internationally agreed "freeze" or reduction could impede a power such as the Soviet Union, which seeks to equal or surpass an opponent stronger in major types of military capabilities.

Another range of problems, unrelated to the adequacy of information on military spending, further reduces the chances of Soviet-American agreement to accept limits on military budgets. Such agreements would probably have to include all the significant military powers. Yet the antipathy of Communist China toward current disarmament negotiations, and its almost certain rejection of any such agreement, could ruin whatever prospects might otherwise exist of placing a ceiling on expenditures. Besides, the fact that Communist China is increasing its military capabilities while remaining hostile to the Soviet Union may reduce Moscow's interest in a Soviet-American agreement to limit military expenditures.[10]

A related difficulty of more immediate importance renders prospects poor for any agreement. The asymmetrical military activities of negotiating states would always hinder attempts to pair military spending trends. The heavy involvement of the United States in Vietnam illustrates the more general problem, namely, that a state expensively involved in military activities that are tangential to its rivalry with a major adversary cannot tie its spending level to that of its adversary. Put another way, the breakdown of bipolarity worsens prospects that senior states of opposed military alliances might agree to financial limits for military efforts. For most of the period since World War II, the United States and the Soviet Union have been able to organize their military preparations with some confidence that they knew the likely line-up of foes and allies. Neither has this confidence today. Communist China is the great unknown, but there are others, both East and West.[11]

If these difficulties regarding availability of information and congruity of policy could be overcome, the budget-cut approach would have some advantages for countries seriously favoring arms reductions.

---

[10] Considerations revolving about China have probably had little effect on either Soviet or American total military expenditures since the Korean War, but the development of Chinese nuclear weapons capabilities and the increased prospects of American-Chinese or even Soviet-Chinese military collisions make the Chinese factor more important.

[11] See, for example, the declaration on January 27, 1968, by President de Gaulle that France sought a defense covering "all azimuths." See *Le Monde, Sélection Hebdomadaire,* XXI, No. 1007 (February 1–7, 1968).

It would allow them to combine an actual reduction, or at least a stabilization, of the human and material resources devoted to military purposes, and maximum national freedom to decide which armaments or forces should be reduced.[12] Theoretically, at least, this would allow for a better fit between decisions on military spending and the varying interests of the opposing sides. Each power accepting a ceiling on spending could then concentrate on those forces it deemed most vital to its national security, and could cut down or cut out activities of marginal importance.

Budget cuts lend themselves easily to a method of "disarmament" often recommended by those impatient with the slow process of diplomatic negotiations, that is, to unilateral but reciprocal steps, or "the arms race in reverse." Downward spirals have occurred in the arms spending of both the USSR and the U.S. in the period since World War II. The most recent of these shifts downward occurred in 1964, when both the U.S. and the Soviet Union announced reductions of defense spending in a period when the successful conclusion of the 1963 test-ban treaty created favorable prospects for additional arms limitation measures.

Although the 1964 cuts were not jointly agreed on, they could be viewed as reciprocal measures creating a basis for additional steps. Their fragility was soon demonstrated, as the escalation of the war in Vietnam caused a steeply upward movement of American and Soviet military spending. But even apart from such dramatic turning points, a rhythm of reciprocity has proved difficult to sustain. This is partly because a regime that reduces its arms budget may label this a step toward disarmament inviting emulation from the other side, but such a move will usually be regarded by adversaries (and often quite rightly) as a decision governed by national considerations and judged wise irrespective of any response or reciprocation from rival states.

LIQUIDATION OF FOREIGN MILITARY BASES

Proposals aimed at the liquidation of "foreign military bases" and the withdrawal to their homelands of troops stationed abroad have been a staple of Soviet policy since 1946, and, in more absolute form, since 1953. They became more sweeping as the division of Germany

---

[12] The sums involved are not petty. According to one computation, $140 billion was spent world-wide on military establishments in 1965, with the United States and the Soviet Union accounting for two thirds of the total, or $92 billion; the addition of NATO and WTO powers would bring the proportion to 84 per cent. In the same year, about $7 billion was spent on foreign aid. See the ACDA report *Worldwide Military Expenditures and Related Data* (for calendar year 1964), December, 1967.

became more permanent. With its relinquishment of bases in China and Finland in 1955 and 1956, the USSR considered that it no longer had any foreign military bases.[13] Soviet troops were still stationed outside the Soviet Union, however, in three Warsaw Pact states: East Germany, Poland, and Hungary; and Soviet forces, along with those of four other Warsaw Pact states, occupied Czechoslovakia in August, 1968. (Soviet troops were withdrawn from Rumania in 1958.) Conceivably the Soviet position on foreign military bases could change as the USSR increases its military presence (particularly its naval forces) in areas distant from Soviet home bases. But so far such a change has not occurred.

The distinction between stationing of troops and military bases in foreign countries is somewhat artificial, of course, since troops more or less permanently quartered abroad have to be stationed at fixed installations, whether or not these are called military bases. Presumably what Soviet authorities mean by "foreign bases" are military installations, especially naval or air, so located to serve purposes going well beyond—or having little or nothing to do with—the military needs of the host country (e.g., Singapore, the former Soviet base at Porkkala-Udd, Guantánamo). Troops in foreign countries are usually more clearly linked to possible military operations involving the host country.

Through its proposals, the USSR sought to break down the worldwide system of military bases maintained by the United States, and even Soviet proposals for the mutual withdrawal of Western and Soviet troops from other countries in Europe were usually tied to a demand for U.S. withdrawal from non-European bases as well. Short of this dismantling of all military establishments abroad, the USSR also proposed, as in December, 1964, a cutback (either by agreement or by step-by-step mutual example) of troops stationed by the USSR and Western powers in Germany, of Soviet troops in "other European" states, and of Western troops in "other countries." [14]

The United States has rejected all these Soviet proposals for the liquidation of foreign bases and withdrawal or reduction of troops in other countries. The proposal on bases—as defined by the Soviet authorities—would clearly reduce American military capabilities without touching those of the USSR. The proposal for mutual withdrawals in Europe would not be as one-sided in its impact, since Soviet troops too would leave Central and Eastern Europe; but the departure of U.S. troops across the ocean would probably diminish American capabilities and influence in Europe more than Soviet withdrawal to nearby Soviet borders would reduce Soviet capabilities. Apart from the impact in

[13] Soviet troops were also withdrawn from Austria in 1955.
[14] Documents 1964, pp. 510–11.

Europe, Soviet proposals have aimed at U.S. withdrawal from Vietnam, from bases elsewhere in Asia, Latin America, and Africa.[15]

The USSR has received substantial support for its campaign against foreign military bases from many of the nonaligned and formerly colonial countries, but has never been able to get the endorsement of any disarmament forum or of the U.N. General Assembly for its stand. This was not for lack of trying. One of the two resolutions submitted by the USSR to the U.N. Disarmament Commission in 1965 was a call for liquidation of foreign military bases. The Soviet draft resolution was not, however, put to a vote, probably because the USSR foresaw that it did not have enough support for passage.[16] At the 1966 session of the U.N. General Assembly, a resolution on bases in Asia, Africa, and Latin America was submitted by the UAR, Yugoslavia, and India as a substitute for a much stronger Soviet proposal. The substitute was adopted by a vote of 94–0, with the U.S. among 10 abstainers. The title referred to "the elimination of foreign military bases in the countries of Asia, Africa, and Latin America," and the text stressed the importance of foreign bases as an issue. Nevertheless, the resolution lacked teeth: it merely referred the question to the Eighteen Nation Disarmament Committee for "further consideration and report." [17]

It is highly probable that the Soviet authorities do not consider any proposal for liquidation of foreign military bases as negotiable with the United States; it is more likely that their main objective is to build up pressure on the U.S. from the radical-nationalist states of the third world. The element of reciprocity in the "troops abroad" proposal makes it somewhat more interesting to Western states, which have sought for a long time to secure the retreat of Soviet forces from Eastern Europe. Even with this compensation, however, the withdrawal of all Western (and particularly American) troops to their homelands is considered unacceptable by the United States as a basis for negotiation.

Proposals for agreed reductions of troops stationed in Europe seemed until recently to have some promise. They had long been advocated by the USSR, and the United States showed some interest in scaling down troop deployments in Europe. Thus, President Johnson referred to the NATO-WTO confrontation in Europe in an address of October 7, 1966, in which he said, "If changing circumstances should lead to a gradual and balanced revision in force levels on both sides, the revision could . . . help gradually to shape an entire new political

---

[15] For one explanation of the U.S. position, see the statement at the U.N. by ACDA Director Foster on November 28, 1966, *Documents 1966*, pp. 79–97.

[16] Text in *Documents 1965*, pp. 207–8. See Statement by ACDA Director Foster at the ENDC, August 10, 1965; *ibid.*, pp. 322–24.

[17] Text in *Documents 1966*, p. 804.

environment."[18] In 1967 the United States announced decisions to bring back to the United States from Europe some 50,000 troops during 1967–1968.[19] The decision was explained by Administration officials as based on balance-of-payments and other practical considerations, rather than as a move toward a lessened confrontation of Eastern and Western forces in Europe. Secretaries Rusk and McNamara expressed hope for Soviet reciprocity, but thought this unlikely in view of the vulnerability of the USSR to charges that it was aiding the United States in Vietnam.[20]

There apparently has been no answering Soviet reduction of forces in Europe, despite rumors of shifts of Soviet troops from East Germany to the borders of China.[21] Even apart from Soviet vulnerability to Chinese accusations, it is not clear that the Soviet leaders would want to ease America's problems (whether of the balance of payments, or availability of troops for Vietnam, or others) by agreeing to reciprocal reductions. Should they seek mutual reductions, however, it seems likely that they would prefer to gain the political advantages of an agreement on the subject, rather than follow the route of quiet reciprocation of unilateral steps. They might, thus, show greater responsiveness to the more formal overtures recently under discussion.[22] Even a negotiated agreement would make Soviet withdrawals a target for attacks from militant Communists. In Soviet eyes, however, it

[18] *Ibid.*, p. 654.

[19] Of these, 18,000 were reductions effected in connection with the shift of NATO forces and headquarters from France; 35,000 were due to a redeployment from Germany to the United States of a few ground and air units. These were to remain committed to NATO. See the discussion in the Hearings on United States Troops in Europe.

[20] At these hearings (p. 63) Secretary Rusk said:

. . . I am inclined to believe that the Soviets [sic] will not negotiate at this point on mutual withdrawal of forces because they are apparently nervous about being charged with negotiating a mutual withdrawal in Central Europe in a way that would release U.S. forces for Vietnam and bring them under the fire of China.

My guess is that, if there is any prospect of any movement on this, it is likely to come without agreement, but through what is called mutual example—that they simply take certain steps. . . . If the Soviets were to show some real interest in this problem, that could, in turn, be taken into account by NATO in determining what forces are required in NATO.

[21] See *McNamara Posture Statement, 1968.*

[22] At the December, 1967, meeting of the North Atlantic Council, the ministers "reaffirmed their view that, if conditions permit, a balanced reduction of forces on both sides could constitute a significant step toward security in Europe." (*Department of State Bulletin*, LVIII, No. 1489 [January 8, 1968], 49–52.) It was reported from Washington that President Johnson and the NATO Secretary General Manlio Brosio had agreed that NATO should work on a proposal to Moscow for a phased withdrawal of troops in Europe (*The New York Times*, February 20, 1968).

would also have the advantages of greater permanence and of providing a starting point for other East-West negotiations on the future of Europe.[23]

[23] It might be noted in this connection that the Western incentives for a complete Soviet withdrawal from Central and East Europe have lessened somewhat over the years as a result of military and political developments.

11

EUROPEAN REGIONAL ARRANGEMENTS
IN SOVIET ARMS CONTROL POLICY

Since 1964 the Soviet leaders have invested considerable effort in pushing proposals for new political-military arrangements in Europe. To facilitate these efforts, they have studiously avoided military or political steps threatening Western nations and likely to restore cohesion to Western alliances. The USSR has sought instead to take advantage of the lessened fear of war, the "contradictions" among leading Western states, and the absence of any significant American initiative on Europe.

Khrushchev sought to deal with Europe by attacking the most sensitive of all European problems, that of Berlin. His successors, on the contrary, have generally diverted attention from Berlin to German problems and groped for a way of dealing with Europe as a whole. There were occasional reminders, as in the spring of 1968, of the East German and Soviet capability of putting pressure on West Berlin. Basically, however, the Soviet leaders have left Berlin to fall into place as a part of, rather than a prelude to, the constitution of a new order in Europe.

Most of the various proposals on European affairs advanced by or acceptable to the Soviet Union have arms control or disarmament provisions. Therefore, a discussion of European regional proposals is relevant and indeed necessary to this study. But it must be noted that a discussion based on the arms control and disarmament aspects of broad political measures cannot deal adequately with these measures. Yet a complex treatment is well beyond the scope of this work.

A related difficulty is that some arms control and disarmament proposals of general applicability, discussed elsewhere in the volume, have special importance for Europe. The U.S.-USSR draft nonproliferation treaty is one of these. There could not help but be profound reactions in Europe to this spectacle of Soviet-American bridge building. The relative powerlessness of the former leading nations in Europe was evident in the largely bilateral (U.S.-USSR) character of the negotiations leading to the completion of the draft in 1968, in the eventual submergence of the NATO MLF project while these negotiations were going on, and in the seal of acceptance that the draft treaty placed on the division of states into two classes, with the Soviet Union and the United States in one class and most of their allies in the other.[1] There seems little doubt that the Soviet interest in the treaty centered first of all on its European impact. Specifically, Moscow used the treaty negotiations to make the regime in Bonn appear as the stumbling block to a *détente* in Europe, to isolate the Federal Republic from its allies, and to lessen any West German chances of acquiring nuclear weapons.[2] Although Soviet spokesmen and propagandists have occasionally expressed concern over the possibility of a general spread of nuclear weapons to additional countries, most of their attention has focused on the West Germans, whose leaders allegedly thirsted for nuclear weapons.[3]

Along with some new proposals, or at least new versions of old proposals, the Soviet Union has continued in the post-Khrushchev years to back various measures that originated years ago in Moscow and other Eastern European capitals. In the section dealing with atom-free zones, reference was made to the Rapacki and Gomulka proposals for a "freeze," reduction, or elimination of nuclear weapons in Central Europe. The later variants of the Rapacki plan also suggested steps to reduce conventional forces in the same area.[4] All these meas-

---

[1] The full text of the draft treaty is in the *Department of State Bulletin*, LVIII, No. 1493 (February 5, 1968), 165–67. Of course, the nuclear-equipped allies of the United States (the United Kingdom and France) and of the Soviet Union (the Chinese People's Republic) were also classified as "nuclear weapons states" under the draft, which set January 1, 1967, as the cut-off date for classification purposes. Both France and Communist China have indicated that they would not adhere to the treaty.

[2] The role of the treaty as a barrier to German "revanchism" received much more attention in the statements of Soviet leaders and in Soviet propaganda than did any other beneficial effects expected from the treaty. It dominated Soviet references even after the MLF was discarded from Western plans.

[3] See, for example, Premier Kosygin's message of February 1, 1966, to the ENDC (*Documents 1966*, pp. 10–11); the letter of Foreign Minister Gromyko to U.N. General Assembly President Pazhwak, September 23, 1966 (*ibid.*, pp. 645–46); and the statement of Soviet representative Roshchin to the U.N. General Assembly on November 7, 1966 (*ibid.*, pp. 711–20). The German aspect was also stressed in an article designed for an elite audience, L. Ia. Cherkassky, "Iz istorii bor'by Sovetskogo Soiuza za iadernoe razoruzhenie," in *Novaia i noveishaia istoriia*, No. 2 (March–April, 1967), 99–107. There have been only a few allusions in Soviet statements to the "Nth" country problem, i.e., the danger of "ten" or "twenty" additional countries developing or acquiring nuclear weapons. In these references Soviet sources have named likely countries on the basis of Western sources.

[4] The original Rapacki proposal for an atom-free zone in Central Europe was presented to the U.N. General Assembly on October 2, 1957 (*Documents 1945–1959*, II, pp. 889–92), and restated with special attention to the question of control, in a government memorandum of February 14, 1958 (*ibid.*, pp. 944–48). In a second vari-

ures continued at least until recently to have Soviet backing,[5] along
with proposals for disbanding both the NATO and Warsaw Pact alliances, a pact of nonaggression between states of the North Atlantic
and Warsaw treaties, and "measures to avert surprise attack."

NONAGGRESSION PACT BETWEEN NATO
AND WARSAW TREATY STATES

Less far-reaching than many other Soviet suggestions for Europe, the
Soviet-proposed pact of "nonaggression" between member states of the
Atlantic and Warsaw alliances has been given desultory support by the
post-Khrushchev leadership and was not included in the list of suggested partial measures advanced by the USSR on July 1, 1968.[6] The
proposal is one of several largely symbolic measures that have been
viewed with favor in the East and with disfavor in the West. After
several years of exploitation of the proposals, first launched over a
decade ago,[7] Premier Khrushchev attempted in the 1963 negotiations
for a nuclear weapons test ban to tie Soviet acceptance of a partial
test ban to American and British support for a nonaggression agreement. In the end he settled for a mere promise to consult the interested
allies, which meant the end rather than the beginning of negotiations.
Apart from the difference of viewpoint on the value of declaratory
agreements of this kind, the sticking point was the fact that the proposal—like other Soviet proposals on Europe—would have contributed
diplomatic support to the recognition of the division of Germany and

---

ant, the plan foresaw two stages in the denuclearization process, with an initial
freeze and a subsequent elimination of nuclear weapons. This was publicized by
Rapacki on November 4, 1958 (ibid., pp. 1217–19). Rapacki then expressed willingness to reduce conventional as well as nuclear arms, but a plan so modified was
not submitted to the ENDC until March 28, 1962. This retained the idea of a freeze
on nuclear weapons in the first stage and envisaged parallel reductions of conventional and nuclear weapons in the second (Documents 1962, pp. 201–5). A subsequent "Gomulka plan" was announced December 28, 1963 (Documents 1963, pp.
651–52) and circulated officially on February 24, 1964 (Documents 1964, pp. 53–55).
In effect, it made a separable plan of the first stage of the revised Rapacki proposal; i.e., it was limited to a freeze on nuclear weapons in Germany, Czechoslovakia,
and Poland.

   [5] For a Soviet account of the Rapacki and Gomulka plans, see SSSR, SShA, i
razoruzhenie, pp. 80–82. The proposals were endorsed in Soviet government memoranda of January 28 and December 7, 1964 (Documents 1964, pp. 14–15, 513–14),
and in other official statements since that time, but not in the Soviet government
memorandum of July 1, 1968.

   [6] A minor point may have some importance: the proposals always call for this pact
between the states of the rival alliances, not between the alliances, as often described in Western sources.

   [7] A Soviet draft of the proposed nonaggression pact was submitted to the ENDC
on February 20, 1963 (Documents 1963, pp. 57–58).

to the international status of the Communist-led regime in East Germany. It was largely for this reason that the pact was sought by Moscow, Pankow, and other Eastern capitals and rejected by Washington, Bonn, and Western capitals.[8]

A variant of the NATO-Warsaw nonaggression pact was proposed at a conference of European Communist parties in Karlovy Vary (Czechoslovakia), April 24–26, 1967. The parties represented there called for conclusion of a treaty between all European states on "the renunciation in their mutual relations of the application of force or threats of its application, and of interference in internal affairs." The treaty should guarantee, it was said, "in accordance with the principles of the U.N. Charter, the settlement of all disputed questions by exclusively peaceful means." [9] The shift of Soviet attention from a pact with NATO states to an all-European arrangement reflects a desire to minimize any possible role for NATO in promoting *détente* and to focus attention on 1969 as a date for NATO states to reconsider their membership in the alliance.

Whether covering all European states or limited to members of the rival alliances, such a treaty raises difficulties for NATO. Signature of such a treaty by NATO states would constitute an acknowledgment that their Eastern opponents had ruled out the use of force. Since NATO's military efforts are predicated on the idea of repelling aggression from the East, the treaty would be at cross purposes with the rationale for NATO. The treaty might also raise problems regarding access to West Berlin, because the GDR (and the USSR) can interfere with movement by administrative measures, whereas Western efforts to insure access might require application of force.

As already indicated, one of the big stumbling blocks in the past, particularly for the United States and the German Federal Republic, has been the intended participation of the East German regime. With the Federal Republic becoming more flexible in its policies toward Eastern Europe, however, the German barrier may cease to be determinative. Despite qualms and reservations, the Federal Republic and the United States signed the 1963 test-ban treaty along with the German Democratic Republic, and presumably will eventually sign a nonproliferation agreement. The signature of both German states of a nonaggression treaty would, nevertheless, stand out more prominently because of the smaller list of signers.

Although still chary of symbolic agreements of this kind which do not alter the military or political facts of life, the United States and

---

[8] One account of the factors involved in the U.S. government's consideration of a nonaggression pact in 1963 appears in Arthur M. Schlesinger, Jr., *A Thousand Days* (New York: Fawcett World Library, 1967), pp. 836–38.

[9] Declaration in *Pravda*, April 27, 1967.

its allies have come to see more advantages and fewer disadvantages than they formerly calculated. Paradoxically, the prospects of such an agreement are likely to become better as it loses relevancy. This is to say that it is precisely the decline of fears of "aggression" against Western Europe that makes a nonaggression pact conceivable. Nevertheless, there are few prospects that the United States and the Soviet Union, or more generally the NATO and Warsaw Pact states, will soon find a genuinely amicable mode of coexistence. For this reason, a symbolic measure such as a nonaggression pact might be an appropriate recognition of a situation involving intermingled fears and hopes. It would amount to a ceremony in which the partners swore that they did not have the worst of intentions (and kept silent on the fact that they did not have the best of intentions either).

The only recent diplomatic activity centering on a renunciation-of-force agreement occurred in 1967–1968 between the Federal Republic of Germany and the USSR. This came to nothing. The USSR had responded belatedly but favorably to a 1966 West German proposal for nonaggression pacts with the USSR and other Eastern European states (not including the German Democratic Republic). The USSR made its acceptance conditional on inclusion of the GDR and on a reduction of the Federal Republic's presence in West Berlin.[10]

PREVENTION OF SURPRISE ATTACK

Both the United States and the Soviet Union were interested at one time in the problem of reducing the danger, and fears, of surprise attacks, a subject that gave rise to various suggestions of Soviet and Western origin, including conflicting proposals in 1955 on aerial photography. These now seem dead. In 1958 there were fruitless negotiations on the subject of surprise attack between Soviet-allied and

---

[10] *The New York Times,* January 17 and February 3, 18, 1968. The 1966 West German proposal was in a note of March 25 to the USSR and other governments, in *Documents 1966,* pp. 168–74. The Federal Republic then proposed

> that formal declarations be exchanged . . . with the governments of the Soviet Union, Poland, Czechoslovakia and any other East European states, in which either side gives an undertaking to the other people not to use force to settle international disputes.

The Soviet reply of May 17, 1966, brusquely derided the proposal without specifically turning it down. After a restating of the German proposition, the Soviet note said that "peace in Europe does not exist by grace of the German militarists," and implied that the proposal was a "scheme" dictated by animosity against the GDR (a patent reference to the omission of the East German regime from the scope of the renunciation-of-force offer). *Ibid.,* p. 311. The Soviet Government published in *Izvestiia,* July 12–14, 1968, the memoranda to the FRG dated October 12 and November 21, 1967, and July 5, 1968.

American-allied governments. Although Moscow is now largely quiet on the subject, an old Soviet proposal was re-endorsed by the post-Khrushchev regime.[11] It was dropped, however, in the July 1, 1968, listing of measures sought by the USSR. The surprise attack feature of the Soviet plan consists of a system of observation or "control" posts on NATO and Warsaw Treaty territory. Soviet willingness to accept this control system was made explicitly dependent on agreement to reduce the number of foreign troops in European countries and to ban nuclear weapons from German soil. According to the Soviet proposal, the observation posts were to be established initially at transportation and embarkation centers, with air bases included at later stages (after troop and armament reductions had been accomplished). Missile launching sites were completely excluded from the system.[12]

Soviet proposals on the subject obviously have not met major American concerns about the launching of a Soviet surprise attack, conceived not so much as a push westward of Soviet and Soviet-allied troops in Europe, but rather as a sudden launching of nuclear-equipped vehicles, principally missiles. The focus on ground rather than air attacks makes the projected system uninteresting to the United States as a form of security from surprise attack; and the ban on nuclear weapons in Germany runs against American and NATO strategy. This is one of the few Soviet-sponsored partial measures, however, envisaging an international control system functioning on Soviet soil. Even the accompanying proposal for troop reductions would probably not pose a great barrier to negotiations for the Western states. In view of lessened Soviet interest, the prospects for negotiation of a measure on surprise attacks do not now seem at all promising.

NEW PROPOSALS ON EUROPE

In attempting to deal with old problems and to take advantage of new opportunities, the present leaders of the USSR have advanced some new proposals, at least one of which would alter current military arrangements in Europe. This is a proposal for disbanding the military organizations of the North Atlantic and Warsaw treaties. It was advanced in July, 1966, by the Political Consultative Committee of the Warsaw Pact at a Bucharest meeting attended by both Soviet Party

---

[11] *Documents 1964*, pp. 16, 516. See also *SSSR, SShA, i razoruzhenie*, pp. 102–3.

[12] The link between provision for control posts in all NATO and Warsaw Treaty states and the provisions regarding armaments in Germany is very tenuous; presumably the system is geared to the prevention of sudden launching of large-scale conventional war in Central Europe. The real link is probably that the USSR shies away from any measures with control features that do not involve arms reductions.

chief Brezhnev and Premier Kosygin.[13] Conceived as a first step toward the liquidation of both alliances, an objective long sought by Moscow, the proposal would leave the two alliance systems in existence as "old-fashioned" political-military groupings, shorn of their more or less integrated military organizations. Because NATO has a more highly integrated military structure than the Warsaw Pact, the effect of the measure would obviously, and designedly, be greater on the Western than on the Eastern side.

The withdrawal of France from NATO military activities, accompanied by a reaffirmation of its adherence to the North Atlantic Treaty, clearly provided the example on which this proposal is based. Endorsing this "good example," Moscow and allied capitals sought to generalize the French behavior into a European pattern. Nevertheless, even President de Gaulle might not be entirely happy to see his neighbors follow the example of France in regard to NATO.

In any case, the Federal Republic of Germany and the other principal NATO nations place a higher value than does Gaullist France on close ties to U.S. military power, institutionalized in present NATO military arrangements. The proposal has little importance, therefore, as a basis for negotiations, but serves as a convenient goal around which the USSR can organize its diplomatic and propaganda activity. In its basic thrust, the proposal also shows the continuity of Soviet policy toward Europe over most of the postwar period; for the USSR has made repeated efforts to bring about the withdrawal of American forces from Europe, and especially from Germany.

Another recent line of Soviet policy has received even more emphasis than the proposal for abolition of alliance military structures. This must be noted here, although the military and arms control aspects are fuzzy. It is the suggestion for the convocation of an all-European conference to discuss European security questions. The idea has been proposed with some vigor over the past few years by Soviet and East European leaders, as in declarations of the Political Consultative Committee of the Warsaw Pact (e.g., the Warsaw meeting in January, 1965), and the Bucharest meeting in July, 1966.[14]

Moscow's intentions regarding participants and agenda at a European conference are far from clear. When Polish Foreign Minister Rapacki proposed such a conference in an address to the U.N. General Assembly on December 14, 1964, he referred to "a conference of all

[13] The Bucharest declaration was accepted on July 6, 1966 (*Pravda*, July 9, 1966; see also *Documents 1966*, pp. 407–20). Although the document alluded to a number of possible arms control and other agreements between European states, it did not mention the proposed nonaggression pact between NATO member states and those of the WTO.

[14] *Documents 1965*, pp. 5–9; *Documents 1966*, pp. 407–20.

European states, with the participation, of course, of both the Soviet Union and the United States. . . ." [15] In subsequent Soviet and joint Eastern European statements, Rapacki's "of course" (as it had applied to the United States) was forgotten, and the emphasis was usually on the capability of the Europeans to decide such matters for themselves. Soviet planning seemed to aim at excluding the United States: the Europe assigned the task of organizing itself was the Gaullist Europe in reverse, "from the Urals to the Atlantic" and not a fathom further. However, there was not complete consistency on this point. [16]

Soviet intentions about the purpose of the conference are also unclear. In documents expounding on the need for new European security arrangements, very ambitious Soviet objectives are laid out, including the liquidation or truncation of the rival alliances, the departure of American troops from Europe, and the settlement of the German question on the basis of recognition of two German states and of present German frontiers. In contrast, the passages in the Bucharest declaration of July, 1966, on the proposed European security conference presented a very bland menu for nervous stomachs. In this document, the purpose of the conference was defined as issuance of an all-European "Declaration" in favor of peaceful settlement of international disputes, exchange of "information on questions of mutual interest," and "comprehensive development of economic, scientific-technical and cultural ties." [17] (In other contexts, however, there has been mention of a European treaty emerging from the discussions which would establish a new system of collective security.)

Even in the minimal variant, the Soviet leaders probably hope to orient efforts toward a reduction of the American presence in Europe, a consolidation of the territorial status quo in Germany, and the creation of a trans-European superstructure. The latter is clearly designed to undermine ties among the Western European states and those linking Western Europe to America.

Soviet leaders have attempted, without outstanding success, to secure backing for their European security proposals in bilateral meetings

[15] *Documents 1964*, pp. 523–27.

[16] Even Soviet intentions to exclude the United States are not completely clear. Soviet statements avoid mention of American participation. The Bucharest declaration of July, 1966, stated: "As for the participants in such a discussion [i.e., of European security questions] the Warsaw Treaty states make no exceptions. It is for each state to decide whether or not to participate in the discussion and solution of European problems." This was said, however, not in reference to the conference but to the use of diplomatic and other channels for the discussion of the same problems. Nevertheless, the USSR insists on the continued validity of the Potsdam accord on Germany, thus implying a recognition of four-Power responsibilities in regard to Germany.

[17] *Documents 1966*, pp. 418–19.

with Western European leaders, particularly President de Gaulle and Prime Minister Wilson. Using a different and somewhat contradictory tactic, however, they have also emphasized Communist sponsorship of the program. The April, 1967, European Communist conference on European security held at Karlovy Vary passed rather lightly over the proposal for an all-European security conference, and devoted more attention to other means of firming up the situation in Germany and of eliminating the division of Europe into hostile alliances. (This meeting was boycotted by the Albanians, the Rumanians, and the Yugoslavs, among the Communists in power, as well as by some minor Western European parties.)

The present Soviet leaders probably do not themselves believe that suggestions for dismantling alliance military structures or for holding an all-European conference on security are currently negotiable. The Soviet strategy appears to be based on long-range maneuver rather than expectations of immediate negotiations.* Since one of the primary objectives of both measures is the consolidation of the European territorial status quo by adaptation to it of the diplomatic status quo, the Soviet leaders no doubt consider that time is on their side. They gain comfort from the absence of any promising Western plan for peaceful alteration of the situation in Central Europe, i.e., a plan to eliminate the East German regime and unify Germany under a government oriented to the West and allied militarily to the U.S. through NATO.

It is perhaps more difficult at the present time than at any time since the war ended in 1945 to gauge with any confidence the possibilities for agreements on European issues incorporating arms control provisions, or to chart European political trends and their possible impact on the East-West military confrontation. Groping their way to a new bilateral relationship, the United States and the USSR at the same time have had to reconcile themselves to some loss of leverage over their allies, for the boldness displayed by France and Rumania has altered the ground rules in both alliances.[18] The Rumanians have

---

* Some participants in the project believed that the prospects for Soviet success in exploiting opportunities to change political relations in Europe are greater than the report indicates. In contrast, some participants felt that the report minimizes the overwhelming difficulties faced by the Soviet leaders in trying to consolidate the Soviet sphere of dominance in Eastern Europe. These observers hold that whatever course the Soviet leaders adopt in dealing with the problem of Germany or with the problem of containing Rumanian and other divergences, the position of the USSR in Eastern Europe is likely to deteriorate.

[18] Thus, the need to conciliate Rumania forced Soviet leaders to a policy of maneuver with their pact partners; Rumanian resistance on numerous issues accustomed Eastern European states to acceptance of "least common denominator" agreements, and the Rumanian example provided other member states with the opportunity (and sometimes the need) to assert their own national interests.

made life difficult for Moscow on an increasing number of issues, including some touching armament and arms control, such as the proposed nonproliferation treaty and the organization of military activities under the Warsaw Pact.[19] To prevent spread of the Rumanian "infection," the Soviet leaders have had to tread very softly in regard to their allies, while seeking to capitalize on shows of independence from Washington on the part of NATO states. As long as Eastern European Communist regimes—even those independent of or hostile to Moscow—remained in full control of their countries, the USSR tolerated national divergences. But the rapid and far-reaching changes in Czechoslovakia in 1968 appeared to the Soviet leaders as threatening the continuation of Communist Party rule. The events of August, 1968, showed the insufficience of Soviet capabilities to control developments without resort to military force, and also demonstrated that the Kremlin leaders were willing to use such force so as to re-establish the kind of "order" they preferred, even against the opposition of the duly-established Party and government leaders of the country.

In the current atmosphere, when relationships in Europe are being re-evaluated and reconstructed, it may well be that old or new proposals for arms control and disarmament will become negotiable. If such agreements come to pass, they will in turn affect the East-West confrontation in Europe, either by altering the levels and kinds of military dispositions there, or by contributing symbolically to changes in the political atmosphere of the continent.

[19] The Rumanians apparently sought to revise the command structure of the Warsaw Treaty Organization to have rotation of commanders, to give individual countries the right to approve use of nuclear weapons, etc. (*The New York Times*, May 18, 1966). For the Rumanian criticism of the Soviet-American draft nonproliferation treaty, see the statement to the ENDC on February 6, 1968, by Rumanian representative Ecobescu. He mentioned the lack of security guarantees, the omission of any provisions for reduction of nuclear armaments, the requirement that a nation deciding to withdraw from the treaty justify its decision to other signatories, and discrimination on control requirements between the nuclear weapons states and others.

12

SECRECY, INSPECTION, AND INTERNATIONAL CONTROL

Inspection problems have been less prominent in the disarmament negotiations of the 1964–1968 period than in earlier negotiations. Observance of the outer-space treaty—signed in 1967—was left to national means of verification, as in the three-environment test-ban treaty of 1963.[1] Soviet resistance to foreign inspection did not surface as an issue in the negotiations of the U.S.-USSR nonproliferation treaty draft of 1968, since none of the five countries falling within the treaty's category of nuclear weapons powers was to be subject to control or restrictions over its own nuclear arsenal.[2] The absence of serious negotiations in the post-Khrushchev era on "general and complete disarmament," or on the extension of the test ban to cover underground testing, or on any other partial measure involving inspection of the major military states has made it slightly more difficult to ascertain if Soviet attachment to secrecy and antipathy to foreign inspection have lessened in the last few years.

SOVIET ATTACHMENT TO SECRECY

Resistance to inspection under international agreements is one facet of a general preference for secrecy on the part of Soviet leaders.[3] They seek to retain a high degree of control over what is to become

---

[1] "Verification" refers to the means of checking on fulfillment of obligations under an arms control or disarmament agreement. "Inspection" by an international agency or by an adversary is one technique of verifying observance of an agreement. The dispensability or indispensability of inspection depends on the availability of other means of verification, notably national means of checking on observance.

[2] International safeguards were an issue in the negotiations, of course, but the Soviet-American differences that delayed the agreement concerned Western Europe, not the USSR or even the Soviet allies in Eastern Europe.

[3] The chapter "Secrecy and Inspection," in *The Soviet Union and Disarmament*, offers a much fuller examination of the nonrational and rational factors contributing to the Soviet preference for secrecy. The judgments reached in this previous study seem as pertinent today as at the end of Khrushchev's era, when

known about the USSR, either inside or outside the country. In order to account for the Soviet "obsession" with secrecy it is not necessary to delve deeply into ancient Russian history or the peculiarities of the Russian psyche. The historical traditions and psycho-cultural patterns of Russia before the October Revolution no doubt contribute something even today to the high valuation placed on secrecy by the elite, and to its acceptance by the population. In addition, specifically Bolshevik qualities and experiences before and after accession to power fortified tendencies to guard sensitive information from domestic and foreign opponents.

It is actually more useful to analyze the functions performed by secrecy in the Soviet environment than to attribute the Soviet penchant for secrecy to nonrational factors. In regard to military affairs, for example, it is somewhat inconsistent to talk simultaneously about a Soviet "obsession" with secrecy and about the advantages that tight security affords the Soviet regime. If the advantages are real, there is no need to explain as irrational the high value placed upon secrecy.

It is possible to imagine, if not to predict, an evolution of Soviet society in which dedication to secrecy wanes as the society evolves and the system needs change. But the day of a new order is not likely to dawn rapidly.

Secrecy about developments in the USSR extends well beyond the military field to include political, economic, scientific, cultural, and other matters. Information regarding even these latter areas, of course, has potential military importance in the event of war. But war possibilities and war preparations do not go far to explain the scale of restrictive policies adopted by the USSR in guarding information on Soviet affairs generally. The broad scope of these restrictions is owing primarily to two other causes, one international, the other internal.

Internationally, the Soviet Union has played a dual role as a state among states and as the homeland of Communist revolution. Since 1917, Soviet leaders have sought to combine a revolutionary mission with efforts to bring a relatively backward Russia, a "poor relation" in the family of great powers, to the level of the advanced Western states. The USSR has made great achievements; yet 50 years after the Revolution, it has not been able to equal the Western nations in material levels of popular well-being, or to present an image to the world of a flourishing political life. In view of the revolutionary mission Moscow has accepted (and has interpreted largely as setting an example to the world of the wonders of socialism), the persistence

---

the study was completed. Since the problem of control and inspection on Soviet territory has not loomed large in the discussions and negotiations on disarmament in the period since Khrushchev, it received relatively little attention from the experts who participated in this project.

of "communist" poverty in the midst of (relative) "capitalist" plenty in the industrial West has affected many aspects of Soviet outlook and behavior. Notably, it has affected the degree to which the regime has opted for secrecy about its affairs. Openness, in Soviet eyes, is an option of the rich and powerful or a necessity of the poor and weak, but is inappropriate to the poor and powerful Soviet Union.

The internal considerations conducive to a policy of secrecy, although linked to this concept of world struggle, reflect specific features of Soviet society. In all institutions of that society, unity and unanimity are prized and conflict disdained. This is especially true of the Party and government. If unanimity does not exist in fact, it has to be invented for public display. Furthermore, Marxism-Leninism is supposed to provide the Party with a true science of politics and economics; therefore, the mistakes and failures of fallible practitioners, especially of high authorities, have to be concealed as much as possible.[4] The "enemy" seeks to exploit any evidence of disunity in the ranks and of failure in performance; frustration of his designs depends on concealment of disunity and failure where these cannot be eliminated.

MODIFICATION OF STRESS ON SECURITY

To acknowledge the social functions of secrecy in the USSR and thus disparage the nonrational element in security preferences is not to minimize the price paid for maintenance of strict secrecy. None of the successors to Stalin has been willing to give secrecy as high a priority as he accorded it. Under Stalin, restrictions on publication of economic data were so severe that they hampered the functioning of the economic system. Other security restrictions contributed to the stagnation of trade and tourism. The isolation of the USSR from the international flow of people and publications was partly responsible for the stultification of intellectual life and lessened the regime's opportunities to influence developments abroad. Security preferences contributed also to a certain passivity in Soviet foreign policy, and

---

[4] The fact that most former Party and government chiefs are in disrepute means that their fallibility has been acknowledged. But the acknowledgment came only after they had died or been thrown out of office. "Criticism and self-criticism" is encouraged in regard to lower officials, but not at the top. One of the few leaders to criticize himself while in office was—Joseph Stalin! At the end of the war in Europe, Stalin said in 1945: "Our government made not a few errors. . . . A different people could have said to the government: 'You have failed to justify our expectations. Go away!' . . . The Russian people, however, did not take this path. . . ." (J. V. Stalin, *War Speeches and Orders of the Day* [London: Hutchinson & Co., Ltd., 1946], p. 139.)

the accompanying failure to utilize opportunities for maneuver among underdeveloped and advanced states alike.[5]

After 1953, there was a gradual trend toward relaxation of security barriers, marked by freer conditions of travel into and out of the USSR; lightening of censorship of publications originating in the country, or allowed to enter; and lessened use of security police methods in dealing with dissent and deviation. For the last several years, however, including the period since 1964, there has been no trend toward further relaxation of secrecy practices, which remain rigorous in comparison to those of Western societies. In fact, the post-Khrushchev leaders have taken several steps to tighten controls, mostly regarding ideological influences. In an effort to restore a brighter image of Soviet society, past and present, they have prevented publication of works of writers such as Alexander Solzhenitsyn, who dwelt on the dark side of Soviet reality. In addition to stepping up ideological pressures, the regime has brought to trial many obscure dissident and nonconformist writers and intellectuals. (International notoriety did attach to the case of Iulii Daniel and Andrei Siniavsky, who were arrested in 1965, and tried and sentenced to terms of hard labor in early 1966.) Almost all the defendants in these cases were charged with some kind of nefarious connections with foreign intelligence or propaganda agencies.[6] A somewhat ominous publicity campaign, begun in Khrushchev's last years and continued afterward, extolled the services rendered by the Soviet security police and intelligence forces under the KGB and its predecessors.[7] This tightening up was particularly noticeable in 1968, as the regime sought to suppress dissent at home and restore an orthodox pattern of Communist rule in Czechoslovakia.

Soviet policy on foreign contacts and travel has a bearing, even if indirect, on attitudes toward the inspection aspects of proposed arms control agreements. The kinds of foreign contacts alluded to above are not nearly as serious as those involved in inspection on Soviet soil under an arms control or disarmament agreement. Under almost any such agreement providing for international or adversary inspection,

[5] After 1956, Stalin was criticized for many of the practices cited in this paragraph, but there was no general criticism of the secrecy practices of his regime.

[6] A recent case was tried on January 8–12, 1968, and resulted in the conviction and imprisonment of four dissident intellectuals: Aleksandr Ginzburg, Iuri Galanskov, Aleksei Dobrovolsky, and Vera Lashkova (*The New York Times,* January 9–17, 1968).

[7] Most of this material has centered on security police and intelligence activities in the civil war and World War II, in protecting Soviet borders against penetration, or in fulfilling missions abroad. Revelations in the USSR about Soviet agents (such as Sorge, Abel, and Philby) operating in other countries involved a reversal of a long-standing Soviet practice of denying or minimizing such activities.

the USSR would have less control over places, personnel, communications, and supply of information than in the reception of foreigners coming as tourists or diplomats, or entering the USSR under exchange agreements.

Soviet authorities have consistently dismissed protestations from the United States and others that foreign inspection in connection with an arms control or disarmament agreement is not designed for collection of intelligence on military installations. The spokesmen of the USSR assert that military and political needs of foreign intelligence would be served by the corps of inspectors, collecting information both on activities subject to inspection and on other aspects of Soviet life.[8]

SOVIET SECRECY AND ARMS CONTROL
AND DISARMAMENT NEGOTIATIONS

To the extent that the problem of inspection has recurred in the disarmament negotiations of 1964–1968, these negotiations provide no evidence of lessening Soviet resistance to foreign inspection within the USSR. In occasional discussions of a comprehensive ban of nuclear weapons tests, for example, Soviet representatives have repeatedly turned down suggestions for a study of verification requirements. Such a study would examine the extent to which improvement in devices for distinguishing between natural and artificially produced seismic shocks has modified inspection needs for a comprehensive test ban. The USSR has insisted that there is no need for a system of inspection beyond existing national means of verification.[9] In rejecting out of hand such American proposals as those for a freeze on strategic vehicles for nuclear weapons delivery, and for a cut-off of production of fissionable materials for nuclear warheads, Soviet spokesmen have placed major emphasis on the unacceptable inspection demands accompanying these proposals.[10] (It must be noted, however, that the Soviet authorities find it convenient to highlight this motive for rejection of proposals. Other, more important reasons for rejection may be more awkward to acknowledge. Thus, they cannot very well admit that measures to "freeze" armaments would condemn them to

---

[8] See, for example, the statement of Soviet representative Tsarapkin to the ENDC, June 2, 1965, in *Documents 1965*, p. 224, and the statement by Soviet representative Roshchin to the ENDC, August 9, 1966, in *Documents 1966*, p. 530.

[9] Statement of Soviet representative Roshchin to the ENDC, August 25, 1966 (*ibid.*, p. 601).

[10] Interview of Soviet Foreign Minister Gromyko in *Izvestiia*, March 2, 1964, and *Documents 1964*, pp. 72–73.

permanent military inferiority, since they cannot openly admit the superiority of opponents.)

The history of disarmament and other foreign policy negotiations shows that the Soviet leaders are much more indulgent to foreign or international inspection on the territory of their allies than on their own territory. Of various proposals advanced or accepted by the USSR involving foreign inspection, many have envisaged application to countries allied with the USSR, and relatively few to the Soviet Union proper. This has been true, for example, of numerous proposals envisaging arms limitations in Central Europe. (It might be noted that an "inspection" arrangement—through military liaison missions—continues to exist in West and East Germany, although this is not connected with an arms control agreement.) The agreement accepted by the USSR (and rejected by the Castro government) to end the Cuban missile crisis of 1962 offers another example of Soviet willingness to allow foreign inspection on allied territory. A similar stand characterized the position defended by the USSR in the negotiations over a nonproliferation agreement in 1965–1968. The Soviet Union actively supported the assignment to the International Atomic Energy Agency of responsibility for checking on compliance with the agreement, since the verification was limited to non-nuclear weapons states. In contrast, the USSR was critical of, and refused to follow, American initiatives to extend the application of IAEA safeguards to peaceful atomic activities of the nuclear weapons states. (The U.S. announced in 1967 that it would permit such IAEA safeguards to be applied to all nuclear activities in the United States except those "with direct national security significance.")[11]

Proposals contemplating foreign inspection of even Communist-ruled countries (other than the USSR) were naturally easier for the Soviet leaders to accept than for the leaders of some of these countries, as the Cuban affair showed in 1962. This difference in Soviet attitude toward having foreign inspectors in the USSR and in Soviet-allied countries casts some doubt on the idea that the Soviet "secrecy mania" is primarily a function of apprehension about the reliability of control over the people and about the internal stability in Communist-ruled countries. For it is difficult to believe that the Soviet leaders consider the Soviet regime more shaky in its control over the population than such regimes as Walter Ulbricht's German Democratic Republic or the Castro regime in Cuba. Both these countries, and others allied to Moscow, were to be subjected to foreign inspection in various measures proposed or accepted by the USSR. The greater reluctance to allow

[11] For the text of President Johnson's announcement of December 2, see *The New York Times,* December 3, 1967.

inspection of Soviet than of Soviet-allied territory gives weight to the idea that it is Soviet nuclear strategic striking power, almost entirely concentrated at military bases within the USSR, which is being given preferential treatment.

THE CHANGED PROBLEM OF MILITARY SECURITY

The post-Stalin policy favoring greater international contacts and circulation of more information on Soviet (and world) affairs has not extended to military or "national security" affairs, on which the regime continues to maintain a wall of secrecy. Although even this area has been affected by the generally increased freedom of contact, technological developments are more important in reducing Soviet secrecy. The latter receive less attention than espionage agents in Soviet public statements on foreign intelligence activities. This stress on human agents is not because of a Soviet delusion that they are more important than sophisticated techniques of intelligence collection, but because "vigilance" is only peripherally important against the latter.

The testing, for example, of long-range strategic vehicles, notably missiles and satellites, has necessarily involved the use of areas (the Pacific Ocean and outer space) that the USSR did not control, and where opposing powers could operate freely.[12] Even more significant in the degradation of Soviet secrecy is the development of complex instruments and equipment for collection of information. The United States is the principal possessor of apparatus for detecting from outside the borders of the USSR Soviet military and space events both inside and outside the country. The United States has deployed these advanced systems of sensors on a worldwide basis. (The USSR has been active in this area also, although its needs are probably more modest than those of the United States, its resources abroad more limited, and its equipment less sophisticated.)

Unlike the earth's surface and adjacent air space, outer space and the high seas provide free environments for competitive intelligence activities. Thus, both sides have invested large efforts in space activities of direct significance for military intelligence, especially by means of observational satellites capable of photographing the military ground installations and activities of rival states.[13]

By increasing national intelligence capabilities, some of these technological developments have eased the problem of control over certain

---

[12] Thus, the terminal phase of Soviet firings of long-range missiles into the Pacific could be observed at close hand by interested foreigners.

[13] See the *Review of the Soviet Space Program,* which lists Soviet observational satellites (pp. 36–43, 137), and has comparative data on Soviet and American military launches (pp. 33–35).

possible arms control or disarmament agreements. In fact, two of the arms control agreements now in effect were made possible by technological developments extending the capabilities of national intelligence services. The partial test-ban treaty was acceptable to the United States because of the perfection and deployment of devices capable of detecting nuclear explosions in and above the atmosphere, and under water. The United States changed its stand on an outer-space treaty when it developed facilities for keeping track of foreign objects in space. This development allowed abandonment of demands for on-site inspection of space launches. No doubt further technological advances extending such national intelligence capabilities are possible, even likely. Thus, systems capable of detecting earth tremors and of distinguishing between nuclear explosions and natural seismic shocks may be improved sufficiently to remove the verification problem in relation to a comprehensive ban on nuclear weapons tests. Improvements in satellite reconnaissance and other systems of sensors under national control may reduce the need for on-site inspection to police an agreement limiting competition in ballistic missiles and other strategic nuclear delivery vehicles.[14]

Technology yields its favors, however, to those protecting as well as to those penetrating secrets; it is not, therefore, necessarily on the side of arms control. For example, experiments have shown that a state trying to evade a ban on nuclear weapons tests might be able to frustrate detection and identification of underground tests by muffling their seismic effects. There are grave doubts, however, about the practicality of such evasive tactics. In other areas of military activity that might be brought under some international agreement, the problem of verification is more complicated than with tests of nuclear weapons. Testing would probably lose its importance with the outbreak of war, and test sites are not likely to be priority targets. But offensive and defensive missile installations would be targets of first priority. The capability of verifying a possible agreement limiting such missiles would be simultaneously the capability of pinpointing these sites as targets. It is not surprising, therefore, that Soviet technology has been called upon to frustrate opponents' capabilities of gathering such intelligence. This is one reason for the USSR's great interest in the development of mobile ICBMs. Although attempting, like the United States, to secure invulnerability for its striking force by transforming "soft" into "hard" installations, the USSR has also sought security along a very different route, by developing mobile ICBMs.[15] As an incidental effect, mobility of Soviet ICBMs might lessen

---

[14] Speech of Assistant Secretary of Defense Paul C. Warnke, October 6, 1967, in *Documents 1967*, pp. 454–59.

[15] Marshal N. Krylov, the Commander of the Soviet Strategic Rocket Forces, in

American confidence in national capabilities for verifying observance of a possible agreement placing limitations on numbers and types of deployed missiles.

Mobility is not the only technological factor affecting prospects for verification of a missile agreement. These prospects might also be diminished by the planned American (and possible Soviet) equipment of strategic missiles with multiple warheads (called MIRV in the American program). Presumably, current observation capabilities by way of satellites are not sufficient to distinguish between single- and multiple-warhead missiles; and thus it would be difficult to confirm adherence to fixed limits on missile installations.

*   *   *

Neither technological nor political developments give a clear answer to the question of how seriously progress on arms control will be impeded by Soviet attachment to secrecy and the consequent antipathy to foreign inspection. It is far from clear, as has been noted, which arms control or disarmament agreements are being blocked by differences over inspection. The Soviet authorities are fond of explaining their rejection of Western proposals in terms of unacceptable inspection demands when other considerations are at least as important. Nevertheless, the differences on control and inspection are real enough, and may come once again into the forefront of negotiations if proposals acceptable in substance to both sides arouse divergent views on verification.

Certainly, the "secrecy gap" between the USSR and major Western states has been narrowed. This is largely a result of technological developments that have reduced the *value*—rather than the *extent*—of the Kremlin's tight security control over Soviet territory and the adjacent atmosphere. Thus, the Soviet leaders had to put up with "spies in the sky" (observational satellites) even if they did not like them. Their reconciliation to this form of degradation of Soviet security, however, did not make them more willing to accept foreign inspection in arms control or disarmament agreements.

Soviet proposals for "general and complete disarmament," and for less sweeping arms reductions, frequently incorporate provisions for control or inspection on an international or adversary basis. Spokesmen of the USSR insist that foreign control on Soviet soil is acceptable only if the measure involves "disarmament," i.e., substantial arms

---

referring to Soviet successes in solving the problem of mobile installations, said: "An innovation is the creation of mobile starting complexes for intercontinental solid-fuel rockets. . . . Mounted on self-propelled chasses, they are very maneuverable, are easily camouflaged, and therefore can be hardly detected by the enemy's air and space reconnaissance." (*Krasnaia zvezda*, February 16, 1968.)

reductions. Up to this time, none of the four measures agreed to in U.S.-USSR disarmament negotiations has established a control system within the territory of the USSR or other major military powers, and none has provided for arms reductions.

This has meant that, in order to achieve agreements, the United States has had to sacrifice its desire to see international inspection function on the territory of the major military powers. Similarly, the USSR has had to sacrifice its oft-stated desire to reduce armaments and to lower levels of spending for military purposes. Moscow continues to regard secrecy as an important asset, and expects to gain important advantages as compensation for any acceptance of foreign inspection in an arms control or disarmament agreement. Thus renewal of serious negotiations on measures involving inspection requirements may once again make the verification question a stumbling block to agreements.

13

IN RETROSPECT AND IN PROSPECT

Trends in Soviet policy and in Soviet society relevant to arms control prospects support only modest expectations of future progress toward significant disarmament and arms control agreements.* At their optimistic best, arms control measures offer a means of promoting two interrelated but distinct objectives of interest to Soviet and other peoples: avoidance of war (especially between states armed with nuclear weapons), and reduction of the resources allocated to armies and armaments. The achievements have fallen far short of this "best."

The first objective, of averting the danger of war or limiting the scope of war if it comes, has been only *indirectly* advanced by the arms control achievements discussed earlier in the book. None of the measures put into effect has reduced the arsenals of the major powers or the danger of armed conflict in the areas where these powers confront each other most belligerently. Nor has the objective of reducing the economic burden of arms competition been much advanced; the agreed measures have had a miniscule effect on the arms spending of the big powers, whose military budgets have been rising, and rising rapidly.

In contrast to slow and faltering progress of disarmament negotiations, advances in weaponry have been rapid. By 1968 it had become plain enough that increases in inventories of strategic arms and development of more sophisticated weapons systems were outdistancing by a wide margin steps to bring areas of military activity within mutually agreed limits.

Furthermore, beyond measures already negotiated, there is no agreement clearly in sight to follow the nonproliferation treaty. (Major negotiations, such as those on the NPT, absorb so much attention in both Washington and Moscow that follow-up proposals get short

---

* By definition, arms control is a "game" at which at least two must play. This consideration is largely implicit in the present study, which focuses on Soviet behavior and viewpoints and devotes little attention to those of the United States and other interested nations.

shrift.) It appeared in mid-1968 that American and Soviet representatives would begin serious work on measures to limit or reduce strategic weapons delivery vehicles, especially missiles. But there was no indication that Soviet and American thinking went along similar lines. Naturally, agreements follow rather than precede negotiations; but the successful negotiations of the past decade began on subjects where a significant congruence of objectives provided an encouraging basis for agreement, however difficult it proved to translate the shared interests into acceptable text.

HOW SOLID ARE PAST AGREEMENTS?

Although it is not often recognized, there is now even some danger of backsliding on past agreements, such as the 1963 partial test-ban treaty and the 1967 outer-space treaty. Both laid bans on certain kinds of weapons testing and space utilization, carefully segregating prohibited activities from others in the military spectrum left to the free enterprise of the powers.

The 1963 treaty drove the testing of nuclear weapons in both the United States and the USSR under ground, thus spurring maximum use of the sole environment permitted. Not only were large numbers of underground tests mounted, but both countries pushed toward the limits of feasibility in this difficult environment. Partly as a result of this push, a few tests vented above ground, presumably by accident. No American test apparently vented sufficiently to result in the passage of radioactive debris beyond American frontiers. By contrast, amounts of radioactive debris were detected outside the USSR after the venting of three Soviet tests. These events constituted at least a "technical" violation of the treaty. In the incident giving rise to the most prolonged diplomatic exchanges on observance of the test-ban treaty, the USSR refused to acknowledge that the admitted venting had actually constituted a treaty violation, even an unintended violation.[1] With both the American and Soviet weapons laboratories doing underground testing of devices more powerful and sophisticated than had been tried before other environments were placed off limits, there are prospects of subsequent wrangling over treaty violations as accidents

---

[1] This was the January 15, 1965, test. In response to an American inquiry through diplomatic channels, Soviet Ambassador Dobrynin, on January 25, replied orally that the amount of radioactive debris released into the atmosphere was "so insignificant" that the Soviet government excluded the possibility of a violation of the treaty. After subsequent exchanges on the matter, the Department of State announced on November 19, 1965, that the United States had concluded that the effects were the result of "a miscalculation by the Soviet Union" and had asked the USSR to take precautionary measures so that the treaty would be observed.

recur.[2] There have also been some pressures, at least in the United States, for a renewal of nuclear weapons tests in the atmosphere and outer space to permit perfection of anti-ballistic missile systems and other weapons.[3]

Doubts about the observance of the outer-space treaty have also been voiced, mostly "unofficially" and outside diplomatic channels. Even before the outer-space treaty was negotiated, but subsequent to the 1963 U.N.-endorsed outer-space agreement, the USSR displayed what were called "orbital missiles." The United States in November, 1965, asked through diplomatic channels how this development squared with the pledge not to orbit weapons of mass destruction. In reply, Soviet authorities said that production of orbital rockets did not violate the agreement, which the USSR would continue to observe.[4] In 1966 and 1967, a number of space tests apparently advanced Soviet mastery of re-entry problems connected with the use of satellites as weapons carriers. Referring to those tests, Secretary of Defense McNamara announced on November 3, 1967, "the possible development" by the USSR of a space weapon called, in Pentagonese, FOBS—or a fractional orbital bombardment system.[5] (The Kremlin remained silent while the new arrival was christened and its prospects discussed in Washington.) McNamara did not imply that the weapon violated any agreement. As a matter of fact, in reaffirming an earlier United States decision against development of a similar weapons system, McNamara

[2] One of the Soviet tests that vented, that of October 27, 1966, apparently involved the largest underground nuclear explosion ever carried out. On November 14, 1966, the United States tested the most powerful device it had ever exploded underground. The increase in power of devices being tested underground forced American officials in mid-1966 to seek other sites in Nevada (besides their National Nuclear Test Site at Pahute Mesa) and (for still more powerful explosions) in the Aleutian Islands. See the November 30, 1967, speech of Senator Henry M. Jackson.

[3] See Edward Teller, "Planning for Peace," *Orbis*, X, No. 2 (Summer, 1966), 341–59. Dr. Teller was a principal opponent of the 1963 test-ban treaty. It might be noted, however, that some of the most vigorous proponents of ABM deployments in the United States stop short of recommendations that the 1963 treaty be abrogated. Thus, Colonel William R. Kintner, in *Peace and the Strategy Conflict* (New York: Frederick A. Praeger, Inc., 1967), p. 216, merely calls for increased underground testing by the United States "so as to improve its ABM capability as well as its offensive re-entry vehicles." See also *The Changing Strategic Military Balance: U.S.A. vs. U.S.S.R.*, and Senator Jackson's speech to the Senate, November 30, 1967.

[4] In response to the American inquiry, Soviet Ambassador Dobrynin merely said that the USSR would abide by the U.N. resolution on outer space. *Pravda* on December 9, 1965, through its "Observer," noted that the resolution did not apply to the production of orbital or "any other rockets launched into space."

[5] For the text of Secretary McNamara's announcement, see *The New York Times*, November 4, 1967. In describing the system, McNamara said that the vehicles were fired into "a very low orbit about 100 miles above the earth," and that the payload was to be dropped out "generally" before the first orbit was completed.

referred only to considerations of efficiency, not to any doubts about legality.

Nevertheless, to those who did not realize the very limited scope of the ban on military activity in outer space, the Soviet development came as an unwelcome surprise. In developing an orbital missile or the FOBS, the USSR has not needed to hitch any nuclear load to a vehicle lofted on an orbital trajectory; and the FOBS in particular does not seem to be designed for continuous orbit, as in one of the imagined "doomsday machines." From the treaty standpoint, the decisive factor relating to legality is the presence or absence of warheads. The development of such satellites designed as weapons vehicles is apparently legal, but it serves to emphasize that restrictions limiting the military use of outer space will receive a strictly limited interpretation.

This is not surprising, since the test-ban and outer-space agreements were negotiated by states which fully intended to "perfect" and augment their nuclear arsenals, and to increase their military utilization of outer space. As to the latter, outer space is the medium through which ICBMs, the superpowers' principal offensive weapons, would pass en route to target (on a ballistic rather than orbital trajectory). Unlike the atmosphere, outer space is an unrestricted medium for collection, by photography and other means, of intelligence on the offensive and defensive installations of opponents; data so collected are useful for targeting and other military purposes.[6] It is also a superior medium for military communications, by way of satellites facilitating the transmission of intelligence and command messages vital to management of distant and complex military operations on a rapid basis (approaching the military ideal of "real time," or instantaneous communication). Finally, outer space is available as a potential base of operations of the "military man in space," whenever it is discovered what a general or even a sergeant could do better while floating around the earth than standing on *terra firma*.[7]

ARMS LIMITATIONS AS SPUR TO ARMS
COMPETITION

Even if the agreements currently in effect can be made to stick, there remains the troublesome irony that, in discouraging certain specifically defined kinds of arms competition, these agreements have

---

[6] A discussion of Soviet and American activity in use of reconnaissance satellites is contained in *Review of the Space Program*, p. 35.

[7] The American program, currently guided by a directive from President Johnson of August 25, 1965, to develop a "manned orbiting laboratory" for military purposes, has been attacked by Soviet spokesmen as indicative of the military emphasis in the United States space program, and as inconsistent with the outer-space agree-

spurred competition in related military activities. This happened with the partial test ban, which forced weapons testers under ground. Fall-out from the United States and the USSR stopped, but the treaty served as a green light for extensive underground test programs. What will proliferate as a result of the nonproliferation treaty is as yet unknown. The very negotiation of the treaty forced several states to consider seriously issues of atomic development (both in the peaceful uses and military fields) before they otherwise might have faced up to these.[8]

This is not the only irony of arms control achievements. Contrary to many expectations, successes have bred subsequent failures as well as more successes. The elimination of atmospheric tests by the USSR, the United States, and United Kingdom reduced popular pressures for a comprehensive test ban to the not inconsiderable extent that these pressures were based on apprehensions about the dangers of radioactive fall-out from tests. Moreover, in 1963 both the United States and the Soviet Union experienced considerable internal opposition to restrictions on weapons testing. Consequently, the political leaders had to make arrangements conciliating opponents in order to clear the way for the partial ban. These arrangements in turn discouraged and somewhat restricted national leaders from moving toward a comprehensive ban. The process was very clear in the United States —and something similar occurred in the Soviet Union as well. President Kennedy considered it expedient to pledge the maintenance of a vigorous underground test program, and readiness to resume atmospheric testing, in order to gain the approval of the Joint Chiefs of Staff and the consent of the Senate for the partial test-ban treaty.[9] In the USSR, where political bargaining is less open and where the military establishment has less autonomy than in the United States, it was hardly a coincidence that the agreement of then-Premier Khrushchev to a ban excluding underground tests—resisted for years as not in the

---

ments. It clearly was not based on the idea of orbiting weapons of mass destruction.

[8] India, which has not signed the treaty, did not want to foreclose now the possibility of developing nuclear weapons, even though it has not undertaken such a weapons program. Discussions at the ENDC by representatives of certain non-nuclear weapons countries showed their interest in the use of nuclear explosions for civil construction. Even the most advanced nuclear powers have not mastered a technique to make such applications feasible above ground.

[9] The "safeguards" insisted upon by the Joint Chiefs of Staff are enumerated in the report of the U.S. Senate Committee on Foreign Relations on the test-ban treaty, September 3, 1963. (*Documents 1963*, pp. 473–76). President Kennedy is quoted by Arthur M. Schlesinger, Jr. (*A Thousand Days*, p. 839), as saying, on September 9, 1963, that the test-ban treaty "is being so chewed up in the Senate, and we've had to make so many concessions to make sure it passes, that we've got to do something to prove to the world we still mean it."

Soviet interest—was accompanied by a hardening of the conditions acceptable to the USSR for a full ban, i.e., rejection of any foreign inspection. It seems likely that military and other influential forces unenthusiastic about mutual cessation of testing made a bargain in which acceptance of the partial test ban was conditioned on renunciation of the Soviet decision to allow limited foreign inspection of compliance with a comprehensive ban.[10]

POLITICAL EFFECTS OF SUCCESSFUL ARMS CONTROL NEGOTIATIONS

Recognition of the modesty and ambiguity of past steps in arms control must be balanced by an appreciation of their political impact in the East and in the West. The successful negotiation of several arms control agreements has contributed to an easing of the political atmosphere, even as the "lessening of tensions" attributable to other causes helped to make these agreements possible. Due weight must be given to this betterment of the political climate; for otherwise an unjustifiably dark assessment of future prospects would be required. The ups and downs in Soviet-American relations should not obscure a long-term trend toward a marked lessening of tension in these relations, although the objective bases of tension and hostility remain firmly rooted in both Communist and Western societies.

What has gained strength has been an explicit awareness of a certain mutuality of interest—chiefly, in regard to the dangers of cataclysmic war. There has also been increased recognition that decisions of both sides on questions of "national security" emerge from similar calculations of loss and advantage, of opportunities to be seized and risks to be run. Greater sophistication has entered into analyses of decision-making processes in the rival camp. There has been acknowledgment that, in each alliance system and within individual countries, varied and opposing forces affect decision making on alliance problems, on national military policies, and on a variety of international prob-

---

[10] Moscow's rejection, after conclusion of the partial test-ban treaty, of any inspections under a comprehensive test ban was first voiced by Soviet representative Novikov at the U.N. General Assembly on October 17, 1963. Remarks by Premier Khrushchev, long before Soviet acceptance of a partial test ban, intimated that the USSR might be withdrawing its agreement to two or three on-site inspections. Thus in an interview with Norman Cousins on April 12, 1963, Khrushchev predicted a hardening of the Soviet position. (*Saturday Review*, November 7, 1964, p. 58). Ten days later, in an interview with the editor of *Il Giorno* (Milan), Khrushchev said: "There may now arise the question of whether we too should not return, as did the United States, to our own former positions and withdraw our assent to the holding of two to three inspections a year. . . ." (Moscow radio broadcast, April 23, 1963.)

lems. Glorious fictions such as those portraying "the free world" confronting "the slave world," "totalitarianism," or "international communism," or those portraying "world imperialism" as menacing "the democratic and socialist states," continue to have popular appeal and to serve as organizational vocabularies for influential elites. Their relevance, however, has steadily declined as ideological ties have proved insufficient to keep "friends" together and "enemies" apart.

DOUBTFUL AREAS FOR ADVANCES IN ARMS CONTROL

If the international situation permits or encourages further steps in the arms control field involving the USSR, the United States, and other powers, it is necessary to indicate the areas where agreements seem *unlikely* before discussing some possible accords. For reasons discussed earlier, the possibility of "general and complete disarmament" appears even less promising now than it was in Khrushchev's day. Khrushchev's successors have managed to conceal any enthusiasm for negotiating such proposals, and American negotiators have always preferred to concentrate on smaller steps. Apart even from the fact that the American Soviet plans for GCD embody divergent approaches, the very idea of negotiating a millennial plan to alter drastically and on a world scale the relations among the powers has little appeal for state leaders. There seems to be no need, therefore, to examine in detail the differences in approach on specific aspects and stages of the two plans.

As emphasized early in this study, a major difference of outlook on disarmament objectives is likely to bar not only progress on general disarmament but also many proposed partial measures of arms limitation, especially regarding nuclear forces. The United States desires measures that would preserve, although sometimes at a reduced level, the American margin of superiority in strategic forces. The USSR seeks measures to eliminate this superiority.

This incompatibility of concepts about the desired effects of arms limitations on the "relations of forces" between the United States and the USSR has not affected, or has affected much less, prospects for agreements regarding conventional forces, or conventional and nuclear forces in Europe. Both the United States and the USSR have proposed in their GCD outlines that their armed forces be reduced to equal size, although the proposed levels differ. For Europe, the USSR has even supported plans contemplating a "freeze" (stabilization) or equal reduction of Soviet and Western forces. In areas of strategic confrontation where the United States has had a clear military superiority, however, the discrepancy has prevented any *rapprochement*.

It is necessary to emphasize this point, because the idea that the

USSR was prepared to accept permanent inferiority gained currency in Khrushchev's later years, and continues to find expression in the United States. After 1962, this belief became almost gospel among many American strategists and "arms controllers." To take only one example, Secretary of Defense Robert McNamara declared in 1965 that "the Soviet leaders have decided that they have lost the quantitative race, and they are not seeking to engage us in that contest." [11] But the idea has also been basic to many American proposals for arms limitation. Had these been advanced in the expectation of Soviet rejection, they would have been understandable enough, but apparently some were intended to elicit Soviet interest.

Conclusions about Soviet acceptance of permanent inferiority were not derived from Soviet statements, which suggest that parity or superiority is the USSR goal, although these statements were often fuzzed to imply that the Soviet Union had already achieved this status.[12] The myth of Soviet acceptance of inferiority has derived from the fact that the USSR did not build up its strategic nuclear and long-distance conventional forces as rapidly as had once been expected, or as rapidly as the USSR could have done. This lag was particularly noticeable in the aftermath of the 1962 Cuban affair, which demonstrated Soviet weakness in both strategic nuclear and long-range conventional capabilities.

The slowness of the visible Soviet post-Cuba build-up can be explained, however, by reasons other than acceptance of permanent inferiority. Even more than their counterparts elsewhere, Soviet leaders have to consider their arms programs in the light of total state objectives. The early 1960's were years of special economic difficulty in the Soviet Union, when the annual increment of national product fell to levels unknown since World War II. Without the imminence of a military showdown forced on them from the outside, the Soviet leaders were able to tailor their own moves to accord with their resources, and did not need to neglect economic growth in order to concentrate on a crash program to improve Soviet military capabilities.

Even in these years, it now appears, the USSR was initiating programs indicative of Soviet ambitions for overtaking the United States in strategic nuclear power. Secretary McNamara has suggested, for example, that the Soviet decision to begin deployment of an ABM

[11] Interview in *U.S. News and World Report*, April 12, 1965, p. 52.

[12] The strong and long-standing Soviet aversion to admissions of military weakness affects not only public statements but the whole posture of the USSR. The U-2 affair offered the clearest example, because the Soviet authorities had had to tolerate flights over the Soviet Union without uttering a word of public complaint, until the Powers plane was forced down in the Soviet interior in 1960, four years after the overflights began.

system dated back to 1961 or 1962.[13] It seems likely, also, that measures that came to fruition after Khrushchev's departure—the marked increase in numbers and the hardening of Soviet ICBM installations—were in preparation before 1964.

The slowdown in the rate of Soviet economic growth in the early 1960's itself contributed to Western acceptance of the idea that the USSR was reconciled to permanent strategic inferiority. The slowdown appeared to the Kremlin leaders as a serious but temporary difficulty; it appeared to many in the West as a confirmation of the unworkability of the Soviet system of agricultural and industrial production, or at least of the incapacity of the USSR to compete economically with the United States and other Western nations.

Finally, Soviet acceptance of inferiority has seemed fully rational to the school of strategic thought articulated by Secretary McNamara. In this view, the USSR's possession of a secure strike force, even one a poor second to that of the United States, is all that the USSR needs. The significant factor in the strategic equation is said to be not calculations of superiority or inferiority but the possession of a secure deterrent force (i.e., one capable of riding out an opponent's attack and delivering a powerful counterblow, thus, by its mere existence, deterring that opponent from launching the first attack). But the American Secretary of Defense repeatedly insisted, despite the relative insignificance he ascribed to superiority-inferiority calculations, or United States determination to maintain its superiority, come what may.[14] The Soviet Minister of Defense probably does not accept even the framework of McNamara's thinking, but he has almost certainly echoed the determination to escape inferiority, however "meaningless."

Soviet behavior in disarmament negotiations offers confirmation of this interest in changing the ratio of forces. Many American proposals (such as those for a cut-off of production of fissionable materials for weapons, and for a stabilization of the quantity and quality of offensive and defensive strategic nuclear delivery vehicles) have offered the USSR a way out of the strategic arms competition while preserving the nuclear and conventional capabilities it has already built up. Except for agreement on inspection, the only price tag attached has been a renunciation of ambitions to catch up with or overtake the United States in strategic military forces. Furthermore, these proposals have required no public acknowledgment of Soviet backwardness, and Soviet spokesmen could have gone on talking in their habitual vocabulary about the USSR's might. Under some of the proposed agreements,

---

[13] Interview in *Life*, September 29, 1967.

[14] The most recent restatements of this intention were in the Secretary's San Francisco speech of September 18, 1967 (*The New York Times*, September 19, 1967), and in the *Life* interview.

though not all, the USSR might even have been able to protect itself, despite the required inspection, from confirmation to the world and to its rivals of the exact extent of its military weaknesses—and strengths.

Soviet policy makers never displayed the slightest interest in any of these proposed "freezes" of the status quo. Although much emphasis was placed on the unacceptability of inspection if proposals contemplated little or no arms reductions, the real reason lay elsewhere. Soviet negotiators were forced to rely on arguments equating inspection with espionage rather than allude to Soviet inferiority as the factor motivating their behavior.

The validity of the reasoning advanced above may be tested if serious negotiations come to pass on the subject of limiting offensive and defensive missiles. The only specific proposal in this area dates back to 1964; it is the measure suggested by the United States for a "freeze" on strategic nuclear delivery vehicles, encompassing aircraft and naval vessels as well as offensive and defensive missiles.[15] A missile limitation proposal along these lines might be modified by the U.S. to eliminate the inspection requirement insisted upon earlier. That such a modification is not far-fetched may be concluded from the remarks of Assistant Secretary of Defense Paul C. Warnke on October 6, 1967. Warnke said:

> In considering any possible agreement with the Soviet Union to level off or reduce strategic offensive and defensive systems, or even the possibility for parallel action on the part of the two countries, we may have to depend on our own unilateral capability for verification. We believe that a number of possibilities for parallel action and even for formal agreement with the Soviets [sic] would permit our reliance on unilateral means of verification. Other more far-reaching agreements, particularly any involving substantial reductions, would require agreed international inspection.[16]

Warnke's suggestion was pointedly quoted in remarks on December 12, 1967, at the U.N. General Assembly by Adrian S. Fisher, Deputy Director of the ACDA.[17] This seems to betray a willingness to amend the January, 1964, proposal to drop the adversary inspection requirements heretofore firmly insisted upon. Such a change would force, at least, an altered rationale in the Soviet response; but if the analysis presented here is correct, there would be no change from *nyet* to *da*.

---

[15] The Soviet-American public exchanges after signature of the nonproliferation treaty on July 1, 1968, made it clear that negotiations about nuclear delivery vehicles would not be limited to missiles but would encompass other strategic forces.

[16] *Documents 1967,* pp. 454–59.

[17] *Department of State Bulletin,* LVIII, No. 1490 (January 15, 1968), 98.

Conceivably the USSR might have been better off in 1968 (militarily as well as economically) had it accepted in January, 1964, the American offer to stop then and there the competitive race in strategic delivery vehicles. The rejection of this and similar proposals indicates that the Soviet leaders prefer to take their chances on unrestricted competition in arms systems rather than sign up for a stabilization tying the USSR permanently to an inferior status.

The fact that the Soviet leaders hope to change the relations of military power does not necessarily mean, of course, that they will succeed. Over any short period of time, the USSR may not be able to *narrow* the strategic gap; and even over a long period, the Soviet Union may not *ever* be able to achieve parity or better. Changes in the strategic capabilities of world powers depend on many variables, of which national determination to gain or preserve supremacy is only one, and perhaps not the most crucial.

Probably, also, the leadership in the USSR is averse to a greatly stepped-up arms competition, and will be content to make haste slowly in implementing plans for approaching American power. The Soviet leaders may hope that their liberal financing of research and development will result in a technological breakthrough that will enable the USSR to narrow the strategic gap without spending large bundles of rubles on the expensive equipment required by the current "state of the art." [18] They may have been somewhat chastened by past experience, which showed that even innovations first brought to completion in the USSR, such as the ICBM, yielded no long-term advantages, since the United States was able to overcome an initial lag, and then to outproduce and outspend the USSR.* What does seem improbable, however, is Soviet renunciation of the competition by acceptance of a proposal which, in Soviet eyes, made legitimate and permanent the superiority of the United States. It is in the light of this conclusion that the ensuing discussion of possible arms limitation agreements omits mention of proposals on nuclear weapons and delivery systems, including proposals to avert further deployment of ABMs, the most discussed topic in arms control at the present time.

[18] In 1964, Soviet investment in scientific research (including, but not limited to, the important military component) was 400 per cent of 1956 investment; investment in industry in 1964 was 180 per cent of 1956. In 1964, the USSR was spending 3680 rubles per year on equipment for each person employed in scientific research, as compared to 660 rubles yearly per employed worker in industry. See *Soviet Space Programs, 1962–1965; Goals and Purposes, Achievements, Plans, and International Implications,* Senate Committee on Aeronautical and Space Science, 89th Cong., 2d sess. (Washington, D. C.: Government Printing Office, 1966).

* Some participants in the project considered that economic considerations would deter the USSR from competition in expensive strategic weapons systems to a greater extent than is implied in the text.

POSSIBLE AGREEMENTS

Attempts through arms control and disarmament negotiations to deal with the most dangerous forms of arms competition and military confrontation have yielded unsatisfactory results. The history of such negotiations between the USSR and the United States is strewn with the wreckage of attempts to deal with situations of the greatest urgency. In contrast, marked successes have occurred in dealing with questions of lesser priority. The relevant motto seems to be: "Think small." In the following discussion, therefore, attention is centered on measures involving relatively minor limitations on armaments or arms policies. As in the case of past accords, even arrangements limited to peripheral or potential arms confrontations can have considerable political importance.

The measures to be discussed are not new, and the fact that almost all have been on the table in previous disarmament meetings means not only that the interested powers have taken positions, but that the positions taken were in disagreement. Therefore, a policy change by the USSR or the United States, or both (to cite only the two indispensable parties), would be necessary for agreement.

Some of the proposals suggested for possible agreements would require revision of American or Soviet policy; they were included because of the belief that the measures do not violate the fundamental military or political principles of either power, and that their acceptance would leave intact the kind of military establishment that each considers necessary. The United States and the Soviet Union have, in fact, revised their positions over time on various proposals in the arms control and disarmament fields, so that the fact that these and other governments take a certain stand does not mean that such stands are immutable.[19]

1. *Comprehensive test ban.* One of the few measures supported in principle by both the USSR and the United States is a comprehensive ban on all testing of nuclear weapons, underground as well as in other environments. American-Soviet differences on the proposed treaty are narrow but deeply rooted. The Soviet Union now insists that na-

---

[19] Although there are others, only one example need be cited. The United States and the Soviet Union both reversed their initial opposition to an outer-space agreement of the type negotiated in 1963. Thus, in 1958 the USSR refused to discuss the problem of outer space unless the United States would agree to prohibit nuclear weapons and liquidate foreign military bases. Although yielding on these demands, the Soviet Union much later insisted that an agreement on outer space include a prohibition on "spy" satellites. Originally the United States was opposed to an agreement settling for verification that was dependent on national means alone.

tional means of detection are adequate, and rejects any thought of on-site inspections by adversaries or an international agency. The United States insists that some on-site inspection is still necessary, despite improvements in capabilities for detection and identification of underground nuclear tests.

It is not clear whether there is a possibility of movement on this issue. Probably both the United States and the Soviet Union have a greater "vested interest" in continuing underground tests now than they did in 1963, because of the large and successful programs mounted since that date, and the need to perfect new weapons systems now on the horizon. Certainly neither has pushed hard since then to extend the partial test ban.[20] It is barely conceivable, but highly unlikely, that the Soviet Union might return to its former position of agreeing to a few on-site inspections to police a full test ban. Soviet negotiators have in recent years been particularly unyielding in rejecting any discussion of foreign inspection under such an agreement. They now have a much stronger technical argument against the necessity for inspection than they had in 1963.

Apart from the inspection issue, developments of the post-1963 years have not increased American enthusiasm for abandonment of all testing. First, underground testing has yielded results beyond 1963 expectations.[21] Second, free atmospheric testing since 1964 by the Chinese, who in Washington's eyes have replaced the Russians as the most virulent enemy, has not been conducive to acceptance of further restrictions not applicable to all the nuclear weapons states.[22]

Against these trends there is the fact that the American advantage over the USSR under ground may have declined seriously since 1963,

[20] Despite the difficulties of testing underground, the United States and the Soviet Union have been able to keep their nuclear weapons laboratories profitably employed under the 1963 treaty. Abandonment of all nuclear weapons tests would probably hamper greatly efforts to maintain scientific and technical facilities in a state of readiness, i.e., capable of resuming testing immediately if either side decided to do so. Maintenance of such readiness was one of the "safeguards" insisted on by the United States Joint Chiefs of Staff in agreeing to the 1963 ban.

[21] Senator Henry M. Jackson in his Senate speech, November 30, 1967, referred to the "very large number of underground tests" by the United States and said that "very significant advances [were] made in the area of weapons technology development, new and radically different weapon-design concepts, and in the science of peaceful uses for nuclear explosives." Senator Jackson stated that "results are being obtained that were previously thought impossible under the treaty restrictions."

[22] Although Secretary of State Rusk once implied that the United States would not agree to a comprehensive test ban if the Chinese continued free testing, American representatives have continued to call for such a ban without mentioning Chinese participation. See the interview, October 19, 1964, in *Department of State Bulletin*, LI, No. 1324 (November 9, 1964), 654–59.

since the USSR has pursued an active program rivaling that of the United States. In 1963, in comparison to the USSR, the United States was much more experienced in, and had better facilities for, underground testing. The advantage is no longer as obvious. In agreeing to a complete ban, therefore, the United States would not be relinquishing a superiority as clear as that which it once enjoyed.

The United States has already shown flexibility in scaling down its expectations on requirements for verification. American insistence on "in-country" inspection of the USSR's adherence to a complete ban might be reconsidered in the light of (1) advances in the techniques for detection and identification of underground tests, (2) the experience of detecting and identifying Soviet underground tests since 1963, and (3) a re-evaluation of the risks to the national security of the United States from the possible failure to detect or identify individual Soviet tests.[23] A suggestion for American action on the test-ban issue was advanced three years ago by the Committee on Arms Control and Disarmament (headed by Jerome B. Wiesner and including other former scientific, military, and disarmament officials of the United States government) of the National Citizens' Commission on International Cooperation. Wiesner's group wrote, in a report published on November 28, 1965: "New improvements in national detection systems might make it possible to accept a treaty in which inspection followed a challenge based upon a threat of withdrawal; ultimately any quota of inspections is no more dependable than such an arrangement would be." [24]

Although the comprehensive test ban seems to be the subject of a possible agreement, it should be noted that, in both American and Soviet official circles, incentives for a total ban on tests are so ambivalent that even substantial concessions from one side might not clinch an agreement. Thus, it is possible to imagine a situation in which American relinquishment of requirements for on-site inspection would be greeted by a Soviet reversal on the desirability of any agree-

---

[23] Without the benefit of any Soviet announcements, the United States has been able to detect and publicize a large number of Soviet underground tests since 1963. Naturally, this does not eliminate the possibility that some tests have gone undetected. A country would gain a significant advantage over a close rival by violating an agreed ban only if it were able to carry out a series of tests in secret. Thus foolproof verification is a less important feature of a comprehensive test ban than it is of certain other possible disarmament measures. Obviously, to take an example, verification embodied in a system designed to avoid surprise attack must be certain (if a state is in any way dependent for its security on the system) because a single "miss" could be decisive. If an agreement were reached on reduction of missiles and other strategic vehicles, the need for foolproof verification would become crucial as the number of permitted vehicles approached zero.

[24] *Documents 1965*, p. 562.

ment. Were this done, it would probably take the form of making a complete ban contingent upon a GCD agreement, a course followed by the USSR in 1961 when it resumed testing of nuclear weapons.

2. *Germany and Europe.* For almost two decades after World War II, the diplomatic line-up in Europe remained very stable, almost frozen, in spite of pressures for change emanating from the East and West, which were almost equally dissatisfied with the division—and the particular lines of division—between Communist-dominated Europe and the rest of the continent. The postwar line-up proved more stable than the European order following World War I, and this stability contrasted rather sharply with the considerable shifts after World War II in power relationships in Asia, Africa, and the Middle East. Nevertheless, the tension in Europe associated with the existence of hostile alliances under Soviet and American leadership inspired many arms control proposals. Simultaneously, the hostility and tension made it impossible to negotiate any of these.

In the past few years, however, a new fluidity in the European scene has improved the chances of negotiating political agreements involving both Western and Eastern Europe, though the Soviet-led intervention in Czechoslovakia has darkened prospects for the time being. In the context of this discussion of arms control problems, it is possible to treat European possibilities only from a very limited perspective. Yet almost all the proposals—mostly Soviet or Polish in origin—looking toward negotiations on arms relationships in Europe involve fundamental questions of the political future of Europe *tout court.*

The new situation in Europe was shaped partly by changes in the Soviet-American relationship, as the two superpowers and senior alliance states began to negotiate more successfully with each other and to find at least limited points of common interest. It was perhaps affected even more by the growing divergences within each alliance system. Both the United States and the Soviet Union have been forced to take account of allies no longer content to play only the game of "follow the leader." It is no accident, as a Russian editorialist might say, that France and Rumania, the two states which have pursued the most independent policies toward Washington and Moscow respectively, are precisely the states which took the lead in developing relations across the European "continental divide." But other states have also displayed a greater flexibility than had hitherto characterized cross-alliance relations. The fluidity has affected Germany itself, acutely split by the forces that divide most of the continent. In particular, the Federal Republic of Germany has moved to better its relations with the governments of Eastern Europe and, to a much lesser degree, even with the East German regime.

The recession of the threat of armed conflict in Europe may have diminished pressures for new arms arrangements. It is also true, paradoxically, that the lessening of the need for control measures may make them more attainable. Furthermore, the USSR, for understandable reasons, has never been cool toward "freezes" and "equal reductions" in the European context, even to some touching nuclear weapons. The Soviet Union has not felt in regard to Europe the strategic inferiority that made stabilization unacceptable to it in other situations.

Big Soviet schemes, of the type described in an earlier chapter, involving the dismantling of NATO and Warsaw Pact military structures or the dissolution of the two alliances, are not likely to be the subject of negotiations, and clearly not with American concurrence. But almost any conceivable negotiations will require from the West, particularly from the United States and West Germany, a "flexibility" about the Communist regime in East Germany that has heretofore been avoided.

One area which seemed to offer some possibilities of agreement concerned measures to reduce Soviet, American, and other Western forces in Germany. The United States has in recent years indicated its interest in such reductions, but it is not clear whether Washington has envisaged a formal arrangement or merely informal reciprocal cuts.[25] The USSR, despite its basic stance favoring freezes, cutbacks, and withdrawals in Europe, has turned a deaf ear to these American overtures.[26] Certainly the Soviet Union would seek to avoid steps helping or seeming to help the United States to ease its problems of augmenting forces in Vietnam by reducing requirements in Europe. Even before the invasion of Czechoslovakia, the USSR dropped all European arms proposals from its July 1, 1968 list of desirable measures.

Another possible area of arms control negotiations and agreements is that of nuclear weapons in Europe. With a diminution of prospects for early employment of nuclear weapons in any European hostilities, there would seem to be some chance of a stabilization, if not a reduction, of the nuclear weapons stationed in Europe. This might involve arrangements along the lines of the Gomulka "freeze" proposal cover-

[25] President Johnson in an address on October 7, 1966, said: "Reduction of Soviet forces in Central Europe would, of course, affect the extent of that [Soviet] threat. If changing circumstances should lead to a gradual and balanced revision in force levels on both sides, the revision could . . . help gradually to shape an entire new political environment." (*The New York Times*, October 8, 1966.) The final communiqué of the North Atlantic Council, following the ministerial meeting at Luxembourg, December 12–14, 1967, "reaffirmed" the view of the ministers "that, if conditions permit, a balanced reduction of forces on both sides could constitute a significant step toward security in Europe." (*Department of State Bulletin*, LVIII, No. 1489 [January 8, 1968], 49.)

[26] See remarks by Secretary of State Rusk, May 3, 1967, on the "Mansfield resolution" regarding reduction of American troops in Europe, in *United States Troops in Europe*, p. 63.

ing Germany (East and West), Poland, and Czechoslovakia, to be monitored by NATO and Warsaw Pact teams.[27] Such an arrangement would not involve the pullback of American nuclear weapons from Germany, which the USSR claims as the price of an otherwise interesting proposal to "lessen the danger of surprise attack." The proposal, overambitious in its title, links the establishment of control posts on NATO and Warsaw Pact territory, including the United States and the USSR, with denuclearization of Germany and reductions of foreign troops in Germany. (In connection with either of these proposals, the NATO allies might seek to include the Soviet MRBMs and IRBMs targeted on Western Europe.) Such arrangements would not require formal recognition of the East German state by the NATO states, but they would certainly enhance its international status.

The same troublesome and pervasive question of the East German regime affects the acceptability of the idea of alliance negotiations between the North Atlantic and Warsaw Treaty organizations. The USSR for a long time promoted the idea of a pact of nonaggression between the member *states* of the two alliance systems, although it is far from clear that it favors *alliance* negotiations as such.[28] Apart from the Federal Republic of Germany, which has special reasons to look askance at any negotiations of this kind, the maverick states such as France and Rumania are not likely to be enthusiastic about negotiations emphasizing alliance structures. Whatever their possible form, it seems out of the question for the United States and its NATO allies to hope to negotiate without and against the German Democratic Republic. Indeed, a principal objective of the USSR and some other Warsaw Pact states is to use such negotiations and possible agreements to bolster the standing of the East German state and regime.

None of these agreements presupposes millennial changes in the structure of European affairs, and all are compatible with the continued confrontation of American and Soviet military forces on the continent. Further disintegration of the rival alliances, additional manifestation of independent courses by European states, and the strengthening of tendencies in both Western and Eastern Europe toward European unity, might lead in time to arrangements organized without American or Soviet assent. The world is not yet at this point, however; and the Soviet-led occupation of Czechoslovakia in August, 1968, demonstrated again the Soviet willingness to resort to extreme measures against developments perceived by Moscow as threatening the postwar

[27] See *Documents 1964*, pp. 53–55.

[28] Soviet backing of negotiations between NATO and Warsaw Pact member states rather than between the two alliances probably is dictated by the USSR's position that existence of the alliances is harmful, and that both alliances should be abolished.

order in Eastern Europe. For at least the next decade, it appears likely that any European settlement will require the participation and consent of both superpowers.

3. *Use of nuclear weapons.* Another area of possible negotiation involves proposals to "prohibit" the use, or first use, of nuclear weapons.[29] As previously mentioned, such a ban would have little or no effect on the deployment of nuclear weapons, i.e., little effect on nuclear deterrent forces (and probably only minor impact on the use, or time of use, of nuclear weapons in international conflict). However, with nuclear weapons in the hands of adversary powers—notably the United States, the USSR, and Communist China—the likelihood of rapid introduction of these weapons into conflict has diminished. All the nuclear weapons states seek to project their influence far beyond their national frontiers, and the principal adversaries profess to have worldwide interests. For this reason, there are few areas of potential or actual conflict in which any of the five nuclear weapons states could detonate nuclear weapons without running some danger of escalation and retaliation. Both the Soviet Union and the United States have attained a nuclear threshold giving each something approaching a secure deterrent force, and presumably Communist China will in time develop at least a small deterrent force.[30]

A ban on the "use" of nuclear weapons (detonation against an enemy) would affect most of all the diplomacy of deterrence—that brandishing of the threat of nuclear warfare that is called "nuclear blackmail" if the "other side" engages in it. Acceptance of a ban on use of nuclear weapons would probably make unprofitable such diplomatic manipulation of nuclear arsenals. At the same time, the continued possession and enlargement of nuclear weapons stockpiles and delivery vehicles would remind contending statesmen that rival and opposing countries possessing such weapons would no doubt use them, regardless of treaty commitments, if important interests were jeopardized. (Obviously such states would use them "second," but they would also be tempted to use them "first" in case of need.)

The United States has always resisted such an agreement, largely for reasons of European policy. Fearing Soviet resort to force to rearrange the map of Europe, and concluding that Western conventional forces could not prevent Soviet victory, the United States for over two

[29] The pros and cons of no-use agreements have been widely discussed. For some of the relevant literature, see Note 36 to Chapter 9.

[30] The assumptions that Communist China will develop a secure second-strike capability, and that when the Chinese leaders have a greater nuclear armament they will be less tempted to irrational and dangerous employment of these weapons, were spelled out in the address in Detroit by Assistant Secretary of Defense for International Security Affairs, Paul C. Warnke. See Note 16.

decades has held to an explicit first-use doctrine contemplating early introduction of nuclear weapons to counter Soviet conventional superiority in a war launched in Europe.[31]

A number of conditions have changed, however, since the United States adopted its negative position on a declaratory ban against use of nuclear weapons. The prospect has lessened for Soviet initiation of armed hostilities in Europe, and the Soviet advantage in conventional capabilities is no longer as obvious or as overwhelming as it once seemed. Perhaps more important, the American advantage in initiating use of nuclear weapons is no longer clear-cut. The idea of establishing a permissive climate for use of "tactical" nuclear weapons in Europe, separated sharply from exchanges of major blows, has made little headway.[32] Despite strong reaffirmation from Washington, there has also been a decrease in the belief that America is willing to use nuclear weapons for the sake of Europe, and thus to invite retaliation on the United States.

When the United States position on the question was fixed, organized international relations were largely confined to states of rival Communist and Western groups, each of which was more or less closely tied to either the United States or the USSR. Two trends have changed this situation. Alliances East and West have loosened as independent-minded partners have asserted a greater freedom of action and minimized their dependence on the protection afforded by the United States or the USSR. Decolonization has altered the situation by causing many newly independent states to appear on the world scene, none equipped with nuclear weapons and most of them nonaligned, that is,

---

[31] The policy was built into NATO strategic doctrine as formulated in 1956, and received a clear expression of approval by President Kennedy on March 12, 1962 (*The New York Times*, March 28, 1962). The President stated, in an interview with Stewart Alsop: "Of course in some circumstances we must be prepared to use the nuclear weapon at the start, come what may—a clear attack on Western Europe, for example." ("Kennedy's Grand Strategy," *Saturday Evening Post*, March 31, 1962, p. 11.) Other presidents before and since have expressed the same idea somewhat less bluntly. It should be noted that NATO accepted a revised strategic concept in 1967 calling for "a flexible and balanced range of appropriate responses, conventional and nuclear, to all levels of aggression or threats of aggression." Text of final communiqué following the Luxembourg meeting of North Atlantic Council, December 12–14, 1967, in the *Department of State Bulletin*, LVIII, No. 1489 (January 8, 1963), 49–50. The new doctrine did not rule out first use, but made it more problematic.

[32] This is partially because of expectations of great devastation in Europe if both sides used even "tactical" nuclear weapons. For a recent scary picture, see *Report of the Secretary-General on the Effects of the Possible Use of Nuclear Weapons and on the Security and Economic Implications for States of the Acquisition and Further Development of These Weapons*. U.N. General Assembly, Document A/6858, October 10, 1967, a report by a 12-member committee including American, British, and Soviet members.

unprotected by a nuclear ally. This has resulted in increased support outside the Communist group of states for measures designed to "outlaw" nuclear weapons by inhibiting their "use" in international relations and that most classic form of such relations, war.

4. *Regional arms limitations.* The Indian-Pakistani and Arab-Israeli wars heightened interest in negotiation of agreements limiting "local" arms races in order to discourage early resort to force by anxious and antagonistic states, with possible "catalytic" effects elsewhere, and to avoid waste of badly needed resources on expensive armaments. The United States in particular has shown an interest in promoting certain regional arrangements to minimize such competition in "conventional" armament. The principles guiding American thinking were most carefully spelled out by William C. Foster, Director of the United States Arms Control and Disarmament Agency, on April 19, 1966.[33] He emphasized that the initiative for an agreement must come from the states within the region, that the agreement should include all the states whose participation is considered important, and that it should be respected by potential suppliers. These principles appear to have greater relevance to arms competition among Latin American states than to the situation in either South Asia, involving India and Pakistan, or the Middle East. In particular, the insistence that any regional arms limitation agreements originate with the states in an area seems less than promising in these two conflict-ridden areas. In any case, such proposals for agreed self-denial have little importance in terms of negotiations with the Soviet Union.

Of more relevance in the American-Soviet context are proposals occasionally discussed over the years for supplier nations to limit their arms deliveries to states in a particular region. Along with the United States, the USSR has been a major supplier of arms to certain Middle Eastern and Asian states since the mid-1950's. The build-up of the UAR and Syrian forces by the Soviet Union obviously was one decisive factor in the events leading to the June, 1967, Arab-Israeli war. Following the cease-fire, President Johnson on June 19 proposed that the U.N. "immediately call upon all of its members to report all shipments on file for all the peoples of the word to observe." [34] Referring to this proposal, Secretary of State Dean Rusk on July 19, 1967, called for "some sort of understanding—whether in general or in detail (because details are difficult to work out)—that arms-supplying nations will not themselves be responsible for a major renewal of an arms race in the Middle East." [35]

---

[33] Statement to the ENDC; see *Documents 1966*, pp. 226–30.
[34] *Department of State Bulletin*, LVII, No. 1463 (July 10, 1967), 33.
[35] *Department of State Bulletin*, LVII, No. 1467 (August 7, 1967), 161.

Despite the defeat suffered by the armed forces of the Arab countries in the June war, there have been few signs of reciprocal Soviet interest in limiting arms deliveries to friendly Arab states. Soviet military equipment has continued to flow into the area, not only to replenish equipment lost in the five-day war, but also to augment Arab capabilities. In its memorandum of July 1, 1968, however, the USSR alluded favorably to the possibility of agreements for regional arms reductions. It singled out the Middle East as a possible area, but made it clear that an agreement would require evacuation by Israel of Arab territories occupied in June, 1967.[36]

The USSR experience as an arms shipper has not been altogether happy. If one purpose was to encourage a pro-Soviet and pro-Communist orientation of nonaligned countries, some of the results, as in Indonesia, were dubious. Experience with Arab and other states has shown the USSR that Soviet arms do not necessarily provide the margin for victory when client states put the weapons to use against external foes in the region.

Consequently, opportunities may present themselves for agreements to limit dangerous arms races. This will become promising only if the USSR becomes sufficiently nervous about the possibilities for escalation implicit in local wars, or becomes less convinced that its arms supplies to radical nationalist regimes will hurt only the "imperialists." Thus, the USSR would have to alter its calculation that competitive great-power support of local powers will have asymmetrical consequences favoring the USSR.

5. *Peripheral Measures.* "Arms controllers" long ago discovered that limitations are more easily negotiated on potential than on actual areas of rivalry, on exotic and undeveloped pursuits rather than on activities central to the functioning of opposed military establishments. With Antarctica and heavenly space already "discovered" and "exploited" for purposes of arms control, the ocean floor and the seabed have aroused some interest. Establishment of international regulations in this area will probably turn out to be a more difficult task than establishment of comparable regulations concerning outer space, because of the traditional use of oceans for economic, military, and other pursuits. Furthermore, arms control components seem less important in regard to a possible agreement on use of the ocean floor than they did in the regulation of outer space. This is because stationing nuclear or other military installations on the ocean floor appears to be a more remote possibility than stationing weapons in orbit, and because other types of exploitation of the seabed appear to be more feasible than in the case of outer space.

[36] *The New York Times,* July 2, 1968.

Malta proposed in August, 1967, that the U.N. General Assembly initiate steps for a treaty insuring, among other objectives, that the seabed and ocean floor be reserved "exclusively for peaceful purposes." [37] With the Soviet Union initially cool to the whole idea and the United States interested but wary of immediate steps, the U.N. General Assembly voted unanimously on December 18, 1967, to establish an *ad hoc* committee of 35 states (including the United States and the USSR) to study the matter and report at the next session of the U.N. General Assembly.[38] When the committee met in March, 1968, the Soviet representative introduced at the first session a proposal for a ban on any use for military purposes of the seabed and ocean floor "beyond the scope of national jurisdiction." [39] The United States has shown an interest only in a ban on use of the ocean floor for placement of "weapons of mass destruction."

The problem of the "nonmilitarization" of the seabed, or its "nonnuclearization," does not appear to have caused many sleepless nights for statesmen or common folk. It is, however, an example of the kind of potential or exotic problem on which arms control negotiations have achieved past successes and may record others in the future. It would be unwise to disparage such achievements merely because they leave untouched urgent problems of international relations and of military competition and confrontation. Such agreements involve symbolic and "atmospheric" repercussions that may be as important as specific limitations on military operations spelled out in the agreements. Furthermore, since technology advances rapidly and arms control negotiations are notoriously slow-moving, potential problems could become very real if not anticipated in good time.

*   *   *

An assessment of prospects for arms control and disarmament arrangements must take account of possibilities of reciprocal "understandings" as well as formal agreements. (Obviously words not spoken and actions not taken can be as important in such understandings as those expressed.) Thus, reciprocal reductions in expenditures for defense establishments, and reduction of forces and armaments generally

[37] U.N. General Assembly, Document A/6695, August 18, 1967.

[38] The text of the U.N. General Assembly resolution is in the *Department of State Bulletin*, LVIII, No. 1491 (January 22, 1968), 126–27. For the American position, see Ambassador Goldberg's statement, *ibid.*, pp. 125–26, and a statement by Assistant Secretary of State Joseph J. Sisco to the Committee on Foreign Relations of the U.S. Senate, November 29, 1967, in the *Department of State Bulletin*, LVIII, No. 1488 (January 1, 1968), 17–19.

[39] Moscow TASS International Service, March 20, 1968. The proposal was included in the list of suggested partial measures made public by the USSR on July 1, 1968.

or in sensitive areas, might be examples of genuine but informal "disarmament" measures, just as informally-fixed limits on deployment of ICBMs or mutual abstention from installation of ABM systems might constitute forms of "arms control" under similar circumstances. The increased civility of communications between the Soviet Union and the United States in the 1960's, as compared to earlier periods of the Cold War, as well as the recognition of some shared interests, provide a certain basis for development of such understandings.

The kinds of reciprocal understandings suggested here are no panacea for perpetual harmony, and are no substitute for formal agreements. The "understandings" may turn out to be misunderstandings, because the very informality that makes them attractive prevents any precision. Before 1961 it could have been argued, and was argued,[40] that mutual abstention of the great powers from all nuclear weapons tests constituted an informal arms control agreement that was as good as, and better in some ways than, a formal agreement. The illusion was dispelled with Soviet resumption of tests in 1961. In a different area, many Americans talked themselves into believing (until recently) that a kind of tacit agreement on the strategic-nuclear balance of forces existed between the United States and the USSR. The contribution of the United States to this "stability" was seen in the fixing of a finite number of ICBMs it would deploy, and in the abstention from deployment of an ABM system.[41] When it became known in 1966–1967 that the USSR was rapidly expanding its force of offensive missiles and had installed an antimissile system around Moscow, the actions appeared to some American observers as a betrayal of a tacit accord. In this affair, the "misunderstanding" had been based on an earlier misinterpretation of what the Soviet leaders were *doing*, to which a minimization of what they were *saying* had contributed. For the Soviet leaders had not accepted either the unfavorable strategic balance in general or the restriction of competition in strategic systems to offensive weapons alone.

Even if reciprocal understandings exist, they are likely to be fragile. The possibility of unilateral termination allows a policy of "easy in, easy out," which was well illustrated by the history of the tacit moratoriums on testing between 1958 and 1961. Patterns of responsive cuts in military budgets have shown even less "survivability." In another

[40] Thomas C. Schelling, "Reciprocal Measures for Arms Stabilization," in *Arms Control, Disarmament, and National Security,* ed. Donald G. Brennan (New York: George Braziller, Inc., 1961), pp. 167–86.

[41] Secretary McNamara announced a number of years ago that the United States planned to install slightly more than 1000 Minutemen ICBMs, and this number has not been increased, although the planned introduction of multiple warheads for the Minutemen ICBMs would multiply the number of potential targets to be covered by the same number of ICBMs. In contrast, it would not increase the number of targets the USSR would have to take care of in a "counterforce" blow.

area, the negotiated unilateral announcements in 1964 by the United States, the United Kingdom, and the USSR, of reductions in production of fissionable materials for weapons purposes led to mutual recriminations, not to other measures of disarmament by reciprocity.

One reason for the fragility of many informal "understandings" on arms control is that, in the absence of fixed obligations on rival states, national leaders must justify their measures largely in terms of their own state interests. To the extent that these national interests provide sufficient justification, the pressures on rival nations for reciprocation, or for continued reciprocation, are extremely weak. When President Johnson on April 20, 1964, said that the reductions he was ordering in production of fissionable materials for weapons were to bring American "production in line with need," he was undercutting any attempt to use the understanding to press for Soviet fulfillment of Premier Khrushchev's simultaneous pledge "to reduce substantially the production of uranium-235 for nuclear weapons." [42] When Premier Khrushchev announced reductions of Soviet armed forces and of budgetary allocations to defense, the very fact that the reductions were rationalized in terms of Soviet interests undercut his simultaneous attempts to use these unilateral steps to put pressure on the United States for reciprocation.

Some of these deficiencies of informal understandings also inhere in more formal agreements, although to a lesser degree. The vagueness that makes "understandings" capable of divergent interpretations also affects even the negotiated language of documents formally approved and ratified by rival states. If tacit agreements are fragile, treaties are not eternal. Solemn arrangements between the USSR and Western powers have succumbed to the ravages of time and changes of circumstance. Recognition of this temporal quality led to the marking of "exit" doors in the 1963 test-ban treaty and in the 1968 nonproliferation treaty. Both allow unilateral withdrawal when a participating country judges that its "supreme interests" have been jeopardized by "extraordinary events" related to the subject matter of the treaty.[43]

These cautionary words on informal understandings do not mean that viable tacit arrangements cannot be reached between Soviet and American leaders on certain urgent arms control problems. It is conceivable that American-Soviet communications and discussions at various levels might result in some understandings regarding the deployment (and employment) of crucial weapons systems. The discussions

---

[42] For President Johnson's and Premier Khrushchev's statements, see *Documents 1964*, pp. 165–68.

[43] The text of the test-ban treaty is in *Documents 1963*, pp. 291–93; that of the nonproliferation treaty is in the *Department of State Bulletin*, LIX, No. 1514 (July 1, 1968), 8–11.

would necessarily include authoritative spokesmen of both countries, but the resulting understandings would be impossible to fix in any more formal agreement. The poignant word here is "conceivable." For reasons that have been spelled out at some length, such understandings at the present time seem unlikely, in view of the asymmetrical forces and objectives of the rival powers.

Even if the war in Vietnam has not prevented successful negotiations on arms limitations (since two agreements—outer space and non-proliferation—have been reached), it seems likely that these agreements were survivors of the war rather than its products. Their chances of surviving, furthermore, would have been less had the confrontation of American and Soviet military power in Vietnam been more direct and open. The possibility of such an open confrontation is still not excluded, and therefore the war serves as a potent deterrent to more ambitious measures affecting the military establishments of the two superpowers. Likewise, while the Soviet-led intervention in Czechoslovakia may not have long-term effects on arms control prospects, it is certain to make immediate prospects more difficult.

These prospects for further arms control agreements are also affected by the technological instability introduced into the weapons field. Recent advances in means of attack and of defense did not spring, of course, from some supernatural force, but from the technical laboratories of the same states which maintain staffs of arms controllers to worry about the unsettling effects of "destabilizing" innovations. To recognize this is merely to recognize that the great powers prepare simultaneously for two remote if not unthinkable contingencies, making war and making peace. Whatever their origin, military innovations such as ABM deployment, orbital rockets, and multiwarheads for ballistic missiles complicate the task of arms controllers.

Finally, prospects for agreements depend on domestic trends within the states engaged in negotiations. There are in the USSR, as in the United States, opposing forces that pull national policy toward and away from such agreements. (Although internal developments in the United States are just as relevant as previously discussed trends in the Soviet Union, this is a study of Soviet attitudes and behavior, not of American.) In the Soviet Union since 1964, both the mode of collective leadership and the personalities of the leaders affect policy making on arms control and other national security issues. Leaders and groups favoring emphasis on the USSR as a revolutionary power, or committed to unrestricted build-up of Soviet military strength, or inclined to the use of Soviet military power in crisis situations, coexist with others interested in arrangements with opposing states and anxious to check spending for military purposes in order to promote economic expansion or welfare programs. Of course, the emphases characteristic of recent Soviet policy may change as a result of shifts in the composition of the decision-making group, or of untoward events in Soviet or world affairs.

Short of some turn of this kind, arms control and disarmament measures of interest to the Soviet leadership are likely to be those of modest scope, compatible with a policy of "no war, no peace." Already the leaders have virtually dismissed grandiose prospects for a disarmed world, even as a specter useful for haunting the Western states. Arrangements affecting the crucial weapons systems indispensable to the present balance of terror will prove feasible only if calculations of superiority-inferiority between the great powers lose their determinative influence on state leaders. There may be, as President Kennedy once said, "no permanent enemies" among the different nations on our planet. The great powers of the nuclear age have not yet arrived at the stage, however, in which confidence in the viability of peaceful relations enables them to halt competition in military power and to contemplate the eventual liquidation of the awesome machines of destruction on which they currently rely.

APPENDIX A: PARTICIPANTS

Professor Vernon V. Aspaturian
Department of Political Science
Pennsylvania State University

Professor Abram Bergson
Russian Research Center
Harvard University

Professor Severyn Bialer
Russian Institute
Columbia University

†Dr. Karl Birnbaum
Swedish Institute of International
   Affairs, Stockholm

Professor Urie Bronfenbrenner
Department of Child Development
Cornell University

*Professor Alexander Dallin
Russian Institute
Columbia University

†Professor Herbert S. Dinerstein
School of Advanced International
   Studies
The Johns Hopkins University

Professor Loren R. Graham
Russian Institute
Columbia University

*Mr. Thomas B. Larson
Russian Institute
Columbia University

Mr. Wolfgang Leonhard
Department of History
University of Michigan

Professor Richard Lowenthal
Otto-Suhr Institute
Free University of Berlin

Professor Alec Nove
Department of International Economic Studies
University of Glasgow

*Professor Warner R. Schilling
Institute of War and Peace Studies
Columbia University

*Professor Marshall D. Shulman
Russian Institute
Columbia University

* Attended both the conference at Nantucket, Mass., on April 1–5, 1967, and the New York follow-up conference on November 30–December 1, 1967.
   † Attended only the New York conference.

231

Professor Robert C. Tucker
Department of Politics
Princeton University

*Dr. Thomas W. Wolfe
The RAND Corporation

GUESTS

Professor Zbigniew Brzezinski
Policy Planning Council
Department of State

†Mr. Michael Durkee
U.S. Arms Control and Disarmament
Agency

Mr. Harland Moulton
U.S. Arms Control and Disarmament
Agency

*Colonel Kent K. Parrot
U.S. Arms Control and Disarmament
Agency

*Mr. Helmut Sonnenfeldt
Department of State

Mr. Lyman Wooster
U.S. Arms Control and Disarmament
Agency

* Attended both the conference at Nantucket, Mass., on April 1–5, 1967, and the New York follow-up conference on November 30–December 1, 1967.
† Attended only the New York conference.

APPENDIX B: A SELECTIVE BIBLIOGRAPHY

This bibliography lists principally books and articles on Soviet arms control and disarmament policy since 1964. Some basic references to writings on relevant Soviet attitudes during the Khrushchev period are contained in *The Soviet Union and Disarmament: An Appraisal of Soviet Attitudes and Intentions*, by Alexander Dallin and others (New York: Frederick A. Praeger, Inc., 1965); *Khrushchev and the Arms Race: Soviet Interest in Arms Control and Disarmament, 1954–1964*, by Lincoln P. Bloomfield, Walter C. Clemens, Jr., and Franklyn J. C. Griffiths (Cambridge, Mass.: The M.I.T. Press, 1966); and *Soviet Disarmament Policy, 1917–1963*, a bibliography compiled by Walter C. Clemens, Jr. (Stanford, Calif.: The Hoover Institution on War, Revolution, and Peace, 1965).

Many Soviet statements on disarmament are reproduced in English translation in the annual issues of *Documents on Disarmament*, compiled by the United States Arms Control and Disarmament Agency (Washington, D.C.: Government Printing Office). English translations of Soviet writings on disarmament also appear in the monthly, *International Affairs* (Moscow), and in the weekly publication, *The Current Digest of the Soviet Press* (New York).

The most extensive digest of the current literature is to be found in *Arms Control and Disarmament: A Quarterly Bibliography with Abstracts and Annotations*, compiled at the Library of Congress, beginning with the first issue of Winter 1964–1965. The most convenient source for the text of official United States documents of current interest as well as policy pronouncements is the weekly *Department of State Bulletin*, issued by its Bureau of Public Affairs. *Studies in Progress or Recently Completed: Arms Control and Disarmament*, a semiannual publication of the External Research Staff of the U.S. Department of State, provides lists of research projects in the field carried on by Western, mostly American, scholars.

BOOKS AND ARTICLES

Amme, Carl H., Jr. *NATO Without France.* Stanford, Calif.: The Hoover Institution on War, Revolution, and Peace, 1967.

——, "Arms Control Concepts and the Military Balance in Europe," *Orbis,* VIII, No. 4 (Winter, 1965), 832–53.

Aron, Raymond, *The Great Debate: Theories of Nuclear Strategy,* Trans. Ernst Pawel. Garden City, N.Y.: Doubleday & Company, Inc., 1965.

Barnet, Richard J., and Richard A. Falk, eds., *Security in Disarmament.* Princeton, N.J.: Princeton University Press, 1965.

Beaton, Leonard, *Must the Bomb Spread?* Baltimore: Penguin Books, 1966.

——, "Nuclear Fuel-for-All," *Foreign Affairs,* XLV, No. 4 (July, 1967), 663–69.

Becker, Abraham S., *Soviet Military Outlays Since 1955.* Santa Monica, Calif.; The RAND Corporation, 1964 (RM-3886-PR, processed).

Benôit, Emile, ed., *Disarmament and World Economic Interdependence.* New York: Columbia University Press, 1967.

Bloomfield, Lincoln P., Walter C. Clemens, Jr., and Franklyn J. C. Griffiths, *Khrushchev and the Arms Race: Soviet Interest in Arms Control and Disarmament, 1954–1964.* Cambridge, Mass.: The M.I.T. Press, 1966.

Bogatov, S., "Peregovory po razoruzheniiu i iadernye problemy," *Mirovaia Ekonomika i Mezhdunarodnye Otnosheniia,* No. 9, 1966, 29–41.

Bogdanov, Oleg V., *Vseobshchee i polnoe razoruzhenie.* Moscow: Mezhdunarodnye otnosheniia, 1964.

——, "A Soviet View of Disarmament," *World Federalist,* IX (January, 1965), 14–16.

Bondarenko, V., "Voenno-tekhnicheskoe prevoskhodstvo—vazhneishii faktor nadezhnoi oborony strany," *Kommunist vooruzhennykh sil,* No. 17 (September, 1966), 7–14.

Brennan, D. G., "New Thoughts on Missile Defense," *Bulletin of the Atomic Scientists,* XXIII, No. 6 (June, 1967), 10–15.

Brodie, Bernard, *Escalation and the Nuclear Option.* Princeton, N.J.: Princeton University Press, 1967.

Brzezinski, Zbigniew, "Moscow and the M.L.F.: Hostility and Ambivalence," *Foreign Affairs,* LXIII, No. 1 (October, 1964), 126–34.

Buchan, Alastair, ed., *A World of Nuclear Powers?* Englewood Cliffs, N.J.: Prentice-Hall, Inc., 1966.

Bullard, Sir Edward, "Detecting Underground Explosions," *Scientific American,* CCXV, No. 1 (July, 1966), 19–29.

Carter, L. J., "Test Detection: Decoupling Theory Verified, But Does It Matter? *Science,* CLV, No 3761 (January 27, 1967), 438–40.

Cheprov, I. I., "Dogovor o kosmose—pobeda sovetskoi diplomatii," *Sovetskoe gosudarstvo i pravo*, No. 4 (1967), 48–56.

Cherkassky, L. Ia., "Iz istorii bor'by Sovetskogo Soiuza za iadernoe razoruzhenie," *Novaia i noveishaia istoriia*, No. 2 (March–April, 1967), 99–107.

Clemens, Walter C., Jr., "China's Nuclear Tests: Trends and Portents," *The China Quarterly*, No. 32 (October–December, 1967), 111–31.

——, "The Nuclear Test Ban and Sino-Soviet Relations," *Orbis*, X, No. 1 (Spring, 1966), 152–83.

——, "Outer Space, Strategy, and Arms Control," *Bulletin of the Atomic Scientists*, XXIII, No. 9 (November, 1967), 24–28.

——, "The Sino-Soviet Dispute: Dogma and Dialectics on Disarmament," *International Affairs* (London), XLI, No. 4 (April, 1965), 204–22.

——, "Underlying Factors in Soviet Arms Control Policy: Problems of Systematic Analysis," in *Papers VI, Peace Research Society*, eds. Walter Isard and Julian Walpert. Tokyo: Peace Research Society (International), 1967. Paper presented at the 1966 Vienna Conference of the Society.

Coffey, Joseph I., "Stability and the Strategic Balance," *Proceedings of the U.S. Naval Institute*, LMIII, No. 6 (June, 1967), 40–47.

——, "The Anti-Ballistic Missile Debate," *Foreign Affairs*, XLV, No. 3 (April, 1967), 403–13.

——, "An Over-all Freeze on Strategic Forces," *Disarmament*, No. 11 (September, 1966), 5–7, 21.

——, "Strategy, Strategic Forces, and Arms Control," *Orbis*, IX, No. 1 (Spring, 1965), 96–115.

Dallin, Alexander, and others. *The Soviet Union and Disarmament: An Appraisal of Soviet Attitudes and Intentions*. New York: Frederick A. Praeger, Inc., 1965.

Dougherty, James E., "The Nonproliferation Treaty," *The Russian Review*, XXV, No. 1 (January, 1966), 10–23.

——, "The Status of the Arms Negotiations," *Orbis*, IX, No. 1 (Spring, 1965), 49–97.

——, and J. F. Lehman, eds., *Arms Control for the Late Sixties*. Princeton, N.J.: D. Van Nostrand Co., Inc., 1967.

Edeen, Alf, "The Strategy Debate in the Soviet Union," *Cooperation and Conflict*, II (1965), 1–15.

Erickson, John, "The Fly In Outer Space: The Soviet Union and the Anti-Ballistic Missile." *The World Today*, XXIII, No. 3 (March, 1967), 106–14.

——, ed., *The Military-Technical Revolution: Its Impact on Strategy and Foreign Policy*. New York: Frederick A. Praeger, Inc., 1966. See especially essays by Herbert S. Dinerstein, John R. Thomas, and Raymond L. Garthoff.

Ermath, Fritz, "Die Diskussion über die sowjetische Verteidigungspolitik unter Breshnjew und Kossygin," *Europa-Archiv,* XXII, No. 16 (August 25, 1967), 571–84.

Falk, Richard A., Robert C. Tucker, and Oran R. Young, *On Minimizing the Use of Nuclear Weapons.* Princeton, N.J.: Princeton University Center for International Studies, 1966 (Research Monograph No. 23, processed).

Feld, Bernard, "A Pledge: No First Use." *Bulletin of the Atomic Scientists,* XXIII, No. 5 (May, 1967), 46–48.

Foster, William C., "Risks of Nuclear Proliferation: New Directions in Arms Control and Disarmament." *Foreign Affairs,* XLIII, No. 4 (July, 1965), 587–601.

Frank, Lewis A., "ABM and Nonproliferation: Related Issues," *Orbis,* XI, No. 1 (Spring, 1967), 67–79.

Frye, Alton, "Space Arms Control," *Bulletin of the Atomic Scientists,* XXI, No. 4 (April, 1965), 29–33.

Gardner, Richard N., ed., *Blueprint for Peace: Being the Proposals of Prominent Americans to the White House Conference on International Cooperation.* New York: McGraw-Hill Book Company, Inc., 1966. Chapter I contains the report and recommendations of the Committee on Arms Control and Disarmament, chaired by Jerome Wiesner, which also appears in *Documents on Disarmament 1965,* pp. 555–81.

Garthoff, Raymond L., *Sino-Soviet Military Relations.* New York: Frederick A. Praeger, Inc., 1966.

———, *Soviet Military Policy: A Historical Analysis.* New York: Frederick A. Praeger, Inc., 1966.

Gasteyger, Curt, "Ende oder Wandlung der Allianzen? Gedanken zur Krise des atlantischen Bündnissystems," *Europa-Archiv,* XXI, No. 14 (July 25, 1966), 427–32.

Getler, Michael, "Soviets Trying to Close Strategic Gap," *Technology Week,* XVIII, No. 26 (June 27, 1966), 4–15.

Gilpatric, Roswell L., "The Atomic Arms Race: A 'Mad Momentum' May Be Under Way," *The New York Times Magazine,* December 3, 1967, 24–55 ff.

Glagolev, I. S., ed., *SSSR, SShA i razoruzhenie.* Moscow: "Nauka," 1967.

———, "Economic and Social Consequences of Disarmament," in Walter Isard and Julian Walpert, eds. *Papers IV, Peace Research Society.* Tokyo: Peace Research Society (International), 1966. Paper presented at the 1965 Cracow Conference.

———, "Reducing Military Expenses—A Soviet View," *Disarmament,* No. 12 (December, 1966), 1–4.

Griffith, William E., *Sino-Soviet Relations, 1964–1965.* Cambridge, Mass.: The M.I.T. Press, 1967.

———, *The Sino-Soviet Rift.* Cambridge, Mass.: The M.I.T. Press, 1964.

———, *The United States and the Soviet Union in Europe: The Impact of* the Arms Race Technology and the German Position. Cambridge, Mass.: M.I.T. Center for International Studies, 1967 (467–12, processed).

Griffiths, Franklyn J. C., "Inner Tensions in the Soviet Approach to 'Disarmament,' " International Journal, XXII, No. 4 (Autumn, 1967), 593–617.

Grinyov, O., "Soviet Efforts for Disarmament," International Affairs (Moscow), No. 12 (December, 1967), 63–69.

Hahn, Walter F., and Alvin J. Cottrell, "Ballistic Missile Defense and Soviet Strategy," Orbis, IX, No. 2 (Summer, 1965), 316–37.

Halperin, Morton H., China and Nuclear Proliferation. Chicago: University of Chicago Press, 1966.

———, ed., Sino-Soviet Relations and Arms Control. Cambridge, Mass.: The M.I.T. Press, 1967.

———, and Dwight H. Perkins, Communist China and Arms Control. New York: Frederick A. Praeger, Inc., 1965.

Hardt, John P., "Der wirtschaftliche Hintergrund der sowjetischen Diskussion über die militarische Strategie," Europa-Archiv, XXI, No. 4 (February 25, 1966), 127–38.

Herzfeld, Charles M., "BMD and National Security," Survival, VIII, No. 3 (March, 1966), 70–76; reprinted from Harold E. Whipple, ed., Annals of the New York Academy of Sciences: Civilian and Military Uses of Aerospace, CXXXIV (November 22, 1965).

Hsieh, Alice L., Foreword to the Japanese Edition of "Communist China's Strategy in the Nuclear Era": Implications of the Chinese Nuclear Detonations, Santa Monica, Calif.: The RAND Corporation, 1965 (P-3152 processed).

———, "The Sino-Soviet Nuclear Dialogue," Journal of Conflict Resolution, VII, No. 2 (June, 1964), 99–115.

Horelick, Arnold, and Myron Rush, Strategic Power and Soviet Foreign Policy. Chicago: University of Chicago Press, 1966.

Inglis, David R. "Missile Defense, Nuclear Spread, and Vietnam," Bulletin of the Atomic Scientists, XXIII, No. 5 (May, 1967), 49–52.

Iurev, N., "European Security and the German Question," International Affairs (Moscow), No. 10 (October, 1965), 56–60.

Ivanov, Konstantin, and Boris Batsanov, Le désarmement et ce que cela donnera aux pays en voie de développement. Moscow: Novosti [1965].

Jackson, Henry, "Nuclear Test-ban Treaty Safeguards," Congressional Record, LXIII, No. 195 (November 30, 1967), S17415–417. Speech in the U.S. Senate.

Jackson, William E., "The Missile Nobody Needs," The New Republic, October 28, 1967, pp. 13–16.

Kahn, Herman, and Charles Dibble, "Criteria for Long-Range Nuclear Control Policies," California Law Review, LV (May, 1967), 473–92.

Kertesz, Stephen D., ed., *Nuclear Nonproliferation in a World of Nuclear Powers*. South Bend, Ind.: University of Notre Dame Press, 1967.

Kintner, William R., *Peace and the Strategy Conflict*. New York: Frederick A. Praeger, Inc., 1967.

Klein, Jean, *L'entreprise du désarmement depuis 1945*. Paris: Editions Cujas [1964].

Knorr, Klaus, *On the Uses of Military Power in the Nuclear Age*. Princeton, N.J.: Princeton University Press, 1966.

Kolkowicz, Roman, *The Red "Hawks" on the Rationality of Nuclear War*. Santa Monica, Calif.: The RAND Corporation, 1966 (RM-4899-PR, processed). Includes as appendices: Ye. Rybkin, "On the Nature of Nuclear-Missile War," *Kommunist vooruzhennykh sil*, No. 17 (September, 1965); and J. Wiatr, "On the Rationality of Nuclear War: A Polish Comment," *Polityka*, No. 45 (November 6, 1965).

————, *The Soviet Military and the Communist Party*. Princeton, N.J.: Princeton University Press, 1967.

Kramish, Arnold, "The Great Chinese Bomb Puzzle—and a Solution," *Fortune*, LXXIII, No. 6 (June, 1966), 157–58ff.

Kriukov, P., "The German Question and the Present Situation," *International Affairs* (Moscow), No. 2 (February, 1967), 11–16.

Kronech, Friedrich J., "Politische Aspekte des Aufbaus eines amerikanischen Raketenabwehrsystems," *Europa-Archiv*, XXII, No. 19 (October 10, 1967), 697–702.

Lall, Arthur S., "On the Agenda of Mankind: Disarmament," *Columbia University Forum*, IX, No. 2 (Spring, 1966), 32–37.

Lall, Betty Goetz, "Superiority and Innovation in U.S. Defense Forces," *Bulletin of the Atomic Scientists*, XXIII, No. 3 (March, 1967), 11–13.

Lambeth, Benjamin S., *The Argument for Superiority: A New Voice in the Soviet Strategic Debate*. Washington, D.C.: Institute for Defense Analyses, 1967 (N-419 [R], processed). A discussion of an article by Lt. Col. V. Bondarenko, *Kommunist vooruzhennykh sil*, No. 17 (September, 1966).

Luard, Evan, ed., *First Steps to Disarmament: A New Approach to the Problem of Arms Reduction*. New York: Basic Books Publishers, Inc., 1965.

Lvov, M., "Ban Nuclear Weapons," *International Affairs* (Moscow), No. 1 (January, 1965), 9–14.

McGuire, Martin C., *Secrecy and the Arms Race: A Theory of the Accumulation of Strategic Weapons and How Secrecy Affects It*. Cambridge, Mass.: Harvard University Press, 1965.

McNamara, Robert S., "Defense Fantasy Now Come True," *Life*, September 29, 1967, 28–28c.

————, "The Dynamics of Nuclear Strategy," *Department of State Bulletin*, LVII, No. 1476 (October 9, 1967), 433–51. Address given in San Francisco, September 18, 1967.

Maratov, M., "Nonproliferation and NATO Nuclear Plans," *International Affairs* (Moscow), No. 1 (January, 1966), 18–24.

——, "Ways of Solving the Atom Problem," *International Affairs* (Moscow), No. 8 (August, 1966), 9–15.

Margolis, Howard, "From New York and Washington: Talking about Disarmament," *Bulletin of the Atomic Scientists*, XXII, No. 2 (February, 1966), 38–40.

Martin, Laurence W., "Ballistic Missile Defense and Europe," *Bulletin of the Atomic Scientists*, XXIII, No. 5 (May, 1967), 42–46.

——, "Strategic Implications of BMD," *Survival*, IX, No. 7 (July, 1967), 216–18; reprinted from *Spectator*, CCXVIII, No. 7242 (April 14, 1967), 419–20.

The Military Balance, 1967–1968. London: Institute for Strategic Studies, 1967.

Molodye natsional'nye gosudarstva i razoruzhenie. Moscow: "Nauka," 1967.

Morton, Louis, "The Anti-Ballistic Missile: Some Political and Strategic Considerations," *Virginia Quarterly Review*, XLII, No. 1 (Winter, 1966), 28–42.

Moss, Norman, "McNamara's ABM Policy: A Failure of Communications," *The Reporter*, February 23, 1967, pp. 34–36.

Novoseltsev, Y., "European Security and World Peace," *International Affairs* (Moscow), No. 2 (February, 1965), 3–8.

Orlik, I., and V. Razmerov, "European Security and Relations Between the Two Systems," *International Affairs* (Moscow), No. 5 (May, 1967), 3–8.

Osipov, V., "New Trends on the Continent," *International Affairs* (Moscow), No. 7 (July, 1967), 13–19.

Pay, Rex, "Technical Implications of BMD," *Survival*, IX, No. 7 (July, 1967), 219–22; reprinted from *Technology Week*, XX, No. 12 (March 20, 1967), 14–15.

Petrov, M., "Non-Nuclear Zones: A Pressing Demand," *International Affairs* (Moscow), No. 6 (June, 1967), 12–16.

50 let bor'by SSSR za razoruzhenie, 1917–1967. Moscow: "Nauka," 1967.

Ploss, Sidney I., *Soviet Politics Since the Fall of Khrushchev*. Philadelphia: University of Pennsylvania Foreign Policy Research Institute, 1965 (No. 4, processed).

Quester, George H., "On the Identification of Real and Pretended Communist Military Doctrine," *The Journal of Conflict Resolution*, X, No. 2 (June, 1966), 172–79.

R., G., "Le conflit sino-soviétique et le bloc communiste européen," *Revue de défense nationale*, XXII (March, 1966), 466–76.

Rehm, Georg W., *Rüstungskontrolle im Weltraum*. Bonn: Siegler, [1965]. XXV, Dokumente und Berichte des Forschungsinstituts der Deutschen Gesellschaft für Auswärtige Politik.

Remington, Robin A., *The Changing Soviet Perception of the Warsaw Pact.* Cambridge, Mass.: M.I.T. Center for International Studies, 1967 (C/67–24, processed).

Rodberg, Leonard S., "ABM—Some Arms Control Issues," *Bulletin of the Atomic Scientists,* XXIII, No. 6 (June, 1967), 16–20.

Rosen, Steven, "Proliferation Treaty Controls and the IAEA," *The Journal of Conflict Resolution,* XI, No. 2 (June, 1967), 168–75.

Rothstein, R. L., *On Nuclear Proliferation.* New York: Columbia University School of International Affairs, 1966 (processed).

Rubinstein, Alvin Z., "Political Barriers to Disarmament," *Orbis,* IX, No. 1 (Spring, 1965), 140–54.

Schelling, Thomas C., *Arms and Influence.* New Haven: Yale University Press, 1966.

Schlesinger, James R., "The Strategic Consequences of Nuclear Proliferation," *The Reporter,* October 20, 1966, pp. 36–38.

Schwartz, Leonard E., "Manned Orbiting Laboratory—For War or Peace?" *International Affairs* (London), XLIII, No. 1 (January, 1967), 51–64.

Shulman, Marshall D., *Beyond the Cold War.* New Haven: Yale University Press, 1966.

Sokolovsky, V. D., and M. Cherednichenko, "O sovremennoi voennoi strategii," *Kommunist vooruzhennykh sil,* No. 7 (April, 1966), 59–66.

The Soviet Military Technological Challenge. Washington, D.C.: Georgetown University Center for Strategic Studies, 1967 (Special Report Series No. 6, processed).

Stone, Jeremy J., "Beginning of the Next Round?" *Bulletin of the Atomic Scientists,* XXIII, No. 10 (December, 1967), 20–25.

————, *Containing the Arms Race: Some Specific Proposals.* Cambridge, Mass.: The M.I.T. Press, 1966.

————, "The McNamara Story Continues," *Bulletin of the Atomic Scientists,* XXII, No. 4 (April, 1966), 39–42.

————, *Strategic Persuasion: Arms Limitations Through Dialogue.* New York: Columbia University Press, 1967.

Sugg, Howard A. I., "Soviet Disarmament Theory Since 1959: An Analytic Study." (Doctoral dissertation), American University, Washington, D.C., 1967.

Talensky, N., "Anti-Missile Systems and Disarmament," *International Affairs* (Moscow), No. 10 (October, 1964), 15–19.

Tatu, Michel, *Le Pouvoir en U.R.S.S.* Paris: Bernard Grasset, 1967.

Teller, Edward, "Planning for Peace," *Orbis,* X, No. 2 (Summer, 1966), 341–59.

Thomas, John R., "Limited Nuclear War in Soviet Strategic Thinking," *Orbis,* X, No. 1 (Spring, 1966), 184–212.

Trivedi, V. C., "India and Nuclear Proliferation," *Disarmament*, No. 11 (September, 1966), 1–4.

Tucker, Robert C., Klaus Knorr, Richard A. Falk, and Hedley Bull, *Proposal for No First Use of Nuclear Weapons: Pros and Cons*. Princeton, N.J.: Center of International Studies, 1966 (Research Memorandum No. 23, processed).

The 23rd Congress of the CPSU. Moscow: Novosti, 1966.

United Nations, General Assembly, *Report of the Secretary-General on the Effects of the Possible Use of Nuclear Weapons and on the Security and Economic Implications for States of the Acquisition and Further Development of These Weapons*. (22nd Session) General Assembly Document A/6858, October 10, 1967.

U.S. Congress, Joint Committee on Atomic Energy, Subcommittee on Military Appropriations, *Scope, Magnitude, and Implications of the United States Antiballistic Missile Program*, Hearings, November 6 and 7, 1967; 90th Cong., 1st sess., Washington, D.C.: Government Printing Office, 1967. See especially statements by Alice L. Hsieh and Thomas W. Wolfe.

————, Joint Committee on Atomic Energy. *Impact of Chinese Communist Nuclear Weapons Progress on United States National Security*, 90th Cong., 1st sess., Washington, D.C.: Government Printing Office, 1967.

U.S. House of Representatives, Committee on Armed Services, *The Changing Military Balance: U.S.A. vs. U.S.S.R.*, 90th Cong., 1st sess., Washington, D.C.: Government Printing Office, 1967.

————, Committee on Science and Astronautics, *Review of the Soviet Space Program with Comparative United States Data*, 90th Cong., 1st sess., Washington, D.C.: Government Printing Office, 1967. A valuable report prepared by Charles S. Sheldon II, Science Policy Research Division, Legislative Reference Service, Library of Congress.

U.S. Senate, Committee on Aeronautical and Space Science, *Soviet Space Programs, 1962–1965; Goals and Purposes, Achievements, Plans, and International Implications*, 89th Cong., 2d sess., Washington, D.C.: Government Printing Office, 1966.

————, Committee on Armed Services, *Authorization for Military Procurement, Research and Development, Fiscal Year 1969, and Reserve Strength*, Hearings February 1, 2, 5, 7, 15, 16, 20, 21, 27, 28, 29; March 4, 14, 1968; 90th Cong., 2d sess., Washington, D.C.: Government Printing Office, 1968. See especially Secretary of Defense McNamara's statements.

————, Committee on Armed Services and the Department of Defense Subcommittee on Appropriations, *Military Procurement Authorizations for Fiscal Year 1968*, Combined hearings, January 25—February 2, 1967, 90th Cong., 1st sess., Washington, D.C.: Government Printing Office, 1967. See especially Secretary of Defense McNamara's "Posture Statement," pp. 7–215.

————, Committee on Foreign Relations, Subcommittee on Disarmament,

Status of the Development of the Antiballistic Missile Systems in the United States, 90th Cong., 1st sess., Washington, D.C.: Government Printing Office, 1967.

——, Committee on Foreign Relations, and House Armed Services Committee. *United States Troops in Europe,* Combined hearings April 26 and May 3, 1967; 90th Cong., 1st sess., Washington, D.C.: Government Printing Office, 1967. See especially Secretary of State Rusk's comments on the "Mansfield resolution," p. 61.

——, *United States Armament and Disarmament Problems,* Hearings, February 3, 6, 7, 28; March 1, 2, 3, 1967; 90th Cong., 1st sess., Washington, D.C.: Government Printing Office, 1967.

Voslensky, M. S., ed., *Zapadnaia Evropa i razoruzhenie.* Moscow: "Nauka," 1966.

Voznenko, V., "Dialektika razvitiia i smeny form i sposobov vooruzhennoi bor'by," *Kommunist vooruzhennykh sil,* No. 11 (June, 1966), 41–48.

Waterkamp, Rainer, "Die Abrüstungskonzeptionen der Sowjets," *Osteuropa,* XVI, No. 2/3 (February–March, 1966), 153–59.

Wedge, Bryant, and Cyril Muromcew, "Psychological Factors in Soviet Disarmament Negotiations," *The Journal of Conflict Resolution,* IX, No. 1 (March, 1965), 18–36.

Whalen, Richard J., "The Shifting Equation of Nuclear Defense," *Fortune,* LXXV, No. 6 (June 1, 1967), 84–87 ff.

Wiesner, Jerome B., "The Cold War is Dead, but the Arms Race Rumbles On," *Bulletin of the Atomic Scientists,* XXIII, No. 6 (June, 1967), 6–9.

Wilson, George C., "Here We Go Again—Massive Retaliation," *The New Republic,* March 9, 1968, pp. 11–12.

Wolfe, Thomas W., *Evolution of Soviet Military Policy.* Santa Monica, Calif.: The RAND Corporation, 1968 (P-3773, processed).

——, *The Evolving Nature of the Warsaw Pact.* Santa Monica, Calif.: The RAND Corporation, 1965 (RM-4835-PR, processed).

——, "Military Policy: A Soviet Dilemma," *Current History,* IL, No. 290 (October, 1965), 201–7ff.

——, "Problems of Soviet Defense Policy under the New Regime," *Slavic Review,* XXIV, No. 2 (June, 1965), 175–88.

——, *Soviet Influences on an Arms Control Environment.* Santa Monica, Calif.: The RAND Corporation, 1964 (P-2995, processed).

——, *Soviet Military Power and European Security.* Santa Monica, Calif.: The RAND Corporation, 1966 (P-3429, processed).

——, *The Soviet Military Scene: Institutional and Defense Policy Considerations.* Santa Monica, Calif.: The RAND Corporation, 1966 (RM-4913-PR, processed).

——, *The Soviet Quest for More Globally Mobile Military Power.* Santa Monica, Calif.: The RAND Corporation, 1967 (RM-5554-PR, processed).

———, *The Soviet Union and Arms Control.* Santa Monica, Calif.: The RAND Corporation, 1966 (P-3337, processed).

Young, Oran R., "Active Defense and International Order," *Bulletin of the Atomic Scientists,* XXIII, No. 5 (May, 1967), 35–42.

Zorza, Victor, "Arms and the Soviet Union," *The New Republic,* January 14, 1967, pp. 13–15.

APPENDIX C: A SELECTIVE CHRONOLOGY, 1964–1967

1964

October 16: Chinese People's Republic explodes an atomic bomb and announces that "China will never at any time and under any circumstances be the first to use nuclear weapons." Proposes a universal summit conference to discuss prohibition and destruction of nuclear weapons. Chou En-lai sends a note to this effect the next day.

October 18: U.S. Secretary of State Dean Rusk declares that other powers will not sign an agreement eliminating all nuclear tests unless China also agrees to stop testing.

November 15: An "authorized statement" by TASS published in *Pravda* states that the Soviet Union would "take appropriate measures" to safeguard its security if NATO developed an MLF.

November 25: American and Communist Chinese representatives in Warsaw discuss the Chinese A-bomb.

November 27: TASS statement in *Pravda* condemns U.S. "air attacks" against North Vietnam and warns that the Soviet Union is prepared to give "necessary assistance" to North Vietnam.

November 27: Liao Chen-chin, a member of the Chinese Communist Party Central Committee, suggests (in Rome) conclusion of a regional pact to ban nuclear weapons "on either side of the Pacific." States that "partial agreement" on ending nuclear tests facilitated "monopoly and blackmail" by the great powers; insists that all states must meet to discuss a general agreement to outlaw nuclear weapons.

December 3: At a friendship rally of Soviet and Czechoslovak leaders in Moscow, Party Secretary Leonid Brezhnev affirms "firm decision" of the Soviet Union to keep West Germany from gaining nuclear weapons.

December 7: A Soviet government memorandum to the UNGA calls for measures to reduce international tension and limit the arms race. These measures include: reduction of military budgets, withdrawal or cutback of foreign troops and bases, prevention of nuclear proliferation; prohibition of the use of nuclear weapons, establishment of denuclearized zones, bomber destruction; banning underground nuclear weapons testing, nonaggression pact between NATO and WTO countries, prevention of surprise attack, and reduction of total forces. (*Pravda,* December 8.)

December 9–11:   Before Supreme Soviet, Premier Aleksei Kosygin announces a reduction in Soviet military expenditures for 1965 (from 13.3 to 12.8 billion rubles), declaring he has acted after being informed the U.S. is planning to reduce its budget in the coming year.

December 28:   Kosygin, in a message to Chou En-lai, supports the Chinese proposal for a conference calling for prohibition and destruction of nuclear weapons. He asserts that the Soviet Union favors "radical" agreements on nuclear weapons, but he also says that it favors measures to "limit" or "slow down" the nuclear arms race.

1965

January 15:   A Soviet underground nuclear test in the Semipalatinsk area is reported on January 16 by the U.S., which on January 19 reports that venting of radioactive materials into the atmosphere from the Semipalatinsk test has brought an inquiry by the U.S. of the Soviet government. (See also November 19, 1965.)

January 18:   In notes handed to the U.S. and West German ambassadors in Moscow, the Soviet government protests alleged plans for creating "a belt of nuclear mines" along West Germany's border with Czechoslovakia and East Germany.

January 19–20:   A Warsaw Pact conference attended by heads of state and Party leaders meets in Warsaw. Communiqué (*Pravda,* January 22) warns that creation of MLF by NATO will force WTO "to take the necessary defensive measures to ensure their security." It endorses the idea of a Central European nuclear-free zone, a proposal for a conference on European security, a NATO-WTO nonaggression pact, a German peace settlement, the Chinese proposal for a world summit conference to discuss abolition of nuclear weapons, and a nonaligned proposal for a world disarmament conference.

February 7:   U.S. and South Vietnamese planes bomb North Vietnamese military installations for the first time, while Premier Kosygin is in Hanoi.

February 9:   As the bombing of North Vietnam continues, the first formal Soviet government statement on Vietnam declares that the "Soviet Union will be forced, together with its allies and friends, to take further measures to safeguard its security and strengthen the defense capability" of North Vietnam.

February 26:   Kosygin warns in televised speech that unless the U.S. halts aggression against North Vietnam, the war will "inevitably transcend its original boundaries."

March 23:   First Secretary Leonid Brezhnev hints at possibility of Soviet involvement in the Vietnam War, saying that many Soviet citizens have volunteered to serve there.

March 31: Soviet representative at the U.N. requests Secretary-General to convene the UNDC by April 15 (according to *Pravda*, April 2).

April 3: On request of Cambodia, the Soviet government proposes to Britain (as cochairman) immediate convocation of a conference to guarantee the neutrality and territorial integrity of Cambodia.

April 18: A joint Soviet-North Vietnamese declaration issued in Moscow states that the dispatch of Soviet volunteers to North Vietnam depends on intensification of the war by the U.S., an appeal by North Vietnam, and a "necessity" that might yet arise. The declaration confirms that Soviet military shipments have reached North Vietnam.

April 19: Kosygin warns that U.S. air bombardments and use of gas in Vietnam could lead to "retaliation in kind." Kosygin also endorses the "four-point" North Vietnamese proposal April 13.

April 21–June 16: UNDC meets, for the first time since 1960, in New York.

April 26: Nikolai T. Fedorenko, Soviet representative to UNDC, proposes an appeal to all states to conclude an agreement banning the use of nuclear weapons, and, prior to the conclusion of such an agreement, declaratory no-first-use pledge by nuclear states.

April 28: A revised Soviet draft treaty on GCD is submitted to UNDC.

April 30: Communiqué at close of Foreign Minister Andrei Gromyko's visit to Paris indicates Soviet agreement with the French proposal to consider the problem of disarmament in a conference of the five nuclear powers.

May 10: A message in name of Soviet government on the 20th anniversary of VE Day calls for a proclamation by the nuclear powers that they will not use nuclear weapons, a ban on nuclear proliferation, liquidation of foreign bases, reduction of military budgets, a nonaggression pact between opposing military groupings, and GCD.

May 14: Chinese Communist government announces explosion of a second atomic bomb; reiterates that it will never be the first to use nuclear weapons.

May 17: At UNDC, chief of U.S. delegation, Director of Arms Control and Disarmament Agency, William C. Foster, suggests broad program of non-proliferation, including cut-off of fissionable materials for weapons use and a transfer of these materials to peaceful purposes; he endorses Vice-President Hubert H. Humphrey's remarks of February 17 in favor of atom-free zones in Latin America, Africa, and Near East. U.S. opposes atom-free zones in Europe and Mediterranean.

May 19: Soviet representative Semion K. Tsarapkin at UNDC says that the most urgent questions before UNDC are the elimination of foreign military bases and withdrawal of foreign troops from all countries.

May 21: TASS statement declares that "provocation of armed conflicts" and "acts of aggression against socialist countries" are incompatible with agreements with the Soviet Union about "ending tension."

May 27: Two Soviet draft resolutions are submitted to UNDC. One calls for liquidation of foreign bases and withdrawal of forces stationed abroad; the other, for convening a conference no later than June, 1966, to draft a convention banning use of nuclear weapons. Neither resolution is brought to a vote.

June 3: A draft UNDC resolution with 36 cosponsors recommends that UNGA consider calling a world disarmament conference. The resolution is passed on June 11 by 89–0, with 16 abstentions; the Soviet Union voted in favor and the U.S. abstained.

June 14: A provision in a Swedish resolution at UNDC calls for all states to condemn nuclear tests and to adhere to the 1963 test-ban treaty. Tsarapkin criticizes it for its implicit censure of Communist China (which has not signed the test-ban treaty), and its loose wording on proliferation. Soviet Union abstains when the resolution is passed on June 15 by 85–1 (Albania), with 18 abstentions.

June 30: Soviet Foreign Ministry confirms to the British Ambassador in Moscow that the Soviet government, in accord with the wishes of Cambodia, no longer considers a meeting of the Geneva Conference on Cambodia necessary (*Pravda*, July 4).

July 3: Reviewing Soviet military posture, Brezhnev declares Soviet Union has more missiles than Western intelligence estimates suggest, and that "important steps were taken lately" to increase efficiency in ABM defenses.

July 11: In a message to the World Congress for Peace, National Independence, and General Disarmament, in Helsinki (July 11–15), Kosygin calls for prohibition of nuclear weapons, liquidation of foreign bases, dismantling of military blocs, and GCD.

July 17: Kosygin in Riga declares Soviet struggle for peaceful coexistence is "varied and multifaceted" and includes easing of international tension as well as acting against foreign interference in domestic affairs of other countries.

July 27–September 16: ENDC meets in Geneva. France, a member, does not participate.

August 4: Tsarapkin states at ENDC that "there can be no progress here as long as the United States persists in its aggressive policy."

August 9: A conciliatory editorial in *Pravda* asserts that "peaceful coexistence is the only alternative to thermonuclear war in this age." It denounces the idea that aggression is compatible with peaceful coexistence, but develops the argument that closer East-West ties would inhibit imperialists from aggressive war.

August 17: A U.S. draft treaty on nonproliferation tabled at ENDC. Article III obligates all signatory states "to facilitate the application of IAEA or equivalent international safeguards on all peaceful nuclear activities." The draft is rejected by the Soviet Union on August 31 on the grounds that it would not prevent West Germany from gaining access to nuclear weapons under an MLF or Atlantic Nuclear Force arrangement.

August 17:   UAR representative at ENDC proposes that the 1963 partial test-ban treaty be extended to prohibit underground explosions above a seismic magnitude of 4.75, and that a voluntary moratorium on all tests be instituted prior to agreement on a comprehensive test ban. On September 7 the proposal is accepted by the USSR and rejected by the U.S.

August 23–September 2:   The Preparatory Commission for the Denuclearization of Latin America meets in Mexico City.

August 25:   President Johnson announces that he has instructed the Secretary of Defense to begin construction of an orbiting space laboratory for various purposes. A dispatch in *Pravda*, August 26, stresses military aspects.

September 10:   Communiqué signed by the Soviet Union and Rumania in Moscow gives a strong endorsement of GCD and also of an atom-free zone in Europe.

September 14:   At meeting of Soviet and Czechoslovak leaders, Brezhnev says that Eastern European nations will further strengthen WTO as a precaution against resurgence of German militarism. Joint Soviet-Czechoslovak communiqué signed in Moscow endorses the Polish proposals for an atom-free zone and a freeze on atomic weapons in Central Europe, and for a conference of European states on European security issues.

September 17:   Kosygin invites Indian and Pakistani leaders, Prime Minister Lal Bahadur Shastri and President Mohammed Ayub Kahn, to meet in the Soviet Union and negotiate settlement of Kashmir dispute (*Pravda*, September 20). This is the first time the USSR has proposed direct mediation in an international dispute.

September 23:   In the first explicit Soviet criticism of the Chinese role in the Kashmir conflict, *Pravda* expresses concern over Communist Chinese troop concentrations on the Indian border.

September 24:   Soviet Foreign Minister Andrei A. Gromyko presents to UNGA a draft treaty on nuclear nonproliferation, with ban on transfer of nuclear weapons "in any form" through any non-nuclear states or alliance of states.

September 24:   At Soviet-East German friendship rally in Moscow, Brezhnev warns that in the absence of "agreements that would preclude the possibility of military clashes and would guarantee peace," there is "serious danger" of a confrontation between NATO and WTO blocs. Call for a nonaggression pact between the states of the two military groupings is renewed.

September 29:   Vice-Premier Chen Yi declares that China would be willing to render assistance to other countries with nuclear programs for peaceful purposes, but says that "while it would be better for a greater number of countries to come into possession of atom bombs," the question of China aiding other nations in the manufacture of atom bombs is "not realistic."

October 16–22:   WTO military exercises take place, with armies of East Germany, Czechoslovakia, Poland, and the Soviet Union participating. (*Pravda,* October 23.)

November 4:   In the U.N. Political Committee, the eight nonaligned members of ENDC table a resolution (later approved) calling for the earliest possible reconvening of ENDC to negotiate a nonproliferation treaty based upon specified principles.

November 5:   Secretary Rusk expresses feeling that joint American-Soviet-British guarantees "would not be completely reassuring to some nations who may feel that they would be subject to nuclear blackmail."

November 6:   Deputy Premier Dimitri S. Poliansky declares that the Soviet Communist Party has done "everything that is possible" to settle differences with China and that any further conciliatory moves must come from China. He adds that steps are being taken to strengthen "political and military" framework of WTO.

November 7:   Military parade in Moscow displays three new rocket systems. *Pravda* states one of missiles shown can be fired from orbit at any target. On November 8, State Department says it is studying whether Soviet Union has violated, by development of an orbital missile, 1963 UNGA resolution calling on all states to refrain from placing weapons in space and prohibiting stationing of nuclear weapons in orbit. In response to U.S. inquiry, Soviet Ambassador Anatoli F. Dobrynin explains that the Soviet Union will abide by the resolution. *Pravda,* December 9, states that resolution does not apply to production of orbital or "any other rockets launched in space."

November 8:   Indian Prime Minister Shastri affirms the decision of India not to produce nuclear weapons.

November 15–20:   A conference of socialist countries is held in Moscow on the question of research on and use of space for peaceful objectives. Delegates from Bulgaria, Hungary, East Germany, Cuba, Mongolia, Poland, Rumania, Czechoslovakia, and Soviet Union attend. (*Pravda,* November 24.)

November 19:   U.S. Department of State announces, on the basis of discussions with Soviet government, that venting from January 15 Soviet test was result of Soviet miscalculation. U.S. asks USSR to take precautions to assure observance of limited test-ban treaty.

November 19:   UNGA passes by 93–0, with five abstentions (Cuba, Pakistan, Guinea, France, and Rumania), a resolution on nuclear nonproliferation.

November 24:   In response to inquiry by Senator Henry Jackson, AEC states there "was no evidence" that Soviet Union has carried out cutbacks in production of U-235 announced April 20, 1964. On that day, U.S. and USSR announced parallel cutbacks, but no formal agreement was concluded.

November 29:   With France abstaining, UNGA approved by 112–0 a resolution endorsing proposal for world disarmament conference to which all nations would be invited. Preparatory Committee is to be established to convene conference no later than 1967.

December 1:   ACDA Director Foster says U.S. will support UNGA resolution on denuclearization of Africa despite provision calling on states to "refrain from the use, or threat of use of nuclear weapons on the African continent." Foster said that pledges of non-use in general were considered unsound by the U.S., not their application to Africa. Resolution passes, December 3, by 105–0, with France and Portugal abstaining.

December 3:   UNGA approves resolution in favor of suspension of nuclear tests by 92–1 (Albania). All Warsaw Pact countries except Rumania abstain; U.S. votes in favor.

December 8:   *The New York Times* publishes James Reston's interview with Kosygin, who makes sharpest attack on U.S. since he took office, accusing it of subordinating foreign policy to military considerations, thus also forcing Soviet Union to increase military budget.

December 10:   Foster sends a letter to Preparatory Commission for the Denuclearization of Latin America on establishment of atom-free zone in Latin America, saying U.S. does not want Virgin Islands or Puerto Rico included in zone, but would agree to Panama Canal Zone and Guantánamo if Cuba participates. Contends refusal of certain states to participate could render agreement ineffective.

1966

January 10:   *Pravda* statement asserts that intervention by Kosygin after week of deadlock in negotiations is instrumental in achieving Pakistani-Indian agreement on withdrawal of troops from Kashmir. This meeting at Tashkent is the result of Kosygin's invitation of September 17, 1965.

January 25:   Soviet Ambassador Tsarapkin, in Geneva for reconvening of ENDC, says that disarmament talks should not be "interdependent" with events in Vietnam.

January 27–May 10:   ENDC meets in Geneva.

February 1:   Kosygin, in a message to ENDC, proposes in connection with non-proliferation agreement that signatory nuclear powers agree not to use nuclear weapons against countries that do not possess such weapons or have them on their territory; also favors the Polish proposals for denuclearized zone and nuclear freeze in Central Europe; prohibition of underground nuclear tests, with unilateral policing by national systems of detection; elimination of troops and bases in foreign countries; steps toward complete nuclear disarmament, including destruction of existing weapons and production cut-off; and reduction of military budgets.

February 16:   Soviet Union, in a note presented by Gromyko to U.S. Ambassador Foy Kohler, protests January 17 crash of U.S. bomber carrying thermonuclear weapons, off Spain, as contaminating sea, contrary to provision of the limited test-ban treaty and 1958 Convention on the High Seas. It renews Soviet 1958 proposals to ban flights of aircraft carrying nuclear weapons beyond national borders. U.S. rejects protest on February 25.

March 3: In ENDC, U.S. and USSR express opposition to attempts by non-aligned nations to make accord to halt spread of nuclear weapons depend on other disarmament agreements.

March 8: Tsarapkin rejects U.S. proposal that superpowers destroy "thousands" of their nuclear weapons as having "nothing in common with disarmament." Charges Washington's aim is to make room for latest weapons by destroying outdated models under guise of disarmament.

March 25: Secretary Rusk says that Soviet Union, U.S., Britain, France, and "possibly even Peking" agree that proliferation of nuclear weapons is undesirable.

March 29–April 6: XXIII Congress of the Communist Party of the Soviet Union meets in Moscow. Brezhnev recommends initiating talks on European security in attempt to relax "military tensions" and achieve reduction of armaments in Europe. Defense Minister Marshal Rodion Ia. Malinovsky refers to "blue belt" of Soviet defense in connection with Soviet rocketry, but does not elaborate. Gromyko blames U.S. presence in Europe for failure of efforts to reduce East-West tensions on European matters, and calls for settlement of European security problems by nations of Europe themselves. Kosygin says expansion of Soviet trade could help reduce tension.

April 10: Premier Chou En-lai, in interview, attacks U.S. and USSR for acting in collusion to consolidate their nuclear monopoly and deprive and blackmail other countries; says a world disarmament conference would "yield no useful, practical results" under present circumstances.

April 19: At ENDC, Foster outlines six principles for regional arms control measures: countries should undertake not to acquire the military equipment being regulated, initiative should come from the region concerned, all important states in the region should be included, potential suppliers should respect agreements, the arrangement should contribute to regional security and maintain a military balance, and there should be adequate control.

April 26: AEC reports low-yield explosion at Nevada test site. Blast vents and spreads radioactivity over five states, but well below danger levels.

May 5: Preparatory Commission for Denuclearization of Latin America adjourns to reconvene August 30. U.S. and USSR, among other nations, are asked to comment on various proposals. Negotiating committee is to "explore informally" Chinese attitudes toward Latin American denuclearization.

May 7: President Johnson announces that U.S. will seek a treaty in U.N. to prevent sovereignty claims and promote cooperation in outer space. Treaty would prohibit stationing weapons of mass destruction in orbit or on celestial bodies, as well as weapons tests and military maneuvers on celestial bodies.

May 9: Communist China announces detonation of its third nuclear device, which allegedly contains "thermonuclear material."

May 11: Prime Minister Indira Gandhi says India is not forever committed to barring development of nuclear weapons.

May 14: Joint Chinese-Albanian statement issued in Peking reiterates Chinese appeal for world conference to ban manufacture and use of nuclear weapons.

May 16: Kosygin, in Cairo, attacks American "Hitlerite" policy in Vietnam, and demands withdrawal of American troops from both South Vietnam and South Korea.

May 17: Rusk, at news conference, says U.S. has rejected Chinese proposal for ban on first use of nuclear weapons because it believes that such measures "should be carried out under strict and effective control."

May 25: At meeting of American and Chinese diplomatic representatives in Warsaw, U.S. raises possibility of accepting a no-first-use pledge on nuclear weapons if China adheres to 1963 limited test-ban treaty. June 20 article in *Jen Min Jih Pao* rejects American initiative and attacks idea of adhering to test-ban treaty in exchange for agreement on no first use of nuclear weapons as "a big fraud."

May 30: Gromyko, in a letter to U.N. Secretary-General U Thant, urges a treaty banning use of celestial bodies for military purposes, and prohibiting territorial claims upon them. Points suggested are similar to those advanced by President Johnson on May 7.

June 14–August 25: ENDC meets in Geneva.

June 21: U.S. Secretary of Defense Robert S. McNamara says that U.S. will withdraw some of its forces from Europe if Soviet Union reduces the number of its troops in East Germany.

June 30: A joint Franco-Soviet declaration, signed by Presidents Charles de Gaulle and Nikolai V. Podgorny, states intent to cooperate toward a peaceful Europe but avoids details on European security and Germany.

July 9: Declaration of WTO summit conference invites nations of Western Europe to join in general conference to discuss European security questions. Declaration calls for dissolution of NATO and WTO military organizations, as a step toward liquidation of alliances.

July 9: The first official Soviet protest since American raids began near Hanoi and Haiphong on June 29, is delivered to the U.S. Embassy in Moscow, charging that U.S. raids on a fuel depot near Haiphong July 7 "created a direct threat to Soviet merchant ships and the lives of Soviet seamen."

July 30: Chou En-lai, in a message to the Tokyo meeting of the World

Congress Against Atomic and Hydrogen Bombs, calls draft nonproliferation treaties "a scheme to deprive peace-loving countries of the right to develop nuclear weapons."

August 3: Kosygin, in an address to the Supreme Soviet, reiterates that the Soviet Union will "display restraint and calmness" in Vietnam to prevent a third world war, but will do everything in its power to expel U.S. forces from Vietnam "as soon as possible." He stresses Soviet Union commitment to "strengthen its defenses."

August 25: Soviet delegate Roshchin at ENDC declares that the Swedish proposal for a full test-ban treaty, providing for inspection by challenge in case of suspected violation, with permission to abrogate if the other side does not provide adequate assurance of nonviolation, is "absolutely unacceptable." This proposal, which had neutralist support, had been rejected by the U.S. on April 4.

September 1: *Pravda* calls hypocritical President Johnson's invitation to the Soviet Union (August 26) to join in "rational acts of common endeavor" despite the war in Vietnam.

September 12: AEC reports some radiation leakage from a 20-kiloton American underground nuclear test of this date, but doubts that a measurable amount will be found outside the test site. On November 10 the State Department, in response to Soviet inquiry, acknowledges that a "small amount of radioactivity" was released into the atmosphere by the blasts, but stresses that spread is confined to the U.S.

September 23: Gromyko submits two Soviet resolutions to UNGA—on nonproliferation and on eliminating foreign military bases in Asia, Africa, and Latin America. On September 26, the U.S. becomes a cosponsor of the nonproliferation resolution, which is passed, on November 4, by 110–1 (Albania), with Cuba abstaining. Nonaligned countries offer a watered-down substitute for the Soviet bases proposal, passed on November 30; on December 2 the First Committee votes 99–1, with eight abstentions, not to vote on the Soviet proposal.

September 23: At the IAEA General Conference in Vienna, Polish and Czechoslovak delegates announce that they would place their countries under IAEA safeguards if West Germany (whose nuclear facilities are under Euratom safeguards) would do the same. On September 26, East Germany makes a similar proposal (through Czechoslovakia) regarding West Germany.

October 7: President Johnson, speaking in New York, proposes broadening East-West relations and alludes to the possibility of "a gradual and balanced revision in force levels on both sides" in Europe.

October 10: After meeting with President Johnson, Gromyko says that "it looks like both countries . . . are striving to reach agreement" on a nonproliferation treaty.

October 13: Kosygin, at a Soviet-Polish friendship meeting, charges unequivocally that Peking is damaging the effort to help North Vietnam and has prevented a victory over U.S. imperialism. He reiterates the Soviet determination to continue aiding the North Vietnamese.

October 15: Brezhnev declares that Soviet-American ties cannot be improved until the U.S. stops the bombing of North Vietnam, and charges that "U.S. imperialism continues to claim the role of an uninvited organizer of European affairs."

October 20: USSR representative Fedorenko, in the U.N. Political Committee, says there are no major obstacles in the way of a nonproliferation treaty.

October 27: At UNGA, eight nonaligned members of ENDC, plus 24 cosponsors, introduce in the First Committee a draft resolution on nonproliferation that includes a call to the nuclear powers to give assurance against use or threatened use of nuclear weapons on nonnuclear powers. On November 10, the U.S. abstains in the vote on the paragraph referring to Kosygin proposal of February 1, but supports the draft resolution as a whole, which is adopted by 103–1 (Albania), with Cuba and France abstaining.

October 27: Soviet Union sets off largest underground nuclear explosion to date, with a yield of over one million tons of TNT.

October 27: CPR announces a successful guided missile, nuclear weapons test with 20 kiloton yield.

October 30: President Johnson, in Malaysia, asserts that CPR's attempt to build up a nuclear arsenal invites danger for China and that her nuclear striking power will be "deterred." He states the U.S. will give strong support "against any threat of nuclear blackmail."

October 31: Indian Ambassador Trivedi tells the UNGA First Committee that a nonproliferation treaty should impose balanced provisions on nuclear and non-nuclear powers, requiring "that no country . . . produce nuclear weapons."

November 9: U.S. State Department states it is "looking into the question" of whether the Soviet underground explosion of October 27 has vented radioactivity beyond Soviet borders.

November 10: Secretary McNamara reveals at news conference that there is "considerable evidence" that the USSR is building and deploying an ABM system, which will probably require a U.S. response in the form of increased numbers of offensive missiles.

November 11: Poland and the Ukraine cosponsor a draft resolution in the U.N. First Committee calling on all states "to refrain from sending aircraft carrying nuclear weapons and other kinds of weapons of mass destruction on flights beyond national frontiers."

November 14: AEC sets off Nevada blast reported to be the most powerful ever detonated in U.S.

November 15: An authoritative article in *Jen Min Jih Pao* declares that the CPR "would never be a party to a nuclear nonproliferation treaty."

Calling advocacy of such a treaty an example of global Soviet-American collusion, it denounces the Soviet role as "another big exposure of its renegade features." It declares that total prohibition of nuclear weapons, which it advocates, will be possible "only when more or all countries possess them" and when the "United States nuclear monopoly" is broken.

November 17: UNGA adopts a nonproliferation resolution including a call for a conference on non-nuclear powers, to meet no later than July, 1967, to consider security assurances and the use of nuclear devices for peaceful purposes.

December 5: UNGA adopts a resolution on GCD, including a request to U Thant for a report on the effects of nuclear weapons, a Hungarian resolution on chemical and biological weapons, and a nonaligned resolution on GCD.

December 5: UNGA adopts a nonaligned resolution on suspension of nuclear tests by 100–1 (Albania), with Cuba and France abstaining.

December 5: UNGA approves by 80–0 a resolution on convening a conference to outlaw nuclear weapons. The U.S. is among the 23 abstainers.

December 8: The U.S. and the Soviet Union agree on a draft treaty banning nuclear weapons in outer space.

December 9: A joint Franco-Soviet statement, concluding a Kosygin visit to Paris, asserts that the nuclear powers must discuss the means to insure nuclear nonproliferation and disarmament.

December 15: Soviet Finance Minister Vasili F. Garbuzov at a Supreme Soviet meeting announces an increase in military spending of 1.1 billion rubles (8.2 per cent) in USSR budget for 1967, because "the aggressive monopolist circles of the United States have recently sharpened international tensions and increased the danger of a new world war."

December 18: AEC reports another Soviet underground nuclear test. On December 30, the State Department notes an "apparent discrepancy" between U.S. and Swedish estimates regarding radioactive venting.

December 19: UNGA unanimously endorses the proposed treaty on the peaceful uses of outer space.

December 21: Rusk at a news conference says the U.S. wants "some means developed" to avert another upward spiral in the arms race. The long-run effect of ABM system, he says, would be stronger offensive missiles without affecting the strategic balance.

December 28: Communist China conducts another nuclear test.

1967

January 6: The U.S. Department of Defense announces "experimental verification" of the theory that it is possible to muffle the seismic force of a nuclear explosion by firing it in an underground cavity (the "decoupling" effect).

January 18: The editor of *Za rubezhom* (issue of January 20–26) denies President Johnson's contention of January 10 that the USSR and the U.S. have a common interest in "arms control." He asserts that the USSR seeks "disarmament" and has always opposed "arms control."

January 27: The treaty on peaceful uses of outer space is signed in Washington, London, and Moscow.

January 30 to February 14: The fourth session of the Preparatory Commission for the Denuclearization of Latin America meets in Mexico City.

February 9: Kosygin, at a London news conference, states with regard to ABM systems: "The system that warns of attack is not a factor in the arms race. On the contrary, it is a factor that reduces the possibility of the destruction of people." He reiterates the Soviet proposal for a ban on nuclear weapons and stockpiles as a way to solve the ABM problem.

February 11: An unsigned statement issued at the conclusion of the WTO foreign ministers' conference fails to reiterate the minimum conditions for a *rapprochement* with West Germany set at the July WTO summit conference, including a West German pledge to renounce nuclear weapons.

February 14: A treaty to establish an atom-free zone in Latin America is signed by 14 nations at Mexico City, concluding the fourth session of the Preparatory Commission for the Denuclearization of Latin America.

February 15: A *Pravda* article by Fiodor Burlatsky explains that Kosygin's remarks on ABM systems mean that the Soviet Union is "ready to discuss the problem of averting a new arms race, both in offensive and defensive weapons." Burlatsky criticizes Chinese Communist opposition to a nonproliferation treaty and asserts refusal of Chinese leaders to help lessen the threat of nuclear war "proves once again that their plans and schemes are far from being in the interests of the cause of peace."

February 20: McNamara states that it might be desirable for the U.S. to deploy a limited ABM system directed against Chinese nuclear potential and that such a system could also protect U.S. missiles (but not cities) from Soviet attack.

February 21–March 23: ENDC meets in Geneva.

February 26: In a television interview, U.S. General Earle G. Wheeler, Chairman of the Joint Chiefs of Staff, says that the JCS believe technical and financial considerations would dissuade the Soviet Union from developing more offensive missiles in response to U.S. ABM deployment. They do not feel, as does McNamara, that a U.S. ABM system would "necessarily" result in more Soviet offensive missiles.

March 2: President Johnson announces that Kosygin has agreed to bilateral discussions on "means of limiting the arms race in offensive and defensive nuclear missiles." Two days later, New China News Agency denounces Moscow's acceptance as "the latest act of capitulation and betrayal," and says the U.S. aim is to continue blackmailing other nations.

March 9: Foster submits memorandum to ENDC members suggesting that an international organization, rather than individual nuclear powers, decide where and when nuclear explosions would be used for peaceful purposes for the benefit of non-nuclear countries. The purpose of the measure is to assure non-nuclear countries against discrimination under a nonproliferation treaty.

March 29: France launches her first nuclear-fueled submarine, making her the fourth nuclear naval power.

April 15: Western European and Soviet nuclear scientists agree to conduct joint peaceful research on a nuclear accelerator near Moscow.

April 24: Delegates from 25 Communist parties of Eastern and Western Europe, meeting in Karlovy Vary, Czechoslovakia, to discuss European security questions, hear Brezhnev demand the removal of the U.S. fleet from the Mediterranean and declare that for many countries, including those of Northern Europe, neutrality can be an alternative to membership in military alliances. A declaration issued on April 26 outlines a plan to replace NATO and WTO with a system of collective European security based on the principles of peaceful coexistence; calls for a people's congress of all elements opposed to NATO and U.S. presence in Europe; and advocates conclusion of nonaggression pacts among all European nations.

April 29: U.S. reports Soviet objections to a new U.S. draft of nonproliferation treaty that would provide for continued Euratom controls for three years, while agreement is worked out for IAEA verification of safeguards. Roshchin dismisses Euratom scheme as "self-inspection."

May 18: McNamara, stressing the distinction between ABM systems against "light" and "heavy" attacks, at a news conference expresses hope for an agreement with the Soviet Union on ABM systems.

May 18: ENDC resumes discussions in Geneva.

May 18: The Presidium of the Supreme Soviet approves the treaty on the peaceful uses of outer space.

May 23: The Indian Ambassador tells the ENDC that a nonproliferation treaty would be easier to negotiate if it were considered together with a comprehensive test ban and a freeze on nuclear delivery vehicles. He criticizes the great powers for failing to give adequate consideration to the security needs of non-nuclear countries.

June 2: The Soviet Union protests the U.S. bombing of a Soviet merchant ship in a North Vietnamese port. A similar protest is made on June 30.

June 17: CPR successfully explodes a hydrogen bomb. NCNA states that the explosion "dealt a telling blow" to American and Soviet "nuclear blackmail."

June 25: After meeting with President Johnson at Glassboro, N.J., Kosygin declares at a news conference that discussions between the two states regarding arms limitation should center on the "entire complex of armaments and disarmament questions," not only on ABM systems.

June 25: NCNA charges that Kosygin, in talks with President Johnson, "is actually getting near the conclusion of a vicious deal" aimed against China.

June 25:   Editorial in *Jen Min Jih Pao,* in the aftermath of the Arab-Israeli
fighting (June 5–10), denounces Kosygin's references in the U.N. to the
need to prevent nuclear war, interpreting them to mean ostensibly that no
state should resist aggression because to do so would mean to risk destruction by U.S. and Soviet nuclear weapons.

June 29:   Sweden's ENDC delegate states that new seismological developments
have made identification methods so effective that it is now "meaningful to
discuss verification without inspection."

August 11:   At a news briefing in Washington, Foster says that "it is doubtful" that France or China would give nuclear weapons to other nations.

August 24:   U.S. and USSR submit to ENDC separate but identical texts of
draft treaty on nuclear nonproliferation. The draft leaves blank the article
on inspection and does not contain security assurances to non-nuclear
powers.

September 18:   Secretary McNamara, in San Francisco speech, announces
U.S. decision to deploy a light ABM network, to insure against Chinese
Communist attack. He argues the futility of full ABM deployment, but
warns that the U.S. would respond to Soviet extension of its ABM network
by increasing stockpile of American offensive missiles. For the first time,
McNamara links possible U.S.-USSR negotiations on ABM systems with
reducing the size of nuclear arsenals.

September 22:   At UNGA Gromyko submits draft convention prohibiting
use, threat of use, or inducement to use nuclear weapons, and obligating
signatory states to "exert the utmost effort" toward agreement to end production and destroy stockpiles of nuclear weapons under a GCD treaty.

October 10:   At a Supreme Soviet meeting, Finance Minister Garbuzov announces 15 per cent increase in Soviet defense budget for 1968.

October 19:   Splitting with the Soviet Union at ENDC, Rumania proposes
amendments to draft nonproliferation treaty calling for review of treaty
in five years if nuclear powers have not stopped producing nuclear weapons and destroyed their stockpiles, and making it easier for any nation to
refuse to be bound by changes in the treaty.

October 23:   Vice-Admiral William E. Ellis, Chief of Staff of the Supreme
Allied Command, Atlantic, says that the Soviet Union is building its first
aircraft carrier, apparently designed to launch helicopters rather than jets
or bombers.

November 3:   McNamara discusses evidence suggesting Soviet development
of a fractional orbiting bombardment system, and says that a Soviet bomb
fired from orbit could be operational by 1968. He says U.S. has no intention
of developing such a weapon, and contends that Soviet advantages of such
a system are negated by recently installed over-the-horizon radar.

November 7:   Military parade in Moscow reveals five new types of Soviet
missiles, the biggest a rocket about 110 feet long, according to a *Pravda*
account.

November 14:   Alexander Boiko, writing in *Moscow News* (November 25–

December 2, 1967), denounces McNamara's speculation on Soviet use of outer space for military purposes as "fabrication." He says that the USSR is engaged in large-scale space research but has signed treaty on outer space that forbids space orbiting of nuclear weapons; he notes that, since conclusion of that treaty, Soviet leaders have not publicly shown similar suspicion of U.S. space activities.

December 2:   President Johnson offers to place all civilian atomic plants in U.S. under international inspection. Offer comes while U.S. is still attempting to persuade many non-nuclear nations to accept inspection of their nuclear activities by an international agency.

December 5:   UNGA resolution approving the treaty concluded on February 14, prohibiting nuclear weapons in Latin America, and inviting nuclear powers to sign an additional protocol provided for them in the treaty, is passed by 82–0. Twenty-eight abstentions include Cuba and all WTO countries except Rumania. Albania is absent.

December 10:   TASS statement warns U.S. against extending military action from Vietnam into neighboring Cambodia and Laos.

December 13:   John S. Foster, Director of Research and Engineering, U.S. Department of Defense, says the U.S. is developing a missile that could drop multiple separately targeted thermonuclear warheads as it flies over enemy territory; the missile is intended as a reply to new Soviet offensive missile and ABM deployment.

December 19:   UNGA adopts by 103–1 (Albania), with seven abstentions, a resolution, introduced by nonaligned powers, on ending underground nuclear tests "as a matter of urgency." Two nonproliferation resolutions are also approved: one requesting ENDC to report by March 15, 1968, on progress toward a nonproliferation treaty; the other calling for a conference of non-nuclear states in August, 1968, to study ways to prevent nuclear spread and guard against nuclear threats. The first is passed by 112–1 (Albania), with four abstentions, the second by 110–0 with eight abstentions.

December 24:   AEC announces a seventh Communist Chinese nuclear test, but there is no announcement by Peking. A Peking broadcast the next day refers to six successful tests and says the United States and Soviet Union "have colluded" in their attempt to "contain and destroy" Communist China ever since CPR succeeded in its first nuclear test.

APPENDIX D: THE IMPACT ON THE USSR OF CHINESE DISARMAMENT POLICIES, 1964–1967

by Kenneth Lieberthal

The issue of nuclear disarmament and nonproliferation played a major role in the Sino-Soviet dispute through the end of 1963; and this role has been both documented and analyzed in depth in a number of sources.[1] Since this time, however, major changes have taken place. Khrushchev has been deposed; the Chinese have exploded six nuclear devices; the war in Vietnam has grown to major proportions; and the Sino-Soviet dispute has advanced to an unprecedented stage of animosity.

How have these developments changed Chinese attitudes toward nuclear disarmament and nonproliferation, and the Soviet response to them? What will be the future impact of the Sino-Soviet dispute on disarmament policies? This essay is an attempt to give at least tentative answers to these questions.

The fundamental argument of the Chinese with respect to disarmament and nonproliferation runs as follows: "Modern imperialism," headed by the United States, is *by nature* aggressive. While modern imperialism (joined by its collaborators) has an effective monopoly on the use of nuclear weapons, it will continue to use nuclear blackmail to thwart the "legitimate aspirations of all peace-loving people." The prime consideration, therefore, must be to break the nuclear monopoly of the imperialists; and the more thoroughly it is broken, the better. Any partial steps toward nuclear disarmament or nonproliferation will only serve to consolidate further the predominant nuclear power of the imperialists. The only hope for disarmament, therefore, lies in measures that will immediately produce a "complete prohibition and thorough destruction of nuclear weapons." Finally, expectation of general and complete disarmament prior to the worldwide victory of

---

[1] See, for instance, *The Sino-Soviet Rift* especially pp. 60–66, 154–206, 326–420, 481–90; and *The Soviet Union and Disarmament*, especially the Appendix; and *Sino-Soviet Relations and Arms Control,* ed. Morton Halperin (Cambridge, Mass.: Harvard University Press, 1966).

socialism is completely unrealistic, since the imperialist powers will remain aggressive as long as they exist.[2]

The Soviet Union, according to the Chinese Communists, has erred in the evaluation of the current stage of development of the world balance of forces. It has failed to recognize the impossibility of reaching any lasting agreements with the United States, and it has overestimated the dangers inherent in wars of national liberation. Because of these mistakes, the USSR has taken an incorrect approach toward the types of struggle that must be waged against the West, and has propagated the line of peaceful coexistence and *détente*. It is Peking's view that this misjudgment, and the "incorrect" policies attendant upon it, have made the USSR a *de facto* accomplice of the United States in the latter's attempt to subjugate the people of the world.[3]

The Chinese Communists have been remarkably consistent, during the period under consideration, in their advocacy of this basic line on nuclear disarmament and proliferation. Within this general framework, however, there has been considerable room for subtle shifts in emphasis, and the use of this latitude by the Chinese is worth documenting.

Specifically, there have been four areas in which policy shifts by the Chinese People's Republic have been discernible: the desirability of nuclear proliferation, the feasibility of atom-free zones, the possibility of convening a world summit conference on nuclear disarmament, and the role of a no-first-use pledge by the nuclear powers.

NUCLEAR PROLIFERATION

Prior to their first explosion of a nuclear device, on October 16, 1964, the Chinese were strong advocates of nuclear proliferation.[4] After this test, Peking's attitude did not change, but the Chinese rarely ex-

---

[2] These basic tenets are repeated constantly in Chinese discussions of disarmament and nonproliferation. See, for instance, "Exposing New U.S. Fraud Over Nuclear Weapons," by "Observer," *Peking Review*, IX, No. 26 (June 24, 1966), 23–38; hereinafter cited as "New Fraud"; Karachi *Dawn*, April 27, 1966, quoted in U.S. *Disarmament Document Series*, No. 420 (May 18, 1966); "Break Nuclear Monopoly, Destroy Nuclear Weapons," *Jen Min Jih Pao*, October 22, 1964, quoted in *Survey of China Mainland Press*, No. 3325; hereinafter cited as "Break Nuclear Monopoly." See also, Walter C. Clemens, Jr., "China's Nuclear Tests: Trends and Portents," *The China Quarterly*, No. 32 (October–December, 1967), 111–31.

[3] Whether or not the Chinese consider the Soviet leaders to have become imperialists themselves is a moot point, which will be discussed below. The important fact is that the USSR, by its policies, has worked *de facto* to consolidate the effective monopoly of nuclear weapons shared with the U.S.; thus, in Peking's view, the USSR is not using its formidable nuclear power to aid revolutionary movements throughout the world.

[4] Two aspects of Communist China's concept of proliferation should be noted

pressed their opinions on the issue.[5] In fact, for the first five months of 1965, until the second Chinese nuclear test on May 14, leaders in Peking made almost no mention of the issue of proliferation.[6]

Peking's bypassing of an issue that had played a very important role in its polemics with the USSR may simply have been part of an overall Chinese attempt to dampen the Sino-Soviet dispute in the aftermath of Khrushchev's fall. It might also be taken as an indication that the CPR's advocacy of proliferation had been designed primarily to legitimize its own acquisition of nuclear weapons, and this propaganda line therefore decreased in importance once China had exploded its first bomb.

In May, 1965, however, the Chinese again started enumerating the blessings to be gained from the further acquisitions of nuclear weapons by "peace-loving" countries. Since the previous October, the CPR had maintained at least some degree of ambiguity about the desirability of proliferation (the ritual incantation regarding the U.S. nuclear monopoly was that ". . . the more thoroughly it is broken, the greater will be the possibility of completely prohibiting and thoroughly destroying nuclear weapons").[7] Now, however, the Peking leaders became increasingly explicit about what constituted "more thoroughly breaking [the U.S.] monopoly."

This new trend culminated in a rather remarkable press conference held by Vice-Premier and Foreign Minister Chen Yi on September 29, 1965. In response to a question from a London *Times* correspondent, Chen declared that the CPR had already been approached by "several" countries asking for nuclear assistance and that it was "ready to render them assistance" in "the peaceful use of atomic energy and the building of atomic reactors." The foreign minister stated that the idea of China's helping other countries to build atomic bombs was "unrealistic," but added that "any country with a fair basis [sic] in industry and agriculture and in science and technology will be able to manufacture atom bombs. . . . China hopes that Afro-Asian countries will be able to make atom bombs themselves, and it would be better for a greater

---

here. First, proliferation is desirable only insofar as it protects the right of all "peace-loving" (i.e., "progressive," anti-American) countries to possess nuclear weapons. Secondly, China's concern with a class principle leads her to lay primary stress on the *type* of countries to acquire nuclear weapons rather than on the *number* of countries to do so. Thus, a "pro-proliferation" policy in the context of this paper means advocating the right of all "revolutionary" countries to possess nuclear weapons. These qualifications should be borne in mind as China's attitude toward "proliferation" is discussed below.

[5] "Break Nuclear Monopoly," p. 25.

[6] Oran K. Young, "Chinese Views on the Spread of Nuclear Weapons," *The China Quarterly*, No. 26 (April–June, 1966), 146.

[7] "Break Nuclear Monopoly," p. 25.

number of countries to come into possession of atom bombs." [8] Although no other Chinese statements are as explicit as Chen's, the CPR has consistently maintained the above attitude since September, 1965.[9]

ATOM-FREE ZONES

The issue of atom-free zones has been given very little attention by the Chinese press since early 1964. It is interesting to note that two favorable references were made to the concept of atom-free zones during the week of October 22–29, 1964,[10] just after the first detonation of a Chinese nuclear device. In the second of these, China explicitly advocated the establishment of an Asian and Pacific atom-free zone that would include the United States, the Soviet Union, China, and Japan. In an editorial of November 23, 1964, however, *Jen Min Jih Pao* put a number of restrictions on the establishment of such zones (such as that a no-first-use pact on atomic weapons be agreed upon as a precondition),[11] and since then the whole question seems to have been dropped completely.

WORLD SUMMIT CONFERENCE AND
NO FIRST USE

The changes in the Chinese attitudes toward the convening of a world summit conference and the necessity of adopting a no-first-use clause have been closely intertwined. Ever since 1961, the CPR had been advocating "the complete prohibition and thorough destruction

[8] "China Is Determined to Make All Necessary Sacrifices for the Defeat of U.S. Imperialism," *Peking Review*, VIII, No. 41 (October 8, 1965), 8. The Chinese were undoubtedly aware of how easily peaceful nuclear technology could be adapted to military purposes, since they had accomplished this very task themselves. See Arnold Kramish, "The Great Chinese Bomb Puzzle—and a Solution," *Fortune*, LXIII, No. 6 (June, 1966), 157–58 ff. There is reportedly evidence that the CPR began giving nuclear information to Indonesia during or just prior to Foreign Minister Subandrio's visit to Peking in January, 1965. This aid no doubt stopped after the abortive coup in Indonesia during the following September.

[9] See, for instance, "New Fraud," p. 27, which states that "Such things as . . . the prevention of nuclear proliferation . . . are . . . aimed at restricting and depriving China *and all other peace-loving countries* of their legitimate right . . . to possess and develop nuclear weapons." (Emphasis added. K.L.)

[10] "Break Nuclear Monopoly," p. 24; and "Text of Joint Statement Between Chinese Institute Delegation and Japanese Socialist Party Delegation," New China News Agency, October 29, 1964, reproduced in *Survey of China Mainland Press*, Nos. 3330 and 3333; hereinafter cited as "Sino-Japanese Statement."

[11] Alice L. Hsieh, *Foreword to the Japanese Edition of "Communist China's Strategy in the Nuclear Era": Implications of the Chinese Nuclear Detonation*, (Santa Monica, Calif.: The RAND Corporation, 1965, P-3152, processed); also see Young, p. 154.

of nuclear weapons." The signing of the partial test-ban treaty in 1963 brought forth renewed Chinese emphasis on the convening of a world summit conference to achieve its own expressed goal. Another basic stand of Peking had been that it would never be the first to use nuclear weapons.

With the first Chinese nuclear test in October, 1964, the basic attitudes toward a summit conference and a no-first-use clause were united, and for the first time the Chinese government insisted on common agreement to the latter as the first item to be settled by the former.[12] The emphasis was now placed on multilateral acceptance of such an agreement.

The year 1965 witnessed a rapid escalation of the Vietnam conflict, and the evolution in China's thinking concerning a world summit conference and a no-first-use agreement can be viewed as a reaction to the increased threat that the CPR perceived from this quarter.

This change in attitude followed two lines: (1) from advocating the convening of a summit conference, to barring such a conference in the foreseeable future; and (2) from calling for a multilateral agreement on a no-first-use pact, to stressing a bilateral U.S.-CPR agreement. These shifts seem to have occurred during the period from April to June, 1966, although some wavering was evident even during this period. On April 10, 1966, Chou En-lai implied that U.S. withdrawal from Vietnam was now a precondition to Chinese participation in a world summit conference.[13] A statement released after the third Chinese nuclear test on May 9, 1966, was ambiguous in that it mentioned the CPR's past advocacy of a summit conference but failed to renew this appeal.[14] A Sino-Albanian joint communiqué on May 14 reaffirmed, however, Chinese support for the convocation of such a conference.[15]

An article by "Observer" in *Jen Min Jih Pao* on June 20 finally cleared up this question by stating that ". . . China will definitely not attend any world disarmament conference at the United Nations or outside it." [16] The same article, after discussing various disarmament proposals, suggested that the United States and China conclude a no-first-use agreement; no mention was made of other countries adhering to this pact.[17] The Chinese communiqués following the nuclear tests of October 27 and December 28 made no mention of a summit

[12] Hsieh, p. 9; and "Sino-Japanese Statement," p. 33.

[13] "Interview with Premier Chou with Karachi *Dawn* Correspondent [extract] April 10, 1966." Karachi *Dawn*, April 27, 1966, cited in *Documents 1966*, pp. 211–12.

[14] Government Statement, NCNA, May 9, 1966.

[15] "Chinese-Albanian Joint Statement," NCNA, May 14, 1966.

[16] Quoted in "New Fraud," p. 27.

[17] *Ibid.*

conference at all.[18] The escalation of the war in Vietnam has thus caused the Chinese to bar any possibility of a summit conference on nuclear disarmament; concurrently, the greater danger to China arising from this war has evidently made the Peking leaders concentrate their efforts on eliciting a nuclear no-first-use pledge from the United States.[19]

BASIC TENETS OF CHINESE FOREIGN POLICY

The outstanding feature of Chinese propaganda on disarmament and nonproliferation in 1964–1968 has been the relative paucity of official statements on this issue as compared with the previous four-year period. The change in emphasis and content of Chinese propaganda can be explained in two ways. First, certain lulls or shifts in emphasis have clearly been triggered by specific events that occurred during this period. Additionally, these changes may have been dictated by Peking's view of the function of disarmament and nonproliferation proposals in its over-all strategy.

Before going into this question, it is necessary to highlight several aspects of Peking's view of the international situation. This *Weltanschauung* contains a major internal contradiction, but, as the Chinese leaders are wont to say, "Such is the dialectic of the development of things." [20]

The Chinese world view has several basic elements, the most important of which is the recognition of the desirability of change. The CPR is, above all, an anti-status quo power. It sees the major driving force for change in the restlessness and dissatisfaction in underdeveloped countries, and a primary goal of its foreign policy is to capture and lead this "revolutionary upsurge."

In Peking's eyes, the major opponent of change is the United States, which is viewed by the Chinese leaders as willing to use its immense power in a vain effort to quash the flames of revolution that have been ignited in the so-called third world. One of America's major tools in waging this battle is considered to be the threat of using nuclear weapons—that is, "nuclear blackmail." Memories of the Quemoy crisis of 1958 undoubtedly serve to remind the Chinese of the potency of this threat.

---

[18] Government statements, NCNA, October 27 and December 28, 1966. For an interpretation of the shift in contents of the Chinese communiqués after each nuclear test, see "Fifth Chinese Nuclear Test," *Asahi,* December 30, 1967, reproduced in *Daily Summary of Japanese Press,* January 7–9, 1967, p. 18.

[19] Whether or not the Chinese *actually* take any of their disarmament proposals seriously is a moot point, but the shift to advocating a bilateral no-first-use agreement is of interest in either case.

[20] "Break Nuclear Monopoly," p. 25.

Using a simple, if somewhat distorted, logic, the Chinese have reasoned thus: (1) the United States uses its overwhelming advantage in nuclear weapons to subdue revolutionary change; (2) as more of the revolutionary countries acquire nuclear weapons, the relative advantage of the United States will decrease; (3) acquisition of nuclear weapons by "progressive" countries will, therefore, improve the chances of success for revolutions in the underdeveloped countries.

Another fundamental tenet of the Chinese *Weltanschauung* in favor of a pro-proliferation policy is the notion that an imperialist power (e.g., the U.S.) is by nature aggressive and warlike. The greatest danger of nuclear war arises, therefore, when nuclear power is concentrated in the hands of an imperialist country. Proliferation of nuclear weapons to nonimperialist countries will, in this view, help to redress the balance of power and make the United States more hesitant to unleash the nuclear war that it would otherwise contemplate.

On a lower level of abstraction, it can be cogently argued that their experience has tended to make the leaders in Peking discount the possibility of an accidental nuclear war and emphasize the possibility of a deliberate American nuclear attack on China. Reasoning in these terms would lessen Peking's fear of increased possibilities of accidental war through the spread of nuclear weapons, and would put a premium on China's building up its own deterrent to any deliberate American attack.[21] The CPR might then attempt to use advocacy of nuclear proliferation as a propaganda tool in its effort to win over the developing countries.

From several different points of view, therefore, China can be shown to have a vested interest in a policy that upholds the right of "peace-loving" countries to acquire nuclear weapons. There is, however, one major contradiction in the above analysis—that is, this policy might encourage nuclear proliferation to countries such as India and Japan. Should such proliferation occur, it would add to the potential of those countries as centers rivaling China for leadership of the third world, or as opponents on interstate issues (disputed territories and the like). In this context, it seems probable that the CPR's great emphasis on its no-first-use pledge has been designed at least in part to forestall the "panic proliferation" that its policies and actions might otherwise precipitate.[22]

The chief part that remains to be fitted into the puzzle is the atti-

[21] This point is argued in detail by Morton Halperin in *China and Nuclear Proliferation* (Chicago: University of Chicago Press, 1966), pp. 17–36.

[22] Hsieh, p. 12. For an interesting illustration of the effectiveness of this tactic, see Manabu Hattori, "Significance of China's Nuclear Missile," *Economist*, November 15, 1966, reproduced in *Summaries of Selected Japanese Magazines*, November 21, 1966, pp. 46–62.

tude toward the Soviet Union in China's evaluation of the current international situation. In the late 1950's, the Chinese Communists seemed to believe that the USSR was simply following an incorrect policy of *rapprochement* with the West, a policy based on a misevaluation of the strategic balance of forces. They have since adopted the view that the USSR has become a definitely conservative and pro-status quo power which, in collusion with the United States, is actively seeking to consolidate its position as one of two unrivaled superpowers.

The basic foreign policy tenets of the CPR can thus be summarized as: a passionate desire for revolutionary change; the hope of assuming leadership of the third world; fear of United States "nuclear blackmail"; a lack of concern over the danger of an accidental nuclear war; and extreme concern over the collusion of the United States and the Soviet Union. (The Chinese now consider the U.S. and the USSR to be working in at least tacit collusion.)

REACTIONS TO ENVIRONMENTAL CHANGES

The four major environmental changes with which the Chinese Communists have had to deal during the period under consideration have been: their own acquisition of nuclear weapons, the ouster of N. S. Khrushchev, the escalation of the Vietnam war, and the concurrent "escalation" of China's dispute with the USSR. Each of these events significantly influenced the Chinese attitude toward nonproliferation and disarmament.

The explosion of a nuclear device in October, 1964, made China the fifth member of the nuclear club. At the same time, it brought new pressures to bear on the CPR, and these new pressures were reflected in shifts on the disarmament and nonproliferation issues. Chinese statements at the time of and shortly after the country's first nuclear explosion indicate that the Peking leaders sought to ameliorate negative foreign reactions to their feat. The fact that the 1963 test-ban treaty had been very well received throughout the third world increased Chinese concern in this area. As a consequence, the propaganda surrounding this test was very subdued in tone, heavily stressing the themes that Peking's development of nuclear weapons was for purely defensive purposes and that it represented a strengthening of the position of the third world vis-à-vis the developed countries.

In addition, it is probable that China realized that, during the early stages of development of its nuclear arsenal, its vulnerability to attack by foreign powers would actually be *increased* (because the incentive to attack China would be greater, whereas the CPR's capacity for retaliation would not have grown significantly).[23] This realization

---

[23] Hsieh, pp. 15–16.

encouraged China to place great emphasis on a no-first-use agreement among all the powers.[24] The combination of these several pressures resulted in the CPR's urging the desirability of a world summit conference on nuclear disarmament, with general agreement that a no-first-use pact should be the first item considered by such a conference.

The ouster of Khrushchev, which occurred almost simultaneously with the first Chinese nuclear explosion, placed different demands on the Peking leaders. The CPR now had an interest in soft-pedaling the main sources of contention with the USSR until the new Soviet leaders had clarified their positions on key issues.

In the realm of disarmament and nonproliferation, the most contested concrete issues between the two Communist powers had been the test ban and a ban on nuclear proliferation. The Chinese nuclear test made it definite that China not only rejected the test-ban treaty (as did the two other Asian Communist states, plus Cuba and Albania) but was determined to arm itself with nuclear weapons. The nonproliferation issue became even more important with China's entry into the nuclear club.

It is significant, therefore, that the Chinese press, as noted above, made almost no mention of the issue of proliferation between October, 1964, and May, 1965. The renewed vigor with which Peking, after its second nuclear test (May, 1965) supported the right of "peace-loving" countries to acquire nuclear weapons was a direct reflection of its increasing disillusionment with the new Soviet leadership.

The role of Vietnam within this framework is highly complex. It seems very likely that at least by the end of 1965 the Chinese leaders had become greatly concerned about the possibility that a war with the United States might grow out of the Vietnam conflict. This situation lent new urgency to the CPR's quest for an effective deterrent against United States nuclear power. With the Russian nuclear umbrella rapidly losing its protective force for China, the Peking leaders placed renewed stress on a no-first-use clause, and shifted the proposal's context from multilateral to bilateral (aimed directly at the U.S.).

The war in Vietnam also tested the value of "wars of national liberation." Vietnam, in the view from Peking, called for wholehearted Chinese support and for greater Chinese militancy against the West in every sphere—when such militancy would not prove too costly. It is interesting to note in this context that the CPR in this period still bought wheat from Canada, and increased its trade in general with the West. At the same time it rapidly lost interest in, and then completely

[24] This stress on a no-first-use agreement had the beneficial side effect, of course, of allaying India's and Japan's fears and making the CPR seem generally less bellicose.

rejected, the idea of a world summit conference on nuclear disarmament. China's continued intransigence on the subject of conventional
disarmament also fitted in well, of course, with its fears and hopes in
Vietnam.

The war in Vietnam has had a dual influence on the Sino-Soviet
dispute. On the one hand, by forcing China to assume a "hard line"
on many issues, it has served to polarize the Chinese and Soviet positions; this polarization has "objectively" contributed to increased tension between the CPR and the USSR, which was advocating "peaceful
coexistence." On the other hand, it has been consciously and deliberately *used* by the Chinese to show both the incorrectness of the
Soviet line and the basically "capitulationist" outlook of the "revisionist ruling clique" in the USSR. As such, Vietnam has served
functionally to exacerbate the already strained relations between the
CPR and the USSR, and has also been used deliberately by each side
to flay the other. This observation leads us to consider the role of disarmament and nonproliferation in the Sino-Soviet conflict as a whole,
and its effects on the Soviet attitudes toward these issues.

CHINESE IMPACT ON SOVIET ATTITUDES

Discussions of nuclear disarmament and nonproliferation policies
have played several roles in the Sino-Soviet dispute. There are some
indications that the USSR has been genuinely concerned about the
"Nth-country" problem,[25] and that this is one of Moscow's reasons for
seriously advocating a nonproliferation treaty. As shown above, Peking has manifested a rather different attitude toward it.

On another plane, both sides have used their disagreement over
arms control measures to gain propaganda advantages in the third
world. Here, the Russians have concentrated on the themes of Chinese
bellicosity and ignorance about the destructiveness of nuclear weapons.
The Chinese, in turn, have pointed to the test-ban treaty, the hot-line
agreement, the U.N. resolution banning weapons in orbit, and the
simultaneous U.S.-Soviet announcement in April, 1964, of a cutback
in the production of fissionable materials, to show that the Soviet
Union has in fact been working in collusion with the United States to
dominate the world. Soviet support for a nonproliferation treaty,
like Soviet agreement to a partial test ban, has been portrayed by the
Chinese as part of a USSR "smokescreen" designed to cover up United
States aggression in Vietnam.[26]

---

[25] For a good summary of the Soviet position on this question, see M. Maratov,
"Nonproliferation and NATO Nuclear Plans," *International Affairs* (Moscow), No. 1
(January, 1966), 18–19.

[26] A number of points in this section have been drawn from the excellent analyses

On yet another level, specific stands on arms control issues have been used either to exacerbate or to moderate the Sino-Soviet dispute itself. Thus, in spite of its strong nonproliferation policy, the Soviet Union made no negative comments after the Chinese nuclear tests, and resisted proposals at U.N. disarmament talks to condemn Chinese testing. Thus, in the spring of 1965, when Brezhnev and Kosygin were still seeking (or so professing) to improve relations with their Chinese comrades, the USSR secured a suspension of the ENDC talks in Geneva, and a shift to the U.N. Disarmament Commission, where the Soviet representatives concentrated their efforts on two proposals more to Chinese liking—elimination of foreign military bases and a ban on the use of nuclear weapons. The Soviet campaign on behalf of nuclear nonproliferation was resumed at the 20th U.N. General Assembly, in the fall of 1965, at which time the Sino-Soviet dispute was already raging again.

The almost total Chinese neglect of the proliferation issue from late 1964 to May, 1965, coincided with a phase of lessening Sino-Soviet tension; Peking's subsequent emphasis on this issue coincided with a heightening of tension.

If any conclusion can be drawn from these and other, earlier examples (such as the conclusion of the test-ban treaty of 1963), it is that the influence of the Sino-Soviet dispute on specific Soviet arms control postures has been multidirectional in practice. At certain times, the USSR has apparently been willing to bend to Chinese demands and subordinate arms control issues to larger policy purposes—either to improve Sino-Soviet relations, or to assume a "hard line" because of sensitivity arising from Chinese accusations of Soviet cowardice or Soviet collusion with the United States. At other times, the USSR has deliberately used arms control issues as a weapon to goad, expose, or isolate Peking, or to prove the validity of the Soviet "general line."

To complete the discussion of the past "uses" of arms control issues in the Sino-Soviet dispute, it should be noted that these polemics have served as a concrete way of discussing broad disagreements about the nature of the present historical stage. In this way they may be compared to the earlier role played by Albania and Yugoslavia when they were, in effect, used as surrogates for talking about China and the Soviet Union directly. Thus, in the past few years, disputes over the likelihood of nuclear war have been a convenient way of discussing

published by Morton Halperin. These include *Sino-Soviet Relations and Arms Control*, and his Introduction to "Sino-Soviet Relations and Arms Control," *The China Quarterly*, No. 26 (April–June, 1966), 118–22. I have significantly altered a number of Halperin's points, but the intertwining of the two analyses is too complex to footnote in detail. This general recognition of Halperin's influence should *not* be construed as implying that he would agree with the arguments presented here.

general problems of dealing with the United States and promoting wars of national liberation.[27] Arguments in favor of and against arms control have served a similar function. This function of arms control discussion has been decreasing since mid-1965.

The change in the general status of arms control issues since mid-1965 has been similar to the earlier change in the Sino-Soviet dispute when the issues of Albania and Yugoslavia were phased out in favor of direct attack by the Chinese and Russians on each other. Arms control issues even today retain some vestigial utility for the two sides; but since 1965, the Sino-Soviet rift seems to have moved beyond the stage where differences over arms control measures could be considered to have central importance. Essentially, each country gave up any hope of a near-term reconciliation with the other, barring a major change in the leadership of the opposing country. Thus, in a very real sense, the Sino-Soviet dispute had moved *beyond* the "arms control" stage.

Chinese propaganda since this time has called for the overthrow of the Soviet leadership, and Peking's diatribes against the nuclear test-ban treaty and the projected nonproliferation agreement have become at best weak auxiliaries to China's main propaganda line.[28] The Soviet Union has likewise become less sensitive to Chinese attacks as Mao's regime has experienced one setback after another in foreign policy, both within and outside the Communist fold, since the fall of 1965. In addition, the USSR has lost any incentive to woo its Communist neighbor with a "hard-line" position on arms control. (There is a possibility, of course, that this situation could alter with a radical change in the Chinese leadership—but this contingency is too unpredictable to warrant discussion here.)

The Sino-Soviet dispute has thus moved to a stage that essentially frees the USSR from any imperative to cater to the wishes of Mao Tse-tung and his colleagues. This fact should not, however, be construed to mean that China will have no influence on Russia's policies toward arms control in the future. While there exists a major power claiming to be the true guardian of the revolution and thus challenging Russia's hegemony in the Communist world (and in the third world), the Soviet Union cannot afford to ignore the threat that this poses to its authority. Although it would be foolish to predict how Russia's arms control policies in the future will reflect this challenge, certain considerations can be pinpointed.

The existence of China as an alternative to the Soviet Union in

---

[27] Alice L. Hsieh, "The Sino-Soviet Nuclear Dialogue," *The Journal of Conflict Resolution*, VIII, No. 2 (June, 1964), 103.

[28] I would argue that the same situation had been reached by the end of 1963, but that Khrushchev's ouster reopened the possibilities of a *rapprochement* and, therefore, temporarily made arms control a significant question once more.

world Communist leadership affects Soviet behavior even in Europe, where the USSR must be sensitive to the desires of the local Communist regimes.[29] But these regimes push in different and sometimes opposed directions, so that Moscow cannot possibly hope to conciliate some without alarming others.

Likewise, while the Chinese challenge remains, the Soviet policy makers may feel some impetus to sign agreements with the West simply to prove the validity of their "general line." This reasoning may have figured in Soviet agreement on the nonproliferation treaty. And it may also promote other possible arms control measures, such as arms embargoes or the creation of a viable international "police" force under the auspices of the U.N. Security Council. The Soviet leaders' recently-evident freedom to sign agreements with the West uninhibited by considerations of the possible Chinese reaction, provides additional cause for hope of a positive Soviet stance on certain disarmament issues in the future.[30]

The prospects for the future, however, are not all bright. As shown by Soviet policies toward the third world in 1963–1964, and toward Vietnam in particular since then, the USSR is fully capable of promoting revolutionary changes in the third world while seeking general agreement with the United States. The USSR is likely to continue to be anxious to show that the Chinese attacks against it are groundless; moreover, it remains true that the Russians argue with the Chinese over the best means of achieving revolutionary change in underdeveloped countries, but *not* over the desirability of this change. Soviet strategy in the third world will thus probably increase world tensions and therefore somewhat inhibit movement toward some, but not all, arms control agreements.

Last but by no means least is the fact that Russia must consider the direct military threat that China may pose to itself in the future. This threat can take either (or both) of two forms.

First, as the test-ban treaty has illustrated, China will not feel bound by any arms control agreements that the Soviet Union may conclude. Thus a nonproliferation agreement signed by the USSR would give the Chinese some advantage by preserving for China a greater freedom of maneuver; China could, for example, offer to provide nuclear weapons to those countries in the third world which refused to adhere to the treaty.

Second, there is the possibility that China might become a significant direct military threat to the USSR, over the next several decades, should

[29] It is still too early to determine to what extent the Great Proletarian Cultural Revolution will eliminate the Chinese as such an alternative.

[30] Cf. Helmut Sonnenfeldt, "The Chinese Factor in Soviet Disarmament Policy," *The China Quarterly*, No. 26 (April–June 1966), 135.

the latter be restricted by agreements hindering its development or deployment of weapons or forces. Although consideration of this prospect may still be premature, the idea is certainly not nearly as fantastic as it would have appeared ten years ago. There is every reason to assume that the men in the Kremlin are at least giving thought to this possibility. Should the Soviet leadership perceive an actual or potential threat from Peking, there is little likelihood of their concluding meaningful new disarmament pacts that would reduce their effective power vis-à-vis China or restrict their own programs of research and development.

ABBREVIATIONS

ABM	anti-ballistic missile
ACDA	[U.S.] Arms Control and Disarmament Agency
AEC	[U.S.] Atomic Energy Commission
BMEWS	ballistic missile early warning system
CC	Central Committee
CP	Communist Party
CPR	Chinese People's Republic
CPSU	Communist Party of the Soviet Union
EEC	European Economic Community
ENDC	Eighteen-Nation Disarmament Committee
FOBS	fractional orbital bombardment system
FRG	Federal Republic of Germany
GCD	general and complete disarmament
GDR	German Democratic Republic
GNP	gross national product
IAEA	International Atomic Energy Agency
ICBM	intercontinental ballistic missile
IRBM	intermediate-range ballistic missile
JCS	Joint Chiefs of Staff
KGB	Committee of State Security
MIRV	multiple independently guided re-entry vehicle
MLF	multilateral nuclear force
MOBS	multiple orbital bombardment system
MRBM	medium range ballistic missile
NATO	North Atlantic Treaty Organization
NCNA	New China News Agency
NPT	nonproliferation treaty
R & D	Research and Development
SAM	surface-to-air missile
UAR	United Arab Republic
UNDC	United Nations Disarmament Commission
UNGA	United Nations General Assembly
WTO	Warsaw Treaty Organization

INDEX